POST-IMPRESSIONISM

GRAFTON GALLERIES
SECOND POST-
IMPRESSIONIST
EXHIBITION
BRITISH FRENCH
AND RUSSIAN
ARTISTS
OCT·5-DEC·31
10·AM-6·P·M·
ADMISSION
1 SHILLING
GRAFTON
STREET
W

POST-IMPRESSIONISM

THE RISE OF MODERN ART

THOMAS PARSONS and IAIN GALE

Foreword by BERNARD DENVIR

STUDIO EDITIONS · LONDON

Publishers' Note

While it is hoped that the text of this volume is seamless, the publishers feel that the independent work of the two authors should be identified. Thus, Thomas Parsons was responsible for the major part, writing the introduction, chapters 1–4, 6 and 9, while Iain Gale wrote chapters 5, 7 and 8. Each has dedicated their work individually. Thus, this book is for:

Alan and Anne – T.P.

Sarah (my dear wife) – I.G.

Acknowledgements

The publishers are obviously most grateful to all the people and institutions who have so kindly granted permission for their pictures to be reproduced in this volume, thus making the survey as broad and colourful as it is. They would also particularly like to thank Juliet Brightmore for her outstanding efforts and achievements on the picture research for this title and Luci Collings and Hilary Martin for their editorial assistance.

The authors would like to express their gratitude to Sarah Sears for the major part she played throughout the creation of this book – for her dedication and stamina. They would like here to acknowledge their debt to the staff of the London Library, the National Art Library at the Victoria and Albert Museum, the British Library, the Ashmolean Museum, Oxford, the Museum of Modern Art, New York, the Baltimore Museum of Art and the Pushkin Museum of Fine Arts, Moscow. Independently, Tom would also like to thank the staff of the English Department at the University of York and – for different reasons – Richard Parsons and Nick Ross. Iain would like to thank Seamus Collins.

First published in Great Britain in 1992 by
Studio Editions Ltd, Princess House,
50 Eastcastle Street, London W1N 7AP.

Copyright © 1992 Studio Editions

The rights of Thomas Parsons and Iain Gale to be identified as authors of this work have been asserted by them in accordance with the Copyright, Design and Patents Act, 1988.

ISBN 1 85170 861 8

Edited by Sarah Sears
Designed by Christine Wood, Dutjapun Williams and Joy FitzSimmons
Typeset by Goodfellow & Egan, Cambridge
Printed and bound in Hong Kong

Half-title page: Poster for Roger Fry's Second Post-Impressionist Exhibition, held at the Grafton Galleries, London, 1912.

Frontispiece: Detail of Piet Mondrian's Still-Life with Gingerpot II, 1900 (see also plate 263).

Facing foreword: Spencer Gore's Gauguins and Connoisseurs, 1900 (see also plate 361).

Endpiece: Ernst Ludwig Kirchner's The Manifesto of Die Brücke, 1905 (see also plate 218).

Contents

Foreword

Of all periods of art history there are few more difficult to write about than that which gave birth to Post-Impressionism. The concept was conceived in 1910 by Roger Fry, the forty-four-year-old son of a Quaker judge, one of the leading lights of Bloomsbury, and at the time, well on the way to becoming the heir-apparent of John Ruskin. It emerged in a moment of anguished frustration during the difficult search for an exhibition title that would be both vague and comprehensive enough to embrace a collection of contemporary French paintings which Fry had gathered from a handful of Parisian dealers, and some of which he had not even seen until they arrived in London. They were to form a memorable exhibition at the Grafton Galleries in the summer and autumn of that year; the title of the show 'Manet and the Post-Impressionists' ensured that the term was to become part of the art historian's vocabulary.

The name was a very English creation – the French, for instance have never used it. Like the Anglican Church and the British Consitution, it was at once pragmatic and ambitious, admirable and effective. No attempt to fit the vital, personal and idiosyncratic activities of the creative mind into tidy historical categories has ever been totally successful. Impressionism itself is full of contradictions. What really do the works of Degas and Monet have in common? Where in the neat categories of commentators and critics does Cézanne come? A self-acknowledged Impressionist, an exhibitor at many of their exhibitions, a shy but confirmed participator in their gatherings, he is also accepted as a Post-Impressionist; in Fry's exhibition there were twenty-one examples of his work. Manet, on the other hand, had never participated in any of the Impressionist exhibitions, and did not paint *Argenteuil* – his first truly Impressionist painting (in the accepted sense of the word) – until he was forty-two.

But whatever its inconsistencies, Impressionism had broken the unity of Western painting, just as the Reformation had broken the unity of Christendom. And when in the 1880s it lost its internal momentum, and its external appeal, it was succeeded by a host of warring sects, as disputatious as any of those which had shattered the hegemony of Rome in the sixteenth century. In the twenty years which followed the last Impressionist exhibition of 1886, French innovative painting produced Neo-Impressionism, Divisionism, Pointillism, Synthetism, Cloissonism, Symbolism, Neo-Traditionism, Idealism, Naturalism, the School of Pont-Aven, the Nabis, the Fauves, and eventually Cubism. Moreover, many of these new groups or movements – all of which can be classified as Post-Impressionist as they were in the exhibition devoted to the movement at the Royal Academy in 1979 – were not only concerned with stylistic innovations, but postulated an ideology of some kind to justify their work. Maximilien Luce, for

instance, was an anarchist. Maurice Denis and others were moved by strong religious impulses; some were Rosicrucians, others believers in a scientific orthodoxy, which – or so they thought – could supplement, or even supplant aesthetic impulses. But, above all else, they shared an emphasis on the primacy of feeling, an emphasis which led to the dramatic emancipation of colour from its purely descriptive role, which was to lead to Expressionism in all its many varieties, to abstraction and – eventually – to that twentieth-century phenomenon: Abstract Expressionism.

What is so remarkable about this book is that its authors have succeeded in imposing on this complex mass of artistic activity a coherence and a clarity, expressed in prose free of jargon, uncontaminated by the evasive circumlocutions which all too frequently camouflage confusion of thought, and accessible to what Virginia Woolf called 'the common reader'. Moreover they do not insulate artistic phenomena from the environment which surrounds them; rather they sharpen our sensibilities by referring often to literary models drawn from a whole range of writers ranging from Dickens through T.S. Eliot to Angus Wilson.

Above all else, they never fail to realize that fundamentally they are writing about actual paintings, tangible works of art. Their captions to the entrancing collection of illustrations which document this book are models of informed percipience, catching – with an artist's eye – the subtleties of composition, the nuances of colour, the echoes of sentiment and feeling, which justify the belief that anyone writing about art aims to enhance the feeling as well as the understanding of the reader.

To have succeeded in performing what is visually a superb juggling act in giving coherence and intelligibility to an episode in the history of art more complex in its manifestations and more varied in its motivations than anything that had gone before, is in itself a considerable achievement, but the authors have gone beyond that. Understanding the extent to which Post-Impressionism was an international phenomenon, finding expression outside the confines of Paris, they have skilfully and persuasively interwoven these aspects of the movement into the general flow of the narrative. Of particular interest and importance is the section devoted to Russian art of the period, so often neglected in books on this subject.

There is no aspect of twentieth-century painting which cannot be traced back to one or other of the consitutent elements of Post-Impressionism, and anyone who wants to understand the significant nature of that movement could find no better guide to it than this perspicacious and finely illustrated book.

Bernard Denvir
London, 1992

The Naming of a Movement

The timing of profound cultural changes, of far-reaching shifts in human consciousness, do not respect our own more arbitrary chronological markers. We speak without hesitation, for example, of Charles Dickens (1812–1870) as a nineteenth-century novelist. James Joyce (1882–1941), on the other hand, we locate firmly in the twentieth. Yet in such matters, it would evidently be absurd to give 31 December 1899 as the point where the nineteenth century ended and the twentieth century began. Nonetheless, in a lecture given at Cambridge University in 1924, the English novelist Virginia Woolf (1882–1941) hazarded a guess as to the date of this crucial turning point:

In or about December, 1910, human character changed. I am not saying that one went out, as one might, into a garden, and there saw that a rose had flowered, or that a hen had laid an egg. The change was not sudden and definite like that. But a change there was, nevertheless; and, since one must be arbitrary, let us date it about the year 1910.[1]

For all that Woolf couches her assertion with qualifications, she is strikingly, even suspiciously, precise in her choice of date. She is bold enough to specify a month as well as a year: December 1910. It is at this point that, as far as the subject of this book is concerned, her remarks take on particular significance. For it was then that the Post-Impressionist painters earned their name – at a notorious exhibition held in London and organized by a middle-aged painter and critic called Roger Fry (1866–1934). The exhibition, entitled 'Manet and the Post-Impressionists', opened in London in November 1910. It closed in January 1911.

The two events – Fry's exhibition and Woolf's choice of December 1910 as a pivotal date – are not unrelated. Woolf and Fry were close friends. They were also central figures in a set of liberal, highly civilized, monied British intellectuals

1 VINCENT VAN GOGH Portrait of Dr Gachet 1890.
Dr Gachet, an old friend of Cézanne and Pissarro, looked after van Gogh for the last months of the painter's life. Van Gogh wrote to his brother Theo about this portrait: 'I am working on his portrait, his head with a white cap – very blond hair, very bright; his hands also light in colour, with a blue coat and a cobalt blue background. He is leaning against a red table on which there are a yellow book and a foxglove with purple blossoms . . . M. Gachet is absolutely crazy about this portrait and wants me to do another for him, if I can, exactly like it.' To Gauguin van Gogh wrote that he had painted Gachet, 'with the sad expression of our time'. (John Rewald, Post-Impressionism, London, 1978, 367 and 370.)

known as the Bloomsbury Group. Indeed, she was later to acknowledge the particular significance of Fry's influence in her own creative efforts as a writer. Her choice of December 1910, given in her lecture at Cambridge in 1924, thus stands as a veiled tribute to Fry's exhibition. The artists whom Fry featured in this exhibition – the generations of avant-garde European painters working between c. 1880 and 1914 – will form the subject of this book.

Roger Fry: an Unlikely Figure

In 1910 the names of Henri Matisse (1869–1954) and Pablo Picasso (1881–1973), the acknowledged leaders of avant-garde painting from Paris to Moscow, were as yet more or less completely unknown in Britain. Even those of the preceding generation of the avant garde, such as Vincent van Gogh (1853–1890), Paul Gauguin (1848–1903) and Georges Seurat (1859–91), who had come of age just as the leading Impressionists were beginning to earn official acceptance and to make a reasonable living from the sale of their pictures, were little heard of.

Only very few recent French paintings could be seen in Britain in the first decade of the twentieth century. They were usually shown in London at exhibitions put on by bodies such as the International Society or in the galleries of Goupil and Company, the firm of picture dealers from The Hague at whose London branch van Gogh had worked in 1873.

Yet it was in Britain, despite her almost complete isolation from developments in painting then taking place in the rest of Europe, that the Post-Impressionist artists were to earn their name – baptized by Fry at his infamous exhibition.

Fry was in some ways an unlikely figure for such a role. Born into a rich Quaker family, he took some time to decide on a career. Eventually he persuaded his parents that he wanted to become an artist, but there was little to suggest that he would tread anything other than a conservative path. As a student he spent some months at the Académie Julian in Paris. This was an independent art school where many of the most famous avant-garde French painters had already or were yet to meet. But Fry seemed completely unaware of what was happening around him. He had never heard of Paul Cézanne (1839–1906), already something of a legendary figure to a growing number of younger French artists. Fry returned to London and struggled to make a living as a painter. He then turned his attention to writing, and from the turn of the century he steadily began to build a substantial reputation as a critic and connoisseur of Old Master painting. Later, following his growing success as a critic, he took up the post of Curator for the Metropolitan Museum of Art in New York, with particular responsibility for purchasing works by the European Old Masters. It was a task he accomplished brilliantly, acquiring for the museum a number of superb paintings by Giovanni Bellini (1430–1516), Hans Holbein (1497–1543), Lorenzo Lotto (c.1480–1556) and Francisco Goya (1746–1828) among others, along with works by Pierre Auguste Renoir (1841–1919) and James McNeill Whistler (1834–1903). Nonetheless, his activities as buyer for the Metropolitan and as a critic kept him constantly in touch with a network of European galleries and picture dealers. It was through these contacts, together with the handful of opportunities on offer at home in London, that he was first exposed to the work of contemporary painters.

Fry's responses to modern art, however, were very much those of someone whose visual tastes had been formulated through close study of older European traditions that centred, inevitably, on Italian Renaissance art. Initially he had always felt that the most modern European painting had suffered in comparison. 'The more I study the Old Masters the more terrible does the chaos of modern art seem to me',[2] he wrote to his father in September 1894. A little later, however, having seen a handful of works by Cézanne and Gauguin at one of the International Society exhibitions in London, Fry began to revise his opinions. Here at last, he felt, were two painters at least who were doing something different.

The Chaos of Modern Art

Roger Fry's dissatisfactions with modern art focused on Impressionism. It was these misgivings which led him to coin the phrase 'Post-Impressionism'. This was intended as a means of identifying certain tendencies in some recent French painting which he felt corrected the failings of Impressionism. However, as these artists were so obviously directly descended from the Impressionists (some, like Cézanne in his early years, had even been part of that group), the term Post-Impressionism would serve to indicate both these artists' ancestry and their divergence from that inheritance. In order to understand Fry's reasoning, it will be necessary to take a brief look at some technical terminology: to peer under the bonnet, as it were, at the engine of a picture.

A painting, any painting, can be broken down into three constituent parts – line, tone and colour. In a traditionally illusionistic painting, these elements will be used in two particular ways in order to build up a convincing image of reality. Firstly there is perspective – whereby the lines of a composition are ordered so as to suggest the way figures or objects or natural forms diminish in size the further they recede from the eye. Secondly, modelling – whereby a sense of volume or solidity can be given to the figure or object by shading its form in a graduated succession of different tones, progressing from light to dark. Furthermore, it is with these two elements that the painter can clearly and properly organize the design or composition of his picture. These two specific procedures, perspective and modelling, had formed the cornerstone of European painting since the fifteenth century.

2   WALTER SICKERT   Roger Fry Lecturing   c. 1911.
Fry had studied briefly under Sickert in 1893 soon after he returned to England following his time at the Académie Julian in Paris. By c. 1911, when this drawing was executed, Sickert had already long assimilated into his painting all that he wanted from French Impressionism. His stylistic debts to Whistler and Degas thus separated his art from the bold distortions and heightened colour Fry so admired in the Post-Impressionists; and the two periodically clashed in the British press. Sickert attacked Fry's second exhibition with characteristic wit in an article for the English Review *in January 1912. Something of this acerbity can be discerned in this drawing which also successfully conveys the nervous energy of Fry's oratorical performances.*

Thus, of the three basic elements that make up a painting, tradition placed the most emphasis on just two: line and tone. Once these had been properly applied, using perspective and modelling, the painter could then move on to establish the desired colours that would, as it were, sit on top of this linear and tonal framework.

The Impressionists had broken decisively with this tradition. They more or less banished the traditionally dominant role of line and they modelled more with colour itself, rather than with tone. They constructed their paintings with colour as the primary, guiding factor. This they had done for the purpose of greater realism. They realized that everything we see is the result of light reflecting off an object which then forms an image on the retina. Thus they believed that the artist who wanted to paint things as we see them should devote himself to the study of light. Natural light is made up of colour, the different colours of the rainbow known as the spectrum. The artist should therefore restrict himself just to those spectral colours, combining them on the canvas in the same way that the different colours of the light reflected off an object enable us to see things in nature.

This was where Fry felt that things had gone wrong. He was unhappy with the Impressionists' exclusive emphasis on the rendering of optical or visual reality. Such an approach, he argued, precluded the full expression of the artist's emotional responses to nature. Furthermore, the Impressionists' way of building up their pictures through a multitude of small, flecked brushstrokes seemed to him to jettison the traditional virtues of design and composition. It was these two aspects, the expression of emotion coupled with a strong sense of a picture's internal architecture, that Fry felt Gauguin and especially Cézanne were restoring to modern painting.

'The Twitch of a Paralytic'

Tall and gaunt, with small silver spectacles and highly charged curly grey hair, Fry exuded enormous energy and an almost boyish enthusiasm in whatever he did (see plate 2). It was he who was to provide the essential drive in the speedy arrangements for the exhibition: an achievement all the more remarkable, because in many other ways 1910 was a disastrous year for him.

Within a period of twelve months he had resigned from the board of the Metropolitan Museum after disagreements with its chairman, the tyrannical American tycoon Pierpont J. Morgan; his application for the post of Slade Professor at Oxford had been turned down; and after years of anxiously and tirelessly nursing his wife, who had suffered from repeated attacks of mental illness since their marriage in 1896, he had finally had to have her admitted to an asylum.

Until 1910 Fry's feeling that some painters were developing away from Impressionism remained an unconfirmed suspicion, though the idea of holding a large exhibition in London of the most recent French painting (so as to be able to test his theory more fully) remained at the back of his mind. Then, in one of those fortuitous meetings, Fry was encouraged to realize these somewhat vague possibilities. In January 1910, on the train from Cambridge to London, he struck up a conversation with a fellow passenger, a gentleman named Clive Bell (1881–1964). Conversation turned to matters of art, and Fry happened to mention his idea of an exhibition. Bell, who had spent some time in Paris and particularly enjoyed visting the avant-garde dealers' galleries and talking with the artists in the cafés, was very enthusiastic. The two men parted on friendly terms – though nothing was done about the exhibition until later that year.

In June, however, a small number of contemporary French paintings were shown in an exhibition that opened in Brighton, organized by the mayor Robert Dell as an attraction to the many French visitors to the seaside town. Dell had had problems getting the Parisian dealers to lend their stock: they were unenthusiastic about trying to open up a British market while France, Germany, Russia and the United States were already providing them with more than enough buyers. So, although Dell could not get hold of any works by van Gogh or Seurat, he did arrange to show a modest number of paintings by artists like Cézanne, Matisse, Gauguin, André Derain (1880–1954), Edouard Vuillard (1868–1940) and Pierre Bonnard (1867–1947).

The Brighton exhibition determined Fry to hold one of his own in London. It was to open that November. Quickly organizing a gallery, an exhibition committee and sufficient financial backing, Fry and his friend Desmond MacCarthy (1878–1952), secretary to the exhibition committee, were to select the necessary pictures from various dealers and collectors in Paris, Amsterdam and Munich. In July, after an early champagne breakfast, Fry and MacCarthy set off for Paris to meet Bell, who provided many of the contacts. They began a rapid and exhausting trip to various dealers' galleries and collectors' homes. MacCarthy recalls:

In Paris we spent day after day looking at the pictures and nearly all those Roger preferred were at our disposal. I remember his raptures. He would sit in front of them with his hands on his knees groaning repeatedly, 'Wonderful, wonderful.'[3]

Back in London, when all the pictures that he, MacCarthy and Bell had chosen had arrived, it was time to choose a title for the exhibition. MacCarthy again records:

What was the exhibition to be called? That was the next question. Roger and I and a young journalist who was to help with publicity, met to consider this; and it was at that meeting that a word which is now safely embedded in the English language – 'post-impressionism' – was invented. Roger first suggested various terms like 'expressionism', which aimed at distinguishing these artists from the impressionists; but the journalist wouldn't have that or any other of his alternatives. At last Roger, losing patience, said: 'Oh, let's just call them post-impressionists: at any rate, they come after the impressionists.'[4]

The exhibition, entitled 'Manet and the Post-Impressionists', opened on 8 November 1910 at the Grafton Gallery, just off Bond Street in London. Edouard Manet (1832–1883), eight of whose paintings were shown, was the one representative of the previous, Impressionist generation. His work would already have been familiar to the English public, but it was also hoped that his inclusion would indicate how more recent generations both stemmed and had progressed from their illustrious predecessor.

The core of the show was made up of works by Gauguin, who was represented by thirty-seven paintings, including *Agony in the Garden* and *Manao tupapau* (*Spirit of the Dead Watching*) (see plates 21 and 22); Cézanne by twenty-one, including (probably) *Madame Cézanne in a Red Armchair* and *The Great Pine* (see plates 13 and 119); and van Gogh by twenty, including *Portrait of Dr Gachet* and *Crows over Wheatfields* (see plates 1 and 23). Matisse had three paintings shown, one of which was *Girl with Green Eyes* (see plate 14), and Seurat two, one of which was *Lighthouse at Honfleur* (see plate 16). Among the other artists represented were Derain, Maurice de Vlaminck (1876–1958), Picasso, Othon Friesz (1879–1949) and Maurice Denis (1870–1943).

The show proved a 'succès de scandale' – even before it had officially begun – at a critics' preview held a few days before the doors were opened to the public. The effect of such boldly distorted and wilfully unnaturalistic paintings upon critics, the majority of whose experience of modern painting hitherto consisted of the more photographically realistic works of late Edwardian artists, such as Sir George Clausen (1852–1944) and Sir John Singer Sargent (1856–1925) was not surprisingly one of outrage and shock.

Robert Ross of the *Morning Post* noted the date of the preview, 5 November, and wrote that the exhibition revealed 'the existence of a widespread plot to destroy the whole fabric of European painting'. *The Athenaeum* [12 November 1910] described van Gogh's paintings, presumably unaware of its unfortunate choice of image, as revealing 'the twitch of a paralytic'. The critic for the *Connoisseur* [December 1910] was equally unimpressed, writing:

The walls are hung with works which are like the crude efforts of children, garishly discordant in colour, formless, and destitute of tone . . . [we] regret that men of talent . . . should waste their lives in spoiling acres of good canvas when they might be better employed in stonebreaking for the roads.

3 PABLO PICASSO Buffalo Bill 1911.
One of the few identifiably Cubist works by Picasso shown at the second Grafton exhibition. Fry described the fragmentation of the image into a multitude of planes in the preface to the catalogue. He went on to say: 'The logical extreme of such a method would undoubtedly be the attempt to give up all resemblance to natural form and to create a purely abstract language of form – a visual music.' In this way, he revealed a limited understanding of the realistic aims of Cubism. Mondrian, however, was soon actually to evolve just such an abstract style after his studies of the Cubists' formal language.

The press response was enormous. In November alone (the show was to run until January 1911) over fifty reviews appeared, almost all of them hostile. The public, in its turn, crowded to see the exhibition. As Frank Rutter (1876–1937), one of Fry's few supporters in the press, described in the *Sunday Times* [13 November 1910]:

Every day people flock to the galleries and most of them give vent to their feelings in language more audible than polite. Angry old gentlemen shake their fists in their impotence and cry aloud that all this is just done for advertisement . . . Scandalised ladies murmur their disgust and wonder how anybody dared to exhibit such disgraceful daubs . . . Fashionably dressed young men pry closely into the canvas in the hope of discovering some immorality to explain the uproar, and find nothing there so shocking as their own prurient imagination.

Post-Impressionist art – all the reviewers adopted Fry's neologism – was described as subversive, revolutionary, as the product of anarchists, as though the artists involved were a coherent group committed to political violence. Parallels were drawn with the Suffragette movement, who marched on Parliament a few days after the exhibition opened, and with the threatened strikes of the South Wales miners. After all, Petr Alekseevich Kropotkin (1842–1921) the Russian theorist and exponent of anarchism, was lecturing in London at the time, while the activities of the anarchist groups in France, Russia and Italy were widely reported in the papers. The satirical magazine *Punch* projected a Post-Impressionist novel: an extended nursery rhyme complete with baby noises.

Another favourite stance adopted by hostile critics was that such paintings could only have been produced by lunatics. More than being merely one more example of media hysteria, this proposition was in fact treated quite seriously. The chief psychiatrist at the Royal Hospitals of Bridewell and Bedlam went so far as to give a public lecture demonstrating the parallels between Post-Impressionist art and that of the insane. Fry was invited to attend and to reply – which he did, although unfortunately his remarks do not survive.[5]

Fry had raised the necessary capital for the exhibition from the Yorkshire Bank. While he had assured them that he thought it would be a success, privately he admitted to being rather worried. The immense popular success generated by all the press reaction of 'Manet and the Post-Impressionists' of course proved him wrong. In fact the owners of the Grafton Gallery were so pleased that they made an autumn slot in their galleries available to Fry for any exhibition he chose to mount in the future.

As far as Fry was concerned the somewhat frenetic preparations for the exhibition had resulted in a slightly unbalanced selection of paintings – Picasso and Matisse in particular, he felt, had been under-represented. He therefore determined to hold a second exhibition, especially after he had seen many Cubist works at the Salon d'Automne in Paris in 1911. In any case, as he wrote to his mother in June 1912: 'The British public has dozed off again since the last show and needs another electric shock. I hope I shall be able to provide it.'[6]

The next month Fry made the trip to Europe to choose the paintings. This time, however, he decided to broaden the scope. Clive Bell was to choose a selection of English artists' works to hang alongside those of the French; and after some of the English painters refused to lend their work, another friend, Boris Anrep, was asked to choose a selection of modern Russian paintings.

The 'Second Post-Impressionist Exhibition' opened on 5 October 1912 at the Grafton Gallery. Cézanne was represented by eleven works, including *Le Château Noir* (*see plate 15*). The greatest emphasis, however, was placed upon Picasso (sixteen works), including some of his most recent Cubist creations such as *Buffalo Bill* (*see plate 3*), and Matisse (twenty-six works), including *Le Luxe II* (*see plate 4*). This last picture can be seen in an oil sketch painted by Vanessa Bell (Clive Bell's wife, Virginia Woolf's sister and Roger Fry's lover) depicting the rooms of the Grafton Gallery at the 1912 show (*see plate 5*).

Just as popular as the first show, it ran until the end of December and was then extended to the end of January the following year. Despite Fry's hopes of providing another 'electric shock', critics and public alike were on the whole much more tolerant and sympathetic in their reactions. Stories of old men having to be escorted from the gallery suffering apoplectic fits, as had happened to one elderly gentleman in 1910 when he saw *Madame Cézanne in a Red Armchair* (*see plate 13*), were far fewer.[7]

'Humming-bird Hawkmoth'

As far as Fry himself was concerned, the two exhibitions completely altered the course of his life. As a public figure he had changed from being the connoisseur of the Old Masters to become the spokesman, in England at least, for modern art. Indeed, one of his exceptional qualities was a voracious desire not just to learn, but also then to share and explain the reasons for his own excitement and enjoyment of these disturbing and demanding works of art. Woolf, in the biography she was later to write of Fry, describes him at one of the Grafton exhibitions:

> And there was Roger Fry, gazing at [the pictures], plunging his eyes into them as if he were a humming-bird hawkmoth hanging over a flower, quivering yet still. And then drawing a deep breath of satisfaction, he would turn to whoever it might be, eager for sympathy.[8]

There are many accounts of Fry spending his days at the Grafton Gallery trying to explain to quizzical visitors why these works of art were so important. Taking around the 1912 exhibition one young lady who had complained of the ugliness of three nude figures (possibly referring to Matisse's *Le Luxe II*), Fry replied, 'Yes . . . but just look at the gaps they leave'[9] – in other words, the pattern created by the intervals between the figures. He also spent a whole afternoon sitting in the basement with Henry James (1843–1916), the illustrious writer's portly frame crammed into a tiny chair, explaining over a cup of tea what it was he thought was so significant about the works on view above them.

Fry's new position as spokesman, however, did not just confine itself to guided tours but was really built up through his writing and lecturing. In a number of articles and letters published in the wake of the furore elicited by the exhibitions (especially the first), Fry attempted to formulate his defence before a wider audience.

The Post-Impressionists, he argued in a letter to *The Nation*

in December 1910, had reacted against more established trends in the late nineteenth century in which paintings were made to seem as photographically realistic as possible. This sort of realism, whereby the artist, through skill and sleight of hand, managed to trick the viewer into believing that the image on the canvas was real, Fry himself in fact considered to be something of a deception.

The issue centred around the status of the work of art in relation to nature. Fry concluded that a literal, illusionistic description failed to capture or to express the intrinsic reality or vitality of nature and thus that nature's reality had to be translated into terms of what was real in painting. The image, there-

4   HENRI MATISSE   Le Luxe II   1907.
Matisse bought a small Bathers picture painted by Cézanne in 1899 (see plate 115), and reworked its Arcadian subject matter on various occasions. Here, the insistent textures and awkwardness of Cézanne's drawing style have been relinquished, and Matisse chooses to describe his figures with a monumental, decorative grace. He retains, however, Cézanne's reticence regarding the identification of his figures as particular mythological characters. Standing majestically by the sea, receiving the homage of the other two, Matisse's principal bather hints, however, that she might be Venus, who was born from the Aegean, and looked after by attendants.

fore, should remain faithful to its own material qualities – paint should clearly be paint, a painting should not seek to deny the flatness of the canvas – whilst still being descriptive of nature.

In the catalogue to the second Grafton exhibition, for example, Fry wrote:

These artists seek . . . to arouse the conviction of a new and definite reality, not . . . to imitate form, but to create form; not to imitate life, but to find an equivalent for life.[10]

And in a reply to an enquiry someone had made after hearing one of his lectures, he wrote:

Let us say you go out, you see a scene which appeals to you as beautiful, with all the trained skill and power you possess you faithfully put down all the various values as you see them . . . you measure by eye each tone and colour and get them all relatively right. You know the original scene seemed to be beautiful, you find the faithful transcript dull. There is nothing surprising in this . . . Your impression from the original scene was not purely visual; it was a complex of innumerable sensations made up partly of scenes you had come from. It was part of the vivid reality of your whole actual life. But the sketch is a thing isolated from the stream of life. It cannot have the same reality. If you want to give to any other person the exact impression that the scene made on you, you can't be satisfied with a remi-

niscence, an echo, weakened and dulled; you must find an equivalent. An *equivalent* in pure visual effect for a whole which had much besides its purely visual qualities. It is this discovery of an equivalent for life that occupies the Post-Impressionist artists.[11]

Fry had developed such ideas before 1910 in pieces he wrote about non-illusionistic art from other cultures – most notably in reviews of exhibitions of Islamic and Bushman art – where he praised its emotionally expressive powers achieved at the expense of traditional realism.

When he applied these notions to the Post-Impressionists he was effectively turning current opinion on its head. Most writers considered Post-Impressionism (if, that is, they had heard of it) as a decadent and worthless development arising from the achievements of the Impressionists – as can be seen in the influential writings of a Frenchman Camille Mauclair, whose books were being published in English from 1903 onwards. Fry, on the other hand, considered that by turning their backs on accepted standards of realism and returning to traditions of non-illusionistic representation, the Post-Impressionists had achieved incomparably more than their Impressionist forebears.

The origin of Fry's arguments can be traced directly to France, and in particular to patterns of thought developed by the nineteenth-century poets Charles Baudelaire (1821–1867) and Stéphane Mallarmé (1842–1898) (*see chapter 1*) and taken up by subsequent writers and artists such as

5   VANESSA BELL (sometimes attributed to Roger Fry)
A Room at the Second Post-Impressionist Exhibition   1912.

Denis and Gauguin. In some respects, therefore, Fry's activities could be characterized as the concentrated injection of particular aspects of French culture into British life. (Considering the endemic suspicion and hostility with which these two nations have usually regarded each other from either side of the Channel, it is not surprising that Cézanne, Gauguin, Picasso and the rest provoked such angry reactions in London at the two Grafton exhibitions.)

On a more mundane level, for instance, Fry had introduced the Bloomsbury Group of British writers and intellectuals, whose set he had joined through his friendship with Bell, to the delicious French dish of 'bœuf en daube', a stew of marinated beef cooked very slowly and flavoured with herbs and wine. By all accounts, Fry was a rotten cook, but the 'bœuf en daube' was later to achieve literary immortality in Virginia Woolf's description of Mrs Ramsay's dinner party in her novel *To the Lighthouse* (first published 1927).

There, Mrs Ramsay's genius manages to create a temporary sense of harmony and civilized unity among her guests, while her 'bœuf en daube' assumes a symbolic role as the instrument of her powers. In a similar manner, a passionate belief in the lasting, spiritual value of art as a civilizing influence underpinned Fry's writings. His delivery as a lecturer, so the records state, was no less passionate. Brought up as a strict Quaker, Fry had lost his faith while an undergraduate at Cambridge – but in the end art was to provide the consolation and fulfilment which orthodox belief could no longer satisfactorily endorse in the modern age. As he wrote in the catalogue to the second Post-Impressionist exhibition:

It [Post-Impressionism] is the work of highly civilised and modern men trying to find a pictorial language appropriate to the sensibilities of the modern outlook.[12]

As Fry indicated here, the Post-Impressionists, like artists of any other age, were nurtured in particular material and social conditions. Some sort of acquaintance with these conditions is essential to understanding the background forces and influences that operated upon these artists. By way of summary, it can be said that the dynamic nature of European society from the 1880s to the outbreak of the Great War encouraged artists to experiment and break new ground. On the other hand, the latent violence of many of the period's upheavals and transformations contributed just as significantly to the tendency among artists to reject old conventions and to revolutionize the nature of their work.

Technological and Social Change

Europe suffered no major Continental war during the period 1880–1914 with which this book is concerned. Military conflicts between the various European powers were confined to overseas quarrels, invariably to do with clashes of interest over colonial expansion. Nonetheless, a number of fundamental social changes can be identified at home that affected communities in a multitude of different ways.

The growth of industrialization, begun earlier in the nineteenth century, continued apace. Along with relatively rapid population growth (caused mainly by a falling death rate), industrial output rose enormously: in the period between the

6 GIACOMO BALLA Abstract Speed – The Car Has Passed 1913.
Balla's subject was not the car or the landscape through which it has just carved a path, but rather, as the title indicates, the car's speed, which seems to have left dynamic, quivering echoes of its presence in the sky and trees. The means by which Balla and others of the Futurist group sought to depict the dynamism they perceived as the central characteristic of modern life owe much to Picasso and Braque's Cubism. Futurism's ideological commitment to the machine, however, differentiated their endeavours from the more purely painterly concerns of the Cubists. For they firmly believed in the positive potential of technology and the machine.

turn of the century and the outbreak of war, for example, it rose by almost two-thirds. In the same period half the world's trade was made up by the imports and exports of just seven European nations – Great Britain, Germany, France, Belgium, The Netherlands, Switzerland and Denmark.

In the absence of any significant policies of protectionism, trade between the industrialized nations flourished. Exchange rates were kept stable through the mechanism of the international gold standard; this and the dominance of London's money markets acted as the central pivots in the free worldwide flow of capital and goods. The decades before 1914 were, as the economist John Maynard Keynes (1883–1946) portrayed them, something of a golden age of prosperity:

What an extraordinary episode in the economic progress of man that age was which came to an end in August, 1914 . . . The [prosperous] inhabitant of London could order by telephone, sipping his morning tea in bed, the various products of the whole earth, in such quantity as he might see fit, and reasonably expect their early delivery upon his doorstep; he could at the same moment and by the same means adventure his wealth in the natural resources and new enterprises of any quarter of the world, and share, without exertion or even trouble, in their prospective fruits and advantages . . . He could secure forthwith, if he wished it, cheap and comfortable means of transit to any country or climate without passport or other formality, could dispatch his servant to the neighboring office of a bank for such supply of the precious metals as might seem convenient, and could then proceed abroad to foreign quarters . . . and would consider himself greatly aggrieved and much surprised at the least interference. But, most important of all, he regarded this state of affairs as normal, certain, and permanent, except in the direction of further improvement . . . .[13]

7 FERNAND LÉGER   The Mechanic   1911–18.
Unlike Duchamp, who had reduced human relationships in The Large
Glass *to absurd mechanistic exchanges, Léger visualized man and
machine living in harmony, even after the war had displayed modern
technology's atrocious potential for destruction. Léger himself had fought
in the trenches, so his optimism was not based on ignorance or wishful
thinking. Instead he created an heroic race of manual workers to operate
the new machinery whose capacities, if properly harnessed, could be used
to ameliorate life rather than destroy or devalue it. In the end, his was a
vision located in a metallic, not a verdant, Arcadia.*

Keynes pictures the sort of material ease and moral noncha-
lance enjoyed by the characters in the novels of P. G.
Wodehouse (1881–1975), nostalgically recalled after that
world had passed. Keynes's comments could just as easily
have applied to the prosperous inhabitants of Paris and
Berlin, Continental counterparts of the city he described.

The economic boom of the pre-war years was aided by, if
not actually based upon technological progress, especially
new sources of energy such as oil and electricity. Transport
was revolutionized by the internal combustion engine.
Tractors began to replace the horse in agriculture, taxis the
horse-drawn cab in the cities. The pace of change was extraordinary. The Wright Brothers (Orville 1871–1948 and Wilbur
1876–1912) first flew in 1903. Louis Blériot (1872–1936)
crossed the Channel in 1909 and by 1919 there were regular
passenger flights between London and Paris. In 1897
Guglielmo Marconi (1874–1937) sent a radio signal over a
distance of eighteen miles; by 1901 the first message had
been passed across the Atlantic.

A group of revolutionary Italian artists, the Futurists,
reflected these changes the most directly in their cult of
machine worship. 'A racing car, its body ornamented by great
pipes that resemble snakes with explosive breath . . . is more
beautiful than the Winged Victory of Samothrace [the famous
ancient Greek sculpture in the Louvre]', proclaimed their
manifesto of 1909 (*see plate 6*).[14] Elsewhere the new aeroplane
often appeared in the works of the French artists
Robert Delaunay (1885–1941) and Roger de la Fresnaye
(1885–1925) (*see plates 17 and 18*). By 1918 Matisse would
include the windscreen in a number of landscapes he painted
from the front seat of his new car – an invasion both literal
and symbolic of modern technology into the rural. Much of

the faith and optimism invested in the machine at this
stage was lost, however, after the war's horrific demonstration
of technology's destructive capability (*see plate 7*). While
Fernand Léger's (1881–1955) work was unusual in depicting
harmony between man and machine, growing numbers of
artists after 1914 visualized the machine in inhuman, even
demonic terms (*see plate 28*).

Increasing industrialization and wealth brought large movements of people from the country to the city, both to provide
the necessary labour and to enjoy the material benefits of
urban life. Cities were made healthier and safer through
improved lighting and sanitation. In Germany the expansion
of the urban population was the most prolific: between 1850
and 1914 its rural population remained more or less static,
while its total population almost doubled from 35 to 60 million over the same period. Similar shifts, though not as spectacular, occurred in Great Britain and France. In Russia, on
the other hand, in 1913 80 per cent of the population still
worked on the land.

More generally, increased urban populations created a
wealth of new social pressures that demanded changes. These
were to be reflected in the arts. The new material abundance,
the higher standards of living and increased amounts of
leisure-time had made poverty seem unacceptable. The economic boom was to stimulate social reform: first of all in elec-
toral reform and the principle of universal (male, at least)
suffrage, achieved by most European states by the turn of the
century.

A larger franchise demanded educated voters and thus
helped bring about the state's provision of free and increasingly secularized education – again, something which most
north-western countries had accomplished (at least in primary education) by 1900.

Under Bismarck in the 1880s Germany had instituted a
national system of social insurance. It was an example the
majority of European states was to follow. Schemes such as
these demanded an extension of state intervention into the
life of the community. More practically they had to be paid
for. In 1871 Britain had been the exception in Europe in levy-
ing an income tax. By the 1890s France was unique in not
having one at all.

The same period also saw the emergence of organized
political power for the urban working classes in the growth of
the socialist movement and trade unionism. In Great Britain
and Germany the formation of socialist or Labour parties had
taken place before 1900; in France and Italy they were born
slightly later where, traditionally split from the trade unions,
they developed more extremist tendencies. By 1914 membership of the various socialist parties of industrialized Europe
had doubled and in some cases trebled.

Many of the artists with whom we are concerned deal with
these particular issues; all were affected by them. Camille
Pissarro (1830–1903) and Paul Signac (1863–1935) were
committed anarchists. Pellizza da Volpedo (1868–1907) and
Maximilien Luce (1858–1941) pictured the sites and communities of the new working classes (*see plates 19 and 20*).
Picasso and Henri de Toulouse-Lautrec (1864–1901) chose
subjects both from the urban underworld and from those
groups who had been marginalized by the convulsions of
social change (*see plates 26 and 27*). Ernst Ludwig Kirchner
(1880–1938) and August Macke (1887–1914), meanwhile,

produced images of the new urban prosperity (*see plates 8 and 25*). Many others simply turned their backs on it all to retreat into a world of artifice and the imagination.

The absence of a Continental war – and the relative stability that brought – did not prevent some of these changes occasionally and inevitably slipping into manifestations of violence. In the quarter of a century before 1914 large-scale strikes broke out in Great Britain. Strife over Ireland and the Home Rule Bill erupted violently in Ulster in 1913 and, but for the outbreak of European war the following year, might easily have led to more widespread civil war. In France, the Third Republic almost split apart as a result of extreme right-wing support for General Boulanger (1837–1891) in the 1880s. Further polarization ensued as extraordinary forces were unleashed by the Dreyfus Affair in the 1890s, in particular those of anti-clericalism and anti-Semitism. This last culminated in an abortive coup d'état in 1899 and eventually led to the formal separation of Church and State in 1904.

Clashes between all the major powers in the Far East led to the outbreak of war between Russia and Japan in 1904 and, following defeat in 1905, to the first Russian revolution.

France and Germany quarrelled over their respective colonial interests in Morocco in 1906 and 1911: declarations of war were only narrowly averted. As one historian has written:

Anti-semitism and anti-clericalism were the domestic counter-parts to militarism and imperialism in international affairs. It is not mere coincidence that Bolshevism, the prototype of revolutionary movements aiming at single-party dictatorship, dated . . . from 1903, and the ideas of Lenin were shaped during the twenty years before 1914 . . . The war itself, in some aspects, was a consistent if vastly exaggerated form of a nihilistic, destructive trend inherent in European civilization.[15]

Other examples of political violence deserve mention. There was the rise of organized urban violence: the gangs of Apaches, for instance, that terrorized Paris in the first decade of the twentieth century. In one of their first appearances, in the Parisian suburbs of Nanterre in 1909, twelve people were attacked and robbed in one night. One of the Apaches, named Liabeuf, was only arrested after he had killed one gendarme and wounded three others. As the terrified press reported the next day, he was found to be armed with a revolver, a knife and leather wrist-bands studded with spikes.

Following the theoretical writings of the exiled Russian Prince Kropotkin, anarchist groups formed in Russia, Italy, Japan and France. Their activities were widely reported in the press and fictionalized in the novels of Joseph Conrad (1857–1924). One recorded incident that took place in Paris seems worthy of fiction in itself: the Affaire Leauthier. In November 1893 an anarchist shoemaker refused to pay his bill at the famous restaurant of Marguery's on the grounds that he had lost all his money to the 'dirty bourgeois'. He then 'walked to the Avenue de l'Opéra where he stabbed the Serbian Minister "because", he said, "he was well dressed and wore a decoration."'[16]

Among the artistic community, Signac, Vlaminck and Pissarro were all closely associated with the anarchist movement (*see plate 24*). The painter Luce and the critic Félix Fénéon were both arrested in an anti-anarchist purge that followed a spate of anarchist bombings in Paris and the assassination in July 1894 of President Carnot. Fénéon was released

8 ERNST LUDWIG KIRCHNER Five Women in the Street 1913.
Kirchner's elegantly dressed women prowl a luridly lit Berlin street, their fashionable costumes and feathered hats made angular and jagged according to the raw, expressive style of the 'primitive' art he had studied. This violent and incongruous juxtaposition of styles – those of urban fashion and the 'primitive' – was deliberately jarring. Through it Kirchner was able to release his neurotic and sarcastic vision of modern city life. The women on this claustrophobic, flattened street are viewed almost as predatory animals; they are certainly dehumanized. If indeed they represent prostitutes waiting for customers (as some writers maintain), these feral associations assume further resonance.

shortly afterwards but Luce was sentenced to a short term of imprisonment (*see plate 9*).

In the broadest terms, then, the innovations and the spirit of restless experimentalism that characterizes so much of the avant-garde painting of the period can be viewed as a reflection of the forces of dynamism and latent violence that were animating European society.

The Rise of an Avant Garde

How and where did the Post-Impressionists fit into such a society? Certainly the uneasy relations between them acted as a catalyst in all the innovation and experiment. More generally, the fundamental changes and transformations outlined above caused artists to question their role and even the value of art in modern, industrial society.

In the past, artists had always maintained strong, direct links with society's structures of political and economic power. Painters, sculptors and architects had generally worked on commission for specific patrons – the Church, the guilds, the State or the monarchy. Many of the finest statues of Donatello (1386–1466) had been made for a number of the wealthiest and most influential guilds in fifteenth-century Florence. At roughly the same time, some of the finest paintings by Vittore Carpaccio (1455–1522) and Gentile Bellini (c.1429–1507) were commissioned to celebrate the splendour of the Venetian Republic. In the early sixteenth century the Sistine Chapel frescoes were commissioned from Michelangelo Buonarroti (1475–1564) to proclaim the glory of the pope, Julius II. In seventeenth-century Spain Diego de Velázquez (1599–1660) was employed for the whole of his working life to immortalize the nobility of the king, Philip IV, and the Hapsburg royal family.

The artist's social status had risen enormously through the continuous patronage of such exalted and powerful institutions or individuals. The painter in fourteenth-century Europe was considered to be no more important than any other artisan. He was on a par with the barrel-maker, the apothecary and the stone mason. Three hundred years later Peter Paul Rubens (1577–1640), an eminent diplomat as well as a painter of international repute, was courted by just about every European monarch. When Charles I of England (1600–1649) could not persuade Rubens to work for him, he was forced to turn instead to the services of Sir Anthony van Dyck (1599–1641) to act as his official royal painter.

9 PAUL SIGNAC   Portrait of Félix Fénéon   1890.
Fénéon was a prolific writer and an ardent defender of the avant garde in the Parisian press. He contributed to scores of journals and periodicals, founded some of his own, and edited the poetry of Rimbaud, Laforgue and Lautréamont. He was especially interested in the divisionism of Seurat and Signac, and a close friend of both painters. The swirling abstract patterns in the background, including references to the Stars and Stripes, the 'Uncle Sam' profile with which Fénéon is shown and the flower he is holding (probably a cyclamen) evidently refer to various arcane, private interests shared by sitter and artist alike.

Despite these changes the artist had always remained linked to persons or groups that were themselves closely connected to the reins of power. In the nineteenth century these ties were embodied in the Academy. A brief look at the workings of the Académie des Beaux-Arts in France, and the growth of a community of artists operating outside its influence – the avant garde – will serve to illustrate the predicament of the Post-Impressionist generations within European society before the outbreak of the First World War.

The Académie des Beaux-Arts, or as Cézanne use to call it in his strong Provençal accent, the 'Bozards', operated as a regulatory body concerned with all aspects of the production and consumption of art. It functioned in two ways: firstly in the teaching and training of artists and secondly in the provision of a marketplace for their work. As the artists' only representative body its authority and power over the management of these functions was complete.

As an educational establishment it rigidly followed a programme of instruction that had been developed from those of the very first academies established in Renaissance Italy. Its students, whether at the Ecole des Beaux-Arts in Paris or at any of the other provincial schools, all followed the same course, based on the imitation and emulation of the past. Having gained admission, students spent their first two years drawing – first from antique sculptures or plaster casts taken from these statues, and later from the model. There was great emphasis on the correct placing of the contour or outline and the corresponding skill of modelling: that is, the gradual shading from dark to light with pencil or charcoal to describe volume. Students were expected to be able to perform both these skills with precise anatomical correctness. It was only after a student's ability in drawing was deemed satisfactory that the handling of colour was introduced.

Teaching here centred on the practice of copying the paintings of the Old Masters, especially those in the former Royal Collection housed in the Louvre. Art students performed this task for a number of reasons. Firstly it was the most effective way of teaching them the technical skills of composition or design, of perspective, and of modelling – this time with oil paint rather than charcoal. Secondly, and more pragmatically, it was a good way of filling provincial museums and townhalls with cheap copies of the masterpieces held in the Louvre. Students, too, were usually very grateful for the 400 francs or so that the state was willing to pay for a good copy of a Nicolas Poussin (c. 1593–1665) or a Jean-Baptiste-Siméon Chardin (1699–1779).

Students were also taught about different types of subject matter. These were classified according to a strict hierarchy that had also been developed and modified from the original Renaissance academy's model. Thus, at the top of the list were narrative paintings of a religious or historical character. Below these came landscape, only recognized as a separate genre in the seventeenth century, and portraiture. At the bottom of the list came still-life. In each case teaching was rigid and authoritarian. Any kind of non-conformism displayed by students in the application of these methods was frowned upon; but such students were jeopardizing their chances of future success in any case, as the Academy also controlled the principal market place – the Salon. It was here that artists were able to display their work before the public.

Held once a year in Paris, the Salon was indispensable to an artist's commercial success. It was here that works could be sold, commissions for new pieces won from either private or public patrons, and reputations and market value enhanced if an artist were to win one of the various prizes on offer. Admission to the Salon, however, was gained by submitting work to a jury made up of the same individuals who were responsible for the Academy's teaching programmes. The Académie des Beaux-Arts thus prescribed not only the subject matter artists should adopt, but also the style or manner in which these subjects should be depicted.

As a result the Academy directly connected the production of art with society, and, in the case of public patronage, with society's political structures. In so doing it provided artists with stability, security and a well-defined route to success. On the other hand, as we shall see, by its very rigidity it also unwittingly prescribed those areas of non-conformism that were to be explored by the avant garde.

The first blow against the authority of the Academy was struck by the painter Gustave Courbet (1819–1877) in 1855. Two of his paintings had that year been rejected by the jury presiding over the official display of French art to be held at the International Exhibition in Paris. Undaunted, he had exhibited his work in his own private pavilion. Courbet's defiance did not prove commercially successful. His pavilion attracted few visitors from the thousands who had flocked to Paris; the painter Eugène Delacroix (1798–1863) remembers standing alone in the tent for almost an hour, entranced by one of his canvases. Courbet's example, however, sent a powerful signal to future generations – art could exist outside the Académie des Beaux-Arts. In this sense, this was the first act of the avant garde. His successors were to be Claude Monet (1840–1926), Renoir, Pissarro, Cézanne, Edgar Degas (1834–1917) and Alfred Sisley (1839–1899): in other words, the Impressionists.

The first Impressionist exhibition took place in 1874 in the former studios of the contemporary photographer Nadar (1820–1910), on the Boulevard des Capucines in the centre of Paris. It opened on 15 April, two weeks before the Salon. But though it was independent of the Academy and the Salon, the artists who exhibited at Nadar's old studio were not making a collective stand of premeditated defiance. They were not a coherent group of artists who shared a set of ideas and beliefs. They did not even choose the name 'Impressionists', which was given them by the critic Jules Castagnary. In fact they called themselves the Société Anonyme des Peintres, Sculpteurs et Graveurs, the name of the limited company they had formed in order to defray the costs and limit the risk of their enterprise.

The first Impressionist exhibition, rather than being a calculated attack on the authority of the Academy, was a commercial venture designed to attract the monied crowds who thronged the Boulevard des Capucines. Industrialization and urbanization had enormously increased the art-consuming market of the bourgeois classes: a market with which the Salon alone was no longer big enough to cope. The Impressionist exhibition adopted somewhat unusual opening times – from 10 am to 6 pm and from 8 pm to 10 pm – in an effort to attract visitors (and therefore buyers) from those at work during the day. Eschewing large proportions, most of the works on view were small and eminently portable – designed to hang in a bourgeois, not a palatial setting.

Nevertheless, even though they were not deliberately antagonizing the Academy, the first Impressionists were inadvertently continuing a tradition of avant-garde tactics inaugurated by Courbet. Seven more 'Impressionist' exhibitions were held: the eighth and final one took place in 1886. Some of the artists involved, such as Camille Pissarro, rarely sought official recognition at the Salon because of their political sympathies. Others, like Cézanne, simply never had any of their works passed by the Academy's jury (though not for want of trying), and so were obliged to show their work at these independent exhibitions. Others still, like Renoir and Monet, were to show their paintings both at the Salon and at some of the Impressionist ventures.

Avant-Garde Institutions

By the end of the 1880s the avant garde had created a network of structures specifically geared to the marketing and consumption of art outside the circuit established by the Academy. Three particular institutions can and should be identified.

The new, large urban populations themselves provided new markets for art, markets that sustained and eventually encouraged innovation and experiment. The demand for avant-garde art generated by these markets was supplied in the first place by a growing number of specialist picture dealers and secondly at the artists' own independently organized exhibitions. Moreover, the new bourgeois patrons were kept informed by the writings of a new breed of specialist art critics. In each case the avant garde was given the opportunity to operate most effectively outside traditional and established systems, either run by or closely connected to the state.

More and more picture dealers had set up businesses in Paris, specializing in avant-garde art. Figures such as Paul Durand-Ruel (1831–1922) and Georges Petit (c. 1835–1900) had patronized most of the leading Impressionist painters in their early days and by the close of the century were beginning to see a return on their investment. Other dealers followed these pioneers to handle the work of subsequent generations. Ambroise Vollard, for example, opened a gallery on the rue Laffitte in Paris in the early 1890s and was to earn his fame (and fortune) as Cézanne's principal dealer (see plates 29 and 30). The Bernheim-Jeune brothers were to deal with Matisse and Bonnard, Daniel Kahnweiler with the Cubists. Elsewhere, Paul Cassirer devoted his gallery in Berlin to exhibitions of work by contemporary French and German painters.

These figures were a new breed. Private picture-dealing had in the past been undertaken by existing businesses very much as a sideline – usually by people selling artists' materials. Père Tanguy, for example, a friend of many of the French Post-Impressionists, ran just such a business in Paris in the 1880s and 1890s and used to accept the otherwise unwanted works of van Gogh, Gauguin and Cézanne in return for canvas, brushes and pigment.

Durand-Ruel, Vollard and the rest were different because their entire business activities centred on the buying and selling of works of art. Shrewd practices were adopted in order to keep the market for avant-garde painting buoyant. Painters would become contracted to a particular dealer; and while the dealer would pay a fixed sum for anything the painter

10   Photograph of pictures being viewed by the jury of the Salon des Indépendants, 1903.

produced, the painter was prohibited from selling his work to anyone else. In this way, although the painter would be sure of a regular income, the dealer – with a monopoly of that artist's work – would be in a position to control their market value. Matisse had this type of contract with Bernheim-Jeune, for example, as did Derain with Vollard; indeed, with charac-teristically sound business instincts, Vollard had bought the entire contents of the young painter's studio in 1906. Vollard is also known to have bought back paintings from his own stock when they failed to reach a sufficiently high price at auction, thus artificially inflating the market for a particular artist. Such strategies were not uncommon.

Apart from the dealers, other outlets were devised, follow-ing the Impressionists' example, for the independent exhibi-tion of art. The painters Signac and Seurat had helped set up the Salon des Indépendants in 1884. Held from 1886 just off the Champs-Elysées in the spring of each year, it distin-guished itself by having no jury. Any painter who paid a small subscription became a member of the Société des Artistes Indépendants and this entitled him to show up to six works at the annual salon (*see plate 10*).

This strict policy of unrestricted entry naturally proved very popular with artists and over the years the number of works exhibited rose dramatically. Within a few years many felt that their work was being swamped and that the sheer bulk of material on show was indigestible both for prospective buyers and for the critics whose reviews could help boost sales. As a result, two painters who had begun their careers in the 1890s on the fringes of the avant garde, Frantz Jourdain (1847–1935) and Jacques-Emile Blanche (1861–1942), decided in 1903 to set up an alternative: the Salon d'Automne. It was held annually in Paris in October so as not to conflict with the Salon des Indépendants that ran from March to April. Unlike the Indépendants, the Salon d'Automne had a jury, chosen by lot by the entire society which comprised not only artists but also writers, collectors and connoisseurs (as for its predecessor, membership was by subscription). Members were allowed to submit ten works each for the jury to examine and decide whether or not to show. In this way the Salon d'Automne intended to promote some sort of quality control over the art it presented to the public. In 1905, for example, while the Indépendants exhi-bited 4,236 works, the Salon d'Automne limited itself to 1,625.

The first Salon d'Automne had taken place in 1903 (*see*

plate 11) in the galleries of the Petit Palais. Raymond Escholier, a friend of Matisse and a future Director of the museum that is now housed in the same buildings, recalls the opening night:

A night in October, 1903. A long line of carriages parked at the entrance of the Petit Palais . . . under the dazzling brightness of arc lamps, broken up by the scattered foliage of the trees, the bustle of the elegant crowd: beauti-ful ladies in grand evening dresses who covered their shivering shoulders in coats of skunk or mink, well-heeled gentleman in frock-coats or tails.[17]

Thus, only sixty years after Courbet's pavilion, unofficial exhi-bitions such as the Salon d'Automne had become a fixed part of the art-going public's calendar, frequented by the same bourgeois crowds as filled the rooms of the official Salon – the crowds Escholier describes. Even if the bourgeois classes only came to laugh or ridicule the work put on show at exhi-bitions like the Salon d'Automne (*see plate 12*), these had nonetheless become established events.

As well as the dealers and the new display cases, the third essential part of this network was made up by the growing number of magazines and journals that reviewed and evalu-ated the work of the avant-garde artists. Within the press the nature and role of the critic had undergone a change similar to that of the picture dealer. Here, too, the amateur had given way to the professional:

Previously Salon reviews had been a literary challenge accepted by almost every writer, but amateurs were now replaced by men who were beginning to make a profession of writing about art, such as Fénéon and Aurier who were, above all, critics with expert knowledge gained from direct contact with the artists they defended.[18]

Most of the journals concerned, however, were not specifically devoted to the visual arts but could be described more generally as literary reviews. It was chiefly here that avant-garde painters found their work discussed:

Literary magazines were already numerous when, in the 1880s and 1890s, there flowered large numbers of new reviews, often with miniscule circula-tions, founded by young writers (singly or in groups) whose main charac-teristic was fierce opposition to accepted values of society and to the views of all others. They seem to have considered Impressionist, Neo-Impressionist and Symbolist art as the only kind worth writing about. All

11   Photograph of the opening of the Salon d'Automne, 1903.

— Le difficile, ce n'est pas de faire un tableau... c'est de savoir le regarder !

12   At the Salon d'Automne: Cartoon in *Le Figaro*, October 1907.

this in strong contrast to the art periodicals which, though claiming to favour change and progress and to have a strong interest in the new, almost without exception saw no contradiction between their belief in progress and their attachment to the established conventions and to the consensus of opinion. They sometimes attacked the obtuseness of juries or governments [. . .] but they seldom looked beyond the Salon.[19]

Thus, while publications such as the prestigious *Gazette des Beaux-Arts* or the more popular *Art et Décoration* tended to ignore what was going on in avant-garde circles, progressive literary journals such as the *Mercure de France* and *La Revue Blanche* provided extensive coverage of the independent exhibitions like the Salon des Indépendants and reviews of smaller shows put on at the dealers' galleries.

Critics such as Charles Morice at the *Mercure de France* and Thadée Natanson at *La Revue Blanche*, who knew most of the artists about whom they were writing, thus fulfilled an important task as mediators between the public and the avant garde. An artist's commercial reliance upon such figures was extensive. In 1906, for example, Matisse was so upset by Denis's review of his monumental painting *Le Bonheur de Vivre* (*see plate 134*) that he challenged the critic face-to-face at the Salon des Indépendants where it was hanging to justify his comments.

In this and many other cases, the close links between the writers and editors of such journals and the artists themselves encouraged artists to put pen to paper; in fact the editorial offices of these journals became as important as the café as a forum for the lively exchange of ideas. Gauguin and Emile Bernard (1868–1941), as well as their respective supporters, engaged in a lengthy battle in the pages of the *Mercure de France*, arguing over the paternal rights to the innovations of the Pont-Aven school of painters. In 1898 Signac published his defence of his pointillist style of painting in the pages of *La Revue Blanche*, and in 1908 Matisse was obliged to defend his art in an enormously influential article published in *La Grande Revue*.

Thus, even though the mainstream art journals remained silent, the avant garde showed a certain ingenuity in bringing its views before the public. If their painting was particularly

revolutionary and audacious, as in the case of the Cubists, the role of the critic assumed enormous importance in explaining and demystifying it for the rest of the community. The immense success and importance enjoyed by the Cubists would have been unthinkable, for example, without the prolific and energetic defence it received from the critic and poet Guillaume Apollinaire (1880–1914).

The avant garde, then, developed institutions and structures to sustain its own growth outside the traditional and established milieu of the Académie des Beaux-Arts. But all of these, being unconnected either to the State or to the Church, left artists with no defined moral, theological or political philosophy to promote. Artists were cut off, in this sense, from the rest of society. This was bound to cause them to question their role and their function; but it was also this very detachment that stimulated the extraordinary energy behind the innovation and experimentation that characterize this period of European culture.

Picasso and Georges Braque (1882–1963) invented Cubism, thus formulating a visual language which has come to influence, in architecture and design, just about every facet of modern life. Marcel Duchamp (1887–1968) and before him the Futurists celebrated the new technology in ways that anticipate the activities of the Pop Art movement in the 1960s. Other iconic names spring to mind: Cézanne, van Gogh, Gauguin, Matisse, Wassily Kandinsky (1866–1944) and Piet Mondrian (1872–1944) . . . . Even the shortest list of some of the greatest names involved in the visual arts between 1880 and 1914 suggests that this period was an extraordinarily fertile one, comparable in riches to those of any age.

NOTES

1 Virginia Woolf, 'Mr Bennett and Mrs Brown' in *Virginia Woolf: Collected Essays*, Volume I, London, 1966, 320.

2 Denys Sutton (ed.), *The Letters of Roger Fry*, London, 1972, I, 159.

3 Desmond MacCarthy, 'The Art-Quake of 1910' in *The Listener*, 1 February 1945.

4 Ibid.

5 For this and all the other media reactions to the Grafton exhibitions, I am indebted to J. B. Bullen (ed.), *Post-Impressionists in England*, London, New York, 1988.

6 Denys Sutton (ed.), op. cit., I, 359.

7 Desmond MacCarthy, op. cit.

8 Virginia Woolf, *Roger Fry: A Biography*, London, 1940, 159.

9 Benedict Nicolson, 'Post-Impressionism and Roger Fry' in *Burlington Magazine*, (XCIII), January 1951, 15, note 44.

10 In J. B. Bullen, op. cit., 348.

11 20 February 1913, in Denys Sutton (ed.), op. cit., 364.

12 In J. B. Bullen, op. cit., 348

13 J. M. Keynes, *The Economic Consequences of Peace*, New York, 1920, 10–11.

14 Filippo Marinetti, *Le Figaro*, 20 February 1909, quoted in Norbert Lynton, 'Futurism', in Nikos Stangos (ed.), *Concepts of Modern Art*, London, 1985, 97.

15 David Thomson, *The New Cambridge History, Volume XII, The Era of Violence 1898–1945*, Cambridge, 1969, 560-61.

16 R. H. Wilenski, *Modern French Painters*, London, 1939, 146.

17 Raymond Escholier, *Henri Matisse*, Paris, 1937, 63.

18 Hans Brill, in T. Fawcett and C. Philpot (eds.), *The Art Press*, London, 1976, 27.

19 Hans Brill, op. cit., 25.

13 PAUL CÉZANNE Madame Cézanne in a Red Armchair 1877.
While this painting was to cause apoplexy and consternation among the
British public, Fry could write of it in a letter published in The Nation *on*
3 December 1910: 'It has that self-contained inner life, that resistance and
assurance that belong to a real image, not to a mere reflection of some
more insistent reality.' The painting, in other words, achieved more than
just a photographic reproduction of the sitter, though Fry never clearly
defined exactly what this extra quality was. Unfortunately, Madame
Cézanne's opinion on the matter is not recorded.

14 HENRI MATISSE Girl with Green Eyes 1908.

This is one of a number of portraits of anonymous professional models wearing exotic costume that Matisse painted during the early months of 1909. The model here, a young Italian woman, is wearing an elaborate Chinese robe. Above and behind her on a shelf are examples of ceramic pots that Matisse decorated, as well as what looks like a plaster cast. It is a painting rich in colour, and yet all the hues remain subordinate to the vivid emerald green of the model's eyes. And despite its sumptuous palette, this is not one of Matisse's more radical works, which perhaps explains why Fry chose it for his first exhibition – so as to reassure the British public – and also why Matisse chose to exhibit it at the Salon des Indépendants in 1909.

15 PAUL CÉZANNE Le Château Noir 1904.

Le Château Noir was a ruin, set in a large estate near Cézanne's home in Aix; he painted it many times during the last years of his life. The subject is a romantic one: the empty shell of the château, with its pointed, Gothic windows silhouetted against the sky, seems about to be engulfed by the swirling masses of foliage and the dynamic thrusts of the branches. During this final phase of his career, the same natural motifs he had depicted with such poise and classic stability in the 1880s seemed now to Cézanne to be animated by turbulent, even violent energies.

16 GEORGES SEURAT Lighthouse at Honfleur 1886.
*Seurat's divisionist technique was well suited for describing atmospheric
conditions: the small dots of pigment capture the animation and flicker of
sunlight whilst also seeming to interpose an almost grey veil between us
and the scene, as though our eye must penetrate an atmospheric curtain.
Any emotional associations the subject might hold are ignored; the
picture is really only accessible to the eye. At the same time, however,
the artificiality of this style is apparent – in this depopulated scene art
triumphs over the chaos of nature. Where the Impressionists testified to
the instability of nature, Seurat uses nature to create his own abstract
world of order and permanence.*

17 ROGER DE LA FRESNAYE Conquest of the Air 1913.
The two figures, the painter and his brother, seem to be contemplating and planning the projected conquest of the title. De la Fresnaye's brother was passionately interested in yachting and aviation, as the boat and balloon indicate. For the painter, conquest was more a question of artistic goals than any physical or mechanical achievement. The title of the picture is also a veiled homage to Picasso and Braque, the pioneers of Cubism, whose stylistic traits are evident in de la Fresnaye's work; the first review in the Parisian press to mention Cubist painting was printed above an article describing one of the Wright Brothers' latest aerial feats.

18   ROBERT DELAUNAY   Homage to Blériot   1914.

The propellor and undercarriage of Blériot's monoplane can be seen
emerging from the brilliantly coloured discs in the lower left-hand corner.
These circular, abstract shapes seem to emulate the engineered turbulence
produced by the propellor, translating the means by which man finally
learnt to raise himself from the earth into sumptuous, rainbowed eddies of
colour. Already airborne, what looks like the Wright Brothers' first
aeroplane floats in the sky far above, hovering over the Eiffel Tower, the
most conspicuous monument to architectural modernity in Paris. Air
travel is pictured in lyrically beautiful terms only a few years before the
discovery of its destructive potential.

19   GIUSEPPE PELLIZZA DA VOLPEDO   Fiumana   1895–96.
Pellizza used the peasants from his native village of Volpedo as models
throughout the long gestation of this enormous painting (it was abandoned
in 1896). It was always intended to be a massive statement of his political
ideals, a monumental gesture of sympathy with the oppressed agricultural
workers of his home. It was also meant to show the inevitable progress of
the working classes within society, striding forward en masse to claim
their political and material rights. Of his chosen subject Pellizza wrote:
'I am attempting a Social painting . . . a crowd of people, workers of the
soil, who are intelligent, strong, robust, united, advance like a torrent,
overthrowing every obstacle in its path, thirsty for justice.' (A. Scotti,
Catalogo dei Manoscritti di Giuseppe Pellizza da Volpedo *, Tortona,*
1974, 40.)

20   MAXIMILIEN LUCE   The Iron Foundry   1899.

Luce visited the mining areas in southern Belgium in the early 1890s and thereafter painted a number of industrial subjects. This one was painted in his Paris studio. Occasionally he painted similar industrial scenes emphasizing the devastation and suffering that factory, mine and mill had wrought both on the landscape and on the lives of those who worked in them. In others, as in this picture, Luce described the workers in heroic terms. Here the outstretched arm of the main figure to the right recalls the poses of one of the most famous Neo-classical paintings of the eighteenth century: David's Oath of the Horatii (1785, Louvre, Paris).

21 PAUL GAUGUIN Agony in the Garden 1889.
Gauguin erupted as a new leading figure within the Parisian avant garde the year before this self-portrait was painted. The following year he returned to Brittany where he had been painting in 1888. He was followed there by an increasing number of disciples anxious to absorb something of his audacity. Gauguin was in some ways glad of this attention, not least because it meant that his bills at the inn where he was living were paid by someone else. At the same time, however, fame had not brought him fortune; and he felt the loneliness and isolation of the innovator as a burden that not even the most ardent of his apostles could alleviate. It was these feelings that prompted him to picture himself, not unflatteringly, as Christ suffering alone in the Garden of Gethsemane.

22 PAUL GAUGUIN Manao tupapau (Spirit of the Dead Watching) 1892.
Gauguin painted this work during his first trip to Tahiti. It was based on a real experience. One evening he had found his wife Tehura stretched out on the bed in their hut, terrified of the dark which the Tahitians believed was populated by the spirits of dead souls. Fascinated by such 'primitive' beliefs, Gauguin attempted to formulate them in a painting that would operate both in an abstract and a narrative manner; or, as he wrote himself: 'The musical part: undulating horizontal lines, harmonies of orange and blue brought together by yellows and purples, their derivatives, which are lighted by greenish sparks. The literary part: the spirit of a living soul united with the spirit of the dead. Day and night.' (From his own notes, cited in J. de Rotonchamp, Paul Gauguin, Paris, 1925, 253.)

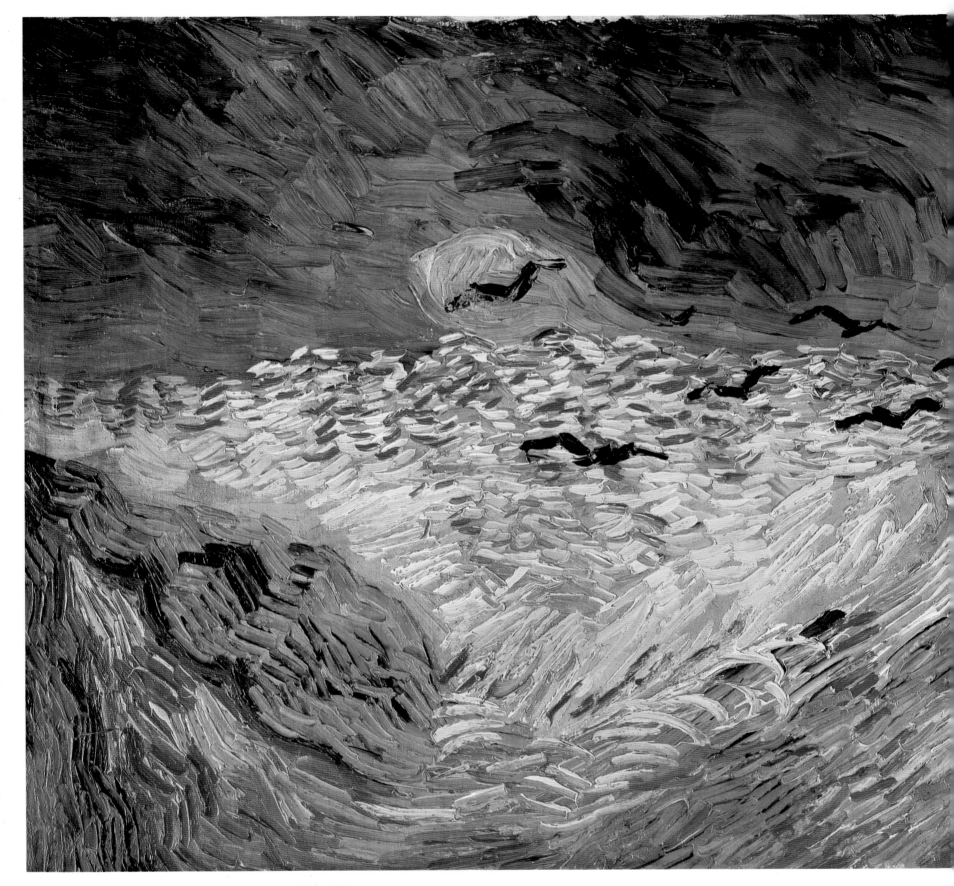

23 VINCENT VAN GOGH   Crows over Wheatfields   1890.
*As John Berger has pointed out in his book Ways of Seeing
(Harmondsworth, 1972), our reaction to this and other van Gogh
paintings of wheatfields has been irrevocably conditioned by the knowledge
that he shot himself only days after completing them. The black birds
become prophetic symbols of the painter's imminent death. The crowded
composition, in which the paths in the corn seem to approach the viewer
rather than recede into space, suggests the mental anguish that provoked
that terrible, final act. Even the deep blue of the late summer sky, pregnant
now with biography, appears heavy and storm-laden.*

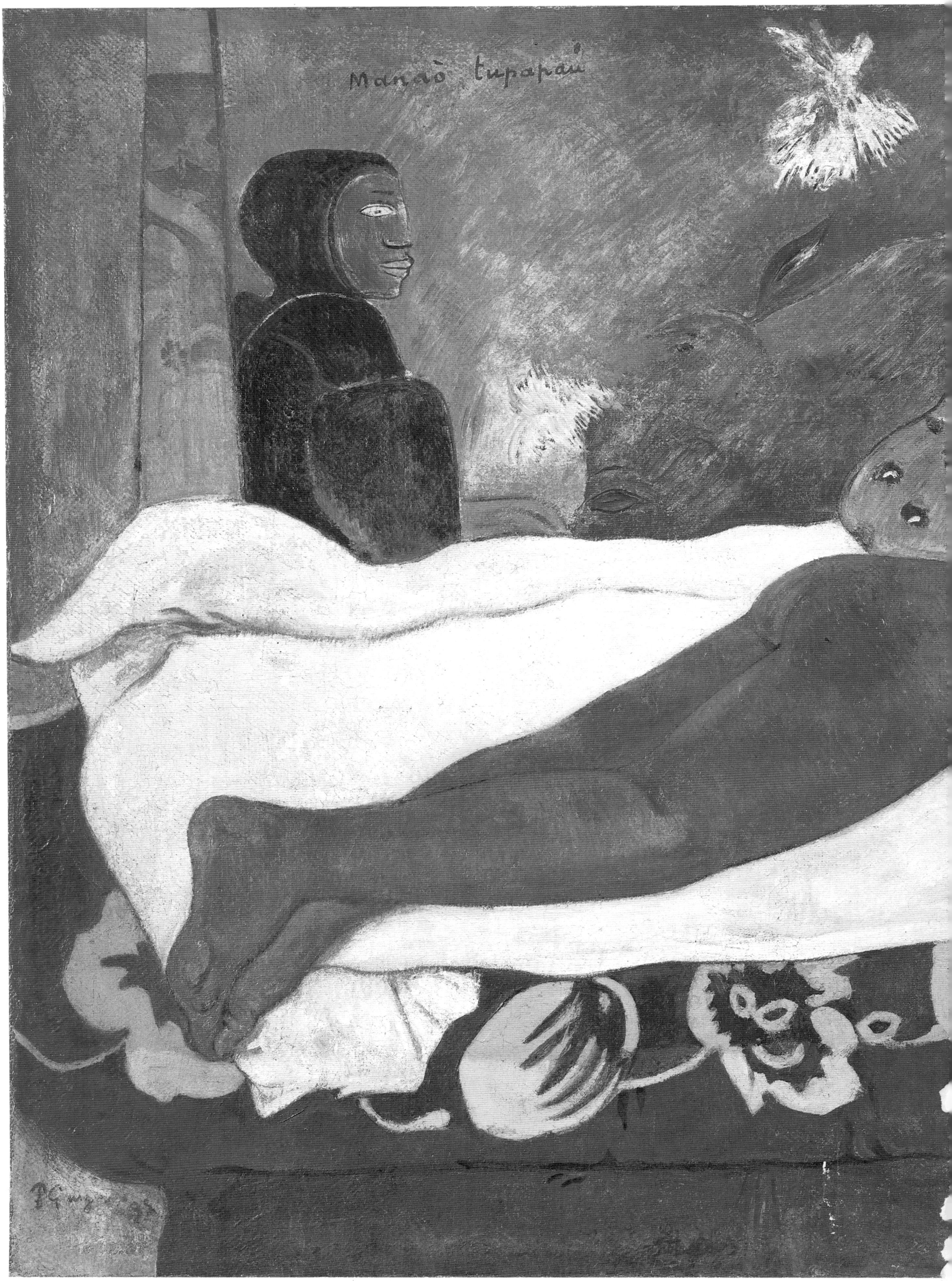
Manaò tupapaù

24 CAMILLE PISSARRO   Ile Lacroix, Rouen – Effect of Fog
1888.

More than any other Impressionist, Pissarro painted many works whose
subjects reflect the changes undergone by the French landscape as a result
of the Industrial Revolution. He also often pictured the working men and
women who lived in these radically altered environments. The lyrical,
poetic qualities so evident and attractive in Impressionism's description
of natural light have tended to camouflage the political flavour of much
of Pissarro's subject matter. His conviction was shared by a number of
younger artists with anarchist sympathies, such as the painter Paul
Signac. It was from Signac that Pissarro learnt the new technique of
divisionism – or 'pointillism' – which he has employed here.

25 AUGUST MACKE Large, Well-Lit Shop Window 1912.
If Kirchner's images of the fashions of the modern city were acerbic and
bitter (see plate 8), Macke was subtler in his approach to broadly similar
subject matter. A gentle irony replaces violent polemic as Macke seems to
describe the hypnotic attractions of a window display in a Munich street.
The materialist urge to possess and consume, foisted upon us by the
mesmeric power of modern commercialism, is depicted here in all its
brilliance and false glitter. Both this painting and Kirchner's work,
however, reveal the extent to which the modern urban environment was
transforming everyday life.

26 PABLO PICASSO Acrobat with Ball 1905.
Picasso moved to Paris in the early 1900s and settled in Montmartre.
It was at this time that he and his friends used to frequent the Cirque
Médrano, and it was there that characters from the world of the circus
began to dominate his choice of subject matter. Suffused with gentle pink
tones, Picasso paints these circus figures in an ideal, unlocalized
landscape. This gentleness seems delicately tinted with a certain elegiac
melancholy as the muscle-bound athlete in the foreground contemplates
the deft grace with which his younger companion balances on the ball.

27 HENRI DE TOULOUSE-LAUTREC Rue des Moulins 1894.
Prostitutes in Paris were regularly checked for syphilis – a disease from
which Lautrec himself suffered and which contributed to his early death.
Lautrec's methods, the hasty execution and thin paint, are often minimal.
Coupled with his use of pale tones, this description of the tired, anaemic
bodies of the prostitutes who are forced to undergo one more physical
degradation in the course of their professional lives seems painfully
eloquent. Yet Lautrec's refusal to flinch from the more squalid side of their
existence was exceptional. He shunned the titillating and avoided all
censure, depicting these women with compassion and sympathy.

29 PIERRE AUGUSTE RENOIR Portrait of Ambroise Vollard 1908.

Vollard is seen here lovingly handling a small statuette, caressing it in the same way that Renoir's soft brushwork caressed almost every form or object he ever painted. Renoir's benevolent touch notwithstanding, Vollard was one of the shrewdest of the new picture dealers who set up their businesses to cater for the growing demand for art in the last quarter of the nineteenth century. He made his reputation and his fortune handling the works of Cézanne – at a time when no one else would touch them. In this portrait, Vollard's commercial acumen cedes as he poses as both connoisseur and art-lover.

30 PABLO PICASSO Portrait of Ambroise Vollard 1909–10.
In this portrait of the picture dealer Ambroise Vollard, Picasso shows that the Cubist style was certainly not incapable of the finer demands of the art of portraiture. There is more psychological subtlety in this image of the man than there is in the portrait Cézanne made of the same sitter (see plate 123). Picasso centres his composition on the tightly closed lips and heavy jowls of this notoriously secretive dealer. As early as 1901, Vollard was displaying Picasso's work in his tiny gallery in the rue Lafitte, although Daniel-Henry Kahnweiler's gallery was later to become Picasso's principal showcase.

28 MARCEL DUCHAMP The Bride Stripped Bare by her Bachelors, Even (The Large Glass) 1915–23.
Duchamp left much documentary material to explain this, his most enigmatic and important work of art, which he constructed out of oil, wire, lead foil and glass. To the left of the upper chamber the bride strips while below her the nine bachelors, represented by the peg-like forms to the left, release their sexual frustration by pumping 'love-gasoline' through tubes into the 'Bachelor Machine', the three-drummed contraption in the centre of the lower panel. Duchamp left the work unfinished, but when the glass shattered in 1927 when the piece was in transit from an exhibition, he restored it, declaring that it had finally been completed 'by chance'.

Chapter 1

Science and Symbolism

In 1910 Roger Fry (1866–1934) had sought to separate the generation of artists of the 1880s and 1890s from their Impressionist forebears – with his new term. Paul Gauguin (1848–1903), Vincent van Gogh (1853–1890) and Georges Seurat (1859–1891) differed, according to Fry, from Pierre Auguste Renoir (1841–1919), Camille Pissarro (1830–1903) and Claude Monet (1840–1926), because rather than seeking to describe the way the eye perceives light, they had used colour and line to express their emotional responses to the scene before them.

In some respects this new generation was reacting to the dissatisfactions and disarray of the Impressionists themselves. For by the early 1880s it seemed as though the strong collective spirit that had held the group together since their first exhibition in 1874 was beginning to weaken. The artists were dispersing geographically. Paul Cézanne (1839–1906) was spending less and less time in Paris, preferring his native Provence in the south of France. Pissarro, Alfred Sisley (1840–1899) and Monet were living in disparate suburbs of Paris. And in the centre of the city Edgar Degas (1834–1917) lived as a hermit, hardly ever seeing his old friends and only exhibiting once after 1891 (*see plates 32 and 50*). The group meetings at the Café Guerbois and Nouvelles Athènes, which had fostered and sustained them in the 1870s, had ended, and though once-monthly dinners were held at the Café Riche, these were irregularly attended.

Furthermore, while the succession of Impressionist exhibitions in the 1870s had given rise to a spirit of artistic defiance – it was an article of faith that none of the group should show their work at the official Salon – by the early 1880s financial hardship had forced some of them to compromise.

Renoir had had a work shown at the Salon in 1878 – a society portrait for which he had received 1,000 francs.

31   CLAUDE MONET   Rouen Cathedral at Sunset   1894.
It is undoubtedly unfair to present, even in reproduction, one isolated canvas of the twenty that Monet painted of Rouen Cathedral. They were intended to be seen all together, as they were when they were hung at Durand-Ruel's gallery in 1895 – their first public appearance. As a series the paintings are able to generate all sorts of meanings which are lost when they are seen each in isolation. There were twenty views of the same motif, viewed under different lights and weathers, but always from the same standpoint. Thus Monet 'discovered his continuities within change rather than in permanence, in becoming rather than in being.' (George Heard Hamilton, Painting and Sculpture in Europe: 1880–1940, *Harmondsworth, 1981, 38.)*

Considering that in 1877 Pissarro had been forced to sell some of his canvases at auction for as little as 10 francs a piece, Renoir's action was quite understandable. Paul Durand-Ruel (1831–1922), the Impressionists' dealer, was on the verge of bankruptcy and unable to provide his painters with anything like a reasonable income. Monet, who had been the most adamant of them all about refusing to seek official recognition, was obliged to follow Renoir's example

32   EDGAR DEGAS   Woman Drying Herself   1903.
Degas first exhibited a number of pastels of women at their toilet at the Salon des Indépendants in 1886. It is a subject and a medium to which he would return many times before his death. Some of the first commentators on these pastels noticed how the privacy of the women's actions and the composition of the images combined to place the spectator in the position of voyeur: '. . . as if you looked through a keyhole', as Degas himself explained. (John Rewald, The History of Impressionism, *London, 1985, 525.) Others saw in them evidence of deep misogyny. Here, however, the woman's pose is a deliberate borrowing; it is taken from a rather tragic figure in Delacroix's* Entry of the Crusaders into Constantinople *(1840) in the Louvre, which Degas had copied in about 1860.*

and regularly exhibited his work at the Salon from 1880 onwards.

As far as the Impressionist cause was concerned, 1880 seemed something of a disastrous year. In April the fifth Impressionist exhibition was held. Pissarro and Degas showed work there but Renoir, Monet, Cézanne and Sisley, all anxious for Salon success and unwilling to risk jeopardizing their chances, decided not to participate. Furthermore, Edmonde Duranty died that year; as he had been one of the few critics who had defended their efforts in the press, they were thus deprived of a much-needed ally. Worse was to come. Renoir and Monet felt that their works at the Salon had been badly hung and would not attract attention. They asked the novelist Emile Zola (1840–1902), who had a growing reputation now in literary circles, to write an article on their behalf. Six years earlier Zola had lost his first journalistic job by passionately defending the Impressionists in the Parisian press. In 1880, in a series of four articles published in the newspaper *Le Voltaire*, Zola criticized the whole group for what he described as a lack of adequate technical skill in their craft, instead of complying with the wishes of Renoir and Monet.

Six years later Zola's betrayal seemed complete. In 1886 his novel *L'Oeuvre* was published. It described the tragic decline of a fictional painter Claude Lantier, whose failure to succeed as an artist ends in madness and suicide. Despite the melodramatic conclusion, it was widely recognized that Zola had modelled Lantier on two real figures – Manet and Cézanne. Cézanne, one of Zola's closest friends since their schooldays together in Aix-en-Provence, never spoke to him again.

That year, 1886, also saw the eighth Impressionist exhibition. Monet, Sisley, Cézanne and Renoir did not participate. Those who did were more or less divided into two opposing factions – one led by Pissarro, the other by Degas. A Dutch painter, Vincent van Gogh, recently arrived in Paris, wrote to a friend of their 'disastrous squabbles . . . each member getting at the other's throat with a passion worthy of a nobler and better aim'.[1] It was to be the last Impressionist exhibition.

Zola had earlier written of the Impressionists in *Le Voltaire* in June 1880:

The real misfortune is that no artist of this group has achieved powerfully and definitely the new formula which, scattered through their works, they all offer . . . We can see what they intend, and find them right, but we seek in vain the masterpiece that is to lay down the formula . . . This is why the struggle of the impressionists has not reached a goal; they remain inferior to what they undertake, they stammer without being able to find words.[2]

What must have been particularly galling about Zola's words was that they repeated the criticism levelled by more conservative critics against the Impressionists from the very beginning. This line of argument was essentially that the Impressionists never finished their paintings to the degree usually demanded of a fully fledged work of art. Instead they exhibited works that never progressed beyond the swift notations of a sketch. Of course, the Impressionist artists' practice of *plein-air* or open-air painting demanded that they work quickly to capture the fleeting effects of light and shade they had set themselves to describe. Their lack of traditional standards of finish was thus an intrinsic and central part of their aims. For Zola to criticize them on this point revealed a disturbing lack of comprehension on his part of all they had tried to achieve.

At the same time, however, their practice of painting only in the open air was beginning to cause problems. As the eye became more perceptive to minute changes in the quality of natural light and the hand more skilled in translating these changes into paint, so the length of time the artist could spend on any one canvas grew shorter and shorter. Monet, for example, would usually work on a number of different canvases at different points during the day, each one corresponding to particular conditions of light, shade and weather. But whereas in the early 1880s he spent on average fifteen minutes each day working on any one particular canvas, by the beginning of the 1890s this had shortened to about seven minutes. By 1918 the average was three or four minutes.

In other respects, *plein-air* painting was occasionally a hazardous occupation. Monet had once nearly drowned when painting from a secluded beach in Normandy, because he had misread the tide timetable. The novelist Guy de Maupassant (1850–1893) described Monet at work in a piece he wrote for the Parisian newspaper *Gil Blas* in September 1886:

I often followed Claude Monet in his search of impressions. He was no longer a painter, in truth, but a hunter. He proceeded followed by his children who carried his canvases, five or six canvases representing the same subject at different times of day and with different effects. He took them up and put them aside in turn, according to changes in the sky. Before his subject the painter lay in wait for the sun and shadows, capturing in a few brushstrokes the ray that fell or the cloud that passed.[3]

Monet the hunter is here combined with a figure reminiscent of the Pied Piper of Hamelin: if there was heroism in *plein-air* painting, it was also sometimes mingled with the absurd.

This method of painting had other disadvantages. By refusing to work on pictures away from nature, away from the 'motif', the Impressionist was obliged to work quickly, denied the benefit of having time to spend in the studio peacefully and calmly pondering what he had produced out of doors, and if necessary, correcting it.

By the early 1880s many of the Impressionists were beginning to modify their methods – working outside initially and then later finishing their works in the studio. Pissarro wrote to his son Lucien in April 1892, that he was, 'more than ever in favour of the impression via the memory – things become less material – vulgarity disappears, and lets float there only the truth as it is perceived and felt'.[4] In an interview the same year he said: 'The unity which the human spirit gives to vision can only be found in the studio. It is there that our impressions – previously scattered – are co-ordinated . . . in order to create the true poem of the countryside.'[5]

Renoir too decided that some alteration in his approach was called for. In 1882 he had travelled to Italy and spent part of his time there studying the Roman frescoes at Pompeii and those by Raphael (Raffaello Santi 1483–1520) in the Vatican apartments in Rome. Returning from Venice to Marseilles he decided to pay a visit to his old friend Cézanne who was at that time working in the nearby seaside village of L'Estaque. The two artists worked together for a while until Renoir became ill with pneumonia and had to be nursed back to health by Cézanne and his ageing mother. Renoir wrote to a friend: 'At lunch Madame Cézanne made me eat a ragoût of cod; this is, I think, the ambrosia of the gods. One should eat this and die.'[6]

33 PIERRE AUGUSTE RENOIR Dance at Bougival 1883.
A comparison between this painting and The Luncheon of the Boating
Party *(see plate 62) painted two years before reveals that while the
subject of this later work has not essentially changed – it is still a scene
under sunny skies, of easy, uncomplicated and festive intercourse between
the sexes – Renoir has tightened up his brushwork. After his visit to Italy
in 1882, he determined to give his compositions greater tautness. Thus
while the background couple are described in typical Impressionist style
with characteristic soft, slightly blurred brushwork, the outlines of the
main couple are much more cleanly defined – the silhouette made by the
man's dark clothes and the woman's pale arm against his breast.*

Renoir's experiences in Italy had prompted a feeling of profound dissatisfaction with his work. He later recalled: 'Around
1883 a sort of break occurred in my work. I had gone to the
end of impressionism and I was reaching the conclusion that
I didn't know how either to paint or to draw. In a word, I was
at a dead end.'[7] The frescoes he had studied in Italy, in the
way in which they depicted the human figure, had placed
great stress on contour and outline – precisely the qualities he
felt were lacking in his own work. In other words, he felt that
by concentrating on light and atmosphere, he had sacrificed
qualities of definition and clarity. A year before his trip to Italy

Renoir had painted a large canvas at the Restaurant Fournaise
in the town of Le Chatou situated on an island on the Seine a
few miles outside Paris (*see plate 62*). Returning to the nearby
town of Bougival in 1883 he tried to correct what he felt his
earlier work had lacked (*see plate 33*).

Renoir's decision to reorientate his painting and to give
line and contour a more prominent role was taking him a step
closer in one way to the practices advocated by the Academy,
which stressed the priority of line over colour. In other ways
too Renoir moved closer to the standards of the Academy. On
his return from Italy he decided to attempt a painting depicting a group of idealized female nudes set in a landscape. With
all its classical and mythological associations, and with a tradition going back at least to the Italian Renaissance, this was
a favourite and revered subject in the eyes of the Académie
des Beaux-Arts and one far removed from the Impressionists'
committed stance only to record the contemporary, only to
paint what was before their eyes.

Renoir clearly intended his *Bathers* (*see plate 34*) to signal a
major change in his painting. It took him three years to complete. Numerous preparatory sketches and studies survive,
indicating the seriousness and deliberation with which Renoir
applied himself. Though some of these studies were made
outside in front of the model, the finished work was painted
entirely in the studio. This procedure, of course, has nothing
to do with Impressionism; it rejected the artist's spontaneous
response to nature in favour of a much more considered
statement of what is in any case a patently artificial theme.

The Bathers, with all its compromises (with the standards of
the Academy), brought Renoir some modest success after he
first exhibited it in 1887. Real financial security for him and
his family followed a few years later, after a triumphant one-
man show at Durand-Ruel's gallery in 1892. Nevertheless,
The Bathers is in many ways an unhappy painting. Pissarro's
comments on it, recorded in a letter to his son Lucien in May
1887, are characteristically astute: 'I do understand what he
is trying to do, it is proper not to want to stand still, but he
chose to concentrate on the line, his figures are all separate
entities, detached from one another without regard for color.'[8]
To these criticisms we might add that the figures also seem
rather flat and silhouette-like, as if cut out and laid on to a
background, overlapping rather than occupying a truly three-
dimensional space. Their flesh also seems rather wan and
bleached, chilled by an unaccustomed intellectual rigour that
contradicts their playful gestures and energetic poses.

Renoir did not, though, to use Pissarro's phrase, stand still.
In this picture he found the subject, the timeless female
nude, that was to occupy him for the rest of his life. But it
was one he was to reinvest with his characteristic sensuous
touch and with glowing, breathing flesh (*see plate 35*).

Even Monet, who of all the Impressionists was the one
who remained most consistently faithful to the doctrine of
plein-air painting, was not unaffected by the changing practices of his friends. After first showing his works at the official
Salon in 1880, he had found financial security by the end of
the decade. This was largely due to Durand-Ruel's success in
finding buyers for his work in America rather than to the
recognition of the Academy. By 1901, at the age of sixty-one,
he could afford to buy his first car. While he never drove himself – he had a chauffeur – he did succeed in getting charged
for speeding in 1904.

34   PIERRE AUGUSTE RENOIR   The Bathers   1883–87.
The more emphatic linear definition he had introduced in Dance at
Bougival *(see plate 33), Renoir now applies to a deliberately major
painting. Leaving aside Impressionism's usual commitment to subjects
taken from life, Renoir here tackles a traditional, pastoral subject – nude
bathers in a landscape – as though he wanted to measure his own talents
against those of the Old Masters. The figures are modelled with smooth,
fused brushstrokes, their forms enclosed within neatly interlocking, yet
individually distinct arcs. This careful description seems somewhat at odds
with the much freer rendering of the landscape behind them.*

As far as his painting was concerned, not having to worry
any longer about selling his work gave him the freedom to
experiment – in particular in a series of paintings of the same
motif made at different times of the day or year, and under
different atmospheric conditions.

The first of these series – of grainstacks in a field close to
his house in Giverny – was painted in *c.* 1890–91 and fifteen
of the paintings produced were exhibited together at Durand-
Ruel's gallery in May 1891 (*see plate 51*). Others followed – of
Rouen Cathedral *c.*1892–93 (*see plate 31*), of poplars on the
banks of the River Epte *c.*1891, of a stretch of the Seine at
Giverny (*see plate 52*) – culminating in the lilies in the water
garden he had been building for himself since the early
1890s (*see plate 53*).

In one sense these series represent the logical extreme to
which the Impressionists' commitment to depicting the particular moment of nature could be taken. Monet worked on
the Rouen Cathedral series in the winter of 1892–3; he
rented a room in the square opposite, setting up his easel
there in order to record the multitude of different effects
his eyes registered of the light falling on the ancient stone
façade. And he worked on up to fourteen different canvases
each day.

One effect that this determined and methodical way of
working had on Monet's endeavours was to enable him to
focus unequivocally on his essential subject – light. For it
becomes apparent in these series paintings that nothing else
held as much interest for him. The towering Gothic façade of
Rouen Cathedral, for example, inspires numerous ideas that
an artist might conceivably wish to exploit: as a monument to
man's faith or to any number of spiritual or romantic associations. All these Monet ignores. Likewise, in the series of grainstack paintings, which he produced during the different

seasons of the year, Monet dismisses both any specific references to nature's cycle or to man's involvement with it –
there are never any labourers working in his fields.

Earlier in the 1870s Monet's paintings had maintained certain links with the society of his own day. He had painted the
great Parisian stations of the new railways; he had described
the elegant bourgeois crowds filling the recently built boulevards in the centre of the city, or enjoying themselves in the
river resorts in the outskirts. Now, in the series paintings of
the 1890s and beyond, with a secure market for his work,
Monet could push all these social issues to one side and
could concentrate simply on describing the way in which
light constantly modifies and alters the objects of our gaze.
As he explained to a visitor to the exhibition of grainstack
pictures in 1891:

For me, a landscape does not exist in its own right, since its appearance
changes at every moment, but which vary continually . . . For me, it is only
the surrounding atmosphere which gives objects their real value.[9]

It was this atmosphere, this envelope of air and light, that was
his real subject. But if these series paintings refined
Impressionism to its purest statement, they also pinpointed
the final futility of the whole enterprise. Monet worked on
fourteen different canvases a day for the Rouen Cathedral
series. But why stop there? Why not one hundred and forty,
why not fourteen hundred, if the painter was truly to capture
the constant changes of the light as it either grazed, illuminated or was absorbed by the aged, pitted stone?

Renoir probably reacted to this same intrinsic contradiction
when he decided to concentrate on the timeless nude from the

35   PIERRE AUGUSTE RENOIR   The Bathers   1919.
*In this much later version of the theme he had tackled rather
unsuccessfully between 1883 and 1887 (see plate 34), Renoir clearly
did not see the integration of his figures into the landscape as being as
problematic as before. He was also less concerned about giving these
figures clear, sharply focused outlines That sort of painterly treatment of
two such evidently fecund goddesses would have been rather niggardly.
Instead, Renoir has lavished on figures and landscape alike a fullness of
colour and a richness of brushwork that makes this painting a teeming,
fertile paradise of fleshy and abundant health. Matisse called it Renoir's
masterpiece: 'one of the most beautiful pictures ever painted'.*
(D. Fourcade, 'Autres Propos de Matisse', Macula, 1 (1976), 97.)

early 1880s onwards. In this way he could keep all the exuberance and spontaneity of Impressionist colour and brushwork without being tied to the depiction of one particular moment of nature. Monet was not insensible to this impasse either.

The freedom enjoyed by Monet at the start of the 1890s – as a result of his recent prosperity – extended not only to the possibility of creating series paintings but also to the direct control of the way in which they were exhibited. He was in a position to decide when and how they were hung. At the 1891 exhibition at Durand-Ruel's gallery, for example, the fifteen canvases of grainstacks were not hung around the walls in chronological order mimicking the cycle of the seasons. Likewise, in 1894, when he exhibited the Rouen Cathedral series, the canvases did not follow the sequence of the hours of the day but followed an apparently random order. In this way, at least, Monet could divert attention away from the problem of time which was intrinsic in his method of working. Each series, hanging together, would not function as a direct representation of linear time – from dawn to dusk or from winter to summer – but rather would suggest a more poetic variety of the artist's responses to nature's constantly changing aspect. In this admittedly rather subtle way Monet could emphasize the artificial over the natural.

He did this in other ways too. Though he rarely admitted it, Monet also worked on these pictures in the studio, away from the motif itself – to finish them to his own satisfaction. He may have worked on the Rouen series on site during the winter of 1892–3, but he finished the paintings in his studio in 1894, and it was this later date that he recorded on the canvases when he signed them before they were exhibited.

By working on the canvases in the studio Monet could concentrate on giving the series its own internal coherence irrespective of the need to describe the motif itself. By accenting a sombre morning scene with the same or similar fiery reds that animated a sunset one, and then by hanging these two side by side, the complete series would display its own inner unity. The series would become a decorative ensemble as well as a precise description of different atmospheric effects. The contemporary critic and painter Maurice Denis (1870–1943) records Cézanne as saying of Monet, 'He is only an eye, but my God what an eye!'[10] It sounds a little disparaging, as though Monet's essential genius was to translate with his hand exactly what his eyes received, without the intervention of the brain's more conceptual, organizing facilities. In the end, however, as his studio reworking and hanging strategies indicate, Monet was well aware that every painting had its own needs that demanded satisfaction – needs that were distinct from those of copying or reproducing nature.

Scientific Impressionism

Pissarro's solution to the problem of painting in the open air was more radical than were Monet's subtle modifications of Impressionist practice. Like Renoir, he had become dissatisfied with his work in the early 1880s. In 1883 he wrote to his son Lucien: 'I am much disturbed by my unpolished and rough execution; I should like to develop a smooth technique, while retaining the old fierceness.'[11]

Two years later in 1885 he had met two young painters, Paul Signac (1863–1935) and Georges Seurat, and had adopted their new technique of divisionism – as for example in *Ile Lacroix, Rouen – Effect of Fog* (see plate 24). It was a remarkable brave step. Signac and Seurat were in their twenties, both fired with a young man's desire for novelty and change. Pissarro was in his mid-fifties and – unlike either of the other two – had a family to support. He had enjoyed a very modest success following the Impressionist exhibitions of 1881 and 1882. So his decision to change the style of his painting just as he seemed on the verge of winning some material gains for all the years of struggle and hardship was courageous if not commercially foolhardy.

Divisionism was essentially the invention of Georges Seurat. At the age of twenty-four he finished his first major work, *Baignade, Bathers at Asnières* (see plate 63). Seven years later, in 1891, he was dead, having completed five more major works and having seen the technique adopted by numerous artists in France, Belgium, Holland and Italy. Pissarro was in fact to abandon divisionism a few years after having taken it up (see plate 60), but with typical generosity and foresight wrote to Lucien the day after Seurat's death: 'I think it [divisionism] will have consequences later on which will be of the utmost importance to art. Seurat really added something.'[12]

Seurat, as deliberate and methodical in character as the style of painting he engendered, set himself the task of systematizing Impressionism according to strict scientific principles. He was in fact one of the few avant-garde painters of this period who underwent the rigours of an Academic training, first at a municipal art school in Paris and then, for two years, at the Ecole des Beaux-Arts. Following a year's military service in Brittany he returned to Paris and devoted the next two years solely to drawing. With characteristic discipline and patience he applied himself to the description of subtle effects of light and shade using only tonal contrasts – without any line or contouring. One of these drawings, the portrait of his friend and fellow artist Aman-Jean, was exhibited at the official Salon of 1884 (see plate 36). His other entries, however, including the monumental *Baignade*, were rejected.

Contrary to Impressionist practice, though not surprising for a work measuring nearly 7 by 10 feet, the *Baignade* was not painted from life but was born in a studio after lengthy preparation; ten drawings and fourteen oil sketches exist for this work alone. The subject matter, though, is certainly Impressionist. Asnières was a popular bathing resort on the Seine outside Paris and many of the Impressionists had painted there in previous years. Thus this painting is concerned with recording contemporary mores (like much Impressionist art) and it could be compared, for example, with a work by Renoir of a similar subject – *The Luncheon of the Boating Party* (see plate 62).

Though pictures share similar subject matter, in spirit they could hardly be more different. While Renoir's picture is full of noise, movement and animation, Seurat's seems timeless, silent and solemn. Renoir's picture contains characters, people with distinctive personalities who are enjoying the sun, the food and each other's company. The Seurat painting is curiously static. All the figures – except one – face the same way and all are in profile. They seem depersonalized like figures in an ancient frieze. They are emotionally isolated from one another; their only connections are purely formal ones of rhyming curves and lines. For instance, three of the principal

36 GEORGES SEURAT Portrait of Aman-Jean 1883.
Seurat executed this drawing using conté crayon, a kind of synthetic chalk, on a heavily pitted paper. The strokes of the crayon do not entirely cover the white surface, producing a grainy, stippled effect. Seurat exploited this to evoke a delicate, gentle luminosity. Light seems to emanate from behind the figure rather than striking it from in front, giving the image a mysterious stillness. In drawings such as this Seurat also revealed an enjoyment of texture, of the sensual potential of his medium that is not apparent in his large oils. This is particularly discernible in the velvet-like texture of the deepest blacks of the shadows.

figures are so placed that the curves of their backs are repeated across the canvas and echoed by the shape of the cloud of smoke drifting across the sky above them. Moreover, Seurat's desire for formal harmonies extends to less important parts of the picture too. So, when he comes to paint a tab on a boot in the foreground, it is hard to decide whether he did so because it added a vernacular, contemporary touch to the image or quite simply because he liked the shape. Next to it the hat certainly seems to have been deliberately tipped on its side in order to rhyme with the shape of the central figure's head.

Seurat's brushwork displays as much formality and premeditation as the design. His technique is in effect a systematization of Impressionist practice. Instead of Renoir's sensual, benevolent touch, which seems to caress his forms, Seurat's purifies, distills and in the end transfixes them.

His colour follows as rigid and doctrinaire a system as his brushwork. Applying recent and contemporary scientific theory on the physiological effects of colour to the bright Impressionist palette, he devised his own system of divisionism. Amongst the various theoretical writings on colour that Seurat studied, most important was the research carried out by Michel-Eugène Chevreul, first published in 1839. As the Director of Dyeing at the state-run tapestry factory at Gobelins, Chevreul had been asked to investigate why some

colour dyes lacked the brightness necessary for tapestry production. He discovered that any individual colour's brightness or luminosity depended more on its neighbouring colours than on the intensity of that colour itself. He also demonstrated that certain colours, when paired together side by side, each achieve maximum luminosity. These are the complementary colours – red and green, blue and orange, yellow and violet. These he organized on a colour wheel, adding intermediate tones to the colours of the spectrum, so that any colour or tone on the wheel is positioned opposite its own complementary (*see plate 37*).

Complementary colours placed side by side in a painting react to each other with vigour and strength, creating an immediate and powerful visual sensation of light and brightness. Painters had used these pairings long before Seurat. Eugène Delacroix (1798–1863) had used them in the ceiling decorations in the Church of St Sulpice in Paris which he had completed in 1861 (*see plate 38*). The Impressionists had also used them in many of their works during the 1870s.

Chevreul had gone on to show how any area of strong colour produces its own complementary in its immediate surroundings. Thus, intense yellow generates a sort of faint aura of violet. This phenomenon had also been noticed by the Impressionists during the course of their open-air studies. Hence, yellow sunlight falling on white snow produces a violet shadow – precisely the sort of effect Renoir and Monet had recorded in their paintings of the 1870s. But where previous artists had discovered these kinds of colour relationships by intuition, Seurat was able, using Chevreul's research, to determine them with scientific precision.

To this Seurat added the principle of optical mixture – whereby instead of mixing colours and tones from the colour wheel on the palette, two adjacent colours are put down on the canvas and 'mix' on the retina to produce the third, desired colour. It was for this reason that Seurat developed what is known as the pointillist stroke – a simple dot of paint – because he found that he could only achieve the optical mixing he sought with a very small brushstroke.

All this had been imperfectly applied in the *Baignade*. He

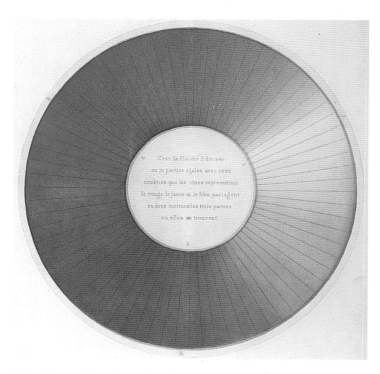

37 Chevreul's Colour Wheel, 1864.

had not used a pointillist stroke, nor had he limited himself solely to the spectral colours of Chevreul's research. In any case the jury of the 1884 Salon had rejected it. Seurat was not alone, however. Hundreds of other artists were in the same position and they determined to hold their own exhibition in a barracks building in the Tuileries – the first Salon des Indépendants opened later that year.

It was a chaotic event. Contributors were given no proper accounts by a patently disorganized organizing committee whose list of expenses at the end of the exhibition unaccountably included a fishing-rod. Fights broke out between various committee members; others tried to have them arrested. The alternative Salon ran at a loss and the group was unable to organize an exhibition for the following year. However, after the debacle of the first show, Seurat and Signac were instrumental in founding a proper society and a second exhibition – in the spring of 1886 – made a modest profit of 700 francs.

With no jury the Indépendants was a popular showcase for many artists unable to get their work past the official juries or unwilling to get involved in the in-fighting that was tearing the Impressionist group apart. Seurat entered the *Baignade* in the first Indépendants where it hung in the canteen, more or less unnoticed . . . except that a young twenty-one-year-old painter called Paul Signac was struck by it and introduced himself to its creator.

Signac noticed that Seurat had employed both the pure colours of the spectrum and the earth colours (browns, ochres etc.) favoured by Academic painters. He himself had been painting in an Impressionist manner and urged Seurat to limit his palette solely to the colours of the spectrum. Seurat heeded the advice and set to work on another vast composition; he completed *A Sunday Afternoon on the Island of La Grande Jatte* in late 1885 and exhibited it the following year both at the Indépendants and also at the eighth Impressionist exhibition (*see plate 54*).

Set on an island on the Seine at Asnières – visible in the far right-hand corner of the *Baignade* – the scene depicted by Seurat is again one of urban leisure, more bourgeois in character than the earlier work which was populated by factory workers. As for the *Baignade*, Seurat painted numerous preparatory oil sketches on wooden panels on the island itself and then returned to the studio to work on the huge canvas. Armed with his own colour wheel, adapted and amplified from Chevreul's, he covered the vast surface with his new system of dots. He was so sure of the accuracy of his colour contrasts that he would work under artificial light late into the night, rarely even stepping back to check their effect.

Scientific Satire

Seurat's ideal could be defined as the reconciliation of art with science. In 1880 he had read a series of articles by David Sutter in the journal *L'Art* which had advocated such a union:

Despite their absolute character, rules do not hamper the spontaneity of invention or execution. Science delivers us from every form of uncertainty and enables us to move freely within a wide circle . . . Since all rules are derived from the laws of nature, nothing is easier to learn or more necessary to know. In art everything should be willed.[13]

38   E U G È N E   D E L A C R O I X   Jacob and the Angel   1849–61. *The working methods employed by Delacroix when he painted the mural decorations in the Chapelle des Anges in the Parisian church of St Sulpice were admired by all the Impressionists. As early as 1857 he had remarked in his diary that all earth colours should be banned – several years before the Impressionists did exactly that. At St Sulpice, knowing that his decorations would only be viewed from a distance, Delacroix allowed himself a freedom in palette and brushwork that he would not have permitted himself in a smaller oil painting made to be seen from closer quarters. In this detail from the decorations, it is quite easy to see how Delacroix based the colouristic structure of his design on the opposition of the complementary pairing of red and green.*

During a period when science, through technological advance, was deeply and ostensibly changing more or less every facet of life in Europe, it seems fitting that Seurat should have wanted to imbue painting with the authority and power that science was displaying everywhere else.

When *La Grande Jatte* was exhibited in 1886, the critics paid attention to it only because Pissarro and other converts had shown their divisionist paintings alongside it. The painting was castigated and attacked. A Belgian painter, Théo van Rysselberghe (1862–1926), then living in Paris, was so irritated by Seurat's picture that he snapped his cane in two as he stood in front of it.

One young critic defended the divisionists: a former bank clerk turned journalist named Félix Fénéon. Fénéon had arrived in Paris in 1881. With a taste for the new and revolutionary, he had acquainted himself with all that was happening within the avant-garde community. He had founded one small literary review – the *Revue Indépendante* – and wrote for a number of others. Having been impressed by the *Baignade* in 1884 he had acquainted himself with both Seurat and Signac, who was later to paint his portrait (*see plate 9*). In 1886, in the newly founded *Vogue* magazine, he put pen to paper on their behalf, arguing that Seurat's new method was a scientific reorganization of Impressionism and coining the word 'Neo-Impressionism' to describe the new style.

Seurat was disdainful of his lack of critical success and also rather haughty towards the growing number of painters who had begun to adopt the divisionist technique. Always introspective, he became progressively more secretive, locking himself away in his studio for weeks on end, refusing even to admit Signac, his closest friend. Above all Seurat wanted to be and to remain original. Indeed, he was to write to Signac in the summer of 1888: 'The more numerous we are, the less originality we shall have, and the day when everybody uses this technique, it will no longer have any value and one will look for something else, as has already happened.'[14]

With *La Grande Jatte*, Seurat had established himself as something of a new, if reluctant leader among the avant garde. He now wanted to extend the scientific theories he had applied to colour to other areas of his paintings – specifically to line and composition. In 1886 Fénéon had introduced him to Charles Henry, a brilliant young scientist and theoretician who had recently published his research work on the emotionally expressive properties of different types of line and colour – correlations that Henry believed he had been able to measure scientifically.

Seurat applied these theories to *La Parade* and *Le Chahut* (*see plates 65 and 56*), both highly stylized images of cabaret performances from the café-concert or nightclubs that were so popular in Paris in the 1880s and 1890s. Although his technique was well suited to describing the animation of natural daylight, as was made apparent by the *Baignade* and *La Grande Jatte*, Seurat had evidently decided to relocate divisionism, moving from the outside to murky, artificially lit interiors, and from day to night.

Theo van Gogh (1857–1891) saw *Le Chahut*, the later of the two works, at the Salon des Indépendants of 1890 and described it in a letter to his brother Vincent: 'Seurat is exhibiting a really curious picture in which he endeavours to express things through the direction of lines. He certainly does express movement, but his canvas has a rather strange aspect and does not seem to reflect a very generous idea.'[15]

Charles Henry had proposed that lines moving upwards from the horizontal and to the right expressed a mood of gaiety and exhilaration. But in the strangely macabre scene of *Le Chahut*, there is no natural joy. Significantly, the upward direction of the dancers' legs moves to the left, not to the right. Instead of gaiety Seurat offers us either the artificial smiles of the performers or the lurid, fatuous grin of a wealthily dressed spectator in the lower right-hand corner.

Similarly, in *La Parade*, the emphatic insistence on the vertical and horizontal elements of the design and the frontal positioning of the performers convey a mood of monotony, even melancholy. The spindly-legged trombonist stands alone on a podium, separated from the crowd below, the frozen musicians to the left and the tail-coated impresario to the right. Nobody in the audience seems to be paying any atten-

39 GEORGES SEURAT Young Woman Powdering Herself 1888–90.

If John Betjeman had been French, he would surely have written a poem in celebration of the bourgeois (or suburban) charms of Madeleine Knobloch. But Seurat loved her. Though he mocks her as she covers her chubby face with powder, her big-boned frame slightly too large for the twee, diminutive furniture, it is, nonetheless, at an intimate moment that Seurat catches her. The framed picture of flowers in the top left-hand corner hides an obliterated self-portrait; Seurat evidently wanted to protect his mistress' privacy. His satire, for once, is gentle and affectionate.

tion at all, but the trombonist, the only figure on the same eye-level as the viewer, seems to implicate us in his isolation. In spirit *La Parade* could not be further removed from paintings of broadly similar subject matter painted a few years later by Henri Toulouse-Lautrec (1864–1901) (*see plates 27 and 64*). Lautrec certainly did not disguise the degradation of the world he chose to describe but he depicted it with warmth, inviting emotional involvement and engaging the sympathy of the spectator with his protagonists. Seurat, like the trombonist in *La Parade*, remains aloof, satirizing the inanity and frivolity of contemporary urban entertainment.

Something of this irony is detectable in *La Grande Jatte* where the bourgeois pomposity of the principal couple on the right is contrasted with the casual, supine pose of a pipe-smoking worker to the left. It is probably no coincidence that after the *Baignade* had been rejected by the official Salon in 1884, Seurat only ever showed his works at independent exhibitions such as the Salon des Indépendants. He also never again attempted to develop the almost heroic lassitude and immobility of the early painting's working-class bathers. Instead he chose to season his subsequent, fully divisionist figure paintings with increasing doses of satire, all directed against the values and pastimes of the urban bourgeoisie.

In landscape, however, Seurat did retain the sense of serene permanence that had infused the *Baignade* (*see plate 63*). From 1886 to 1890 – the year before he died – Seurat spent his summers away from his Paris studio in order, as he told his friend the Belgian poet Emile Verhaeren (1855–1916), 'to wash the studio light from his eyes and to transcribe most exactly the vivid outdoor clarity in all its nuances'.[16] Usually painting in towns far from Paris on France's northern coast, Seurat could refine the few, disparate elements before him – a bollard, a lighthouse, a harbour wall – into sparse images of silent harmony and an almost abstract order. These landscapes, like Cézanne's, were always unpopulated.

In April 1891 Seurat helped to organize a small memorial exhibition of van Gogh's paintings at that year's Indépendants. Van Gogh had killed himself the previous summer. A few days after the Indépendants closed Seurat himself died from an attack of influenza. Thirteen months previously his mistress, the memorably named Madeleine Knobloch, had given birth to their child (*see plate 39*). Not even Signac had known that Seurat was a father.

Tradition and Anarchism

Seurat's secretiveness during his lifetime had made Signac – naturally more extrovert – the principal spokesman among the divisionists. Following Seurat's early death (he was only thirty-one), Signac assumed the position of leader.

Unlike Seurat, his main efforts as a painter were directed towards landscape, first in the outlying regions of Paris and later around St Tropez in the south where he settled in 1892 (*see plate 58*). A committed anarchist, along with other divisionists such as Henri-Edmond Cross (1856–1910) and Pissarro, Signac maintained that Seurat's last figure paintings had been intended as polemical statements about the evils of modern urban life, publishing his views in *Le Révolte*, the anarchist review produced by Petr Alekseevich Kropotkin (1842–1921). He had nailed his own radical colours to the mast as a young man when, much to the annoyance of his mother, he had carved the names of Manet, Zola and Richard Wagner (1813–1883) on the stern of his first boat (he was a passionate sailor throughout his life). Signac's insistence on Seurat's intentions, therefore, may well have been more a reflection of his own ardour than an accurate account of Seurat's aims. Seurat's last paintings seem more ironic criticism than polemical outburst.

Other more politically active divisionists, like Luce, were prepared at times to depict the plight of the working class in heroic terms (*see plate 20*). Signac too, on at least one occasion, was fired by the thought of a reformed art geared towards improving their lot. In 1889 he wrote to van Gogh, whom he had met in 1886, about Charles Henry's theories on the directions of lines:

This will have a great social importance, especially from the point of view of industrial art. We teach the workers, apprentices etc., whose esthetic education until now has been based on empirical formulas or dishonest or stupid advice, how to see correctly and well. I shall send you one of these pamphlets as soon as it is printed.[17]

But in his paintings Signac, like his friend Cross, realized positively anti-urban ideals of a rural Arcadia free from the taint of industrial society (*see plates 57, 59 and 61*). Signac exhibited *Au Temps d'Harmonie* at the Indépendants of 1895 with a line taken from the writings of an anarchist philosopher named Malato as a subtitle: 'The age of gold is not past, it is in the future.' Traditionally, of course, the golden age referred to a mythological age outside of history where man lived in peace and harmony cocooned in a benign and benevolent nature. By reversing the time-scale and locating the golden age in an idealized anarchist future, Signac was doing more than just harnessing an ancient myth for his current political purposes. He was also attempting to connect avant-garde painting to a common European heritage. Classical Roman authors such as Lucretius (first century BC) and Ovid (43BC–AD18) had described Arcadia in their poetry. During the classical revival of the Renaissance, artists like Titian (Tiziano Vecelli c.1487–1590) and Giorgione (c.1478–1510) had depicted it in paint (*see plate 40*), inaugurating the grand tradition in European art that placed the golden age as a subject of central importance. In France the repository of this tradition was the Académie des Beaux-Arts; and it was embodied in the collection in the Louvre. Signac's *Au Temps d'Harmonie*, for all its innovative divisionist style and its explicitly political message, was also attempting to link avant-garde painting to the tradition that the Academy was meant to symbolize and promote.

Signac encouraged such links in a book he published in 1899, *D'Eugène Delacroix au néo-impressionnisme*, relating the

40 TITIAN The Rape of Europa 1559–62.
For all the erotic power in this work, it was not for its eroticism that Titian became such an important figure in the history of European art, if not the founder of modern painting. His crucial contribution was colour: 'for he made oil colour on canvas the main medium of later Western art. He exploited all its possibilities for the first time, from the animation of the picture surface with vigorous brushstrokes on the rough texture of the canvas to the contrast between rich, creamy highlights thickly laid on and deep, dark hues delicately modulated with glazes.' (Hugh Honour and John Fleming, A World History of Art, London, 1982, 370.)

technical innovations of divisionism back to the paintings of Delacroix. Delacroix, though considered a radical in his own day, was seen at the turn of the twentieth century as an important link between French painting and a tradition that wound its way back to sixteenth-century Venice – back again to Titian and Giorgione – and hanging in large part in the Louvre in Paris. Alienation from the Academy did not necessarily imply, therefore, that avant-garde artists wished to exist without any connection with the past.

A European Language

Despite Seurat's desire for originality and his unhappiness with the number of French artists who adopted his new technique, divisionism took root in a number of other European countries, blossoming first in Belgium.

Seurat exhibited *La Grande Jatte* in Brussels in 1887 at an exhibition organized by a group of young artists called Les Vingt, meaning The Twenty. The group had come together in

41 CHRISTOPHER NEVINSON The Towpath, Camden Town, by Night *c.* 1912.
Nevinson saw a landscape of Venice by Signac at the Biennale there in 1907, though he would also have been able to see examples of other divisionist artists' paintings slightly later in London, not least at Fry's first Grafton Gallery exhibition in 1910. While Signac's painting may have been a formative influence, Nevinson has replaced the traditionally romantic associations of Venice's canals with the more sordid, industrial waterways of north London. Smoke and mist rise and mingle above the dirty canal. The factory buildings glower down on the two lovers who are taking some sort of consolation in their embrace for all the oppressive ugliness of their surroundings.

1883 in similar circumstances to those that saw the creation of the Salon des Indépendants in Paris. The Belgian Academy held an annual salon in Brussels that was very much the mirror-image of its counterpart in Paris. In 1883 the jury had been particularly severe. Twenty of the rejected artists, including James Ensor (1860–1949) and Théo van Rysselberghe (see plates 67 and 66), formed a society to exhibit their paintings and decided to hold further shows each year. Whereas the Salon des Indépendants adopted a policy of unrestricted access, Les Vingt limited the exhibitions to the group itself and to a few selected foreign artists. Each member was allowed to invite one foreign artist to participate at each annual exhibition.

Though Belgium had been an independent state for over fifty years, culturally the country was very much dominated by France. Eager to make a stand for independence against the establishment, Les Vingt encouraged French avant-garde painters to show their work alongside their own. Monet and Renoir exhibited there in 1886, Gauguin and Lautrec in 1888, van Gogh and Cézanne in 1889. Les Vingt also published their own review, *L'Art Moderne*, for which Fénéon became the Paris correspondent in 1887.

When Seurat sent *La Grande Jatte* to the 1887 Les Vingt exhibition, its impact was enormous. Van Rysselberghe, who had been so irritated by it when he had seen it in Paris the previous year, immediately took up the technique (*see plate 66*). So did a Dutch painter called Jan Toorop (1858–1928) who was then living in Brussels. Toorop returned to Holland in 1890, settling in a remote fishing village north of The Hague (*see plate 70*). He was instrumental, however, in organizing a number of exhibitions of French and Belgian avant-garde art in The Hague during the 1890s that were to have a decisive influence on the development of the young Piet Mondrian (1872–1944).

Divisionism travelled to Italy (*see plate 19*) and eventually to Britain (*see plate 41*). It also acted as something of an apprenticeship for artists of subsequent generations. Mondrian has already been mentioned in this respect (*see plate 286*) but the achievements of André Derain (1880–1954), Matisse, Wassily Kandinsky (1866–1944), and many of the Italian Futurists would also have been unthinkable without their early acquaintance with this technique (*see plates 68 and 69*).

Pissarro was correct when he said that Seurat had 'really started something'. Divisionism almost became a kind of European language for the avant garde. Seurat himself however had been worried in 1883 that 'the day when everybody uses this technique it will no longer have any value, and one will look for something else, as has already happened'.[18] That was the same year that Pissarro abandoned divisionism because he felt that it did not permit him fully to express his sensations 'of the effects so fleeting and so admirable of nature'.[19] As Pissarro's subsequent paintings indicate 'something else' – as Seurat had put it – was already happening.

In *View from my Window, Eragny*, Pissarro was beginning to move away from the rigours of pointillist paint application (*see plates 42 and 60*). Here, the neat ordering of the landscape elements within the frame suggest that he was also trying something new. The buildings, hedgerows and trees are all precisely positioned along the horizontal and vertical axes of the canvas, lending the work a somewhat naïve, even child-like simplicity. It is as though Pissarro wished to impose a basic symmetrical scheme upon the scene. He described it in a letter to Lucien: 'It seems its subject is not saleable because of the red roof and the farmyard – just what gives the picture all its character; it has a *modern primitive* feel to it.'[20]

A Literary Debate

The idea of the primitive and the deliberately naïve received its seminal pictorial expression not in Pissarro's work but in that of one of his former pupils' – Gauguin (*see plate 43*). In the same year that Pissarro completed his painting of the view from his window – in 1888 – Gauguin produced the *Vision after the Sermon: Jacob and the Angel* (*see plate 79*). If the size and intensity of that expanse of vermilion red are still striking today, it will be no surprise to learn that in 1888 this single painting proved decisive not just in Gauguin's career but also for a number of other artists. Gauguin painted his *Vision after the Sermon* in a remote region of Brittany on the northern coast of France. The circumstances, however, that made this sort of audacity possible began a few years earlier in the sophisticated world of Parisian letters.

Throughout the 1870s Zola's novels and the verse of what was called the Parnassian group of poets had made naturalism the dominant school within French literary circles. Their ascendancy only seemed to be confirmed with the death of Victor Hugo (1802–1885), the towering embodiment of Romanticism. Zola's meticulously researched sociological novels had replaced Hugo's fantastic tales of Gothic horror.

42   CAMILLE PISSARRO   View from my Window, Eragny   1888. *Durand-Ruel refused to buy this picture precisely because of those 'modern primitive' qualities that Pissarro had deliberately sought to express. Pissarro's adoption of the divisionist style was short-lived, lasting only about two years, though at the time his support was very influential. Here, the variety of touch Pissarro has employed suggests that he was beginning to tire of the discipline of the technique, something that is confirmed in his letters of the time: 'How can one combine the purity and simplicity of the "point" with the solidity, the suppleness, the freedom, the spontaneity, the freshness of sensation of our Impressionist art?' (Camille Pissarro, Letters to his Son Lucien, London, 1943, 177.)*

43   PAUL GAUGUIN AND CAMILLE PISSARRO
Portrait of Camille Pissarro, Portrait of Paul Gauguin   *c*. 1880.
Pissarro is seen on the right, smoking a pipe.

The success of the naturalists, both critical and commercial, inevitably brought with it a reaction. Their direct descriptions of the world around them and, in their novels, their refusal to view human character and behaviour as anything other or more than socially conditioned, seemed to a handful of writers to negate the power of the imagination to transcend material reality. Jean Rimbaud (1854–1891), Charles Baudelaire (1821–1867) and Stéphane Mallarmé (1842–1898), all poets in the first instance, were the leading figures of this opposing faction, dubbed 'the decadents' in a generally hostile press. They themselves preferred the term Symbolists. When they were attacked in print in a particularly vicious manner in 1885, the time for some sort of collective retaliation appeared to have arrived.

A young writer Jean Moréas (Yannis Papadiamantopoulos 1856–1910) published his 'Symbolist Manifesto' in August 1886 in *Le Figaro*. Moréas's argument rested on the assumption that the realm of the imagination or the idea was superior to material reality. Literature, he continued, should focus not on this lower, physical plane but rather should attempt to penetrate the idea or the essence that lay behind it.

The notion of a reality residing outside the senses, that could be perceived only through the imagination, is essentially a mystical one. Mallarmé argued that in order to express this higher realm in language, the poet must loosen the bond between words and their normal, everyday meanings. Only oblique allusions and evocations, suggested by the words, and not literal descriptions of objects or feelings, could release the imagination into this higher state. As he said in an interview published in 1891 in the *Echo de Paris*:

The contemplation of objects, the image emanating from the dream they excite, this is poetry. The Parnassians take a thing as a whole and reveal it; by doing this they lack mystery: they deny the human spirit the delicious joy of believing that it is creating.[21]

For some the advent of such a viewpoint was the logical consequence of social change. In the same edition of the *Echo de Paris* where Mallarmé had spoken of mystery and dream, Charles Henry wrote that the immense advance of technology, rationalism and the scientific spirit into most areas of material life demanded an art of mysticism and idealism, 'because our intellects, exhausted by purely rational efforts, will feel the need to refresh themselves with entirely opposite states of mind'.[22]

Others saw the scientific methods of divisionism as the most appropriate painterly response to these same changes. But whatever the case the Symbolists' rejection of naturalism was unanimous. Gustave Kahn (1859–1936), a friend of Fénéon, made this abundantly clear in an article published shortly after Moréas's Symbolist Manifesto in the radical newspaper *L'Evenément*:

We are tired of the everyday, the near-at-hand and the contemporaneous . . . The essential aim of our art is to objectify the subjective [the externalization of the Idea] instead of subjectifying the objective [Nature seen through a temperament].[23]

Years earlier Zola had descibed Manet's art as 'Nature seen through a temperament'. Kahn pointedly alludes to Zola's phrase but replaces its essentially realistic view of art with the Symbolists' imaginative or idealistic standpoint.

A lively debate on such literary matters continued in the Parisian dailies and in numerous smaller reviews; but it soon turned to a discussion of contemporary painting. Most spectacular was the publication in 1884 of a novel, *A Rebours (Against the Grain)* – emphatically Symbolist in character – by a young writer J. K. Huysmans (1848–1907) who had until then been a follower of Zola and firmly resident in the naturalists' camp. In it, Huysmans's hero, the Comte des Esseintes, admires three (real) artists hitherto more or less ignored because their work simply did not fit into es-tablished categories: Pierre Puvis de Chavannes (1824–1898), Gustave Moreau (1826–1898) and Odilon Redon (1840–1916). Huysmans saw in their work, which was nei-ther Academic, Impressionist nor divisionist, a pictorial counter-part to the doctrines of literary Symbolism advocated by his friends.

Redon, the youngest of the three, was a contemporary of the Impressionists. Having trained to be an architect he had then decided to become a painter and had studied at the Ecole des Beaux-Arts. He produced few paintings thereafter, concentrating mainly on lithographs and engravings, working in quiet obscurity. He had shown a number of his lithographs, always printed in black and white, at the first Salon des Indépendants. Their disturbing, fantastic and slightly macabre subjects had first caught the eye of Huysmans and others of the Symbolist group. Redon was somewhat surprised by the subsequent attention of this younger generation (some of whom claimed him as a new Francisco Goya 1746–1828), noting in his diary:

I am supposed to have much more of an analytical mind than I really have, this would at least account for the curiosity that I feel in the young writers who visit me. In contact with me I see them at first somewhat surprised. What did I put into my work to suggest so much subtlety? I placed in it a little door opening on mystery. I made fiction. It is up to them to go further.[24]

This tardy success encouraged him to exhibit more regularly at the Indépendants as well with Les Vingt in Brussels and at other exhibitions in The Hague and Vienna.

Like Redon, Gustave Moreau had received his training at the Ecole des Beaux-Arts. From a wealthy family, he had rarely shown his work in public, last exhibiting at the official Salon in 1880. Thereafter he had lived a very secluded life at his home near the Gare St Lazare in Paris until 1892, when he was made a professor at the Ecole des Beaux-Arts. He taught there for the remaining six years of his life, an outstanding teacher who was to provide decisive encouragement for later generations of French artists.

Puvis de Chavannes, the eldest of the three, had – like the other two – pursued a successful career largely outside the public gaze, winning universal recognition only after the advent of the Symbolists in the 1880s. Eshewing traditional easel-painting techniques he had favoured decorative projects, either panel paintings or large-scale mural decorations. These demanded a different style of painting, one that was suited to their architectural setting. The painting would therefore tend not to emphasize three-dimensional space, nor employ strong contrasts of tone for the description of volume. Instead its somewhat flattened space and cool, neutral palette would complement the flatness of the wall itself, so that the image seemed continuous with it rather than piercing an imaginary hole in it by the strength of its illusion.

The painting of Redon, Moreau and Puvis de Chavannes appealed to the Symbolist writers for a number of different reasons. Redon was admired for the macabre qualities of his imagination and later for the brilliant colours of the oils and pastels he produced in the last years of his life (*see plates 71 and 72*). Moreau was appreciated for the pristine, jewel-like textures of his minutely detailed and highly coloured oils. Later he produced some private watercolours that border on the purely abstract (*see plates 73 and 74*). Puvis de Chavannes was revered for the serene clarity of his bleached classical landscapes and the decorative qualities of his style (*see plates 75 and 76*).

Each of them, however, departed from established norms: Redon in the privacy of his imaginative visions, Moreau and Puvis de Chavannes in the highly individual ways that they tackled more traditionally acceptable subjects.

The Rustic and the Primitive

When this literary debate had broken out in the Parisian press in the mid-1880s Gauguin was living in Brittany struggling to make a living as a painter. His is a colourful biography. Born in 1848, he spent part of his childhood in Peru, and had worked as a merchant seaman in the 1860s before taking a job on the Parisian stockmarket at the beginning of the 1870s. An amateur painter himself he had begun collecting Impressionist works after meeting Pissarro in 1874, and sub-sequently showed his own work at some of their exhibitions.

In 1883, following the stockmarket crash, Gauguin had lost his job and was able to devote all his time to painting – but without success. His Danish wife and children moved to Copenhagen the following year; Gauguin was forced to work as a bill-sticker in Paris because he was unable to sell any of his paintings.

He had remained good friends with Pissarro, learning Impressionist techniques from him in the early 1880s when he went to stay with the older artist at his home in Pontoise just to the north of Paris. He had met Cézanne there as well, though the two did not get on very well. Gauguin's ambitions as a painter were as yet far in excess of his actual accomplishments. As early as December 1884, nearly four years before he painted the *Vision after the Sermon*, he had written to Pissarro. 'I am convinced there is no such thing as exaggerated art. I even believe that salvation lies only in the extreme.'[25] Yet at the same time, while his own work had hardly progressed beyond a conservative Impressionism, Seurat was completing his first concerted effort to develop the Impressionist heritage – in the *Baignade*.

In 1887 Gauguin had travelled abroad, working as a digger on the Panama Canal in order to earn his passage to the French-held island of Martinique that lay nearby. From Martinique he had brought back a modest number of intensely coloured landscapes that had threatened (but only threatened) to go beyond an Impressionist idiom. Gauguin's advance 'into the extreme', however, was to wait until the following year.

Early in 1888 Gauguin returned to the Breton village of Pont-Aven. He had stayed there before in 1886, finding life significantly cheaper than in Paris. Gauguin was not the only painter to find Pont-Aven attractive. Since the 1860s it had become something of an artists' colony for students from the Parisian academies. In general Brittany had profited from the new railways, and by the 1880s it provided the urban bourgeoisie with a number of fashionable seaside resorts. They in turn supported a growing souvenir pottery industry.

Signac visited Pont-Aven in 1889, the year after Gauguin painted his *Vision*. He was most struck by the commercial initiatives of the local community in exploiting the area's popularity with artists. Writing to Luce he described it, perhaps a little unfairly:

It's ridiculous countryside with little nooks and cascades, as if made for female English watercolorists. What a strange cradle for pictorial Symbolism . . . Everywhere painters in velvet garments, drunk and bawdy. The tobacco merchant has a sign in the form of a palette: 'Artist's Material', the maidservants in the inns wear arty ribbons in their headdresses and probably are syphilytic.[26]

Whatever the validity of Signac's misgivings, Gauguin was attracted to the place not simply because it was cheap but also for its picturesque landscape, the charm of its peasant population and all the possibilities these offered a painter. He wrote to an artist friend back in Paris at the beginning of 1888: 'I love Brittany. I find wildness and primitiveness there. When my wooden shoes [Gauguin had adopted the peasants' clogs] ring out on this granite, I hear the muffled, dull and powerful tone which I try to achieve in painting.'[27] Brittany's remoteness and the character of both its landscape and its inhabitants were attractive because they were so different from the modern city – free from all, or at least most of the transformations of industrialism.

In 1888 Gauguin was forty years old. Two years previously an eighteen-year-old art student called Emile Bernard (1868–1941) had been similarly struck by the place:

I returned a devout believer . . . Brittany has made a Catholic of me again, capable of fighting for the Church. I was intoxicated by the incense, the organs, the prayers, the ancient stained glass windows, the hieratic

tapestries and I travelled back across the centuries, isolating myself increasingly from my contemporaries whose preoccupations with the modern industrial world inspired in me nothing but disgust. Bit by bit, I became a man of the Middle Ages, I had no love for anything save Brittany.[28]

Bernard was a student (along with van Gogh and Lautrec) at the Atelier Cormon, a private studio in Paris run by a successful Academic painter called Fernand Cormon (1845–1924). Bernard had first been to Pont-Aven in 1886 and on his return to Paris had tried to apply to his own work some of the stylistic traits he had noticed in Breton art, particularly in the stained glass (*see plates 44 and 45*).

Going back to Pont-Aven again in the summer of 1888, Bernard introduced himself to Gauguin on the advice of a mutual friend, van Gogh. The young man showed Gauguin examples of his recent work, with its thick, dark contours and large patches of bright colour. Evidently Gauguin was impressed. In any case he had himself found it difficult to work earlier in the summer; he was still suffering from dysentery which he had picked up in Martinique; he was alone, cut off from his friends in Paris; and he was heavily in debt. Bernard's enthusiasm for Brittany, his naturally inquisitive mind and eclectic interests must have encouraged Gauguin to get back to work. Bernard would also have been aware of the literary debates raging in Paris at the time. If that was not enough in itself, Bernard also painted a vividly startling picture of a group of Breton women gathered together in a meadow (*see plate 80*).

Bernard's response to the rustic charm of these women in their traditional costumes may not in itself have been particularly original. However, the way in which he realized that response in paint was new. His figures were boldly simplified, painted without any modelling, and silhouetted against flat yellowy greens that signified the grass. Emulating the style of the ancient Breton stained glass he so admired, Bernard renounced traditional standards of realism. Such simplifications and distortions, he felt, better expressed the character of these women than any slickly painted illusion. He gave the finished painting to Gauguin.

Gauguin had written to a friend in Paris in the middle of August, 'Art is an abstraction; derive it from nature by indulging in dreams in front of nature.'[29] These words, clearly Symbolist in tone, probably reflect the conversations he had been having with Bernard. In any case, it seems that Bernard's example inspired Gauguin to paint his first major work – the *Vision after the Sermon: Jacob and the Angel* (*see plate 79*). He described it in a letter to van Gogh:

I believe I have attained in these tiny figures a great rustic and superstitious simplicity . . . To me in this painting the landscape and the struggle exist only in the imagination of these praying people, as a result of the sermon. That is why there is a contrast between these real people and the struggle in the landscape, which is not real and is out of proportion.[30]

Bernard's painting seems somewhat crude seen next to Gauguin's. Where Bernard's figures seem to have come together at random, Gauguin's are there for a reason: the women and a priest are sharing a collective vision inspired, as the title tells us, by the sermon the latter has presumably just preached. Furthermore, while Bernard's haphazard group mingle, or rather overlap in a green field, Gauguin situates his

44 Photograph of van Gogh and Bernard (looking at the camera) at Asnières, 1886.

figures in an unequivocally unrealistic setting. Red lies opposite green on the colour wheel, and thus, by setting his struggling figures in a red field, Gauguin chooses the most emphatic way of telling us that the two wrestlers are visionary, existing only in the minds of the devout women in the foreground. The presence of a cow in this same visionary world is more mysterious; perhaps it is an indication that the women's piety grows naturally out of their rural surroundings.

A Flat Surface Covered in Colours

This picture was to establish Gauguin as the leader of a new Symbolist movement in painting, hailed as such by the same writers and critics who had been debating its literary precedents in the Parisian press. It was a young painter named Paul Sérusier (1864–1927) who carried news of Gauguin's accomplishments back to Paris.

Sérusier was a student at the Académie Julian, a successful private academy that provided its pupils with studio space, regular models and a modicum of supervision from visiting Beaux-Arts professors. Chaotic, noisy and crowded, Julian's studio was notorious for the incessant practical jokes his students played on one another. Polite English students apparently came in for the worst teasing, though every German pupil was forced by his peers to yodel before the rest of the class. Ad hoc performances of bird songs were another favourite pastime. Sérusier, however, along with his friends Jean Edouard Vuillard (1868–1940), Maurice Denis and Pierre Bonnard (1867–1947), formed a more serious group amidst the mayhem. During the summer of 1888 Sérusier went to stay in Pont-Aven. On his penultimate day there he finally plucked up enough courage to approach Gauguin (they were staying at the same inn, the Pension Gloanec), and to ask him about his work. Gauguin invited him to paint with him the following morning.

Earlier that year Sérusier had had one of his paintings accepted by the official Salon, but his painting lesson with Gauguin was to alter the course of his career. They climbed to the top of the Bois d'Amour, a wooded hill overlooking Pont-

Aven. Sérusier began to paint the landscape before him on the wooden lid of an old cigar box with Gauguin looking on. Later in life he recorded Gauguin's advice: 'How do you see those trees? They are yellow. Well then, put down yellow. And that shadow is rather blue. So render it with pure ultramarine. Those red leaves. Use vermilion.'[31] In other words Gauguin was telling his pupil to exaggerate, to take the actual colour he could see and intensify it – pure ultramarine for blue, vermilion for red.

This lesson in exaggeration and the bold unnaturalistic message of the *Vision after the Sermon* Sérusier took with him back to the Académie Julian. There his cigar box sketch, an encapsulation of Gauguin's audacity, astonished his friends and became known as *The Talisman* (see plate 83).

By the following year Sérusier, Denis, Vuillard, Bonnard and others of their friends had formed a group, calling themselves the 'Nabis', which is the Hebrew word for prophet. The Nabis were more an exclusive club than a promotional organization along the lines of the first Impressionists. It was a group for initiates only: they created their own private vocabulary, signed letters with special, formulaic greetings etc. And these initiates shared certain ideas about the course modern painting should take.

The Nabis were to dominate the Parisian avant garde throughout the 1890s, vying with the divisionist painters for supremacy. Their success was remarkably rapid compared with the years of hardship suffered by the Impressionists before they achieved any kind of recognition. Gauguin, van Gogh and Cézanne, the three other principal painters of the time, languished in relative obscurity during this period, only really achieving fame in the following decade.

There were reasons for the Nabis' speedy triumphs. Three of them – Sérusier, Vuillard and Denis – had been educated at the elite Lycée Condorcet in Paris, but the entire group were from wealthy, cosmopolitan bourgeois backgrounds. They were also fortunate to find as quickly as they did a dealer to sell their work from his gallery in the centre of Paris: a flamboyant character named Le Barc de Bouteville. Probably, too, the traditional and explicitly religious Catholic nature of their subjects, certainly in the case of Sérusier and Denis (see plates 81 and 82), though less so for Vuillard and Bonnard, helped to find a market for their work among the conservative bourgeoisie. But just as importantly they also had close contacts with the Symbolist press.

Sérusier, Denis and the others used to congregate with the rest of the Symbolist circle at the Café Voltaire in the Place de l'Odéon, where the group met every Monday at nine in the evening. Their works were well reviewed in the journals produced by Fénéon, Kahn and their friends, particularly in the *Mercure de France* and *La Revue Blanche* (see plate 85), new journals that established themselves in the 1890s as the leading Symbolist organs.

Denis himself published a number of articles on Nabis and Symbolist art in these journals; indeed, he is now more renowned for his writings than his painting, as is also the case with Roger Fry, incidentally. He wrote particularly well on Gauguin and later on Cézanne, in an article translated by Fry and published in the *Burlington Magazine* just before the first Grafton Gallery exhibition. In 1890 he published an important piece about Symbolist painting in which he tried to define its characteristic qualities. Entitled

'A Definition of Neo-Traditionism', the article also attempted to relate this new style of painting back to older traditions.

The essential characteristic of this painting, Denis wrote, was that it was decorative. This idea had a number of implications. First, as the paintings of Puvis de Chavannes had hinted, it constituted an attack on established and cherished traditions of illusionism. Since the Renaissance the main tradition of European painting had been based on two complementary methods of creating illusions of reality: the depiction of space through the use of perspective and the rendition of volume through the careful modulation of light and dark tones. Decorative painting renounced both these technical devices, creating images with flatter, more two-dimensional space and little or no tonal contrasts, so that volume remained unemphatic. Denis related these sorts of characteristics to artistic traditions that did not descend from the Italian Renaissance. By favouring decorative procedures, Puvis de Chavannes, Gauguin and the Nabis were working with traditions that had originated in Ancient Egypt and developed in Europe up to the fourteenth century – up to the eve of the Renaissance. In decorative painting, a picture no longer functioned as a window looking out on to nature, as an illusion of what the eye could or might actually see. Instead decorative painting used colour and line to appeal more directly to the imagination, the emotions, the intellect. Furthermore, with

the rejection of traditional illusionism, greater emphasis was also placed on the formal, abstract qualities of a painting. Or, as Denis put it, in a succinct, aphoristic warning: 'Remember that a painting – before it is a warhorse, a nude woman, or any other subject – is essentially a flat surface covered with colours that have been arranged in a certain order.'[32]

Where Gauguin and the Nabis differed from the older Puvis de Chavannes was in the areas in which they applied these ideas. Puvis de Chavannes tended to avoid easel paintings, which tradition and the Academy demanded be as realistic as possible; instead he chose much larger

45 EMILE BERNARD Bridge at Asnières 1887.
The bright, flat colours that are each enclosed within a dark contour and the surfaces that received a minimum of modelling, were the traits that particularly attracted Bernard to Breton stained glass. He tried to apply these ideas to his own painting when he returned to Paris, as is evident in this painting of the Seine and railway at Asnières, close to his parental home where he lived while a student. It was not far from this site that Seurat had depicted the factory workers resting by the side of the river in his Baignade (see plate 63). It is interesting to note that Bernard painted this picture in the same year Seurat completed his Grande Jatte (see plate 54), also set in Asnières. Bernard, however, ignored Seurat in just about every way. His ghostly couple, silhouetted in black, add a mysterious, slightly disturbing note that is far removed from Seurat's pristine friezes.

formats or took on architectural commissions to decorate a ceiling or a wall.

The Nabis themselves, following Gauguin's example, certainly enjoyed working in media other than the easel painter's customary oil and canvas (see plate 47). They all, for example, produced large-scale decorative panels, and Bonnard found poster design an ideal medium in which to refine his own form of decorative grace and simplicity (see plate 85). At the same time they also applied decorative procedures to their easel paintings. It was in this way that they were original. The Académie des Beaux-Arts had always rigorously separated decorative from easel painting. In the latter the artist was expected to create images as illusionistic as possible, while in the larger formats of panel or mural painting he was expected

46 EDOUARD VUILLARD   Portrait of Toulouse-Lautrec in Oilskins, Cooking   1898.
Knowing precisely why Lautrec wore oilskins when he cooked would probably diminish the humour of this affectionate portrait, faintly tinged as it is with the absurd. Vuillard painted it for Thadée Natanson, editor of La Revue Blanche. *Vuillard usually chose to depict one or two figures in subtly painted, domestic interiors; he executed these with the delicacy and understated refinement with which E. M. Forster was later to portray the English middle classes of southern England. This portrait was undoubtedly an occasional piece, inspired by the striking appearance of the diminutive Lautrec. Fortunately for us this unusual snapshot likeness is captured in paint in an age before the domestication of the camera.*

to adopt a decorative style. Decorative painting, the Academy decreed, was also intrinsically inferior to what was seen as the intellectually more demanding discipline of easel painting.

The Nabis did not devise any rigid programme for their subject matter. While Denis and Sérusier preferred religious themes, Bonnard and Vuillard favoured intimate, domestic scenes (see plates 77, 78 and 84). They shared a commitment, however, to the rejuvenation of traditional easel painting techniques through the adoption of procedures normally reserved for decorative projects, and in this they were instrumental in breaking down traditional distinctions between the fine and applied (or decorative) arts. One result, for example, was that in 1906 the radical Salon d'Automne stopped distinguishing in its catalogue of entries between decorative and traditional easel works. However, because the Académie des Beaux-Arts had created and endorsed these distinctions in the first place, the Nabis' predilection for the decorative also proved further to undermine its authority in matters of taste and style.

Linear Sympathy

When Degas had insisted in the 1880s that his followers be allowed to show alongside him at the various Impressionist exhibitions, his intransigence had played a major role in the quarrels and wranglings that had finally split the Impressionist group apart. Most, if not all of these acolytes have today been forgotten or are simply noted as rather pedestrian imitators of their master. One artist of the 1890s, however, a follower in the more creative sense of the word, built solidly upon Degas's accomplishments to create his own highly distinctive and memorable visual world: Henri de Toulouse-Lautrec.

Lautrec was unusual among the Parisian avant garde of the 1890s for remaining independent of the scientific dogmas of divisionism on the one hand and the decorative ideals of Gauguin and the Nabis on the other. At the same time he was very much one of their number. He exhibited at the Indépendants, with Les Vingt in Belgium and with the Nabis at Le Barc de Bouteville's gallery. He was friends with van Gogh (whose reputation he once defended in an abortive duel against a critical Belgian) and Bernard, and he was well known among the writers and artists associated with the new Symbolist journal *La Revue Blanche*. Yet, as he said of himself in an interview published in December 1891 in the *Echo de Paris*, 'I don't belong to any school. I work in my corner . . . .'[33]

As is the case with van Gogh, Lautrec's tumultuous biography has become an inseparable part of the way in which his art is viewed. Born in 1864 in Albi, near Bordeaux, he was of aristocratic stock. He died of syphilis and alcohol poisoning in Paris in 1901 at the age of thirty-seven. Physical deformity – his legs stopped growing when he was fourteen after a series of riding accidents – has added an element of the grotesque to the sometimes romantic, sometimes squalid, but invariably stylish episodes reported about his adult life (see plate 46).

Having trained as an artist in Paris under two Academy professors at the Atelier Bonnat and then the Atelier Cormon (where he met Bernard and van Gogh), Lautrec moved to Montmartre, setting up in a studio there in 1886. His life among the cabaret singers, dancers and the prostitutes

47 PAUL GAUGUIN Vase decorated with Breton Scenes
1886–87.
*Gauguin's interest in native Breton arts and crafts inspired him to
experiment himself. His other decorative projects included mural painting
– at the Pension Gloanec in Pont-Aven where he mostly stayed during his
time in Brittany – and woodcarving. Leaving the top and bottom sections
in the original earth tone, Gauguin covered the middle section of this
deceptively sophisticated stoneware vase with a white slip, to which he
added the incised, glazed decoration, highlighting its lines and the
embroidered patterns on his figures' costumes in thin gold. Gauguin's
example led other artists to experiment with ceramics: Matisse, for
instance, two of whose vases can be seen in the background of* Girl with
Green Eyes *(see plate 14).*

provided him with a wide variety of source material for the
majority of his work (*see plate 64*).

Earlier in the century Montmartre had been a small village
perched on a hill to the north of the city of Paris. In 1830 it
boasted a population of six thousand. By the mid 1880s its
population had boomed to over two hundred thousand and it
had become an integral part of the city. Through its urban
absorption Montmartre's character had inevitably been transformed. In the 1890s it provided the rest of Paris with enter-
tainments – particularly brothels and café-cabarets. Of these
latter the Moulin Rouge was and still remains the most
famous but many others opened there in the 1890s: the
Cabaret des Assassins which featured the famous dancer La

Goulue (*see plates 48 and 88*) and later became the Lapin Agile
– a favourite haunt of the Cubists; the Chat Noir; the Divan
Japonais for whom Lautrec was to design a poster; and the
Mirliton, owned by Aristide Bruant – famous in his own right.

It was Bruant, notorious for his songs about the miseries of
the poor delivered in Parisian slang or *patois*, who introduced
Lautrec to the world of Montmartrois pleasures. Lautrec,
alienated by his own deformities, seems to have felt an immediate sympathy with the similarly marginalized lives of the
performers – whether dancers, singers or prostitutes – who
served these establishments.

Lautrec was something of a performer himself. He drank
copiously, was witty and sarcastic, and possessed a vocabulary
of obscene expletives as extensive and renowned as Signac's.
His friend Bernard, a devout Catholic, evidently disapproved of
the company he kept at his studio on the rue Tourlaque.
Certainly Bernard's own ideals of a naïve, rustic religiosity
which he (and Gauguin) had glimpsed in Brittany finds its
antithesis in the world that so fascinated Lautrec – the lurid
decadence of Montmartre after dark. Lautrec was attracted to
the contemporary, not to the ideal preferred by the Symbolists.
He even painted a parody of one of Puvis de Chavannes's monumental panels. In the older artist's *Sacred Wood* (*see plate 76*),
draped nudes representing the Arts and the Muses waft and
wander through an idyllic classical landscape. In Lautrec's
much smaller 'copy', he and his friends in their elegant Parisian
costume are seen blustering in on the same scene, only to be
restrained from their violation of paradise by a gendarme.

Puvis de Chavannes's decorations could be seen in the
Sorbonne and the Panthéon. Signac wanted to use his art as
an instrument of political revolution; Denis and Sérusier to
initiate a spiritual revival. Thus, Lautrec's parody of the most
revered of the Symbolist painters and his own commitment to
painting scenes from the life around him in some ways
seemed to question those others' exalted ambitions to the
realms of high art. Although he painted no landscapes and
usually portrayed his figures under the artificial light of the
cabaret or dance hall, this commitment places Lautrec closer
to the Impressionists than to his peers.

Lautrec, however, did much more than tease the aspira-

48 Photograph of La Goulue and others dancing the can-can at
the Moulin Rouge, *c*.1880.

NOTES

1 Letter to Emile Bernard, July 1888, in John Rewald, *The History of Impressionism*, rpt London, 1973, 543.

2 Ibid, 446.

3 Ibid, 517.

4 In John House, 'The Legacy of Impressionism', *Post-Impressionism*, exhibition catalogue, Royal Academy, London, 1979–80, 14.

5 P. Gsell, 'L'Impressionnisme', in *La Revue Bleue*, 26 March 1892, 404.

6 In John Rewald, *Paul Cézanne*, trans. Margaret H. Liebman, London [n.d. c. 1946?], 116.

7 In John Rewald, *The History of Impressionism*, op. cit., 486.

8 Ibid, 548.

9 In John House, *Monet, Nature into Art,* London, New Haven, 1986, 28–29.

10 In John Rewald, *Paul Cézanne*, op. cit., 117.

11 In John Rewald, *The History of Impressionism*, op. cit., 486.

12 In John Rewald, *Post-Impressionism from Van Gogh to Gauguin*, revised edition, London 1978, 398, 400.

13 Ibid, 82.

14 Ibid, 104.

15 Ibid, 349.

16 Emile Verhaeren, *Sensations*, Paris, 1927, 199.

17 In John Rewald, *Post-Impressionism*, op. cit., 125.

18 See note 14.

19 In a letter to Henri Van der Velde, 27 March 1896, in John Rewald, *Post-Impressionism*, op. cit., 404, note 70.

20 In John House, *Post-Impressionism*, op. cit., catalogue entry 153.

21 In John House, *Monet*, op. cit., 223

22 In John Rewald, *Post-Impressionism*, op. cit., 450.

23 In John House, 'The Legacy of Impressionism', op. cit., 20.

24 In John Rewald, *Post-Impressionism*, op. cit., 168.

25 In John Rewald, *The History of Impressionism*, op. cit., 496.

26 In John Rewald, *Post-Impressionism*, op. cit., 266–67.

27 Ibid, 171.

28 Emile Bernard, 'Recits d'un passager au bord de la vie', Lettres de Paul Gauguin à Emile Bernard, 1888–1891, 1954, 30, in MaryAnne Stevens, *Post-Impressionism*, exhibition catalogue, Royal Academy, op. cit., 23.

29 John Rewald, *The History of Impressionism*, op. cit., 548.

30 John Rewald, *Post-Impressionism*, op. cit., 181–82.

31 Ibid, 184.

32 Maurice Denis, 'Définition du Néo-Traditionnisme', in *Art et Critique*, 23 August 1890.

33 In John Rewald, *Post-Impressionism*, op. cit., 462.

34 In Gerstle Mack, *Toulouse-Lautrec*, Paris, 1938, 53.

49   Photograph of three prostitutes, Montmartre.

tions of his contemporaries. At times his work displays elements of a moralist's satire comparable to Seurat's later figurative pieces (*see plate 86*). At others he reveals a sympathetic and compassionate understanding of his subject akin to van Gogh (*see plate 27*). Lautrec's first teacher, Léon Bonnat, said of his pupil (as Lautrec records in a letter written to his uncle in May 1882): 'Your painting isn't bad, it's clever but still it isn't bad, but your drawing is simply atrocious.'[34] Lautrec's use of plunging perspectives and unexpected angles of vision in a painting such as *At the Moulin Rouge* is certainly clever; they are devices that increase the drama of the image. It is hard to agree with Bonnat's verdict of 'atrocious', however, when Lautrec adopts a more abbreviated and condensed manner, as in *Rue des Moulins: The Inspection*, where he as much draws with the brush as paints with it. Rather, even in the degradation of these women waiting to be checked for syphilis, Lautrec's subjects are given grace by his line. It does not flatter but yet seems to discover beauty.

50 EDGAR DEGAS Dancers *c.* 1899.

Degas had a private income and became increasingly misanthropic in his old age. He very rarely exhibited in public after 1890, though his work could be seen at Durand-Ruel's gallery. His independence enabled him to experiment with a variety of different media other than oil. As his eyesight deteriorated he turned more and more to pastel, applying it to the paper with an unprecedented breadth and freedom, and employing more and more vibrant contrasts of increasingly bright colours. The vehemence of his handling was in direct contrast to the delicate modelling and soft, fragile harmonies for which pastel had been used by earlier artists.

51 CLAUDE MONET Grainstacks at Sunset 1891.

It was one of Monet's paintings of haystacks (which have recently been authoritatively identified as grainstacks) that helped to convince Wassily Kandinsky, when he saw them in Moscow in 1895 and failed to recognize the subject of the picture, that a non-objective or purely abstract art was possible. Monet never renounced the study of nature; his essential subject was atmosphere and light so he could hardly dispense with it. But the actual objects he chose to depict seem in themselves to hold little interest for him except as receptacles of light. In this canvas all the forms seem about to dematerialize; the only strong outline occurs where the brilliant yellow of the setting sun silhouettes the top edge of the grainstack.

53 CLAUDE MONET Water Lilies – Reflections of the Willow 1918–25.

In failing health, but with the water garden at his home in Giverny complete, Monet was able to paint his final, most triumphant series paintings – those of the water lilies. The water garden provided him with a piece of nature perfectly suited for the study of light – for the essential subject of this series is not so much the lilies or, as in this painting, the willow tree, but the reflections they produced on the water's surface. The water garden became a sort of hortus enclosus. Nature herself has been landscaped by the controlling will of the artist so that she can be further manipulated with paint on canvas.

52 CLAUDE MONET Morning on the Seine, Giverny 1897.
The coarse, thickly encrusted paint surfaces of Monet's canvases of Rouen Cathedral were probably only partially intended to be analogous to the texture of stone. They probably also testify to the frustrating number of corrections and alterations Monet had to make before he was satisfied that his colours had properly expressed the particular conditions of the light of the moment. The series of river scenes he painted a few years later, however, were executed with superimposed layers of thin, almost transparent pigment, so translucent that it is as if the paint never really dried and still retains its original liquid state.

54 GEORGES SEURAT A Sunday Afternoon on the Island of
La Grande Jatte 1883–86.

*Seurat never concerned himself with portraying individual personalities in
his large figure paintings. In this work, he positioned his various urban
types in a hieratic composition reminiscent of the carved stone friezes of
ancient Greece, or, more recently, the classical decorations of Puvis de
Chavannes. Seurat's frieze, however, removes the static dignity given to
the protagonists by such arrangements both in these particular precedents
and in his own Baignade (see plate 63) completed two years before.
Instead, he gently mocks the bourgeoisie at leisure: the monkey in the
foreground, for instance, subtly implies that the lady holding its leash is
a prostitute and not a respectable bourgeois wife.*

55 GEORGES SEURAT Harbour at Gravelines 1890.

*What is so special about that bollard that it should occupy such an
important place in this sparse composition? Is it because the shadow it
casts is the only diagonal accent counteracting that of the receding road, or
because its shape mimics that of the lighthouse in the top left-hand corner?
Gravelines is a small port on the Channel coast close to Dunkerque.
However, Seurat's insistent emphasis on the shape and position of
something as intrinsically uninteresting as a bollard suggests that he was
not particularly concerned with painting a scene of topographical charm.*

56 GEORGES SEURAT   Le Chahut   1889–90.
This picture was evidently painted as a tribute to the dancer Grille d'Egout
who performed the high-kicking dance of the title at the Moulin Rouge.
But it seems a rather strange trophy, for its attitude to the subject seems
far from laudatory. Seurat moulds all his forms into an upward,
supposedly exhilarating direction: legs, musical instruments and light
fittings, even the bows on the dancers shoes, the tails of a jacket and the
ribbons on the female dancers' shoulder-straps conform to the same
pattern. Yet these last also curl with something of the cynical snicker of the
dancers' smiles.

57 PAUL SIGNAC   The Dining Room   1886–87.

This painting was among the twelve that Signac sent to the exhibition of
Les Vingt in Brussels in 1888. Boldly lit, à contre-jour – against the sun
that streams in from the window – Signac composes his interior through
sharp contrasts of light and dark areas. The careful application of the
points of the divisionist stroke, as well as the strictly frontal and profile
poses of these respectable figures, lends to this bourgeois meal what is
probably (considering Signac's political views) a deliberate feeling of
immobility and artifice. The gentleman sits rigid and impassive, but he is
sufficiently imposing for the seated woman to feel obliged to efface herself
in her teacup.

59 PAUL SIGNAC   Au Temps d'Harmonie   1895.

In Signac's Utopian vision of the future, young and healthy men, women
and children work and play in a beautiful coastal landscape. Two women
and one man can be seen working in the distant fields, while the bearded
man in the foreground has just put down his spade to pick the fruit from
the branch above him The emphasis falls more heavily, however, on play:
on boule, leisurely reading, impromptu dancing, even on painting.
Signac's golden age is set in the future; yet the boat leaning against the
breeze in the background has no smoke-stack. Unlike Luce, Signac firmly
rejects the questionab.e benefits of industrialism in his Utopia.

58 PAUL SIGNAC St Tropez 1893.
During the 1890s Signac began to paint his finished landscapes in the studio, working directly from small studies like this that he had made outside. Later, he refined this process even further, using these plein-air studies only to suggest ideas for the final composition. The speed with which such studies were made is evident in the large amounts of panel left bare of paint. This type of abbreviation and the boldness of the colour employed was later to have a significant influence on Matisse and Derain as they evolved what came to be known as their 'Fauve' style in the summer of 1905.

60 CAMILLE PISSARRO Les Faneuses 1889.

*One of Pissarro's most densely worked and highly finished paintings, Les
Faneuses depicts a number of women making hay in a hot, golden field.
Pissarro painted this work in the studio, working from studies made
outside, a working method most of the other Impressionists had adopted
by this date. The variety of size of the brushstrokes also reveals how
Pissarro was by now moving away from his involvement with divisionism.
Pissarro was as committed in his anarchist convictions as Signac, Luce
and Cross; but in his paintings of rural life, as in this one, he consistently
stressed that living away from the city did not remove the need for work.
Where nature would seem to provide for Signac's Arcadians in his Au
Temps d'Harmonie with very little effort on their part (see plate 59),
and for Cross's with none at all (see plate 61), Pissarro knew differently.*

61 HENRI-EDMOND CROSS   L'Air du Soir   1894.

Cross was a close friend of Signac. The two artists spent many summers painting together at Signac's home in St Tropez. Like so many of his generation Cross admired the work of Puvis de Chavannes, transforming his pale, classical, frieze-like compositions into the brightly coloured idiom of divisionism – though the languid curves of a tree in the middle ground also reveal an interest in the decorative style of Art Nouveau. There are no men in this paradise where the wringing out of hair and the quiet contemplation of an iris or the sea illustrate the height of energetic activity. The stillness of these women, however, matches the stillness of that hour just before dusk when the breeze drops, announcing the imminent setting of the sun – 'A quietness distilled, As twilight long begun . . .', as Emily Dickinson once wrote. (A Choice of Emily Dickinson's Verse, Faber, London, 1979, 59.)

62 PIERRE AUGUSTE RENOIR   The Luncheon of the Boating
Party   1881.

Renoir may have been dissatisfied with the soft edges and lack of linear
clarity that his Impressionist technique bestowed on the forms he described
in this scene. This was something he tried to correct in some of his
subsequent paintings. But the use here of such a technique adds
considerably to this image of a weekend's delightful indulgence. Grapes
lie on the table, the bottle of wine is half-drunk, glasses are empty – all
this food and drink is for consumption. Everybody is replete and they
have moved on to other pleasures: either flirting with another guest,
or gently rebuffing their efforts.

63 GEORGES SEURAT   Une Baignade à Asnières   1883–84.

A brief look at Seurat's description of light will serve to demonstrate how
he departed from Impressionist practice. The shadows in the picture tell us
that the light is falling from right to left, and yet the treatment of the
water, at the point where it touches the limp arm of the central figure, is
not consistent with this. Where the contour of the arm meets the water
Seurat has darkened the blue, thus emphasizing the line. It is certainly
a beautiful and subtle line but Seurat has highlighted its abstract beauty
at the expense of naturalistic description.

Seurat

65 GEORGES SEURAT La Parade 1887–88.
*During the 1890s a large number of new café-cabarets opened in
Montmartre: the Chat Noir, the Mirliton, the Divan Japonais and the
Cabaret Assassins now stood alongside the most famous of all of them, the
Moulin Rouge. Lautrec depicted the somewhat jaded elegance of their most
renowned singers and dancers, as Degas had done before him; the visual
image that has survived until today was one created in that era by these
two artists. Seurat also painted these scenes of nocturnal, urban
entertainment but his images are strangely disconcerting. The expression
of mood dominates any naturalistic concerns; there is little sense of noise
or movement in this sinister performance.*

64 HENRI DE TOULOUSE-LAUTREC At the Moulin Rouge
1892–95.
*Where Seurat's cabaret scenes seem unnaturally stilled, Lautrec's use of a
dramatically plunging perspective and the lurid green light striking the
woman in the right-hand corner together give his painting of the Moulin
Rouge a theatrical, dynamic and dramatic note. Lautrec depicted his
subjects from unexpected angles of vision, a technique he learned from
Degas and the example of Japanese prints. The men sitting at the table are
portraits of his friends. These, the location and the prostitutes combine to
give us a succinct biographical amalgam of the artist's milieu.*

67   JAMES ENSOR   The Entry of Christ into Brussels   1888.
This enormous painting was rejected even by the progressive Les Vingt
when Ensor presented it for exhibition in 1888. Like Seurat's La Grande
Jatte (see plate 54), which had proved so influential in Belgium, Ensor's
massive frieze was an indictment, though an infinitely more ferocious one,
of modern society. With a deliberately crude and ugly technique, Ensor
pictures the violent public demonstrations that might accompany the
arrival of Christ on a new Palm Sunday in modern-day Brussels. Christ is
dwarfed in the centre of the composition, surrounded by hysterical and
inane crowds celebrating a socialist holiday, as the banner flying overhead
and placards below serve to indicate.

66   THÉO VAN RYSSELBERGHE   Portrait of Maria Sèthe at the
Harmonium   1891.
Rysselberghe exploited the divisionist technique to its full, naturalistic
potential in the genre of portraiture. Unlike the fantastically artificial
setting Signac gave to his portrait of Fénéon (see plate 9), van
Rysselberghe used everyday domestic accessories to suggest the personality
and interests of his sitter. Maria Sèthe wears a dress with fashionable
mutton-chop sleeves; the curls of her neatly arranged hair are mimicked by
the pattern on the background wall and the neck of the cello. If Seurat
made a virtue out of immobility, van Rysselberghe seems to have been
hampered by pedestrianism.

68   HENRI MATISSE   Luxe, calme et volupté   1904–05.
*Matisse stayed with Signac during the summer of 1904, and it was
through the older artist's influence that he painted this, his first idealized
subject in the divisionist style. The title comes from Baudelaire's poem,
'L'Invitation au Voyage' (1857), in which the poet invites his mistress to
come away with him to a perfect land. In Matisse's painting, five nude
bathers have come ashore to a picnic presided over by his wife. It is not
clear if they have already arrived at their destination or if they will
continue their journey to the distant hills. There is humour in this
incongruous mixing of elements from the everyday with those of the ideal.
In other ways, however, Matisse has composed an intimate love poem
to his long-suffering wife.*

69 ANDRÉ DERAIN L'Age d'Or 1905.
*The failure of Derain's later work to gain any significant critical or general
acclaim has tended to diminish the important role he played both in the
history of the Fauves and later in that of the Cubists. Here, Derain
combines aspects of avant-garde technical practice, in particular the
lozenged brushwork and the bright palette of the divisionists, with the
traditional subject of the pastoral. He would have seen Ingres's
composition of the same subject at a well-publicized exhibition in Paris a
few months before he executed this large oil. The three foreground nudes
here, however, unhappily separated from the idyllic scene behind them,
could be seen as exemplifying the uneasy relationship that existed between
the avant garde and the Academy.*

70 JAN TOOROP The Shell Gatherer 1891.
*The yellow–violet complementaries employed in this painting lend an
attractively forlorn air. Toorop evidently painted this stark picture as a
tribute to Seurat who had died earlier in 1891 and whose works at the Les
Vingt exhibition in 1887 had proved so important in his development.
Toorop placed his widely spaced dots over thinly painted bands of pigment.
The lone figure drags a heavy cart through the sluggish sand. His body,
arched with effort, is the only vertical accent in this predominantly
horizontal composition. Nevertheless he is dwarfed by the vast spaces
of sand, sea and sky: a configuration that suggests something of man's
insignificance beside the immense scale of nature, which will only
reluctantly provide him with a living.*

71 ODILON REDON The Birth of Venus 1910.
Redon himself explained the particular path of his inspiration in an article published in the journal L'Art Moderne in 1894: 'I have always felt the need to copy nature in small objects, particularly the casual or accidental. It is only after making an effort of will power to represent with minute care a grass blade, a stone, a branch, the face of an old wall, that I am overcome by the irresistible urge to create something imaginary.' (John Rewald, Post-Impressionism: from Van Gogh to Gauguin, London, 1978, 153.) In this late pastel, it is as though the particular natural source for this abstracted image is the teeming, vivid view of life seen under the microscope.

72 ODILON REDON Cyclops *c.* 1898.
Like Degas, Redon used pastel to create effects no one else before had tried to achieve with the medium. Both exploited its potential for bold colouristic effects; but while Degas's contrasts were ferocious, Redon's were more sumptuous. That same richness of colour informed his oil paintings, a medium that he only took up late in life. Redon's preference for the brightest tones in both his oils and pastels was to influence the Fauves in their radical experiments with pure colour. Perhaps it was the sentimentality with which Redon portrayed this lonely, one-eyed giant that prevented the critics from coining the term 'Fauvism' earlier than they did.

73 GUSTAVE MOREAU   The Battle of the Centaurs   *c. 1890.*
Moreau was described by one contemporary critic as, 'an opium-smoker who had at his services the hands of a goldsmith'. (Charles Chasse, The Nabis and their period, Paris, 1969, 21.) The reference to goldsmiths does not really apply in this watercolour but refers to the intricate detailing and smooth, pristine surface of the few works exhibited by Moreau. This watercolour was certainly never shown in public. This was obviously not because he considered this sort of highly abstract work as unimportant, however, for he took the trouble both to sign it and inscribe the title on the lower edge of the sheet. By this time in his life, Moreau had decided that his painting was very much a private concern.

74 GUSTAVE MOREAU   The Temptation of St Anthony
c. 1890.
If it is only after a little while that the two wrestling centaurs in the first watercolour become discernible (see plate 73), in this work the subject is at least marginally more legible. St Anthony stands towards the left clutching his head, surrounded by the terrifying products of his vision. Immediately to his right the head and breasts of a woman, a sexual temptress, are outlined in blue. The nightmare is completed by the goat to the left and the other equally monstrous heads and serpents to the right. Yet the power of these watercolours, not to mention their historical import as precursors of the work of artists like Kandinsky, resides in their use of highly expressive but ultimately abstract means.

75   PIERRE PUVIS DE CHAVANNES   Pleasant Land   1882.
With its pale colours, relaxed and simplified drawing and relatively calm,
uneventful compositions, the work of Puvis de Chavannes might seem a
little anaemic today, yet in the 1880s and 1890s it was held in the highest
regard by establishment and avant garde alike. His classical subjects and
his deliberate emulation of the Italian fresco tradition – by adopting a
decorative style – endeared him to the establishment. Within the avant
garde the serenity of his idyllic settings, and the calm dignity of his figures
was highly influential – in Seurat's Baignade, for example (see plate 63)
– a calm that remains undisturbed in this painting by the two wrestling
boys in the foreground.

76   PIERRE PUVIS DE CHAVANNES   The Sacred Wood Dear
to the Arts and Muses   1884.

*The nine muses and personifications of the three fine arts – Painting,
Sculpture and Architecture – lazily inhabit an idealized classical
landscape, calmly discussing matters as two young boys make wreaths of
laurel from a tree on the right. Lautrec might have painted a parody of
this work (see page 57), but it was more playful than vitriolic in temper.
For many younger painters regarded Puvis de Chavannes with esteem, and
were affected by his characteristic blend of classical subject with decorative
style. Matisse's* Luxe, calme et volupté *(see plate 68) and Derain's*
L'Age d'Or *(see plate 69), for example, despite the brighter colour and
divisionist brushwork, both emulate the achievements of the older artist.*

77 PIERRE BONNARD Madame Claude
Terrasse 1892

*Madame Terrasse plays with her food as her cat
stretches out an inquisitive paw, but her distracted
gaze indicates that her mind is on other things. This
is an after-dinner reverie, a charming domestic scene
that is saved from becoming overly sentimental by the
rough grace of Bonnard's touch. Madame Terrasse's
checkered blouse is rendered as a completely flat
pattern, its folds become autonomous, curling
arabesques echoed by the arched back and neck of her
cat. But both arabesque and pattern, potentially
cloying if over-emphasized, save Bonnard from the
chocolate-box, painted as they are in thick, coarse
slabs of pigment.*

78 EDOUARD VUILLARD Mother and Sister
of the Artist 1893.

*Vuillard enjoyed using pattern in his decorative easel
paintings even more than Bonnard. Regular patterning
on the fabric of a dress or in the design of a wallpaper
could easily be painted to suggest flatness, whilst not
categorically denying the suggestion of depth. Here
the wallpaper is contained within the recessional lines
of the wall, though is seems on the point of breaking
out of these confines to engulf the contorted body of
the artist's sister. She bends over to fit her tall body
into the frame, gripping the wall as if in fear,
nervously glancing out of the canvas. By contrast,
Vuillard's mother sits robustly and confrontational,
receiving her daughter's homage.*

80　ÉMILE BERNARD　Breton Women in the Meadow　1888.
*As his Asnières landscape indicates, Bernard had already generated the
stylistic elements that were to contribute so much to Gauguin's
development in Vision after the Sermon (see plate 79) well before the
two painters met in the summer of 1888. This painting, which Bernard
completed before Gauguin even began his seminal work, also provided the
older artist with his theme. The stature of Gauguin's masterpiece,
however, has somewhat diminished Bernard's pioneering achievements.
Bernard's drawing here is certainly less incisive than Gauguin's. In fact it
is rather flaccid, and his figures remain unconnected by any narrative
thread. Nonetheless, whatever he may have said to the contrary, Gauguin
remains indebted to Bernard's innovations.*

79　PAUL GAUGUIN　Vision after the Sermon: Jacob and
the Angel　1888.
*With this single painting Gauguin, who had hitherto only produced
paintings in a competently Impressionist style, announced the arrival of a
major and original talent to the rest of the Parisian avant garde. There
was simply no precedent in the fine arts for such a vast expanse of bright
vermilion. Gauguin had already hinted at the possibility of what was to
come in some of the landscapes he brought back from the French island of
Martinique in 1887. But it was here that the breakthrough was made
into an unashamedly unnaturalistic kind of painting, where colour and
line could be used as abstract agents for the expression or suggestion
of thought and feeling.*

81 MAURICE DENIS Breton Wrestling (Jacob wrestling with
the Angel) 1893.
*Without the explanatory title, Denis's figures could just as easily be
bucolic swains dancing for joy at the charmed ease of their ideal existence.
Instead, a human struggles with a divine messenger beneath the weight of
God's blessing. For it is only after having fought with the angel through
the night, and having suffered a dislocated thigh-bone in the process,
that Jacob is told by the angel that he has prevailed with God and that
thereafter he shall be called Israel. In contrast to Gauguin's earlier
treatment of the same theme in Vision after the Sermon (see plate 79),
to which Denis is deliberately paying homage here, there is something
decidedly decorous about the grapplings of these biblical characters.*

82 MAURICE DENIS Mary with the Christ Child and St John 1898.

Overlooking what could be Florence and the Arno valley, but what – with its cypresses and churches – is unmistakably an Italian landscape, the Virgin Mary sits on a spacious balcony, tenderly holding the infant Christ. As she looks gently down at him, her modesty suggested by the tilt of her head and lowered eyelids, an infant St John approaches bearing an apple. Three angels witness this intimate scene of maternal love and childish devotion. So far, it could hardly be a more traditional image; but the softly simplified lines, the pale colours and the virtual absence of modelling and volume in the figures reveal Denis's decorative concerns.

83 PAUL SÉRUSIER Landscape in the Bois d'Amour: The Talisman 1888.

Perhaps it was partly because of its physical modesty – Sérusier's tiny landscape was painted on the lid of a cigar box – that this diminutive work assumed such significance for the Nabis in Paris. As the quintessence of Gauguin's instructions and an admittedly indirect embodiment of his genius, this small panel became for them a relic, a sort of Turin shroud of momentous import. Clear reflections of a landscape in water can be somewhat confusing to the eye at the best of times and in the most illusionistic of images. Sérusier, with Gauguin as stepfather and midwife, exploited such spatial ambiguities to the full in this fresh, autumnal, decorative and abstracted scene.

84 EDOUARD VUILLARD   Girl at the Piano   *c.* 1897.
This painting contains none of the disturbing intimations of familial tension and maternal domination evident in Vuillard's double portrait of his mother and sister (see plate 78). Moreover, unlike the figures in the other work, the girl at the piano seems totally unaware that she is posing for the artist; yet Vuillard avoids here the voyeuristic implications that somehow seem to taint the spectator in Degas's nudes. Although his colours are muted, the lively pattern of the wallpaper – the flatness of which is delicately denied at the left edge – suggests the vivacity and colour of the music filling this otherwise rather drab and dull interior.

85   PIERRE BONNARD   La Revue Blanche   1894.
La Revue Blanche was among the most influential of the many new journals to spring up in Paris during the 1880s and 1890s. It was also one of the longer-lived, running from 1891 to 1903. Broadly Symbolist in outlook, it was edited by Thadée Natanson, formerly a lawyer who had defended Félix Fénéon when he was arrested in connection with some anarchist demonstrations and bombings. In Bonnard's poster, a grubby street urchin points with his thumb to the sophisticated, stylish woman holding a copy of the journal. It is a witty and elegant image, composed out of only three closely related tones, and cleverly integrating figures, setting and text.

87 HENRI DE TOULOUSE-LAUTREC   Mme Loïe Fuller Dancing
1893.

*Mme Loïe Fuller was an American who travelled all over Europe
performing her renowned veiled dance. In a costume made of voluminous
swirls of chiffon that she manipulated with unseen wands, Loïe Fuller
waved and twirled the translucent material to musical accompaniment
under changing coloured lights. The effect was entrancing. By abstracting
the movement of figure and costume into a number of simplified,
interlocking arcs, Lautrec almost loses sight of his subject in the
exhilarating, dynamic rhythm he creates. His forms do not so much
capture the dancer's movement – for that would still it – but synthesize
her actions to produce an image of continuous motion.*

88 HENRI DE TOULOUSE-LAUTREC   Jane Avril Dancing
c. 1892.

*The slicing of the composition to the left and the abbreviated description of
the interior – in particular the rapid linear strokes describing the floor –
graphically communicate Jane Avril's speed and energy as she spins on her
painfully thin legs. But there is little that is elegant either about the
dancer's emaciated contortions, or the way in which Lautrec has described
this nocturnal scene. Both performer and description seem thin and
dissipated. Avril's face, the natural focus of the whole composition, is a
portrait of pale, finely chiselled melancholy. Behind her, the seated couple
become grotesque caricatures of the audience feeding on her performance.*

86 HENRI DE TOULOUSE-LAUTREC   Reine de Joie   1892.

*The introduction of colour lithography in the 1880s transformed the
design of commercial posters; figurative elements began to dominate the
printed text. Lautrec, like Bonnard, was quick to realize the artistic
potential of the new medium. The need to create eye-catching images
called for large areas of flatly printed colour, which transformed a
limitation of the technique into a potential opportunity. Jane Avril again
features as the courtesan in this poster advertising Victor Joze's novel of
aristocratic corruption and decadence in 1890s Paris, as she impudently
kisses the balding glutton on his flabby nose.*

Chapter 2

Three Recluses

While rivalries and debates between Symbolists, Impressionists, Nabis and Neo-Impressionists enlivened the avant-garde community in Paris, three of the painters whose pictures would have the most profound effects on later generations were producing work far removed from that city. Paul Gauguin (1848–1903) left France in 1891 for the South Sea Islands, where he was to die in 1903. Paul Cézanne (1839–1906) was spending most of his time painting in his native Provence, rarely visiting Paris or even exhibiting his paintings there. The Dutch painter Vincent van Gogh (1853–1890) also forsook Paris to work in the south, in the small town of Arles.

With a Firm Hand

Nature forgot to shade him off, I think? . . . A little too boisterous – like the sea? A little too vehement – like a bull who has made up his mind to consider every colour scarlet? But, I grant a sledge-hammering sort of merit in him!

So the flighty Mr Skimpole in *Bleak House* by Charles Dickens (1812–1870) describes the more robust and ebullient Mr Boythorn. Dickens was one of van Gogh's favourite authors – and by a happy coincidence there is much in Skimpole's description that might also be applied to the Dutchman.

As an art student van Gogh was sometimes known, in the heat of argument, to strip to the waist in order to prove some anatomical point. He would also, on occasion, squeeze paint directly from the tube onto his canvas, layering it with thick ridges of pigment. Gauguin records being exasperated by his untidiness when they shared a studio together in Arles, in particular his habit of never putting the tops back on the

89 VINCENT VAN GOGH   The Chair and the Pipe
1888–89.
During the long months that van Gogh spent alone in Arles before Gauguin's arrival, Vincent wrote to Theo of the loneliness of the evenings when darkness prevented him from painting: ' I shall find some occupation that will take all my attention. Weavers and basket makers often spend whole seasons alone or almost alone, with their occupation for their only distraction. But what makes these people stay in one place is precisely the feeling of domesticity, the reassuring familiar look of things.' (Letter to Theo, September 1888.) The yellow house in Arles was probably the closest van Gogh got to having a home. The desire to find and keep the security that it would bring informs his depiction of his favourite chair and pipe.

tubes he so mercilessly emptied. In one of the very few articles published on van Gogh during his lifetime, which appeared in the Janurary 1890 issue of the new *Mercure de France*, the young Parisian critic Albert Aurier (1865–1892) cited excess as his dominant characteristic:

What particularizes his entire work is the excess, excess in strength, excess in nervousness, inviolence of expression . . . he is a fanatic, an enemy of bourgeois sobriety and trifling details, a kind of drunken giant, better able to move mountains than to handle bibelots, an ebullient brain which irresistibly pours its lava into all the ravines of art, a terrible and highly strung genius, often sublime, often grotesque, almost always on the edge of the pathological.[1]

The energy unleashed by van Gogh, in person and in his paintings, was terrifying. It emerged, invariably, as some kind of emotional assault upon his audience. As he wrote to a friend in 1885, 'I cannot always keep quiet as my convictions are so much part of myself that it is sometimes as if they took me by the throat.'[2] Yet the man who would suddenly strip to the waist to point out the correct juncture between two bones would also veer to the opposite extreme. Henri de Toulouse-Lautrec (1864–1901) recalled how van Gogh would occasionally visit his studio armed with a stack of canvases under his arm, anxious to discuss them; but out of place amongst the elegant and urbane souls who gathered there, he would sit silently in a corner for half an hour or so before leaving – without having said a word.

Vincent's younger brother Theo, who was without question the one who understood and loved him best, was not unaware of the two sides of his character. He described his brother in a letter written to their sister in 1886 or 1887:

It is as if there are two persons in him – one marvellously gifted, delicate and tender, the other egotistical and hard-hearted! They present themselves in turn, so that one hears him talk first in one way, then in the other, and this always with arguments which are now all for, now all against the same point. It is a pity that he is his own enemy, for he makes life hard not only for others but also for himself.[3]

Van Gogh only decided to become an artist in 1880 when he was twenty-seven years old. His first job had been as an art dealer, working as an assistant for the firm Goupil and Company. This he had left in 1876 after a row with his boss and he had then become a schoolmaster in England, teaching in Ramsgate and Isleworth. His father was a church minister and Vincent's next move was to follow in his footsteps; he entered an evangelical school in Brussels in 1878. He left after only three months to live as a preacher, at his own expense, among the miners of the Borinage in southern Belgium. Life there was particularly squalid. As Kenneth Clark (1903–1983) wrote: 'Like St Francis, he had to share the poverty of the poorest and most miserable of his fellow men – and conditions in industrial Belgium were probably more degraded than in thirteenth-century Umbria.'[4] In fact, his future sister-in-law later recorded how, after he had been given a temporary nomination as a lay preacher in 1879, Vincent decided to put Christ's teaching literally into practice. He gave away his money, his clothes and even his bed – and was promptly dismissed by the Church for excessive zeal.

Thereafter, as one writer has put it, 'Van Gogh's own life could be considered a surrogate religious experience.'[5] Throughout the many letters that survive, most of which were written to his brother Theo, Vincent's responses to nature are often described in religious terms; in one letter, for instance, he talks of the coming of spring as a deliverance after the oppression and anxiety of winter. 'If one pays attention,' he wrote, 'one sees that such a first spring day is a kind of Gospel message.'[6] These kinds of emotions and ideas certainly seem discernible as the motivating forces behind many of his landscapes. More generally, as Theo's wife was to say, his overwhelming desire to serve others was transmuted after his failure as a preacher into an equally powerful desire to bring consolation through his art. The ideals, in fact, that had prompted him to go into the Church infuse all his paintings, landscape and portraits alike.

Having decided to become a painter, van Gogh moved back to the family home in Holland, where his parents let his increasing eccentricities pass without comment. Despite their tolerance, it was not a particularly happy arrangement. Vincent was a difficult person to live with, at the best of times, and at that stage the situation was not helped by his unrequited passion for his cousin. He moved away to Neunen, a small village in the Brabant region near Eindhoven. Here his painting directly reflected his religious and social ideals. He painted the little church there no less than ten times (see plate 90), and it was here that he completed his first masterpiece, *The Potato Eaters* (see plate 103), a large work that Theo proudly hung above the mantelpiece in the dining room of his Paris flat.

In *The Potato Eaters* van Gogh depicted, with brutal sympathy, the squalid existence of the rural dispossessed – the peasant family who can afford nothing to eat except those bland, swollen tubers. While living at Neunen van Gogh had noticed peasant women gleaning potatoes after the diggers had worked the fields. If the meal endured by the family in this painting were procured in the same way, this image of modern suffering might also have seemed in van Gogh's mind a reincarnation of the Old Testament story of Ruth and Boaz.

Whether or not any biblical associations lurk behind the work, van Gogh has certainly chosen to emphasize his figures' suffering and degradation. The way their faces are described seems closer to caricature than portraiture, as though they have been disfigured by squalor and a mean diet. When Theo reported that a friend of theirs named Serret had criticized the structure of the figures in the picture, Vincent countered that 'this was an impression gained after having

90　VINCENT VAN GOGH　Old Church Tower　1885.
Van Gogh wrote of this painting: 'I wanted to express how these ruins show that for ages the peasants have been laid to rest in the very fields which they dug up when alive . . . I wanted to express what a simple thing death and burial is, just as simple as the falling of an autumn leaf – just a bit of earth dug up – a wooden cross. The fields around, where the grass of the churchyard ends, beyond the little wall, form a last line against the horizon – like the horizon of the sea. And now these ruins tell me how a faith and a religion mouldered away – strongly founded though they were – but how the life and the death of the peasants remain forever the same, budding and withering regularly, like the grass and the flowers there in the churchyard.' (Letter to Theo, June 1885.)

seen the cottage in the dim lamplight for many evenings, after having painted forty heads.'[7] In other words the painting had been the fruit of lengthy study of actual scenes – both the figures and the murky interior of a labourer's cottage. Earlier in the same letter he explained:

Tell Serret that I should be desperate if my figures were correct, tell him that I do not want them to be academically correct . . . Tell him that, for me, [Jean-François] Millet [1814–1875] and Lhermitte are the real artists, for the very reason that they do not paint things as they are, traced in a dry analytical way, but as they . . . feel them. Tell him that my great longing is to learn to make those very incorrectnesses, those deviations, remodellings, changes of reality, so that they may become, yes, untruth if you like – but more true than literal truth.'

From the beginning then van Gogh saw his duty as a painter in terms of distorting visual reality for the sake of expressive truth – a position that unwittingly placed him on a theoretical par with the Parisian Symbolists.

In 1885, the year that *The Potato Eaters* was painted, van Gogh had hardly even heard of the Impressionists, let alone the Symbolists. The following year, however, he travelled to Paris to complete his art 'education'. Van Gogh had studied briefly in Brussels, The Hague and Antwerp but he was largely self-taught. In Paris he entered the Atelier Cormon but he stayed there for only a month. Formal instruction was quite simply too rigid for someone as volatile as Vincent to be able to endure for very long.

For the two years he was in Paris Vincent lived with Theo in his flat in Montmartre. Theo had moved there in 1879 to work for the firm of art dealers called Boussod and Valadon. He supported his brother with monthly payments out of his own meagre salary – from Vincent's beginnings as a painter in 1880 until his death ten years later.

Vincent arrived unexpectedly in February 1886; the two brothers met in the Louvre. He was determined to work and study hard. Emile Bernard (1868–1941), whom van Gogh met at Cormon's, recalls how the Dutchman would stay behind at the studio in the afternoons to work alone from the plaster casts of statues, sometimes rubbing out the mistakes in his drawings so vigorously that he made holes in his paper. But van Gogh's education in Paris was really completed through his contact with the other artists he met – either through Theo at Cormon's, or at Père Tanguy's paint shop.

Van Gogh was also introduced to Lautrec, Paul Signac (1863–1935), Camille Pissarro (1830–1903) and Gauguin among others. He was thus able to acquaint himself with all the leading tendencies within the Parisian avant garde. Pissarro taught him the methods and aims of both Impressionism and divisionism. In the summer van Gogh would go with Bernard and Signac to Asnières to paint (see plate 44). The latter recalls how they walked all the way back to Paris after a day's painting furiously discussing Georges Seurat's (1859–1891) ideas on colour contrasts and complementaries. Van Gogh's intensity and commitment were clearly sometimes something of an embarrassment:

Van Gogh, dressed in a blue workman's blouse, had painted little dots of color on his sleeves. Sticking close to me, he shouted and gesticulated, brandishing his large, freshly covered canvas, and with it he polychromed himself as well as passers-by.[8]

The essential change wrought in van Gogh's work by this first-hand exposure to the French avant garde came in his use of colour. He abandoned the dark, earthy hues and grey tonalities of his earlier work and adopted the bright, pure, spectral palette favoured by the Impressionists and divisionists. Always far too individual to submit to the discipline of divisionism, van Gogh typically transformed the technique to suit his own personal, expressive purposes. In a self-portrait he painted in 1887 this influence is immediately apparent (see plate 104). Here van Gogh adopts the short, lozenge-shaped brushstroke preferred by Signac to Seurat's dot. He does not use it according to their system of complementaries and optical mixtures, however, though he does create vivid and insistent textures, and a kind of aura or halo around his own head. He was later to write to Theo: 'In a picture I want to say something as comforting as music is comforting. I want to paint men and women with that something of the eternal which the halo used to symbolize, and which we seek to confer by the actual radiance and vibration of our colourings.'[9] Whatever his aims, van Gogh seems – here at any rate – to have painted an image of the artist as the seat of a creative energy more demonic than divine.

In the end Vincent found Parisian life a strain, despite all the stimulation provided by his new artist friends and acquaintances. For roughly the same reasons that Gauguin left Paris for Brittany, van Gogh wanted to live in the country away from the city too. But instead of Brittany in the north,

he longed for the bright sunlight and dazzling colour of the south. So, towards the end of February 1888 he left Paris for the Provençal town of Arles, renting rooms in a small yellow house close to the station. He arrived when the town and surrounding country were unusually covered with snow, but soon he was entranced by the beauty of the landscape. He described his impressions in a letter to Theo written in September that year:

Nature here is so extraordinarily beautiful! Everywhere and over all the vault of the sky is a marvellous blue, and the sun sheds a radiance of pale sulphur; it is as soft and lovely as the combination of celestial blues and yellows in Vermeer's paintings. I can't paint it as beautifully as that, but it absorbs me so much that I let myself go without thinking of any rules.[10]

This exhilaration is patently apparent in a number of drawings that van Gogh executed of the landscape around Arles in the summer of 1888 using a variety of oriental reed pens he had recently purchased. In one of these, *View of Arles with Irises in the Foreground* (see plate 91), he adopts a brusque, economic style to find strong pictorial rhythms expressive of his own perceived sense of nature's vigour and energy. In the trees in the middle distance, for example, the thin, closely bunched strokes of the pen convey a sense of branches bursting forth from their trunks.

In fact van Gogh gives everything here a powerful dynamism and energy, conveyed through his forceful, muscular drawing. There are no long, flowing lines, only abrupt and

91 VINCENT VAN GOGH   View of Arles with Irises in the Foreground   1888.
There is an almost aggressive economy in the style of this drawing. The scene has been reduced to a series of curt marks which constitute a sort of visual shorthand. Identical touches are repeated all over the sheet, but such is van Gogh's skill that they can be used to describe very different things. For example, he uses a dot-like mark to describe the grass in the foreground fields. This same dot is used for the trees that can be seen among the distant buildings in the background; but here the dots are closely bunched to create an effect of density, while in the foreground they are separated. Placing them further apart, van Gogh uses the white of the paper to create a sense of movement (as though a breeze were blowing over the field) as well as an exhilarating sense of space.

determined short marks. The forms are all sharp and taut; there are no soft angles, no passage where his forms become limp or fall away. A high pitch of rhythmic activity is maintained all over the paper.

During these first months in Arles van Gogh worked with what was for him a new intensity and drive. Though he assured Theo that he thought for a long time before putting brush to canvas, even he was surprised at the speed with which paintings seemed to pour from his hands:

I must warn you that everyone will think that I work too fast. Don't believe a word of it. Is it not emotion, the sincerity of one's feelings for nature, that

92 VINCENT VAN GOGH Peasants Shearing Sheep 1889.
While he was at Saint-Rémy van Gogh painted copies of works by Delacroix, Millet, Rembrandt and Daumier; Theo sent him lithographs, woodcuts and various other printed reproductions from which to work. Sometimes – as here – the reproductions from which van Gogh made his free copies were in black and white, and hence he had to invent the colours himself. This painting was made from a woodcut engraving after a famous picture of the same title by Millet. Millet had portrayed French peasants at work in many of his paintings, romanticizing their labours somewhat to create images of the God-given dignity of manual work. Van Gogh had profound sympathy for such an attitude, and Millet remained one of his favourite artists throughout his life.

draws us? And if these emotions are sometimes so strong that one works without knowing one does so, when sometimes the brushstrokes come with a sequence and a coherence like words in a speech or in a letter, then one must remember that it has not always been so. . . .[11]

Van Gogh worked in the open air in all weathers; he used to have to weight his easel down against the force of the mistral. On one occasion, in order to paint the stars reflected on the waters of the Rhône, he sat at his canvas all through the night with a crown of candles stuck in the brim of his hat.

For all this frenetic activity, van Gogh missed the company of other artists. He dreamed of a colony of painters living and working in the south in much the same way as was already happening in Brittany. After Gauguin's disastrous stay in Arles later that year it became clear that the dream was never to be realized.

In the autumn of 1888 Theo had inherited a small amount of money from an uncle. Now temporarily in a position to offer Gauguin the same financial support he was already giving his brother, Theo encouraged Gauguin to make the journey from Pont-Aven to Arles.

Gauguin arrived towards the end of October. Van Gogh, highly excited at the prospect of his friend's arrival, had painted a series of flower pieces, of sunflowers, to decorate his new guest's room (*see plate 105*). The sunflower, 'earthbound metaphor of the sun's energy',[12] expressed all his optimism. Gauguin liked and admired these paintings. He painted a portrait of Vincent, choosing to show him at work on one of them; twelve years later, in 1900, when he was living five thousand miles away in Tahiti, he ordered sunflower seeds from Paris and painted the flowers himself. Van Gogh recorded Gauguin's reaction in a letter to Theo written early the following year:

You will see that these canvases will catch the eye . . . It is a kind of painting that rather changes character, and takes on a richness the longer you look at it. Besides, you know, Gauguin likes them extraordinarily. He said to me among other things – 'That . . . it's . . . the flower.'[13]

High praise from the usually loquacious Gauguin who was, perhaps, taken aback by the way van Gogh almost sculpted the flowers with thick cusps of paint and seemed to scent an essential, simplified rhythm in their forms. For van Gogh the flowers seem to have held religious associations. As Robert Rosenblum has pointed out, van Gogh referred to them in a letter describing a projected triptych (which was never completed) as 'illuminating candelabra' – as though they were the natural equivalents to the symbolic lighting of a church. Rosenblum goes on to mention a copy made by van Gogh of the *Raising of Lazarus* by Rembrandt van Rijn (1606–1669) where he has replaced the healing figure of Christ with a fiery yellow disc – a modern version of the ancient biblical conflation of sun and Godhead.[14]

Gauguin had himself finished his *Vision after the Sermon* (*see plate 79*) earlier in 1888 while he was still in Brittany and he would have been particularly sensitive to any such symbolic qualities. And van Gogh would indeed be claimed as a Symbolist in the article that Aurier was to write about him in January 1890. However, long before Gauguin's arrival in Arles, van Gogh himself was already very aware of the emotive associations that colours could suggest. He wrote to Theo in September 1888:

I am always hoping to make a discovery there, to express the love of two lovers by a marriage of two complementaries, their mingling and their opposition, the mysterious vibration of kindred tones. To express the thought of a brow by the radiance of a light tone against a sombre background. To express hope by some star, the eagerness of a soul by a sunset radiance.[15]

But whereas Gauguin created his symbols, as in *Vision after the Sermon*, using patently abstract and artificial means, van Gogh always remained closer to nature. In any case, while Gauguin was happy to find pictorial equivalents for his ideas about rustic piety, van Gogh felt a stronger need to draw his inspiration from direct contact with reality. Later, in November-December 1890, he wrote to Bernard:

When Gauguin was in Arles, I once or twice allowed myself to turn to abstraction . . . and at that time abstraction seemed to me to offer a charming path. But it's an enchanted territory, old man, and one quickly finds oneself up against a brick wall.[16]

Van Gogh's symbolism was always felt as an intrinsic part or an emotional extension of that slice of nature he had before him. He distrusted the more intellectual flavour of Gauguin's theories which denied the central importance of nature as the artist's primary inspiration. Van Gogh expressed these misgivings in terms of an opposition between city and country, artifice and nature (*see plate 92*). It was always clear where his sympathies lay:

For a long time I have thought that in our damned artist's trade we have the greatest need for people who have hands and stomachs like workers, more natural appetites, temperaments more loving and charitable than those decadent and rotten Parisian boulevardiers . . . there are other means of attempting to convey an impression of anguish without making straight for the historic Garden of Gethsemane; to create something gentle and consoling it is not necessary to portray the figures of the Sermon on the Mount.[17]

This last was a reference to Gauguin's *Agony in the Garden* (*see plate 21*). Van Gogh's misgivings about the abstract qualities of Gauguin's paintings and his own preferences for a symbolism derived more directly from nature herself were encapsulated in two pictures he painted of chairs – his own and Gauguin's (*see plates 89 and 93*). The paintings function as thinly disguised portraits. Gauguin's chair, though not luxurious, is curved, its arabesques more elegant than the squatter, sturdier lines of the one van Gogh chooses for himself.

Gauguin's chair stands against a brightly coloured carpet, and on its rush seat lie two novels; van Gogh's stands on raw, terracotta tiles, the artist's pipe and tobacco signifying simpler pleasures than his friend's more literary leanings.

Though the portrait of Gauguin's chair was as much a tribute as a criticism, relations between the two had been getting increasingly antagonistic. Gauguin was exasperated by van Gogh's untidiness and Vincent was suffering from nervous exhaustion as he made every effort to make his friend's journey south seem worthwhile. His lifestyle over the previous few months had also been a seriously debilitating one. He had been eating very irregularly, often surviving for long periods on just coffee and tobacco. He had been working exceptionally hard since his arrival in Arles and had begun to drink heavily at the end of the day in order to forget the exhaustion. The disaster, when it came, was cataclysmic.

On 23 December, a few days after he had finished the portrait of Gauguin's chair, the two friends argued. Gauguin left the house to have a walk in the square. Van Gogh followed him, but then returned to the house, and cut off part of his left ear with a razor. He wrapped it in paper and went to present it to one of the prostitutes (named Rachel) at the brothel that he and Gauguin patronized. When Gauguin returned home the following morning he found van Gogh in bed. He telegraphed Theo and left for Paris. Vincent, meanwhile, was taken to hospital by the police. Theo arrived the next day and stayed with him over Christmas. Theo wrote to his fiancée: 'There were moments when I was with him that he was well, but very soon after he fell back into his worries about philosophy and theology. It was painfully sad to witness, for at times his suffering overwhelmed him and he tried to weep but could not. . . .'[18]

93 VINCENT VAN GOGH Gauguin's Chair 1888.
Despite his passion for the portrait and his express intent to create a new, modern type for that genre, van Gogh never painted Gauguin's likeness. Instead there is only his 'empty place', as this painting was called by the Dutchman. Perhaps Gauguin refused to sit for him; or perhaps van Gogh was a little afraid to ask. Whatever the case, this portrait by proxy is an eloquent enough testament to the power of Gauguin's personality: 'Gauguin and I talked a lot about Delacroix, Rembrandt, etc. Our arguments are terribly electric, we come out of them sometimes with our heads exhausted as an electric battery after it has run down.' (Letter to Theo, December 1888.)

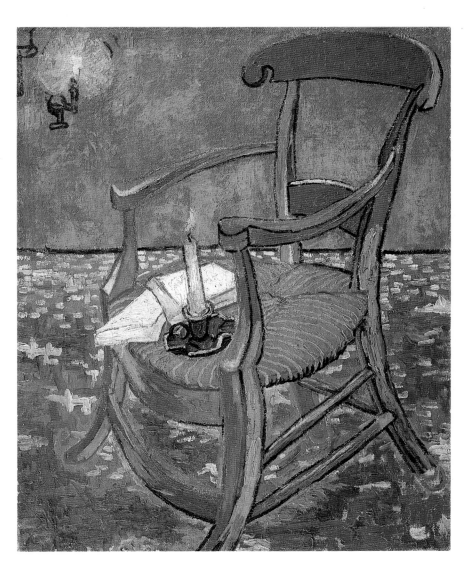

Gauguin's decision to leave Arles immediately may seem callous but it would be unjust to hold him responsible for van Gogh's first attack. A few days earlier Theo had announced his engagement, an event in itself that was likely to upset his brother; for Vincent was supported not only financially by Theo but was heavily dependent on him emotionally as well. Theo's forthcoming marriage, and Vincent's forebodings about the family commitments that that would entail – in which Vincent would have no place – must have played a large part in determining the artist's behaviour that night. This is a theory reinforced by J. Olivier, in his book about the artist; he has pointed out that the victorious matador will offer the vanquished bull's ear to the lady of his choice [19] – a suggestion that van Gogh's self-mutilation was directed by a desire to replace the potential loss of Theo's love with that of a prostitute.

Van Gogh left hospital in January 1889. His neighbours in Arles were not happy with him returning to the yellow house and Vincent, fearing another attack, admitted himself to an asylum outside the nearby town of Saint-Rémy. He was to live there for just under a year.

Van Gogh's responses to the southern landscape, as he expressed them in his paintings and in drawings such as *View of Arles with Irises in the Foreground* (*see plate 91*), indicate that he saw in nature the display of a sort of robust and unsentimental health. Nature seemed to exude a kind of uncomplicated, unpretentious moral strength and vitality. This attitude is reflected in his letters and seems to have been personalized as an ideal code of behaviour. Van Gogh signed all his letters to his brother Theo with the words: 'with a firm handshake, Vincent'. His words and the style of this drawing are very alike in spirit. It is not hard to imagine his sense of despair, therefore, when he himself failed to live up to such standards. His *Self-Portrait* (*see plate 106*) was painted in September 1889, shortly after his second attack. The despair really speaks for itself – in the eyes, the colour and the swirls of cold blue and white in the background that seem to illustrate the mental anguish that lies behind the stern and passive expression.

Of course a portrait such as this demanded as much of a mastery of paint and brush as did the earlier drawing of pen and ink. Six years before van Gogh had described to Theo how he had been struck by certain portraits by the Dutch seventeenth-century painter Frans Hals (1580–1666):

It is so sober that it seems cold; but when you look at it for a short while you are astonished to see how someone working with apparently so much emotion and so completely wrapped up in nature had at the same time the presence of mind to put it down with such a firm hand.[20]

Van Gogh's disease has since been diagnosed as a particularly violent form of epilepsy, one that was accompanied by both visual and auditory hallucinations. The attacks would sometimes last two weeks, sometimes as long as a month. Afterwards, although exhausted he would be totally lucid. Van Gogh was neither the first nor the last to suffer from such attacks; but whatever the scale of the personal tragedies of his life, an image such as this portrait can only have been the result of comparable discipline and detachment. It, like the Hals he described, was certainly painted with a firm hand.

Van Gogh described himself as a cobbler rather than as a musician and the emotional impact of this painting is cer-

tainly anything but refined. Nonetheless, his bravery and honesty about his condition, and his ability to translate these qualities into paint, are utterly compelling.

Three months before his first attack in September 1888, Vincent had written to Theo about the beneficial effects of tackling particularly difficult subjects from life, and had gone on to say, 'That does not prevent me from having a terrrible need of – shall I say the word? – of religion? Then I go out at night to paint the stars. . . .'[21]

In June 1889, soon after he had arrived in Saint-Rémy, he did exactly that and produced a study of the night sky made in pen and ink (*see plate 94*). If in the *Self-Portrait* he had focused internally on his own despair, here he was able to project on to the night scene before him a powerful, transcendent hope. If the making of the *Self-Portrait* was cathartic, drawing the *Starry Night* would have been therapeutic:

I did . . . a new study of a starry sky . . . in colour and draughtsmanship that is more intentional than the exactness of trompe l'oeil, one can express a rustic nature that is purer than the suburbs, the taverns of Paris . . . Gauguin, Bernard, or I, we may all devote our lives to this and we may not win, but we will not be vanquished either; we may not be destined for one or the other, being here to console or to prepare a more consoling art.[22]

Van Gogh, in fact, never went 'further than this in transforming observed fact into ecstatic spirit, where palpable substance becomes flame-like energy'.[23] Though he was wary of the word 'religion', religious seems the only word that fits.

The night sky is convulsed by the fiery revolutions of the stars. Beneath this heavenly activity rises a cypress tree, around which the tiny village huddles; but its incendiary shape is mimicked by the church spire and the smoke curling upwards from the chimneys. The conjunction of heaven and earth is achieved. But the cypress, like the yew, is a symbol of death. Only after life had ended would this union exist.

After nearly a year at Saint-Rémy Vincent decided to return north. He was hoping his attacks were symptoms of a southern disease, as though blown in on the mistral from an infected Africa. Rather than live in Paris he decided, on Pissarro's advice, to live in Auvers, a town about an hour from the city, where he could be looked after by a Dr Gachet. Gachet was an old friend of the Impressionists. Pissarro and Cézanne had stayed with him in the 1870s. Apart from his medical practice, Gachet had built up a large collection of Impressionist paintings and pursued a multitude of diverse interests. An ardent republican, he was also a Darwinist, socialist, homeopath and supporter of free love.

Van Gogh moved to Auvers in May 1890. He saw Dr Gachet two or three times each week. The two men evidently got on well. Van Gogh was attracted by the older man's innate melancholy, and tried to capture it in a portrait (*see plate 1*). For a time everything seemed perfect. Vincent was much calmer. He had not suffered an attack since February. Theo, his wife and son came to stay in early June. In July, however, Vincent seemed to have forebodings of another attack. In the autumn of 1889 he had written to his sister:

The weather outside is beautiful yet for a very long time – I don't know why – I haven't left my room . . . I need courage which I often lack. It is also because since my sickness a feeling of solitude seizes me in the fields in such a dreadful way that I hesitate to go out.[24]

Nearly a year later he wrote to Theo: 'I have painted three more big canvases . . . fields of wheat under troubled skies, and I did not need to go out of my way to express sadness and extreme loneliness.'[25]

In *Crows over Wheatfields* (*see plate 23*) the crowded forms and deep, pregnant colours convey an impression of chaotic compression. It is, in any case, impossible now to look at such a picture and forget that van Gogh shot himself soon after it was painted on 27 July. The bullet missed his heart; but he died two days later.

94 VINCENT VAN GOGH Starry Night 1889.
Dynamic circular forms, similar to those that animate the background of the 1889 self-portrait, trace their paths across this night sky. But if in the self-portrait they speak eloquently of sickness and febrile anguish, in this visionary drawing they are turned into a swirling mass of revolving stellar energies. The short, stubby mark of the pen, however, prevents these curves and discs from developing any languid, decorative grace that might muffle the extraordinary, pulsating energy they discharge. Soaring amongst them into the sky, the branches of the cypress seem to respond in kind to this circular dance in the heavens, joined too by the church spire and columns of smoke.

A Toast to the Future

Van Gogh's dreams of a community of artists living and working together in the south died with him in the summer of 1890. In fact, his plans had effectively been put to an end over a year before, when Gauguin left the yellow house in Arles for Paris on Christmas Eve 1888. But if van Gogh was impossible to live with in Provence, Gauguin had his own ideas about establishing a colony of painters in the tropics, far from any taint of European civilization. Ever since his trip to the French island of Martinique in 1887 he had become more and more obsessed by the idea – and was prepared to realize it on his own if no one else was willing to join him.

Gauguin had initially planned to travel to Tonkin, then thought about going to Madagascar, before eventually settling on the South Sea island of Tahiti – but in each case the enterprise would require funds he did not possess. So, on his return to Paris after his unhappy stay with van Gogh, Gauguin set about raising the necessary sums.

The following year, 1889, saw the opening of another International Exhibition in Paris. Marking the centenary of the Revolution, it was to be an enormous event; in the end, 33 million visitors travelled to Paris to see it. As far as Gauguin was concerned, the prospect of so many people filling the capital provided a supreme opportunity to sell his paintings. The practicalities, however, were more challenging, for the same jury that controlled entry to the official Salon would also preside over the choice of works to be shown at the International Exhibition. There was clearly no conceivable way that Gauguin's paintings, especially his recent Breton works, would be hung in the official pavilion on the Champs de Mars, just to the south of the specially erected Eiffel Tower.

At the International Exhibition of 1855, faced with exclusion from the official pavilion, Gustave Courbet (1819–1877)

101

had exhibited his paintings in his own private enclosure. Forty-five years later Gauguin's funds did not stretch far enough to replicate Courbet's defiant gesture. He did, however, manage to find a café situated next to the Champs de Mars whose owner, an Italian named Volpini, was willing to let Gauguin and his friends hang their pictures there. This impromptu exhibition of paintings, offered by what their posters described as the 'Groupe Impressionniste et Synthétiste', opened in June 1889 at the same time as the International Exhibition itself. Both were to run until the end of October.

Gauguin carried his paintings there, all framed in white, in a cart. The effect of such brightly coloured and simplified works as his *Vision after the Sermon* (*see plate 79*) or Bernard's *Bridge at Asnières* (*see plate 45*) on Volpini's pomegranate-red walls must have been startling. Commercially, however, the exhibition was not a success: not one painting was sold; no reviews appeared in the daily papers. The young Symbolist critic Albert Aurier, who wrote a short piece on the show in the journal *La Cravache* on 6 July, described how difficult it was to see the paintings amidst all the usual crush and bustle of a busy café:

It is not easy to approach these canvases on account of the sideboards, beer pumps, tables, the bosom of M. Volpini's cashier, and an orchestra of young Moscovites whose bows unleash in a large room a music that has no relation to these polychromatic works.[26]

If the Volpini show was a financial failure, it did nonetheless establish Gauguin as a major figure amongst the Parisian avant garde: alerted by Paul Sérusier's (1864–1927) reports, they flocked to see his strange new interpretations of the Breton landscape and people. Enhanced reputations, however, do not pay for the groceries, let alone lengthy painting trips to the tropics – and Gauguin left Paris to return to the quieter, cheaper life of Pont-Aven. Here he continued to develop his work of the previous summer, exploring ways in which patently unrealistic arrangements of line and colour could serve to express the moods and ideas that his subjects aroused in him.

The notoriety which the Volpini exhibition had brought Gauguin encouraged a number of younger painters to follow him to Brittany as disciples. Gauguin and his acolytes now dominated the painters' colony at Pont-Aven. The young novelist André Gide (1869–1951) remembers joining them for supper one night at the Pension Gloanec, intrigued by their extravagant dress and the powerfully coloured canvases with which they had decorated the inn's dining-room. Gauguin, however, despite all this attention and his new position as an avant-garde leader, felt alone – feelings that he tried to encapsulate in a symbolic self-portrait (*see plate 106*) painted in the summer of 1889. In other paintings he developed his idealized depictions of the Breton people, focusing in particular on the easy, natural interchange between their rural surroundings and their ancient religious beliefs (*see plates 95 and 107*).

Gauguin returned to Paris in November 1890, once again determined to raise the necessary funds to enable him to leave France. This time he was successful. Firstly, he used all his new contacts among the Symbolist writers and critics to promote his art. Through his former teacher Pissarro he got Aurier to publish a lengthy article about him in the March 1891 issue of the *Mercure de France*. In this and other dealings with the Symbolist press Gauguin was less than scrupulous. Furnishing Aurier with the material necessary for the article, he ensured that the stylistic advances he had made in the *Vision after the Sermon* and *Yellow Christ* (*see plates 79 and 95*) would seem more his own original invention than was in fact the case. His artistic debts, both to Pissarro and Bernard, were hardly mentioned, and the lack of such an acknowledgement cost him their friendship.

But Gauguin was undeterred. Capitalizing on all the press coverage he had received (and which he himself had helped to engineer), he then organized a sale of a large body of his work at the main Parisian auction house, the Hôtel Drouot – an enterprise that brought him the sum of 9,350 francs. By now Gauguin had determined to travel to Tahiti, a South Sea island that had become a French protectorate in 1843 and a full-blown colony in 1880. He had read the Colonial Department's pamphlet on the island in the autumn of 1890, shortly before his return to Paris, and communicated his excitement in letters written to his friends:

Tahiti is the healthiest country that exists . . . The future of our children is pretty black – even with some money – in this rotten and mean Europe . . . But the Tahitians, happy inhabitants of the unexplored paradises of Oceania, know only the sweet aspects of life. For them to live is to sing and to love . . . I believe that my art . . . is only in an embryonic stage and hope that down there I shall cultivate it for myself alone in its primitive and savage condition.[27]

Gauguin was clearly full of hope. Early in March 1891 he booked his passage to Tahiti. His new-found literary friends and others of the Symbolist circle organized a grand farewell banquet in his honour at the Café Voltaire. Stéphane Mallarmé (1842–1898), Maurice Denis (1870–1943), Sérusier, Jean Moréas (1856–1910) and Aurier were among the forty guests. Pissarro and Bernard were not invited. Gauguin's toast to the assembled company was recorded in the May issue of the *Mercure de France*: 'I love all of you and I am very deeply touched. I can therefore neither say much nor say it well. Some of you have created great works which everybody knows. I drink to these works, as I also drink to the works of the future.'[28] A week later Gauguin took the train from the Gare St Lazare to Marseille and from there began his second-class passage to the South Seas, a journey that would take sixty-three days.

A European Savage

In 1902 Gauguin was to write from the remote Marquesas Islands to his friend Georges de Monfreid in France: 'And you know the public. It would say right away, "What a shame he did not remain in Brittany."'[29] The French public would presumably have found picturesque scenes of quaint rustics in Breton landscapes much more to their taste than the sort of paintings that Gauguin had been sending back to Paris from the South Seas. Instead, the public's lack of comprehension before Gauguin's work was expressed in ridicule and mirth. When an exhibition of some of his Tahitian works was held in Paris in 1893, one reviewer wrote: 'If you want to entertain your children, send them to the Gauguin exhibition; they will

95 PAUL GAUGUIN Yellow Christ 1889.

Returning to Brittany in 1889, Gauguin pursued his interest in ancient Breton art, often visiting the polychromed wooden sculpture of Christ that hung in the chapel at the village of Trémalo, near Pont-Aven. He transferred this to a landscape painting which he set in the fields outside. Three Breton women meditate on this vision of Golgotha, as Christ looks benevolently down upon them. The landscape is painted in the same yellows as Christ's body, a connection that suggests some inherent link between the women's faith and their setting: a natural interchange between religion and rural life that confounds any separation between the real and the imaginary.

be amused by the coloured pictures of animal-like females stretched out on billiard cloths, the whole thing adorned with words from the local children.'[30]

Two years previously, on hearing of Gauguin's plans to leave for Tahiti, Pierre Auguste Renoir (1841–1919) is reported to have asked, 'Why? One can paint just as well at Batignolles.'[31] (The Batignolles was a cheap area of Paris just to the north of the Gare St Lazare where many artists lived.) Nevertheless, Gauguin had his own reasons for wanting to leave. In 1890, a year before his departure, he had written to Emile Bernard:

If only the day would come soon, soon when I could flee into the forests of a lonely South Sea Island, to live there for my art alone, in rapture and peace . . . It seems to me that down there I shall find new strength. At present the West is rotten; everything that is healthy can gain strength if it touches the ground down there.[32]

Gauguin arrived at the Tahitian port of Papeete on 8 June 1891. The paradise he had been expecting was not immediately apparent. Papeete was too Westernized for him. He wrote of the European women there: 'Dowdy from head to foot, vulgar hips, tumbledown corsets, imitation jewellery,

elbows that threaten you, they are enough to spoil any holiday in this country. But they are white – and their stomachs stick out.'[33]

In contrast, to him, the native Maori women showed a natural grace and dignity (*see plate 111*). So within a short while Gauguin bought himself a wooden hut in the countryside, 30 miles further down the coast, with the ocean on one side, and on the other a mountain, half-hidden by a group of mangrove trees. He describes the tremendous effect the country had on him in his book *Noa Noa*, which he wrote as a record of his life in Oceania:

The landscape with its bright burning colours dazzled and blinded me . . . And yet it was so simple to paint things as I saw them, to put on my canvas a red and a blue without any of the calculations of former times . . . Why did I hesitate to let all that gold and all the joy of the sun flow directly onto my canvas? Old routines of Europe, timidity of expression of degenerate races.[34]

It is certainly clear that the exotic landscape of Tahiti inspired the complete liberation of Gauguin's painting from naturalism, a liberation that had been heralded in the *Vision after the Sermon* in 1888 (*see plate 79*). Just before he left France he had written:

I only want to do simple, very simple art, and to be able to do that, I have to immerse myself in virgin nature, see no one but savages, live their life, with no other thought in mind but to render, the way a child would, the concepts formed in my brain and to do this with the aid of nothing but the primitive means of art, the only means that are good and true.[35]

Such a statement is characteristically bold and sensational. In many repects it proved true. Gauguin did live the life of the 'savages', dressing like them and marrying a thirteen-year-old Tahitian girl named Tehura. In his early letters home he noted how his feet, unused to being without shoes, were slowly becoming harder and harder.

He also used primitive art in his work. Such borrowings, however, belied both his eclecticism and the sophisticated way in which he combined various and dissimilar traditions within it. Thus we find in his work references to Javanese friezes, the Parthenon in Athens, Tahitian mythology and Egyptian reliefs on the one hand, and to Courbet on the other. Gauguin admitted such borrowings in a letter of 1892 that rather contradicts what he had written before about his desire for savagery: 'You mustn't mention it, but who cares? One does what one can, and when marble or wood engravings draw a head for you, it is so tempting to steal it.'[36]

He is known to have taken with him a large collection of photographs of paintings, including reproductions of Japanese prints, and works by Edgar Degas (1834–1917), Rembrandt, Michelangelo Buonarroti (1475–1564), Hans Holbein (1497–1543), Pierre Puvis de Chavannes (1824–1898) and Edouard Manet (1832–1883). One of his Tahitian neighbours particularly liked the photograph of Manet's *Olympia*, which pleased Gauguin enormously. In *Noa Noa* he contrasts her instinctive enjoyment of the photograph with the prudish reaction the painting had elicited from the Académie des Beaux-Arts in Paris. The Tahitian woman then asked him if the woman in the picture was his wife, to which he replied that she was.

Gauguin of course did not steal from other sources simply because they 'drew a head for you' or because he was lazy. His borrowings are part of his imaginative creations, adding or often intimating further meanings to his works.

At first, however, Gauguin found it difficult to paint and was appalled by the pictures he did manage to complete. But after the first year he began to feel more satisfied. He wrote to his wife in September 1892: 'I can assure you that what I am doing here has never been done by anybody and that it is unheard of in France.'[37]

Gauguin's first major Tahitian work, *Ia Orana Maria* (*Hail Mary*), was painted in 1891 (*see plate 108*). He described it in a letter:

An angel with yellow wings who points out to two Tahitian women the figures of Mary and Jesus, also Tahitians. Nudes dressed in pareos, a kind of flowered cotton which is wrapped as one likes around the waist. In the background somber mountains and blooming trees. To the left some bananas. I am rather pleased with it.[38]

Gauguin had already been inspired by the sincerity and purity he had seen in the simple faith of the people of Brittany; this picture was a direct successor to works like the *Vision after the Sermon* and *Yellow Christ* (*see plates 79 and 95*) with the exotic replacing the provincial in his depiction of the 'primitive'.

Gauguin also included a visual reference to Eastern religion in the figures of the two worshipping women. Their poses, with the rhythmic movement suggested by the position of their feet, and their hands held in an attitude of prayer, have been taken from bas-reliefs from the Buddhist temple of Borobadur in Java. Gauguin had photographs of these reliefs, which he may well have bought at the 1887 World Fair in Paris. We are thus presented with a mixture of Catholicism, Polynesian figures and setting and Javanese Buddhism, all of which have been pulled together by the strength of the composition, colour harmonies and contrasts, and also by the brushwork – flat areas of vivid colour being complemented by delicately modelled details. It seems to be a resplendent celebration of simple faith, regardless of cultural or dogmatic religious barriers.

The words of the Symbolist writer Octave Mirbeau (1850–1917), though not specifically related to this work, seem to capture some of the essential spirit:

Sometimes his work rises to the height of a mystical act of faith; sometimes it shrinks and grimaces in the frightening gloom of doubt. There is a brilliant mixture of barbaric splendour, of Catholic liturgy, of Hindu reverie, of obscure and subtle symbolism; there are sharp realities and sudden flights of poetry.[39]

But if in this painting Gauguin chose to depict an essentially Christian subject, in two others he painted the following year he concerned himself with the faith and superstitions of the islanders themselves. Even here, however, he could not always help casting a glance back to the European traditions that had nurtured him.

A picture like *Manao tupapau* (*Spirit of the Dead Watching*) might not at first appear to belong to one of the oldest traditions in Western art (*see plate 22*). Its immediate sources would seem to lie in the primitive culture of Tahiti. Furthermore, the picture's subject appears to illustrate some

sort of tribal religious belief, with the woman anxiously aware that she is not alone but not daring to look round. The figure behind her has clearly been modelled on non-Western tribal sculpture. In fact, Gauguin wrote of this picture:

I painted a nude of a young girl . . . I gave her face a somewhat frightened expression . . . These people are very much afraid of the spirits of the dead – I had to explain her fears . . . To achieve this, the general harmony is sombre, sad, frightening, sounding to the eye like a death-knell: violent dark blue, orange-yellow . . . There are some flowers in the background but being imagined, they must not be real; I made them resemble sparks. The Polynesians believe that the phosphorescences of the night are the spirits of the dead. They believe in them and dread them.[40]

Gauguin certainly succeeded in describing the girl's awe and fear at the mysterious spirit and has done so without being condescending or supercilious. Visually speaking, he was a highly articulate artist – in the way that both the impersonal profile of the spirit adds to its disturbing character, for example, and the spiky yellow forms on the linen heighten the sense of threat – even of latent violence.

Gauguin was clearly genuinely fascinated by this sort of primitive supernatural belief. The painting could be said, to a certain extent, to constitute an act of self-identification with the culture that produced such a system of beliefs, especially considering his views on the corruption of European culture. Nevertheless this picture does belong – albeit in a rather perverse manner – to the European tradition of the reclining female nude, a tradition that stretches back at least as far back as Titian (Tiziano Vecelli c. 1490–1576) and Giorgione (c. 1478–1510) in the sixteenth century. More recently, about thirty years before, Manet had also aligned himself with that tradition, though not as antagonistically as Gauguin, when he painted his *Olympia*. Gauguin's painting stands in opposition to such a heritage in almost every way: the figure is lying on her front, her skin is dark not milky white, she represents a non-European mythology, she is fearful, rather than self-assured. Even so, Gauguin decided to paint a female nude lying on a bed, and in so doing he placed himself within an old European tradition, even if he did use it to dissociate himself from the very culture which produced that tradition (*see plate 110*).

Not all Gauguin's paintings, however, are as well documented as this. In *Fatata te Miti* (*Near the Sea*) tendencies towards anti-naturalism have been pushed to a violent extreme (*see plate 109*). It is hard to be sure about where the lines and colours in the lower half of the painting originated. It is as though natural objects have gone through a process of stylization to arrive at pure invention. The yellow, curving lines, serrated tooth-like forms, and amorphous orange shapes within the pinks and purples towards the bottom edge of the canvas are full of stylized movement. These forms and the mottled colours along the tree trunk suggest a return to some primordial, germinal and elemental state. Nature here seems to be in an intense state of ferment. Colour is deep and intense throughout the turbulence and turmoil of the canvas – there are no lighter areas to escape to or to relax in. Yet this turmoil is harmoniously and decoratively described: in the graceful curve of the tree and in the absence generally of sharp edges or angularity. It can also be seen that the naked woman throwing herself into the sea is fixed in the decorative design – her movement is checked and balanced by both the branch above her and the purples and pinks below. The other woman seems to be sitting on, or standing close by the tree trunk, offering herself to the sea which is about to engulf her friend. Their barely modelled bodies contrast gently with the pure flatness of the rest of the canvas. There is a more striking and disconcerting contrast in the figure of the man fishing in the top centre, however, who adds an enigmatic, naturalistic note.

The women seem to be involved in a ritualistic, almost sacrificial relationship with the sea of which we, as spectators, can have no conception. Their strange, mystical act, nevertheless, can take place alongside the mundane act of fishing, with the sea thus providing both spiritual and physical nourishment to the islanders.

The Right to Dare Everything

By the end of 1892 Gauguin was reluctantly preparing to return to Paris. For all his efforts to live as a savage, he still needed money, and his friends in France were proving unbearably lax in sending any. In December that year he had run out of canvas and had only 50 francs left. When eventually a little arrived from Paris he was able to buy his passage home. He arrived in Marseille on 30 August 1893 with only 4 francs in his pocket.

For all the dazzling originality of paintings such as *Manao tupapau* and *Fatata te Miti* (*see plates 22 and 109*), the trip to Tahiti had in many ways proved a failure. Gauguin had not found it possible to survive without money; he had been unable to sell his paintings there and his friends at home had similarly failed to find buyers for those he had sent back prior to his return.

But even if there was ignominy in coming back penniless to France after his dramatic and heroic departure two years earlier, Gauguin was determined to try again. He was to return to the South Seas in 1895, to die there in 1903. During the two years he spent in France, he devoted himself tirelessly to self-promotion. He spent part of this time in Paris, living in a large studio that he painted bright yellow, and enjoying the company both of the Nabis and others of the Symbolists, as well as that of his thirteen-year-old Javanese mistress Annah – and her pet monkey. In November 1893 he held an exhibition of his Tahitian paintings at Durand-Ruel's gallery. Only eleven paintings were sold. The following year he held another exhibition, this time at his studio – in the hope that if he was on hand himself to explain these fiery, exotic works to a potential buyer, his chances of a sale would be greatly improved. He also held another auction of his work at the Hôtel Drouot. All of these ventures, however, ended in financial failure. To make matters worse, Annah deserted him, having stolen as much portable property as she could from the Paris studio; and in February 1894, during a trip to Brittany, Gauguin's ankle was badly smashed by a drunken sailor outside a bar in Concarneau.

Gauguin painted little during this period. He did complete one of his boldest, most abstracted works in 1894: *Mahana no Atua* (*The Day of the Gods*), a sort of composite distillation of his Tahitian experiences (*see plate 96*). Most of this time, however, he spent writing an account of his life in Tahiti,

which would be published in 1897 as the book *Noa Noa*. He also worked on a number of woodcuts as accompanying illustrations (*see plate 97*).

Despite the commercial failure of most of Gauguin's activities during this period, he had reason to hope for a better future. He had found in Ambroise Vollard (1863–1939), who had recently opened a small gallery in the centre of Paris, a young dealer willing to accept any works he sent back from Tahiti in return for a small salary and a regular supply of canvas and paint. He had also inherited 13,000 francs from an uncle. Thus he was able to take the boat once again from Marseille to Papeete, arriving there on 9 September 1895.

Renting a plot of land close to Papeete, Gauguin enlisted native help to build a traditional Tahitian hut out of bamboo and palm. Early the next year he took as his 'vahine' or wife a fourteen-year-old local native girl. Gauguin himself was nearing his forty-eighth birthday and his health was beginning to deteriorate. In severe pain from both eczema and his injured ankle, he admitted himself to hospital for a few weeks in July 1896, but was to continue to suffer from these and other illnesses to the end of his life. Late in 1897 he suffered a series of heart attacks. He was also penniless, dependent for money on payments meant to have been sent from Paris but which never seemed to arrive. In December that year he began work on a monumental canvas, intended as a final testament to his endeavours. He planned to commit suicide once it was finished. On the last day of the year, when once again the mail boat had arrived without any money for him, Gauguin walked off into the mountains and took arsenic. Incredibly, he survived and returned to his hut, exhausted, the next morning. The huge picture, *Where Do We Come From? What Are We? Where Are We Going?*, was finished by June 1898 (*see plate 116*).

Its sheer size (in excess of 4 by 12 feet) and the ontological challenge of its title, which Gauguin wrote out in the top left-hand corner, indicate the ambitious nature of the work: it is as though in this single painting Gauguin wanted to embody one massive and comprehensive statement on his philosophy of life. If that was the case, Gauguin was reticent about allocating precise meanings to it. He described the work's appearance in letters but he never interpreted it – ultimately because he believed that colour and line should function as an autonomous language, totally independent of the explanatory potential of words. As he wrote to a friend in Paris: 'My dream is intangible. There is no allegory.'[41]

Having said that, the painting itself does seem to demand to be read as some sort of allegory. Perhaps that was why Gauguin wrote his disclaimer. But whatever the case, he presents us with a cycle from birth to old age – from the sleeping baby in the bottom right-hand corner to the aged lady on the left. Just to the right of centre a somewhat androgynous Eve plucks a red apple from the branches above her. A child to her left is already eating one. In the background and further to the left, a large wooden image of the Maori moon goddess Hina mimicks Eve's pose with her raised arms. There is no Adam to complement this Eve, no angel to banish her from this shadowy, gloomy Eden. Yet even if Gauguin chose to ignore the biblical consequences of Eve's act, the sombre blues and greens of the surrounding landscape, the disinterested, inactive poses of the other figures, and the slightly ominous presence of Hina in the background all combine to indicate that his conclusions (to the questions posed in the

96 PAUL GAUGUIN Mahana no Atua (The Day of the Gods) 1894.

A central, imposing sculpture of a god dominates this canvas. Two women in white bring offerings to it, while to the right two others in red perform a ritualistic dance. The god is not, in fact, a Tahitian god; Gauguin took its shape from a travel book illustrating sculptures from Easter Island and Borobadur. It is a composite god. The most startling part of the canvas, however, is the lower third – its completely abstracted shapes and colours; its precise meaning, and its relationship with the three figures in the centre and the ritual going on above, has never been fully explained.

title) are not necessarily cause for celebration. In fact, the dominant mood seems rather one of static melancholy.

It would be a mistake, however, to suppose that Gauguin, still depressed from his recent suicide attempt, was simply transferring his personal miseries into monumental, mythic form. Recent scholars have cast doubts on the whole suicide episode, questioning whether it actually happened at all: we only have Gauguin's word for it in his letters and he was not always the most meticulously honest correspondent.[42] Furthermore, *Where Do We Come From? What Are We? Where Are We Going?* was first exhibited as part of a decorative ensemble, hanging together with eight smaller canvases at Vollard's gallery in November 1898. In some of these, and certainly in other allegorical works of the same period, the image of Tahiti is unquestionably paradisiacal. In one of these other paintings, *Rupe Rupe (Luxury)*: 'The fruitpicker . . . [stands] in the center of a landscape abounding in luxuriant beauty. Here fruits have already been picked and will be

picked again, and there is no necessity for the fall of man.'[43]

Gauguin pursued these ideas in one of the last major paintings he completed: *Contes barbares (see plate 117)*. The figure on the far left is a portrait of the artist Meyer de Haan (1852–1895), who had painted with Gauguin in Brittany in 1889 and who was fascinated by the occult. The animal claws with which Gauguin has replaced his former companion's foot have been linked to those of the fox, the Indian symbol of perversity. His expression certainly seems devilish; the lock of hair protruding from his temple suggests a horn.

Meyer de Haan's clothed figure is contrasted with the naked bodies of the two women. Smoke or incense seems to flow from the hair of the foremost of these two figures whose fragrance is identified, further up the canvas, with the overhanging pink flowers. Tipped slightly forward on her arms with toes curled, her wonderfully natural attitude contrasts with the stiffer, more formal pose of the 'Buddha' next to her. Furthermore both de Haan and the Buddha are placed frontally, while the other woman is at right angles to them and to us, her head slightly turned. The fixed gazes of these first two are contrasted with the mental activity of the woman in the foreground, whose eyes gaze in different directions. This juxtaposition suggests a contrast between the inanimate, almost emblematic figures and the living world that Gauguin had already depicted in *Manao tupapau (see plate 22)*.

But a larger contrast between innocence and knowledge, civilized and savage, is clearly intended. Where savage innocence has led to physical beauty and Buddhism, civilized knowledge in de Haan has become satanic. The South Seas became in Gauguin's imagination a new Eden, but one that differed from the European root of that ideal garden in one fundamental way. The South Seas offered Gauguin a return to innocence and beauty free from the burden of original sin. His description of his idea of Eve is significant in this respect: 'The Tahitian Eve is very subtle, very knowing in her naviete . . . She is Eve after the fall, still able to walk naked without shame, possessing all of her animal beauty of the first day.'[44]

Gauguin searched for Utopia both in creative – in his paintings – and in practical terms. In 1899 he all but gave up painting to involve himself in the political life of the island. He wrote articles for its newspaper and started his own satirical broadsheet: *Le Sourire*. In 1901, anxious to find an island

97 PAUL GAUGUIN   Te faruru (To Make Love)   1893-95.
There are no precedents for the power and vitality imbued by Gauguin in the medium of the woodcut, no examples of comparable technical innovation and expressive quality until Munch's prints of the later 1890s. Gauguin's example was later to be of central importance to the German artists of Die Brücke in the first decade of the twentieth century. One of ten woodcuts Gauguin made in Paris to illustrate his autobiographical book Noa Noa *(1897), which described his time in Tahiti – all of them were based on paintings or drawings he had made there –* Te faruru *is a dark, ferocious image of the violent, predatory nature of the sexual act. Like all the prints in this series it is opposed to the more Utopian character of Gauguin's Tahitian oil paintings.*

even more remote and less influenced by the West, he left Tahiti for Hivaoa, one of the Marquesas Islands. Here he refused to pay the taxes levied by the French authorities and urged the natives to resist in the same way. Such behaviour was never likely to win him powerful friends and in 1902 he was charged and imprisoned for libel over an article he had published criticizing the governor. He was already very ill, unable to walk and suffering from ulcerated sores on his legs. He died in prison on 8 May 1903. News of his death only reached Paris on 23 August.

The circumstances of his death – in conflict with the colonial authorities busy Westernizing the islands – were appropriate for one who had travelled so far to escape all traces of Europe. But the tropical paradise of which he had dreamt back in France no longer really existed. Where it did remain, French influence had long been transforming it into its own image. Gauguin died, amongst other things, of syphilis, a disease that had been introduced to the South Sea Islands by European sailors in the seventeenth century. He gleaned his knowledge of Tahitian mythology not from the natives who were already rapidly being converted to Christianity, but from a book written by a Frenchman and lent him by a French colonial in Papeete. In the end, Gauguin's quest for a savage, primitive Utopia had to be an imaginative journey.

In a letter written at the end of his life, Gauguin, uncharacteristically self-deprecating, summed up his achievement in an historical context:

My work has little importance compared to its consequences: the freeing of painting from all restrictions. You have known for a long time what I wanted to establish: the right to dare everything.[45]

With Gauguin ends the Western artist's obsession with visual perception. 'Everything takes place within my imagination. I close my eyes to see', he wrote.[46] Cézanne, on the other hand, critical of the oriental, decorative style of Gauguin's work, had this to say: 'It's all nonsense. He's not a painter. All he's ever done is make Chinese pictures.'[47]

A Harmony Parallel to Nature

Kirk Douglas played the part of van Gogh in a Hollywood film made about the Dutch painter's life, and Somerset Maugham (1874–1965) wrote a fictional account of Gauguin's career in his novel *The Moon and Sixpence* (first published 1919). Paul Cézanne's biography, less colourful than those of these other two recluses of the 1880s and 1890s, has received no comparable dramatization outside the art historian's academy. But if his life was emptier of epic or tragic incident and his own sacrifices and sufferings for his art much more mundane than van Gogh's or Gauguin's, it was nevertheless no less heroic. For of the four figures whose achievements dominate our histories of late nineteenth-century French painting – van Gogh, Gauguin, Seurat and Cézanne – it is Cézanne who seems to have had the most widespread and decisive influence on subsequent generations. Cubism, the collaborative creation of Pablo Picasso (1881–1973) and Georges Braque (1882–1963) in the first decade of the twentieth century, and still perhaps the major revolutionary artistic innovation since 1900, would certainly have been inconceivable without Cézanne. As early as the summer of 1905 the painter Paul Sérusier wrote of the artist in an interview in the *Mercure de France*:

Cézanne has managed to strip pictorial art of all the mould accrued in the course of time . . . If – as I dare hope it will – a tradition is born of our times it will be born of Cézanne.

The testaments of many of the greatest figures from the next generation of European artists show that Sérusier's hopes were fulfilled, at least in part. Braque wrote of Cézanne: 'Everything about the man was sympathetic to me, the man, his character, everything.'[48] Paul Klee (1879–1940) described him as 'the teacher par excellence'.[49] Picasso spoke of him as 'a mother who protects her children'.[50] Henri Matisse (1869–1954) called him 'the father of us all'.[51]

Very little ran smoothly for Cézanne during his lifetime. His ardent desire to show his paintings at the official Salon in Paris was never realized;[52] every year his entries were rejected, yet for the majority of his career he refused to exhibit anywhere

98 PAUL CÉZANNE Madame Cézanne 1879–82.

A work admired by Gauguin, who based one of his early portraits on it, this painting was subsequently bought by the American collectors Leo and Gertrude Stein, who displayed it prominently in their Paris flat. There it continued to influence a later generation of painters, most notably Picasso in his 1906 portrait of Gertrude Stein (see plate 182). The Steins must take much of the credit for fostering the enormous interest shown in Cézanne in the first years of the twentieth century. They were among the earliest collectors of his work and they made their collection available to anyone who cared to see it.

else for fear of jeopardizing his chances with the Salon jury. When, towards the end of his life, the enthusiastic attentions of younger painters brought him a modest notoriety and success, he was unable always to accept their tributes as sincere; years of vicious treatment in the press, followed by neglect and obscurity, had made him both highly critical of his own work and profoundly suspicious of praise. Cézanne died working, as he had prayed that he might. On 15 October 1906, at the age of sixty-seven, he was caught in a storm while painting in the open air. He collapsed and was exposed to the rain for several hours before being found and carried home in a labourer's cart. A week later, on 22 October, he died at his home in Aix-en-Provence. As the historian John Rewald has noted, it was one of the few wishes life granted him.[53]

Paul Cézanne was born in 1839 in Aix, the capital of Provence in southern France. His father, Louis-Auguste Cézanne, originally a hat-maker, had made his fortune after buying the town's only bank in 1848. Paul had first been intended to be a lawyer, and then expected to find a career in his father's prospering bank. But once he had finished his formal education and after studying drawing at Aix's municipal art school, he decided to become an artist and moved to Paris in the early 1860s to continue his training. Here he met Pissarro and through him other painters: Renoir, Manet, Monet and Degas – later to become known as the Impressionists. Cézanne was very much one of their number, exhibiting at the first three Impressionist exhibitions.

At this stage Cézanne cut a bohemian figure among his new friends. Tall and thin, with a fine, aquiline nose, balding but with a full, dark beard, his appearance was striking. So was his broad, Provençal accent and rude, blustering manner. His roughnesses, however, were more a defence for a brittle and sensitive pride than the expression of a genuinely aggressive personality. He was shy and timid, in fact, rarely joining in the theorizing and loud discussions enjoyed by the other Impressionists at the Café Guerbois.

His paintings at this time were also very different from those of his colleagues. Thickly painted, the pigment often so heavily applied with the palette knife that it seemed Cézanne might have been confusing sculpture with oil painting, they are turbulent and passionate works. Though he did paint some landscapes, still-lifes and portraits, his principal efforts were expended in a number of highly charged, poetic and imaginary subjects, often of a violently erotic nature, as though painting offered some sort of release for his mind's darker imaginings.

Cézanne made little effort to exhibit or sell these powerfully original and disturbing works, apart from his attempts to be shown at the official Salon. He was still spending part of each year at his parental home in Aix, and still living off a modest, monthly allowance from his father. In 1869 he fell in love with a model, Hortense Fiquet (*see plate 98*), who moved in to live with him in his flat in Paris – his father was not party to this secret especially after the birth of the couple's son, Paul, in January 1872.

At the outbreak of the Franco-Prussian war in 1870 Paul and Hortense left Paris to hide in L'Estaque, a small seaside village about 30 miles from Aix. Here Cézanne spent most of his time painting landscapes and realized that if his densely painted, frenetic style of work was well suited for feverish, imaginative subjects it was rather a crude instrument for rendering the subtler effects of nature. He also realized that if he were to change his way of painting, he would need technical advice. On his return to Paris he went to Pissarro for help.

At this point, in the early 1870s, Cézanne's painting underwent a crucial transformation. He abandoned the palette knife and dark, earthy tones of his earlier works and took up the brighter, purer colours and smaller, dabbed brushstrokes advocated by his new teacher. Above all, he ceased painting in an impetuous, almost reckless frenzy and began to work slowly and methodically in front of nature; he adopted Pissarro's practice of always working outside in the open air in order to be able as faithfully as possible to attend to intricate effects of light and shade. All his former turbulent energies were now directed in a different direction, subsumed and contained in the careful, meticulous study of nature.

Cézanne's new paintings met with as little success as their predecessors, and in the late 1870s and throughout the 1880s, he spent less and less time in Paris, preferring instead to live with his mother and sister in Aix, or renting premises in L'Estaque. Hortense and their son Paul generally lived in Paris, although Cézanne and Hortense were eventually married in 1886, after the liaison had been discovered by Cézanne's father. Louis-Auguste Cézanne died the same year leaving his son a sizeable fortune; Cézanne would certainly never have to worry about selling his paintings in order to make a living. Cézanne's financial security, his own intrinsic independence of thought and his increasing isolation from the Parisian avant garde made it inevitable that, once he had learned Impressionist techniques from Pissarro, he should then develop concerns rather different from those of his Impressionist peers, and through these a style of painting very much his own.

His pictures were certainly still shocking to the ordinary amateur. Indeed, Gauguin used to tell a story of how, one afternoon in the late 1870s or early 1880s, Cézanne was painting a landscape near the country house of his old friend Emile Zola (1840–1902) – the two had met at school in the 1850s. A man happened to walk by, while Cézanne was working at his easel:

The pretentious and shocked passer-by looks at what he thinks is a lamentable daub by an amateur and, a smiling teacher, says to Cézanne: 'You are painting.'
'Certainly, but so little . . .'
'Oh! I can see that. Here, I am a former pupil of Corot, and if you will allow me, with a few deft touches I will straighten all this out for you.'
And the vandal impudently puts some stupid strokes on the glittering canvas. Dirty greys cover the Oriental silks. [. . .] Cézanne takes up his palette and scratches out with his knife all the mess made by the gentleman . . . After a silence he lets out a terrific fart and turning to the gentleman he says: 'What a relief!'[54]

If Cézanne was justly intolerant of that unfortunate gentleman's lack of comprehension, he was also growing critical of his Impressionist colleagues. He disapproved of Pissarro's ventures in the divisionist style, was unhappy with Monet's series paintings, and described Renoir's landscapes (see plate 99) as 'cottony'.[55]

And while the other Impressionists had developed their small, fluent brushtrokes and bright, spectral palette to describe the fleeting effects of the light's flickering action, Cézanne adapted these same means for different ends. In 1897 he was to write to a young admirer, the Provençal poet Joachim Gasquet (1873–1921): 'What is one to think of those fools who tell one that the artist is subordinate to nature? Art is a harmony parallel to nature.'[56]

It is a characteristically gruff and pithy statement, but one which reveals that Cézanne was concerned with the precise status of the work of art in relation to nature. Cézanne was very aware that his was not an illusionistic art. Maurice Denis (1870–1943), who visited him in the early years of the twentieth century, quoted him as saying: 'I wanted to copy nature but found that I couldn't. But I was satisfied when I discovered that sunlight, for example, cannot be reproduced, but must be represented by something else – by colour.'[57]

Cézanne recognized that a traditional, literal description of a natural motif would not be able to capture or express the intrinsic reality or vitality of nature, and came to the conclusion that nature's reality would have to be translated into terms of what was real in painting. This was why he spoke of equivalents and parallels – because if nature and a painting of nature are intrinsically different, then direct transcription is bound to fail, making a translation necessary and essential. The painter would therefore have to mediate between the demands of nature on the one hand, and those of the picture – the painted surface – on the other.

The principal aspect of this question, which Cézanne recognized, was the two-dimensionality of the painted canvas.

99 PIERRE AUGUSTE RENOIR Rocky Crags at L'Estaque 1882.

Cézanne's description of Renoir's landscapes as 'cottony' sounds disparaging. Yet more eulogistic phrases such as 'diaphanous charm' and 'honeyed translucence' probably refer to the same thing. In this sense, Cézanne was right, though perhaps a little ungracious in his choice of adjective. A landscape such as this, which Renoir painted during his stay with Cézanne in the early 1880s, is almost the complete antithesis of the qualities Cézanne sought in his work at the time. The softness of Renoir's touch, as it mollifies the craggy rocks, could not be further removed from the tough, granite-like compositions that Cézanne distilled from the harsh Provençal landscape.

This was the basic demand of pictorial reality that he sought to placate, though at the same time this concession to artifice went hand in hand with a descriptive concern. Thus, in the *Blue Vase*, a still-life painted in the mid-1880s, Cézanne described his chosen objects and their surroundings in such a way that he stressed the illusion of three-dimensional space, but at the same time compromised this illusion, subtly moulding it to the flat surface of the canvas (*see plate 112*). Hence, the diagonal line which describes the point where the back wall meets the floor carries with it a sense of recession. Yet this suggestion of depth is not without ambiguity, for as this line approaches the left-hand side of the picture it is cut off, disappearing behind a vertical strip of mottled green and olive. This strip would seem to describe another wall, yet its position in space is nowhere unequivocally stated. Instead of rising clearly from the floor, this 'wall' grows out of the table top in the area of dark green near the bottom of the bottle. Thus Cézanne fixes areas which in the fictive space of the picture are disparate, onto the same plane – that of the canvas, the real space of the picture.

In the *Blue Vase* Cézanne effectively contained the flowers' natural vigour, harnessing their lyrical movement within a stable, balanced composition. Throughout the 1880s he enjoyed lending to each motif he tackled what his first critics were to describe as classical repose. A similar sense of order, immobility and propriety is also discernible in his landscapes of this period.

In *Pine, Viaduct and Mont Sainte-Victoire* (*see plate 118*) Cézanne's desire to express comparable qualities of grandeur and serenity, irrespective of the more ephemeral effects of light and atmosphere that occupied painters such as Monet and Pissarro, separates his endeavours and achievements from those of Impressionism. A painting such as this seems premeditated and deliberate, born out of lengthy contemplation – almost the exact opposite of Monet's speedy and fluent transcriptions of the subtlest nuances of light and shade. Certainly it seems inconceivable that a cloud, with all the transience and change that its presence would imply, should ever cross Cézanne's empty blue skies.

The attitude of stillness and dignity that Cézanne desired to discover in landscape and still-life he also sought in portraiture. The dealer Ambroise Vollard, whom he painted in 1899, recalled that he had over a hundred sittings for his portrait (*see plate 123*). Cézanne was an incredibly slow worker. In an effort to encourage Vollard to keep still during their interminable sessions, Cézanne repeatedly told him to be like an apple, in other words, not to move. When Vollard found it impossible to remain still or to keep himself from falling asleep, the artist perched his sitter's chair on a precariously balanced pile of boxes and tables. The least movement would mean disaster. Vollard still managed to nod off and fell with a terrible crash to the floor, thus ending that particular day's sitting. And while still-lifes were thus obviously easier to paint than people, Cézanne still found it necessary to use wax fruit and paper flowers. The real things simply rotted or faded long before he had finished his picture.

Cézanne left Vollard's portrait unfinished. When the dealer asked him if he was satisfied with what he had done, he replied that he was not displeased with the shirt front. Cézanne had been getting increasingly frustrated by what he judged to be his inability to bring his pictures to a satisfactory

level of finish. This frustration led to a feeling of profound disdain for his work, a tendency some of his friends found distinctly worrying. Renoir's son Jean, in the biography he wrote of his father's life, records:

> Once when he was out working in the countryside at Aix with Cézanne, his friend was seized with an urgent need to relieve himself. He went behind a rock with a watercolour he had just finished in his hand. Renoir rushed over and snatched it from him, refusing to give it back unless he promised not to destroy it.[58]

Cézanne acquiesced on this occasion but there is no telling how many other watercolours or oil paintings were lost when there was no one there to prevent their destruction.

By the 1890s Cézanne had become so isolated that to the generation of painters who succeeded the Impressionists at the forefront of the avant garde – figures such as Bernard and the Nabis – he had become something of a legend (*see plate 124*). Rarely seen in Paris, and often anxious to avoid meeting his old friends when he did visit, Cézanne pursued his lonely studies, so engrossed in his work that he did not even attend the funeral of his beloved mother.

During the final decade of his life, the qualities of stability and order characteristic of his work of the 1880s ceded to a more dynamic interpretation of nature (*see plates 113 and*

100 EUGÈNE DELACROIX *Roses and Hortensias* 1848–50. *Vollard gave Cézanne this Delacroix watercolour in 1902. Formerly owned by Victor Chocquet, it had been bought by Vollard when Chocquet's collection was sold in 1899. Cézanne, who had wept over this work in Chocquet's drawing-room, later copied it in oil. Cézanne's wife was called Hortense, which may have influenced Vollard when he came to choose this gift, although the two were estranged by this date. Cézanne is known to have said of her: 'My wife likes only Switzerland and lemonade.' (John Rewald, Paul Cézanne, London, n.d. [c. 1946], 99-100.) For curt dismissiveness, his remark takes some beating.*

121). It is as if, towards the end of his life, he was no longer afraid of disorder; or, that sensing nature's power as a force so vast and, if not inimical then at least indifferent to man, he no longer felt the need to control it.

Many years after Cézanne's death, Louis MacNeice (1907–1963) was to write a poem entitled 'August', in which he criticized our capacity to force our experience into too neatly ordered parcels:

For the mind, by nature stagey, welds its frame
Tomb-like around each little world of a day;
We jump from picture to picture and cannot follow
The living curve that is breathlessly the same.

While the lawn-mower sings, moving up and down
Spirting its little fountain of vivid green,
I, like Poussin, make a still-bound fête of us
Suspending every noise, of insect or machine.

In these stanzas from the poem, MacNeice laments this tendency which, dividing our lives into static, artificial tableaux, proves in the end to cut us off from a more dynamic, organic understanding of life, the 'living curve that is breathlessly the same'. He also relates this habit not only to picture-making in general but specifically to a classical tradition of painting, as the reference to Nicolas Poussin (*c*. 1593–1665) indicates. Poussin, the seventeenth-century French master of the classical landscape, was an artist Cézanne particularly admired; he used to say that he wanted to 're-do Poussin according to nature'.[59] In other words, he wanted to discover in paintings made directly from nature those qualities of order and calm that Poussin had invented in his imaginary landscapes.

But in the final decade Cézanne, recognizing the limitations of this classical vision, relinquished it for one of cataclysm and apocalypse. In the late pictures of the Mont Sainte-Victoire, *Cézanne* seems to have become sensitive to geological, even seismological forces (*see plate 120*); in others he discovers a turbulent, uncontrollable energy in the twisting branches of a pine tree (*see plate 119*), and in others still, nature seems to express unbearably claustrophobic forces of compression (*see plate 15*). It is as though the quest for control over the painted landscape, and the concentration of gaze demanded by this, revealed to his sensibility more and more of nature's complexities (and eventually, nature's driving energy), and that these in turn had to be controlled. In the late works this process finally seems to break down; Cézanne, that is, allowed it to break down. In the end, Cézanne became visionary.

In January 1905 Cézanne wrote to thank the critic Roger Marx for an article he had written in praise of the ageing artist's paintings in the prestigious *Gazette des Beaux-Arts*. Having expressed his gratitude, Cézanne went on to write:

My age and health will never allow me to realize the artistic dream that I have pursued throughout my entire life . . . In my opinion one does not replace the past, one merely adds a further link to it.[60]

One of the ironies common in the history of painting becomes apparent here, for Cézanne's paintings were to help spawn, in Cubism, one of the most revolutionary movements of the period.

101   PAUL CÉZANNE   Self-Portrait with Beret   1898–1900.
Van Gogh's self-portraits engage the viewer with a degree of intensity and candour that borders on the frightening. Cézanne's image of himself, on the other hand, could hardly be more aloof and withdrawn. He even passes over the opportunity offered by his elegant moustache to whip up a swirl or animated arabesque; this moustache seems, rather, to be made of the same substance as the flesh. If Vollard failed in Cézanne's eyes to behave sufficiently like an apple, the artist seems to have posed for his own self-portrait in a passive, still, fully fruit-like manner. Yet this detachment has its own emotional power – one of absence, suppression and implosion, one that combines the terrible human cost paid by his vocation with the desire to dignify his efforts by portraying himself as an Old Master.

Yet Cézanne himself, who regularly attended mass, who was profoundly conservative in his politics, and who desired for his art only to be able to show it at the Salon, defined his aim as wanting to link his painting to that of the past.

Eugène Delacroix (1798–1863), along with Poussin, Peter Paul Rubens (1577–1640), Paolo Veronese (1528–1588) and Jacopo Tintoretto (1518–1594), was one of the painters from the past to whom Cézanne felt strongly drawn. His son-in-law, Georges Rivière, described one day when Victor Chocquet, a friend of Cézanne and collector of Delacroix's works, laid out a number of his watercolours on the living-room rug in his flat in Paris, in order to show them to Cézanne (*see plate 100*). Rivière recalls: 'These two supersensitive beings, on their knees, bent over the sheets of yellowed paper which for them were so many relics, began to weep.'[61]

Cézanne had planned a painting which would show Delacroix ascending to the heavens, with himself, Pissarro, Monet and Choquet looking on as witnesses. While he never completed this projected apotheosis, in others of his works he consciously emulated past traditions. His pictures of card players (*see plate 122*) deliberately rework a favourite subject of the seventeenth-century brothers Le Nain, whose pictures he studied at the museum in Aix. In some of his self-portraits

102   Photograph of Cézanne in front of *Large Bathers*, 1904.

(*see plate 101*) Cézanne even seems to picture himself in the guise of an Old Master. However, it is in his pictures of bathers that he concentrated most emphatically on relating his own painting to the past – in this case, to the ideal nudes situated in a idyllic landscape setting by Giorgione, Titian and other artists of the sixteenth and seventeenth centuries.

Cézanne painted these pictures in the studio, rarely even working from a live model. It was a subject he depicted throughout his career. Most of them are modest in size, such as the *Trois Baigneuses* Matisse was to buy and cherish (*see plate 115*). Others, which he painted in watercolour, are tiny – miniaturist, jewel-like versions of the same theme (*see plate 114*). It was only towards the end of his life that Cézanne attempted to paint the subject on a monumental scale, as though the hundreds of other versions he had produced during the previous thirty or so years had been so many preparations for a final, massive and conclusive treatment. Three large bather pictures were painted in the last decade. Emile Bernard photographed Cézanne in front of one of them in 1904 (*see plate 102*). Another version hangs in the National Gallery in London. The final, majestic exposition, so large that a hole had to be knocked through the wall of Cézanne's studio to remove it, was left unfinished (*see plate 125*). It now hangs in Philadelphia, but would be equally at home in the Louvre – perhaps more so – alongside the works that Cézanne had studied so often and wished, above all, to emulate himself – the paintings of Titian, Giorgione and Veronese.

NOTES

[1] John Rewald, *Post-Impressionism: from Van Gogh to Gauguin*, revised edition, London, 1978, 342.

[2] Ibid, 35.

[3] Ibid, 40.

[4] Kenneth Clark, *Civilization*, London, 1969, 343.

[5] Robert Rosenblum, *Modern Painting and the Northern Romantic Tradition*, London, 1975, 74.

[6] Letter to Theo, 8 February 1883, in Mark Roskill (ed.), *The Letters of Vincent Van Gogh*, Glasgow, 1963, 185.

[7] Letter to Theo, July 1885, ibid, 237, 236.

[8] G. Coquiot, *Vincent Van Gogh*, Paris 1923, 140, in John Rewald, op. cit., 55.

[9] Letter to Theo, September 1888, in Mark Roskill, op. cit., 286.

[10] John Rewald, op. cit., 194.

[11] Ibid.

[12] Robert Rosenblum, op. cit., 87.

[13] Letter to Theo, 23 January 1889, in Mark Roskill, op. cit., 309.

[14] Robert Rosenblum, op. cit., 87.

[15] Mark Roskill, op. cit., 287.

[16] In John Rewald, op. cit., 233.

[17] Letters to Emile Bernard, October–November 1888 and December 1889, ibid, 221, 338.

[18] Ibid, 246.

[19] Ibid, 248 n45.

[20] Letter to Theo, 8 February 1883, in Mark Roskill, op. cit., 183.

[21] In Robert Rosenblum, op. cit., 93.

[22] In John Rewald, op. cit., 312.

[23] Robert Rosenblum, op. cit., 96.

[24] In John Rewald, op. cit., 316.

[25] In Mark Roskill, op. cit., 338.

[26] In John Rewald, op. cit., 261.

[27] Letters to Emile Schuffenecker and Odilon Redon, September 1890, ibid, 417.

[28] Ibid, 452.

[29] In Robert Goldwater, *Symbolism*, New York, 1979, 116.

[30] Paul Gauguin, *The Writings of a Savage*, New York, 1974, 47.

[31] Paul Gauguin, *The Intimate Journals of Paul Gauguin*, London, 1985, 24.

[32] In K. Mittelstadt, *Gauguin, Self Portraits*, Oxford, 1968, 31.

[33] Paul Gauguin, *The Intimate Journals of Paul Gauguin*, op. cit., 35.

[34] In John Rewald, op. cit., 458.

[35] Paul Gauguin, *The Writings of a Savage*, op. cit., 19.

[36] John House, in *Post-Impressionism: Cross Currents in European Painting*, Royal Academy of Arts, London, 1979–80 77.

[37] Paul Gauguin, *The Writings of a Savage*, op. cit., 24.

[38] In John Rewald, op. cit., 466.

[39] Ibid, 440.

[40] Ibid, 488–89.

[41] Paul Gauguin, *The Writings of a Savage*, op. cit., 53.

[42] Richard Bretell, in *The Art of Paul Gauguin*, National Gallery of Art, Washington D.C., 1988, 417.

[43] Ibid, 394.

[44] Robert Goldwater, op. cit., 143.

[45] In Alan Bowness, *Gauguin*, Oxford, 1978, introduction.

[46] Robert Goldwater, *Paul Gauguin*, op. cit., 86.

[47] In P. M. Doran (ed.), *Conversations avec Cézanne*, Paris, 1978, 63.

[48] In William Rubin, 'Cézannisme and the Beginnings of Cubism', in *Cézanne: The Late Work*, Museum of Modern Art, New York, 1977, 167.

[49] In Theodore Reff, 'Painting and Theory in the Final Decade', ibid, 13.

[50] Ibid.

[51] Ibid.

[52] In fact he did succeed in showing at the Salon on two occasions, in 1882 and 1889. On both occasions, however, he got in somewhat by the back-door and not even under his own name.

[53] John Rewald, *Paul Cézanne*, London, n d. [c.1946?], 185.

[54] Ibid, 104.

[55] Ibid, 122.

[56] John Rewald (ed.), *Paul Cézanne: Letters*, trans. Seymour Hacker, New York, 1984, 261.

[57] In P. M. Doran (ed.), op. cit., 173.

[58] Jean Renoir, *Renoir, My Father*, translated by R. and D. Weaver, London, 1964, 335.

[59] Charles Camoin, *Mercure de France* 56 (1 August 1905), 23.

[60] John Rewald (ed.), *Paul Cézanne: Letters*, op. cit., 309.

[61] From Rivière's biography of Renoir, quoted in John Rewald, *Studies in Impressionism*, London, 1986, 147.

103   VINCENT VAN GOGH   The Potato Eaters   1885.

*In a long letter written to Theo in November 1882, three years before this,
his first major picture, was painted, Vincent draws his brother's attention
to a passage in Harriet Beecher Stowe's* Uncle Tom's Cabin *(1851)
where the slave draws consolation for his sufferings from his faith in God.
He goes on to say: 'This is far from theology, simply a fact that the poorest
little wood-cutter or peasant on the heath or miner can have moments of
emotion and inspiration which give him a feeling of an eternal home to
which he is near.' Christian charity evidently also exists in this dark, dirty
cottage. The wife looks sympathetically at the drawn features of her
husband under the light of the central lamp, while to her right another
figure offers a steaming potato to the woman pouring the tea.*

104 VINCENT VAN GOGH Self-Portrait 1887.

It is rare for a painter to use the self-portrait as an exercise in self-mutilation and yet that is what van Gogh seems to be doing here. The raw rhythm of his brushstrokes scores the flesh, stripping the skin off his own face. There is something horrifying and fascinating about the intensity of this expression. Van Gogh has not tried to comment on the nobility of his vocation by including the tools of his trade – palette, brushes, easel – as some artists had before him. If the aura of reds around his head was meant to suggest a halo, as he said it did, van Gogh has turned himself into a martyr.

105 VINCENT VAN GOGH Sunflowers 1888.

The frame cannot quite contain the vigorous, organic growth of these flowers. Some, those most thickly encrusted with paint, have lost their petals and are about to die as though consumed by the fiery energies they have released. Others are mature; others still have just broken out of their buds. Here then is the cycle of life and death, symbolized by nature, that Monet spurned in his series paintings. If the flowers also held religious associations for van Gogh, the picture presents an optimistic image of the divine, directing will that lies behind that cycle.

106   Vincent van Gogh   Self-Portrait   1889.
Here van Gogh abandons the halo effect that he had used in the self-
portrait of 1887. Instead he fills the background with swirling eddies of
the same glacial blue as his jacket and waistcoat. Figure and background
are connected in this way, most substantially by colour, but also by the
way the creases and folds on van Gogh's clothes, especially over the right
shoulder, are described with the same linear rhythm that pulses more freely
behind. Moreover, his hair and beard stand out particularly against these
pale blues and greens because they are painted orange and red – the
relevant complementaries. Just above the centre, the fearful knot in the
brow stiffly arched over the eyes completes this terrifying self-portrait.

107   PAUL GAUGUIN   Self-Portrait with Yellow Christ
1889–90.

In Agony in the Garden (see plate 21), Gauguin portrayed himself as
a new Messiah of painting. The same conflation is suggested here as he
paints himself in front of the Yellow Christ (see plate 95 – but seen
in reverse because here he is looking at it in a mirror). To the right he
included one of his ceramics: a tobacco jar he had moulded into a
primitive, grotesque self-portrait earlier in 1889. In this way, Gauguin
uses the background, more than his own inscrutable expression, to explain
his intentions. On the one hand he views himself as Christ, whose head
tilts towards his own, and whose outstretched arm frames his figure. On
the other, the jar symbolizes the uglier, primitive side of the painter's
personality, with all its material needs.

108   PAUL GAUGUIN   Ia Orana Maria (Hail Mary)
c. 1891–92.

The Virgin and Child have here been given a rich, luxuriant setting. A
small wooden altar in the foreground is piled high with an offering of wild
red bananas called 'fei' (considered a great delicacy), breadfruit and yellow
bananas. Gauguin fills the canvas with colour. An angel with bright yellow
wings, dressed in a lavender gown, hides behind a small tree. In the
background are pink sands, blossoming trees and thatched huts. The
wealth of detail is successfully contained within a strong, simple design of
vertical tree trunks and a horizontal path. Simple colour patterns also help
the coherence of the design: closely related blues appear in the foreground
path, tree trunks and distant mountains; yellows in the bananas, the
angel's wings and the clouds. Against these the red of Mary's pareos is
strongly emphasized.

IA ORANA MARIA

P. Gauguin 91

109 PAUL GAUGUIN Fatata te Miti (Near the Sea) 1892.
*Gauguin himself had to buy back this painting at an auction of
his Tahitian works held in Paris in February 1895 at the Hôtel
Drouot. Perhaps its high degree of abstraction put off any potential buyers.
Gauguin at least was clear in his own mind about what he
was attempting: 'I borrow some subject or other from life or from nature,
and using it as a pretext, I arrange lines and colours so as to obtain
symphonies, harmonies that do not represent a thing that is real, in the
vulgar sense of the word, and do not directly express any idea, but are
supposed to make you think, the way music is supposed to make you
think, unaided by ideas or images, simply through the mysterious affinities
that exist between our brains and such arrangements of colours and lines.'
(The Intimate Journals of Paul Gauguin, London 1985, 39.) Both
the abstract means and the reference to music anticipate Kandinsky's
paintings and theories.*

111 PAUL GAUGUIN Aha oe feii? (What! Are You Jealous?)
1892.
*Gauguin considered this to be one of the best paintings he produced during
his first trip to Tahiti. Despite the somewhat aggressive question of the
title, there is little suggestion in the painting that one or other of the nude
women is jealous of her companion. Rather it seems as though it is the
spectator – the male spectator in particular – whom is addressed,
challenged by the erotic, tropical paradise he is presented with – one that
stands in deliberate opposition to European notions of decorum and
sexuality. The resolutely unnaturalistic style, in particular the flat expanse
of pink sand and the patterns created by the ripples and reflections on
the surface of the water, serves to intensify the challenge.*

110 PAUL GAUGUIN Nevermore 1897.

Produced in 1897, this painting might be called a companion piece to Manao tupapau (see plate 22). Gauguin described the work in a letter: 'I wanted to make a simple nude suggest a certain barbaric splendour of times gone by. The whole painting is bathed in colours that are deliberately sombre and sad. For a title, "Nevermore"; not "The Raven" of Edgar Poe, but a bird of the devil who watches.' (Robert Goldwater, Paul Gauguin, New York, 1957, 114.) As in its sister-picture, the foreground figure can sense a presence behind her without actually looking at it. Her fearful and suspicious eyes encourage us to empathize with her unease. We, like the nude, wonder what the two figures are talking about. Yet our entry to their conversation is denied by the back and profile views. Similarly, we cannot see the head of the bird, which only increases our feeling of anxiety.

112 PAUL CÉZANNE Blue Vase 1883–87.

*Cézanne has avoided the obvious and simple juxtaposition of the
horizontal and vertical inherent in the motif and has constructed a
pictorial balance in which all the elements in the picture play a part. Thus
the diagonal of the receding wall, for example, helps to neutralize the slight
diagonal tilt of the vase. But this diagonal together with that of the table-
top and the two strips to either side, also effectively frames the motif and in
framing it, stills it. Not completely, however, for the flowers are enclosed on
three, not four sides. At the top the flowers hit the top edge of the canvas
itself, rather than a fictional wall or table. Their upward energy hence
finds some sort of release, despite being buttressed and hemmed in
elsewhere. Cézanne thus injects a dynamic energy into a still-life whose
objects are solidly painted and stably composed, thereby combining lyrical
movement with classical repose.*

**113 PAUL CÉZANNE Still-Life with Apples, Bottle and
Chairback 1900–06.**

*It is surely quite easy to understand, looking at this, why Renoir refused to
let Cézanne take one of his watercolours behind a rock to spoil it; why, too,
Renoir and Degas fought over another at Vollard's first exhibition of
Cézanne's work in 1895. Cézanne built up his watercolours with layer
upon layer of successive, overlapping strokes of colour. Following only the
barest linear skeleton made in pencil beforehand, he allowed each layer of
wash to dry before adding the next. It was in this way that he was able to
construct objects more or less entirely with colour, leaving his outlines
broken and incomplete. For if things only exist by virtue of their relation to
the things around them, a contour would be too static and constricting.
Line, therefore, is – by its very definition – both limited and limiting.*

117 PAUL GAUGUIN Contes barbares 1902.

The enigmatic and poetic images that Gauguin distilled from his years in the South Seas changed in character during his time there. Many of his later works – and this is one of his last paintings – were executed in much softer, paler colours than the brighter palette he had favoured earlier. The aggressive nature, both thematic and technical, of a painting such as Aha oe feii? (see plate 111) cedes here to the gentlest of approaches. Whatever the nature of the contrasts intended between the three figures, the painting exudes a delicate, subtle and above all scented resonance. Colours are handled so as to release natural fragrances that waft deliciously into the imagination.

118 PAUL CÉZANNE   Pine, Viaduct and Mont Sainte-Victoire
1885–87.

*This was Cézanne's answer to what he felt was Renoir's penchant for
cotton (see plate 99). If, in Renoir's landscape, a warm scented breeze
can be felt to blow through the parched rocks and trees, no such
momentary, transient phenomenon animates Cézanne's resolutely stilled
and ordered rendering of nature. There is little or no concession to
atmospherics. Cézanne's landscape may be airless, but it lives more as an
intellectual construction or reorganization of nature's vagaries. Thus, the
road that tapers up through the middle ground is made to mimic the shape
of a branch of the central tree; and the slight tilt of the tree itself is
balanced by the thrust of the viaduct. There is little sense of foreground,
for we relate to this view from on high; we are encouraged to dominate
it with the eye and the mind – physically uninvolved.*

119 PAUL CÉZANNE   The Great Pine   1892–96.

The terrific energy unleashed by the interlocking coils and twists in the
branches of this tree seem more inherent in the tree itself than the result of
the battering of a storm or high winds. The writhing branches become
metaphors for the natural forces of growth animating the tree, itself the
visible manifestation of these unseen energies. Centred within the
composition, the tree towers above us: these energies are thus felt to be
working with such a power and on such a scale that human endeavours
are made to seem, if not irrelevant, then at best puny.

120 PAUL CÉZANNE   Mont Sainte-Victoire seen from
Les Lauves   1904–06.

*Whatever is said or written about them, Cézanne's last views of the Mont
Sainte-Victoire remain extraordinary, baffling paintings. He translates the
simplest of landscape structures – mountain, horizon, diagonal road and
foreground trees and houses – into a rough and complex multitude of
small touches of colour. The individual texture of any one thing is totally
ignored: the substance of rock, tree, stone, sky and grass are all treated
in the same way. At around the time that Cézanne produced this painting
he explained to one visitor that he wanted to use colour – and colour
alone – to express distance, to describe the space between things, without
resorting to the linear device of perspective. There is certainly virtually
no linear definition here. Finally we are tempted to allocate more
visionary meanings to such works.*

121 PAUL CÉZANNE Three Skulls 1902–06.

Even in a subject as morbid as this, Cézanne manages to find a spark of life. For the same diminutive curves with which the pattern on the cloth has been described are used to build up the forms of the skulls. The most heavily worked part of the paper is the passage where bone and pattern meet; a charge of energy seems to pass between the lively rills of skull and cloth. Just as extraordinary, most of the skulls are left untouched by the brush; their smooth, rounded white surfaces are described by blank paper. Nothing, of course, exists except in relation to its surroundings; without the description of the cloth, the skulls would disappear.

122 PAUL CÉZANNE   Card Players   *c.* 1892–95.
In this rustic and yet immensely grand, immobile scene, it seems
inconceivable that any cards should ever fall from the hands of these
statuesque players. We are not even allowed the vicarious pleasure of
identifying what cards the pipe-smoking player has in his hand, as would
have been customary in the type of genre painting Cézanne was here using
as his model. Yet he holds them up to our gaze: it is as though he is
teasing us, frustrating our expectations. In the end, though, Cézanne is
more interested in the way the dirty cloth falls in a jagged fold over the
corner of the table, highlighted along its lower edge, than in creating a
dramatic moment in a narrative piece.

123   PAUL CÉZANNE   Portrait of Ambroise Vollard   1899.
When Cézanne expressed a degree of satisfaction with the shirtfront in this
portrait of the dealer Ambroise Vollard, it was not a remark made out of
any false modesty; Cézanne was a stringent critic of his own work. On
another occasion Vollard asked him why there were two spots of unpainted
canvas on the knuckles of his right hand (still visible today). Cézanne
replied that he had to think very carefully before covering them, because if
he chose the wrong tones he would have to begin the whole picture again.
That sounds like fastidiousness taken to an extreme, but Cézanne's
method of working was to build up the sense of space and volume
through precise tonal relationships between one colour and the next.
The whole image thus depended on the most exacting, rigorous and
consistent balancing of his meticulously researched strokes: the slightest
error would upset them.

124 MAURICE DENIS Hommage à Cézanne 1900.

*Denis's tribute to Cézanne is set in Ambroise Vollard's gallery. Odilon
Redon (far left), Vollard (perched behind the easel) and – from left to
right – Vuillard, Denis, Sérusier, Ranson, Roussel and Bonnard are
among the figures gathered around a still-life on an easel. Other paintings
in Vollard's stock can be seen on the far walls: a Tahitian landscape by
Gauguin and a Renoir portrait; but pride of place goes to the still-life by
Cézanne. This had formerly been in Gauguin's collection and he had
vowed never to sell it until forced to do so through financial necessity.
Cézanne wrote Denis a touching letter of thanks for this, his tribute on
behalf of the Nabis painters. Within seven years Picasso and Braque were
to pay him a very different kind of homage in their creation of Cubism.*

125   PAUL CÉZANNE   Les Grandes Baigneuses   1906.
John Carey began The Violent Effigy *(1973), his book on a famous nineteenth-century English novelist: 'Dickens is infinitely greater than his critics.' The same praise can be applied here to Cézanne. For in this work, his final statement on the Bathers theme that had occupied him for over forty years, Cézanne goes beyond the austere and rarified classicism of Poussin with which his painting has most frequently – and with some justification – been compared. Here is the inspired majesty of a Gothic cathedral. The bathers group themselves beneath this arched vault of trees, unconsciously arranging themselves in harmonious accord with their surroundings.*

Chapter 3

Wild Animals

While the solitary giants of the last decade or so of the nineteenth century – Vincent van Gogh (1853–1890), Paul Gauguin (1848–1903) and Paul Cézanne (1839–1906) – lived and worked in relative obscurity, the forefront of the Parisian avant garde had been dominated, on the one hand, by the Nabis under Maurice Denis (1870–1943), and by the divisionists under Paul Signac (1863–1935) on the other. When, eventually, fame and recognition did come to these recluses in the first decade of the twentieth century, for the most part it came posthumously. Their achievements were to have a decisive influence not so much on their peers as on the next generation of avant-garde painters, who were about to make an explosive and successful bid for attention.

Established in 1903 as the second major avant-garde exhibition forum, the newly founded Salon d'Automne was to play a crucial part in these developments. For as well as giving contemporary painters the opportunity to show their own work, it also exposed them to the works of major figures from the recent past; retrospective exhibitions of their art were hung alongside the other exhibits. Younger painters were thus able to measure themselves against their predecessors. It was also here, in 1905, that the group of painters known as the Fauves, meaning wild animals, was to emerge before the public eye.

The first Salon d'Automne had been held in 1903 in the rooms of the Petit Palais, off the Champs Elysées in the heart of Paris. The following year, however, the use of the Petit Palais was refused; Eugène Carrière (1849–1906), an established artist, exerted pressure on the Académie des Beaux-Arts, and the Salon d'Automne was held at the Grand Palais – across the street. It was Carrière and Pierre Auguste Renoir (1841–1919), who had also by now gained acceptance at the

126 HENRI MATISSE Woman in a Hat 1905.
Madame Matisse sat for this portrait wearing a hat made by Matisse himself. Her right hand rests on the arm of a chair as she holds a fan over her bosom. She looks out at the spectator, as if momentarily surprised. So far the pose, with its slight psychological drama, is conventional enough. It is the way in which it has been described that was to prove so shocking when the picture first appeared. The ferocious manner with which the paint had been applied, thickly ridged in places, barely covering the weave of the canvas in others, was deemed totally unacceptable. And then there was the colour itself. The green shadows on the face, the orange on the neck – enlivened by the adjacent blue – that fiery orange-red of her belt: every individual colour, placed next to its complementary, is brought to its maximum intensity.

official Salon, who made sure that the Salon d'Automne was given space at the Grand Palais again in 1905.

Thus, it was the third Salon d'Automne that opened on 18 October 1905. Henri Matisse (1869–1954), shortly to be dubbed 'King of the Fauves' in the critical press, exhibited ten works, the maximum allowed. Of these, one in particular, a portrait of his wife entitled *Woman in a Hat*, attracted a great deal of attention (*see plate 126*).

Frantz Jourdain (1847–1935), the president of the Salon, had tried to dissuade Matisse from showing the picture because he thought it too 'excessively modern' and feared that it might cause the artist great trouble. Jourdain was right. One critic spoke of 'a pot of colours flung in the face of the public'; another of the 'barbarous and naïve games of a child playing with a box of colours'.[1] Along with six other works from the exhibition that were considered scandalous because of their extremely bright colours, formal incoherence and lack of finish, the portrait was reproduced and ridiculed in the pages of a popular daily publication, *L'Illustration*. Even Leo Stein (1872–1947), the brother of the modern American writer Gertrude Stein (1874–1946), who bought the painting on the last day of the exhibition, described it as: 'The nastiest smear I had ever seen.'[2]

Critics who had usually shown themselves more sympathetic towards Matisse's paintings this time expressed incomprehension. It was one such, Louis Vauxcelles (b.1870), who christened Matisse and the painters whose works hung next to his in Room VIII of the Salon. He called them the Fauves: the wild animals.

Vauxcelles had become art critic for the respected liberal daily publication *Gil Blas* in 1903. A man of left-wing sympathies, he used this position to defend passionately developments in avant-garde painting – rather as Guillaume Apollinaire (1880–1914) would do a few years later for the Cubist painters. Like Jourdain, Vauxcelles had foretold the furore Matisse's *Woman in a Hat* would provoke, in a piece published the day before the Salon opened.

At this point, it was the public that Vauxcelles described as wild animals, saying that they would devour Matisse for his audacity and innovation. It was only later in the same article that he used the word in reference to Matisse and those artists grouped around him – André Derain (1880–1954), Maurice de Vlaminck (1876–1958), Henri Charles Manguin (1874–1949), Charles Camoin (1879–1965) and Jean Puy (1876–1960). But it was in this context that the name stuck. Thus the first artistic movement of the twentieth century came into existence not because the artists involved regarded themselves as a group or had published a manifesto of collective aims (as others had done before and would do later) but rather because of one journalist's witticism. The similarities with the birth of Impressionism are considerable.

Such was the outcry and indignation provoked by *Woman in a Hat* (see plate 126) that Matisse only dared visit the Salon once. His wife did not go at all. In 1905 Matisse was thirty-five years old. He was married with three children. Though not rich, he dressed smartly and respectably. With his neat beard, calm manner and round glasses he had earned the nickname of 'the professor' from his fellow artist friends and acquaintances. This is not exactly the received image of the modern artist; neither radical, subversive nor bohemian, it might almost be deemed disappointing. A reporter for the *New York Times Magazine*, who interviewed Matisse a few years later, was surprised by the conventional nature of his appearance, his house and his way of life. And Matisse, anxious to live down his reputation as a revolutionary, told her: 'Oh, do tell the American people that I am a normal man; that I am a devoted husband and father, that I have three fine children, that I go to the theatre, ride horseback, have a comfortable home, a fine garden that I love, flowers etc., just like any man.'[3] Not long after this statement was published, outraged art students in Chicago burned Matisse's *Blue Nude* (see plate 150) in effigy. Yet the early years of Matisse's life were, by contrast, remarkably uneventful.

One of this century's most illustrious artists, Matisse was something of a late starter. He was born on the last day of 1869 in a small town close to France's border with Belgium, in a grey flat landscape. His family intended him to pursue a worthwhile bourgeois career as a lawyer and sent him to Paris at the age of eighteen to pass the requisite qualifying exams. Matisse then returned home and began to work as a clerk in a small lawyer's firm. For someone who was later to receive the accolades of two of this century's most radical artists, Pablo Picasso (1881–1973) and Marcel Duchamp (1887–1968), anything that might be deemed a rejection of a bourgeois lifestyle or values was thus far limited on Matisse's part to protests of a rather adolescent character. As a law student, he had been caught flicking balls of glue from his sixth-floor apartment window in Paris down on to the shiny top hats of passers-by below. And, as a clerk, he had copied pages of La Fontaine's fables into the law reports he was meant to be compiling in an effort to stave off the unutterable boredom of his work.

After a year as a clerk, Matisse suffered a particularly violent attack of appendicitis, from which he had suffered as a child, and he was forced to spend the best part of 1889 convalescing in bed. It was here that his career as an artist began, when his mother gave him a box of paints and a sort of painting-by-numbers book to help pass the time. In a curiously neat way, Matisse would also end his long career in bed. As an eighty-year-old invalid, he would draw portraits of his grandchildren on the ceiling above his bed with a pen attached to a long bamboo pole, and he would cut rarified, abstracted shapes out of coloured pieces of paper for his final, monumental and triumphant collages.

Back in 1889, at the age of twenty, the experience led Matisse to decide to give up law and become a painter. Not that his legal training had been a complete waste of time. A

127 ANDRÉ DERAIN   Portrait of Henri Matisse   1905.
The almost autumnal colouring, subdued in tone, suggests that Derain probably painted his friend towards the end of the summer they spent together in Collioure. Some brighter orange tones burn a little more fiercely in his full, heavy beard, intimating perhaps that the sun is about to set. With his stern expression and round glasses, his pipe determinedly clenched between his teeth and that concentrated stare in his eyes, Matisse here appears very much 'the professor'. Only the open-necked shirt suggests a more bohemian occupation.

copy of the first contract he signed with the Parisian picture dealers Bernheim-Jeune bears Matisse's own adjustments and alterations. Even Ambroise Vollard (1868–1939), one of the shrewdest of the new dealers who set themselves up to handle the works of the Impressionist and Post-Impressionist generations (it was Vollard who had 'discovered' Cézanne in the early 1890s), respected Matisse's grasp of legal detail. Moreover, many who met the artist in his later years were struck by his small, bird-like eyes, encased in thin gold-framed spectacles, that seemed to pierce the particular object of their scrutiny.

Initially, Matisse's father objected to his son's new plan but he yielded after the intercession of his wife. Thus, in the autumn of 1891 Henri Matisse found himself back in Paris with a year's grace. His father had promised him an allowance for one year, during which he was to try to gain a place at the Ecole des Beaux-Arts.

Having failed to gain admission Matisse was advised to get in by the back door. In order to do this you had to position yourself in the courtyard of the Ecole and begin drawing one of the sculptures there. When the professors crossed the courtyard on the way to the studios, you would then stand up, show your work to one of them and hope that the professor, favourably impressed, would admit you into his 'atelier', or studio, as a student.

128 HENRI MATISSE Portrait of André Derain 1905.
Matisse's portrait of Derain is much bolder than the younger man's of his mentor (see plate 127). The pigment is thinner, allowing light to reflect off the white of the canvas beneath and giving the colour a livelier, breathing energy. The colours themselves are much brighter. In fact, Matisse constructs the whole image – figure and background alike – around pairings of complementaries. He uses the entire canvas, whereas Derain had left the background relatively unstressed. Thus Matisse's colours sing, while Derain's remain more muted. Yet for all the colouristic brilliance, Matisse also succeeds in describing a lyrical, melancholy quality in his friend: through the tilt of the head, the droop of the moustache, the silhouette of the cheekbone.

At that stage there were three professors working at the Ecole des Beaux-Arts: Léon Bonnat (1833–1922), Jean-Léon Gérôme (1824–1904) and Gustave Moreau (1826–1898). While the first two were notoriously indifferent to students, Moreau had only recently taken up the post of professor and had a reputation for being a gifted and committed teacher. It was Moreau that Matisse approached in the courtyard one spring morning of 1892, and he was duly invited to work at the professor's studio.

Matisse studied at Moreau's atelier for five years. He drew from casts, sculpture and the model, copied oils in the Louvre and occasionally went out onto the streets of Paris with his fellow student Albert Marquet (1875–1947) to sketch. It was during these years that the painters who would later form the core of the Fauves came together. Many of them passed through Moreau's studio – Manguin, Camoin, Réné Piot (1868–1934), Jules Flandrin (1871–1947) – and all of those that did were to benefit from Moreau's open-minded approach to teaching.

Moreau himself was something of a maverick within the Ecole. He usually painted exotic or literary subjects, but the

pictures were so brilliantly coloured, intricately detailed, and painted on such a small scale, that they could hardly be said to conform to Academic standards. As a teacher, however, Moreau was exceptional. He encouraged his students to develop their own personal style, positively criticizing them if their work showed signs of merely imitating his own. It was a lesson Matisse never forgot. About ten years after he left Moreau's atelier, he himself eventually closed down the school he had been running – partly because the students were simply producing pastiches of his own style.

Off into the Jungle

Accounts of the friendships that have played a major part in stimulating change have delighted the historians of modern French painting. There is Pissarro's meeting with Cézanne in the early 1870s when he urged his friend to leave behind his earlier, dark, turbulent, imaginative works and to study nature. Later, more famously, there is the friendship betweeen Georges Braque (1882–1963) and Picasso which was instrumental in the evolution of Cubism – a friendship so close that Picasso later described it as being like a marriage.

As far as the Fauves are concerned, there is the friendship between Matisse and André Derain, one that is recorded in the two portraits they made of each other in 1905 (*see plates 127 and 128*). They did not meet at Moreau's atelier but at a private studio known as the Académie Carrière, where artists clubbed together to pay for the hire of a model.

That was in 1899. The following year, when Derain was stuck on a broken-down train just outside Paris, he struck up in conversation with a fellow passenger. His companion turned out to be another painter, called Maurice de Vlaminck, and the two became firm friends. Before the year was out they were sharing a studio (*see plate 129*). When Derain introduced Vlaminck to Matisse at a van Gogh exhibition in Paris in 1901, the three central protagonists of the Fauve group had met.

Looking back it seems strange that another four years were to pass before their paintings were to take the Salon d'Automne by storm. On the other hand, it does seem that what they would produce was so revolutionary that they would definitely need each other's support in order to carry it off. And in 1901, Derain was called up for national service. In those days, it was quite literally a lottery for those who were eligible (Matisse failed the medical examination), and Derain, unlucky enough to draw the short straw, found himself down for a three-year stint.

Returning to Paris in late 1904 Derain got back in touch with Matisse and the two became close friends. In the spring of 1905 Derain, who was ten years younger than Matisse, asked 'the professor' to persuade his parents to allow him to pursue a career as a painter. Matisse, dressed in his most respectable suit, obliged. Derain's parents, both part-time musicians, were suitably impressed and thus the young man was free to join Matisse a few weeks later at the village of Collioure on the Mediterranean coast.

It was the canvases that Matisse and Derain produced there during that summer, and which they exhibited at the Salon d'Automne, which were to earn them the title of Fauves. It is the same pictures which are now considered to mark the beginning of the history of twentieth-century painting.

Looking today at pictures like Derain's *Mountains, Collioure* or Matisse's *View of Collioure* (*see plates 141 and 140*), which were both painted early that summer, one is struck by the articulate and deft manner with which the paint has been applied. The range of pigments each has employed is reduced to a handful of the brightest, purest colours, and even these do not cover the whole of the canvas. Matisse and Derain have described the scene before them as much by what they have omitted as by the actual marks of their brushes. But if such abrupt transitions and elisions seem to have flowed easily from the hand, at the time the experience was a fraught one. In the middle of the summer, for example, Derain wrote to Vlaminck, describing Matisse's anxiety over the work he was producing; the letters Matisse himself wrote to Signac seem to confirm this:

In my painting of [*Luxe, calme et volupté*] do you think there is a perfect accord between the character of the drawing and the character of the painting? To me they each seem totally different and even absolutely contradictory. . . .[4]

But what was the cause of their anguish? What was it they were up to that was so revolutionary? In order to answer these questions, it is necessary to retrace a few steps and imagine the situation experienced by avant-garde artists in the years leading up to 1905.

The four giant figures of the preceding generation were either dead or inaccessible. Van Gogh had died in 1890, Georges Seurat in 1891. Gauguin was 5,000 miles away in the South Seas, and in any case he died in 1903, and Cézanne was more or less a hermit in the south of France.

Impressionism was still the style favoured by the majority of artists with avant-garde sympathies, along with the flatter, more decorative manner of the Nabis and the mosaic-like dots of the divisionists. These last were the natural and self-proclaimed successors to the innovations of the 'big four'; as far as the Fauve group were concerned, however, they had failed to develop the discoveries of their predecessors.

As the historian John Golding has shown, the fact that Derain could voice the same doubts in 1906 as Paul Sérusier (1864–1927) had done in 1889 indicates that the older generation had somehow failed to provide the younger artists with enough to chew on.

Sérusier, founder of the Nabis group, had written to Maurice Denis in 1889 clearly in an anxious state of mind:

I find myself all at sea. What worries me above all is this: what part ought nature to play in a work of art . . . Should one work from nature or only look at it and work from memory? Too much liberty frightens me, poor copyist that I am . . . yet nature seems to me poor and banal.[5]

Sérusier seems to have got stuck – daunted by the prospect of loosening the traditional bond between the artist and nature, but dissatisfied with that bond at the same time. Seventeen years later Derain seems worried by essentially the same dilemma when he writes to Vlaminck:

Working from nature I am the slave of things so stupid that my deeper feelings are shattered by them. I can't see what the future should be . . . On one side we strive to disengage ourselves from objective things, and on the other hand we cling to them as both means and end.[6]

129 MAURICE DE VLAMINCK Portrait of Derain 1906.
Having met in 1900 as fellow travellers on a train that had broken down between Paris and their home town, Vlaminck and Derain shared a studio in the suburban town of Le Chatou just outside Paris. Vlaminck gave this painting to Derain who kept it until his death in 1954. But whatever it may have meant to Derain, in the end the portrait seems to tell us more about the painter than the sitter. In temperament the two could hardly have been more different. Derain, classically educated and deeply cultured, was the more diffident and introspective. The crude power of the colour here, however, especially the red, and the primitive savagery of the drawing, are indications of Vlaminck's own more aggressive personality as he stamps his mark on his subject.

Derain's doubts, however, are just one expression of a feeling of uneasiness that was troubling a wide range of artists at the time, as a glance at just one contemporary literary journal – amongst an ever-increasing number – will show.

Charles Morice had become the art critic for the Symbolist journal *Mercure de France* in 1903. One of a new breed of professional, specialist art critics, his articles are of particular interest because he knew many of the figures he chose to write about (he was, for example, a close friend of Gauguin), and he took trouble to reflect their concerns and ideas in his reviews. In the spring of 1905, convinced that avant-garde painting was about to undergo some kind of innovative convulsion, Morice sent out a questionnaire to a large number of artists. Later that year he published their answers.

Though the range of answers given was too broad to allow any precise conclusions to be drawn as to where, if anywhere, contemporary painting was heading, the questions Morice saw fit to pose are in themselves very revealing, as they quantify the debates and discussions then occupying artists' minds. One of them addresses precisely the issue that had troubled Sérusier in 1889 and which would trouble Derain in 1906: 'Should the artist follow nature or only demand from her the plastic means to realize the idea that is within him?'[7]

What connects the letters of both Sérusier and Derain and Morice's questionnaire is a sense of unease about what exactly was or should be the role of the artist. More specifically, the dilemma was felt in terms of whether the artist's duty was to describe nature or to articulate his own reactions in front of nature.

The two landscapes by Matisse and Derain mentioned above could be said to fulfil both categories (*see plates 140 and 141*). One contemporary writer, the painter and critic Maurice Denis, vividly described their use of pure, bright, unnaturalistic colour as analogous to the intense violent glare of the Mediterranean sun: 'What they restore to us is the retinal disturbance of sunlight, the optical quiver, the painful sensation of being dazzled.'[8]

At this point it is worth remembering that both Matisse and Derain were natives of northern France, unused to the bright, sunny weather of the south. Perhaps it was only natural that they should have decided to use pure colour simply to represent the sheer power of the southern sun on their canvases. On the other hand, the unnaturalistic colours and the simplified brushwork they employed could be said to recreate the feeling of exhilaration they experienced when they saw the scene before them. In other words, colour and brushwork were being used to describe an emotional response to the particular slice of nature chosen as the subject of a painting.

The work of Matisse and Derain, then, was radical for the fierce and blatant way that it paraded subjective, emotional responses to nature. In this respect it was a question more of degree than of kind. Van Gogh's landscapes, for example, were clearly highly personal and subjective reactions of the artist to his subject, yet there is a technical difference between his work and that of the Fauves.

Van Gogh certainly used pure, unmixed pigments but his colours are almost always exaggerations of the local colour of the subject in question. In this way, they are still faithful to nature herself. Matisse and Derain, on the other hand, were using colours that were clearly unrelated to local colour. It was this liberation, as much as anything else, that was considered so shocking.

Nonetheless, Matisse and Derain had clearly been looking closely at van Gogh's work, for they were seeking to extend the possibilities it offered. They were given the opportunity when the Salon des Indépendants, following the lead of the Salon d'Automne, put on a retrospective of van Gogh's works in the spring of 1905. They had also been studying the work of both Seurat (who was also given a retrospective exhibition at the Indépendants that year) and Signac. Traces of a divisionist brushstroke can be seen, for example, in the lozenged strokes that Matisse employs in parts of the sea and some of the roofs in his *View of Collioure* (*see plate 140*). The divisionists' insistence upon using only the primary colours and their complementaries is the other legacy Matisse and Derain were happy to inherit from their predecessors.

The methodical, disciplined practice of divisionist technique, however, proved uncongenial to them and they had no hesitation in abandoning it for a more personal, urgent and calligraphic type of brushwork. As Matisse was to say in an interview in 1929: 'Fauvism overthrew the tyranny of Divisionism. One can't live in a house too well kept, a house kept by country aunts. One has to go off into the jungle to find simpler ways which won't stifle the spirit.'[9]

Later in the summer of 1905 Matisse and Derain made a further advance. The sculptor Aristide Maillol (1861–1944), a friend of Matisse, introduced the two painters to an old friend of Gauguin called Georges de Monfreid, who showed the two younger men his collection of Gauguin's early Tahitian paintings. Matisse and Derain already understood that through the juxtaposition of brash and violent contrasts, colour could actually be made to produce light rather than palely imitating the effects of the bright Mediterranean sun. What they realized, having looked at Gauguin's work, was that to make these contrasts stronger and thus emulate the light they were after more effectively, they would have to use more of the stuff – more liberally. In other words, they would have to relinquish the graphic qualities of their broken, dappled brushwork in favour of larger areas of pure, bright, dazzling pigment (*see plates 128 and 139*).

Matisse and Derain pursued this course when they returned to Collioure and its environs the following summer after Matisse's trip to Algeria (*see plates 130, 142 and 143*). Back in 1905, meanwhile, the canvases they exhibited at the Salon d'Automne had a profoundly liberating effect on a number of their contemporaries.

Vlaminck's paintings from 1906 reveal a freedom of brushwork and an intensity of colour that easily bear comparison with the work of Matisse and Derain (*see plates 154 and 155*).

130 HENRI MATISSE Pink Onions 1906.
But for the fact that the diagonal of the table edge suggests that the objects in this still-life stand in a recessive space, this painting is almost completely flat – so flat indeed that the crude highlights on the onions look a little out of place. Matisse painted Pink Onions *in the summer of 1906, having visited Algeria in the spring. He had brought back three jugs which he includes in the picture, and the whole canvas seems to emulate the simplified, flattened style with which they are decorated. Matisse was attempting to integrate some of the stylistic traits of North African, 'primitive' art into his own painting, an exercise that at first caused him considerable anxiety. When, on his return to Paris, he showed Leo Stein a portrait of a fisherman from Collioure that he had painted in the same manner, for instance, he told him that the painting had been given to him by the postman.*

Othon Friesz (1879–1949) and Braque, friends from their childhood days in Le Havre, also painted their first fully Fauve works in 1906, on a painting trip to Antwerp, and they developed their discoveries together in the summer of 1907 in the south of France, in the small town of La Ciotat (*see plates 156 and 157*). And Raoul Dufy (1877–1953) and Marquet travelled together to Le Havre in the summer of 1906 to produce their first landscapes in the new style (*see plates 144, 145 and 146*). Indeed, a number of other artists took up the innovations Matisse and Derain had inaugurated in the summer of 1905 (*see plates 131 and 148*), so that within two years the Fauves had moved to the forefront of the avant garde.

By 1907 Louis Vauxcelles's term 'Fauve' had become a popular label, used by a large number of critics writing for the Parisian papers and journals to describe this significant and burgeoning group of young, avant-garde painters. Moreover, by 1908, the Fauves were also an undisputed commercial success. All of the painters mentioned above were contracted to or otherwise closely involved with one of the growing number of dealers specializing in modern, contemporary art. Vollard purchased the entire contents of Derain's studio in 1906. Braque sold every one of the ten paintings he exhibited

131 CHARLES CAMOIN   Portrait of Albert Marquet   1904. *Camoin studied under Moreau, was a good friend of Matisse and exhibited at the same shows as Matisse, Derain and Vlaminck. Contemporary critics also discussed his painting in the same breath as these others. Camoin has thus come to be considered, somewhat by proxy, as one of the Fauves. His close contacts with Cézanne, however, a painter from the previous generation, and his belief that the artist should first try to imitate nature, rather than recording his subjective response to it, makes the label somewhat misleading. Indeed this portrait of his friend Albert Marquet has more in common with the figures in Cézanne's* Card Players (see plate 122) *than it does with Matisse's* The Green Stripe (see plate 139).

at the Indépendants in 1907. And in 1909, sustained both by a contract with the dealers Bernheim-Jeune, and by the patronage of private collectors such as Gertrude and Leo Stein, and their brother and sister-in-law Michael and Sarah Stein (*see plate 132*), Matisse was able to move his family out of their cramped Paris flat to a spacious house in the suburbs. The Fauves certainly never suffered the prolonged attacks and material hardships of their Impressionist forebears.

Nevertheless, it was also at this time that the group began to disintegrate. From 1907 onwards, most of the artists involved began to abandon the exuberance and gaiety of Fauvism's colouristic excesses for a more sober, structured and traditional style of painting.

At this point, however, it is important to note that Fauvism itself is a somewhat misleading term. It was coined in 1905 by a critic, not a painter, but only came into widespread use in the press in 1907; that is, just as the movement began to fall apart. The idea that the Fauves were a coherent group was also one promoted more by the critics than by the artists themselves. For despite a number of shared stylistic traits, they did not congregate at particular cafés as the Impressionists had done. Nor did they promote their art in the world of letters as the Nabis had done. Predominantly young men in their twenties – Matisse was the exception – they published no manifesto nor codified any specific techniques or practices. Fauvism was a short-lived movement, essentially adolescent in character. As the historian Ellen Oppler has written: 'A movement without very specific and urgent goals, without threatening foes, and with a paradoxical dedication to individualism would exert only a tenuous hold on its members and be apt to fall apart. It is less surprising, therefore, that Fauvism shortly ceased to exist as a movement than that it functioned as such at all.'[10]

Derain was later to describe Fauvism as a 'trial by fire'[11] – as though these artists' respective immersions into a world of exclusively pure, unmuddied colours purged them of former adherences and allegiances. But if, for all these young men, Fauvism was a brief, convulsive liberation from old habits, it also served, a little later, as a necessary apprenticeship for a wide range of artists from all over Europe. Thus, Wassily Kandinsky (1866–1944) and Piet Mondrian (1872–1944) both had to pass through this baptism of fire (*see plates 267 and 260*) before their first, pioneering explorations into abstract painting. Similarly, initiation into Fauvism's excesses was crucial for the German painters of Die Brücke [see chapter 5] and also for a number of British artists working in the years before the outbreak of the First World War (*see chapter 8*).

Matisse and Derain had invented what came to be described as the Fauve style painting landscapes in the open air – 'sur le motif' to use Cézanne's phrase – in the south of France. In fact, landscapes and views of the city were the Fauve painters' preferred subjects, committed as they were to the direct translation of the artist's immediate sensations in front of nature. In this respect, their aims and practices can be considered close to those of the original Impressionists. Furthermore, they revisited a number of sites favoured by the Impressionists: Dufy and Marquet in Le Havre, Derain and Vlaminck at Le Chatou, which lies close to La Grenouillère on the Seine, the resort so loved by Claude Monet (1840–1926) and Renoir in the 1860s and 1870s. Derain even visited London in 1906 in conscious and deliberate emulation of Monet, who had painted views of the Thames there both in the 1870s and as late as 1903 (*see plates 133, 134 and 153*). The Fauves were proud of their forebears and happily paraded their debts to an avant-garde tradition.

By returning to a more spontaneous way of working, one that favoured rapid and intuitive responses to nature, the Fauves were not merely displaying a set of beliefs and ideas akin to those of the Impressionists. For the same reasons, their paintings also constituted an attack on the more theoretical practices of the divisionists on the one hand, and the more mystical leanings of the Nabis and the Symbolists on the other. Initially, then, they largely turned their backs on the achievements of their immediate peers to reconsider those of their more distant predecessors, thus combining the freshness of Impressionism with the more recent advances in colour made by painters such as van Gogh and Gauguin.

It was not long, however, before the Fauves, again led by Matisse and Derain, began to explore the pastoral, imaginary subjects favoured by the Nabis. Matisse exhibited a large oil entitled *Bonheur de Vivre* (*see plate 135*) at the Indépendants of 1906. Here he applied all that he had learned of the abstract, expressive potential of pure colour in the previous summer's landscapes in a sinuously graceful evocation of an earthly paradise. Derain followed suit with his *La Danse* (*see plate 147*), responding to the languid and lazy quality of Matisse's arabesques with his own more violent rhythms and colours.

Avant-garde painters had always enjoyed reworking traditional, classical subjects such as the pastoral in modern terms: Seurat had done so allusively in his *Baignade* (*see plate 63*), Signac more explicitly in *Le Temps d'Harmonie* (*see plate 59*); Gauguin had transferred the subject to the South Seas (*see plate 96*); and Cézanne had represented it in his powerfully awkward Bathers pictures (*see plates 114, 115 and 125*). These references to subjects deeply embedded in ancient tradition probably helped avant-garde painters to gain some sense of continuity with the past – a sense of historical identity which their estrangement from the Academy and the establishment had severed in so many other ways.

During the first years of the new century France was, in fact, undergoing a major cultural realignment with regard to its classical heritage. Within French political and social life the upheavals caused by the Dreyfus Affair and the threats posed by an increasingly belligerent Germany had helped to polarize progressive and conservative tendencies. The vogue for the classical might be seen as a part of the latter. Thus, in the field of letters the poets Jean Moréas (1856–1910) and de Regnier (1864–1936) called for a return to classical clarity and simplicity. Similar developments can be detected in the music of Claude Debussy (1862–1918), Paul Dukas (1865–1935) and d'Indy (1851–1931). In the world of the visual arts the work of Cézanne was to play a fundamental role in this shift.[12]

The Impact of Cézanne

It was fortunate that Cézanne's father died leaving his son a rich man. It enabled him to pursue his own idiosyncratic path as an artist without needing to pay much attention to selling his paintings. Nevertheless, the extraordinary fecundity and originality of his work made it profoundly attractive – even

132   Photograph (left to right) of Michael and Sarah Stein, Henri Matisse, Allan Stein and Hans Purrmann in the Steins' flat in Paris, late 1907.
Michael Stein was the brother of Leo and Gertrude. Their friend Hans Purrmann was also a friend of Matisse. Michael Stein and his wife Sarah collected a large number of Matisse's paintings, amongst them Pink Onions (*see plate 130*) *which hangs to the left above the door, and* The Green Line (*see plate 139*)*, seen here above Hans Purrmann's head.*

indispensable – to a wide range of followers; he became many things to many different men. The timid, sensitive old man of Aix, who was too fearful to find any models to pose for his final, nude figurative paintings, ended by siring a motley variety of artistic progeny. Indeed, an examination of the different ways that his painting was received and understood by the various factions of the young avant garde between 1890 and 1910 provides us with an accurate and fascinating mirror of all the major artistic developments of the period. Histories of early twentieth-century painting have tended to stress Cézanne's exclusive importance for Braque and Picasso in their evolution of Cubism – as though the Cubists became the true and only inheritors of his legacy. The Cubists, however, did not discover Cézanne. His tardy re-emergence from obscurity in Provence into the very heart of the Parisian avant garde was effected at least ten years before Braque and Picasso embarked on their radical voyage of discovery.

Only a few years ago in the late 1980s a major English bank used a Cézanne still-life as the centrepiece for a campaign advertising a new and fruitful type of bank account. Another of his still-lifes has been used to help sell a distinguished brandy. Every year books and articles on the man and his work appear by the score. Yet between the wars it was possible to pick up a Cézanne watercolour at one of the little galleries on the Left Bank in Paris for what would today be about £50. Since then he has become part of the very fabric of French, European and even American culture. Today, when major Cézanne exhibitions are a matter of national prestige, it is hard to imagine the extent of his obscurity at the beginning of the 1890s. Suffice to say that from 1877 to 1895 not a

133 CLAUDE MONET The Thames and Houses of Parliament, Effect of Sunlight 1903.

134 ANDRÉ DERAIN Charing Cross Bridge, London 1906.
Derain was certainly not the first modern French painter to visit London; he was following the example of Courbet, Pissarro, Monet, Matisse and Gauguin amongst others, who had all been there before him. In the spring of 1904 thirty-seven of Monet's paintings of London had been exhibited at Durand-Ruel's gallery. It was their success with both the critics and the public that determined Vollard to send Derain to England in 1906, deliberately to emulate the older artist's achievements. Derain was certainly influenced by Monet's choice of sites. However, while Monet had painted all his later London works either from St Thomas's hospital on the south bank (situated just opposite the Houses of Parliament), or from a room in the Savoy hotel (further down the river) on the north bank, Derain's view of the city was more varied. In this picture, Derain paints a view that had already been described by Monet, but he places his easel a little further to the east, thus bringing himself closer to the bridge and boats, and allowing him to devote less of the canvas to the river itself. For Monet, who was interested above all in depicting the light reflected on the water, such a position would have been counter-productive. Nevertheless, with Monet's example in mind both as an inspiration and a challenge, Derain was able to demonstrate just how far his Fauve style had advanced, in abstract terms, over that of the older Impressionist.

single Cézanne was exhibited in Paris, and until 1895 only twenty-three of them had ever been shown in public.[13]

Until that year anyone wishing to look at his work headed off to Tanguy's paint shop in the rue Clauzel in Montmartre. For Cézanne, like van Gogh and many others, used to exchange his paintings for materials there. Père Tanguy's shop became something of a shrine for a small number of devotees in the 1880s and early 1890s. Pissarro took Signac there in the mid-1880s to buy one of Cézanne's landscapes. And Emile Bernard (1868–1941), Gauguin, van Gogh and Denis were among the other regular visitors to the small, cramped shop where Tanguy would carefully place his beloved Cézannes on a chair for his customers to examine.

When Tanguy died in 1894 and his collection was sold at auction, Cézanne's name was momentarily brought to the public's attention. It was at this point that Pissarro persuaded Ambroise Vollard, who had just opened a tiny gallery on the rue Laffitte (close to the Gare St Lazare), to hold a large exhibition of Cézanne's paintings. Vollard's first Cézanne exhibition opened in November 1895. One hundred and fifty paintings were shown, though Vollard's gallery was so small that only fifty could be seen at one time and the paintings had to be hung in rotation. The show was not a commercial success, but for the avant garde it was the event of the year. Renoir and Degas even fought over a small watercolour of some pears. But it was the Nabis, led by Denis, who proclaimed themselves Cézanne's new disciples; Denis was to immortalize this in his *Hommage à Cézanne*, a large painting that he sent to the Indépendants in 1901 (*see plate 124*).

As the flat space and scarcely modelled volumes of the forms in this picture suggest, Denis and the Nabis saw Cézanne as a decorative painter – as one who was working independently towards the same goals as they were themselves. Cézanne certainly did employ a palette with minimal tonal variations that produced little differentiation between light and dark values. (The range of tones in a painting, especially in work as colourful as Cézanne's, is most easily appreciated in a black and white reproduction, for here the distinctions between light and dark values are apparent to our eyes without the confusing intrusion of the actual colours.) Thus, as the traditional methods employed by artists to describe volume and to indicate a form's relative position in space involved the use of a wide range of tones, one effect of the tonal uniformity of Cézanne's canvases was to flatten the picture space. Apparently, he had wanted to reduce the illusion of a three-dimensional space, and to mould this illusion into the two-dimensional terms of the canvas itself. Hence, Cézanne's first followers, the Nabis, promoted a view of Cézanne (both in their paintings and in the press) that presented him very much as a painter in their own image – that is, as one who wanted to re-examine and rejuvenate the traditional techniques of easel painting through the adoption of decorative procedures. This was, in retrospect, a valid view but it was also a limited one.

The attention which was focused on Cézanne, however, by both paintings such as Denis's *Hommage à Cézanne* and articles published on him by Nabis and Symbolist critics alike, encouraged people to find out more about this newly acclaimed master. Young painters made pilgrimages to Aix to visit the mysterious man himself; they engaged him in correspondence and his letters were published in the press. More

exhibitions of his paintings were held – most importantly the large retrospectives at the Salon d'Automne in 1904 and 1907. All this attention revealed the limitations of the Nabis' original interpretation. Cézanne, it was decided, was more than just a decorative painter. By about 1905, in line with the current predeliction for the classical, Cézanne also came to be seen as the continuation incarnate of the great classical tradition of French painting.

This transformation in Cézanne's reception had much to do with the fact that he himself had defined his work as a modern recapitulation of the art of Nicolas Poussin (c. 1593–1665) (*see chapter 2*). He said as much to the young painter Charles Camoin, who had been stationed at Aix during his national service and who had known him since 1899. Camoin had also studied, prior to that, at Moreau's atelier in Paris and was a friend of Matisse and many of the Fauves. Camoin published Cézanne's statement – about wanting to re-make Impressionism according to Poussin – in the *Mercure de France* on 1 August 1905. And thus Cézanne's own description of his aims, ideals and aspirations was communicated quickly and directly to the Parisian avant garde.

One other result of this change in Cézanne's critical fortunes was that artists and critics became aware that the lack of tonal variety they had discerned in his paintings had not been effected exclusively in order to create a decorative style. Cézanne's achievements were subtler than that – even slightly ambiguous or double-edged. For if the tonal uniformity tended to flatten the illusion of space, Cézanne's intricate and delicate colour contrasts simultaneously modelled his forms and indicated their relative positions in space. It was slowly understood that Cézanne had mediated between a decorative, two-dimensional description of forms and a more traditionally realistic three-dimensional treatment (*see plate 179*).

Fauvism, as has already been mentioned, was an explosive movement that came to an end in around 1907, when many of the artists involved decided that their exclusive researches into raw, expressive colour had been made at the expense of the more classical qualities of order, structure and clarity. Cézanne's art, revealed to the Fauves at exhibitions such as the Salon d'Automne retrospective of 1907 and considered to be the epitome of such ideas, helped to bring about an end to the Fauves' colouristic exuberance. As Friesz was later to say: 'We returned to laws of composition, and of volume – Fauvism was sacrificed . . . there was no other way to get out of the trough of impressionism. We, the creators of Fauvism, were the first to destroy it.'[14]

Matisse, characteristically, was the first to signal this reorientation among the Fauve painters in an important painting that he exhibited at the Indépendants in the spring of 1907: *Blue Nude (Souvenir de Biskra)* (*see plate 150*).

The subtitle – *Souvenir de Biskra* – referred to one of the places Matisse had visited the previous spring during a short trip to Algeria. The full, lush vegetation, with palms and blooming flowers, certainly situates the figure in exotic surroundings. Strong formal correspondences between the figure and this landscape – that between the curve of a hip and a palm frond in particular, which acts as a fulcrum for the whole composition – suggest a thematic connection between the figure and nature's evident vigour and fertility.

This same reclining nude had already appeared in Matisse's only other previous pastoral paintings: *Luxe, calme et volupté* and *Bonheur de Vivre* (*see plates 68 and 135*). In the former Matisse had depicted, albeit somewhat ambiguously, a stage in a journey to a pastoral idyll. But if in the first picture it was not made explicitly clear whether the figures had already arrived or whether they would be continuing their journey to the hills on the horizon, in reworking the same theme in *Bonheur de Vivre* Matisse removed all traces of such ambiguity (figures in contemporary dress and the picnic acting as reminders of the everyday and mundane), and situated his figures unequivocally in an earthly paradise.

In *Blue Nude* Matisse returned to the uncertainties of *Luxe, calme et volupté*. Here, there is also reference to a journey, though this time it is a real one, albeit a journey recalled and suggested, not literally described. The nude thus hovers enigmatically between the realms of memory, reality and the ideal. And as though unsure of where to go after the unequivocally idyllic world of *Bonheur de Vivre*, Matisse translates the overt decorative values he had enjoyed in the earlier work back into Cézannesque terms; as if a return to pictorial tension and constraint were both necessary and more stimulating.

Blue and dull green-yellow hues, smudged into the flesh, model the figure, while the drawing moulds and twists the body both on to the picture surface and into the rectangular format. The distortions are most evident in the right leg and in the upper arm (no wonder he decided to leave out the elbow) and in a passage between the upper shoulder and the prominent hip. In this way the image fuses the decorative and the sculptural. Colour has been muted here, even dirtied; intensity and purity drastically qualified. If in *Bonheur de Vivre* the decorative arabesque was used to indicate the paradisiacal, here it takes on a muscular quality, which lends the figure

135   HENRI MATISSE   Bonheur de Vivre   1906.
Dr Albert C. Barnes made a fortune producing laxatives amongst other things. He spent this fortune on building one of the most extraordinary private collections of modern French painting ever assembled. It is still housed in his foundation outside Philadelphia, although unfortunately none of the works is allowed to be reproduced in colour. This is a shame. The Barnes Foundation holds over 200 hundred Renoir paintings, more than 100 Cézannes, something in excess of 30 Picassos and more than 70 Matisses. Bonheur de Vivre, Matisse's first unequivocal image of a pastoral idyll hangs in a stairwell there – unfortunately inaccessible.

136   Photograph of André Derain in his Paris studio, *c.* 1908.
With a reproduction of a Cezanne Bathers *on the wall behind him, Derain sits holding one of his collection of African sculptures.*

an awkward grace and situates the imaginary locus somewhere between the real and the ideal.

These distortions, and above all the dominant blue hues – used for outline and for modelling – deliberately recall the work of Cézanne. Moreover the finish of *Blue Nude* also parades a debt to the earlier master. Critics had consistently attacked Cézanne's work for its lack of finish; although those sympathetic to his style had explained it in terms of the difficulties the artist had experienced in fully realizing his work. In *Blue Nude* Matisse emulates this tendency quite deliberately – as though leaving evidence of the struggle by which the image was wrested from his memory. Thus *Blue Nude*, specifically intended as an image of a memory of the ideal – as opposed to the direct embodiment he had attempted in *Bonheur de Vivre* – qualifies its idealism by leaving visible the signs of its laboured evolution from the past.

As a Cézannesque revision and distillation of *Bonheur de Vivre*, this painting thus indicates a certain dissatisfaction on Matisse's part with the earlier picture; as though, having completed it, he felt wary of the grand, monumental gesture that might in the end seem merely glib. In *Hemlock and After*, a novel by Angus Wilson (b. 1913), Terence, against his better judgement, moves in to live with his homosexual lover Sherman, and to share in the latter's showy dominance of London's camp community in the 1950s:

It had taken Terence some days to get used to living the desultory, malicious and calculating existence that Sherman's ménage demanded beneath the excessive ecstasy of saints' eyes and the writhing sensuality of martyr's limbs. But the manieristi held the day and whatever held the day took first place in Sherman's house. Nevertheless, though there were moments when

Terence longed to hang up a reproduction of a Cézanne apple, little though such an object would have been to his taste, the first weeks went smoothly enough.[15]

Here Wilson offers a Cézanne reproduction as some sort of foil or antidote to the glitzy mannerism of Terence's adopted milieu. *Blue Nude* stands in a similar relation to *Bonheur de Vivre*. Matisse was unwilling to repeat the unequivocal and direct imaging of a pastoral paradise, and he turned to Cézanne to mediate between the real and the ideal.

The other Fauves followed Matisse's lead. Derain painted his *Three Bathers* (*see plate 149*) in the same year, apparently in competition with Matisse. It was to be their last collaborative effort. Thereafter, while Matisse developed his own brilliantly coloured, decorative style, Derain languished in a dry, almost academic Cézannism (*see plates 137 and 159*).

Friesz and Braque also turned to Cézanne, travelling in an act of homage to the seaside village of L'Estaque where Cézanne had fled during the Franco-Prussian War and where he had painted many of his most influential landscapes. One day in the late summer of 1907 the two friends found traces of old oil paint in a cave where they had taken shelter from the heat of the midday sun; they were convinced that years before them Cézanne had rested there too. In their subsequent works they too, like Derain, retreated from the extremes of their Fauve years (*see plates 158 and 160*).

Ultimately, all the Fauves except Matisse were consumed by the fire they had started. While the others renounced the heat and fury of the Fauve palette, Matisse alone continued his researches into pure colour – as though he alone had been able to withstand the intensity of those brief years.

Fauvism had also brought Matisse financial security. From 1908 onwards he no longer needed to sell his work merely through the two avant-garde salons. Ever since Leo Stein had had the courage to buy *Woman in a Hat* in 1905 (*see plate 126*), a network of private patrons had established itself, all of whom were not only eager to buy more or less anything from Matisse's hand but were also wealthy enough to commission specific paintings from him, usually on a large scale, to decorate their houses (*see plate 297*).

For Matisse, in fact, the Fauve experience had been one of refinement; as though he were purged in its crucible of dross

137 ANDRÉ DERAIN Martigues 1908.
The industrial nature of the subject, the abrupt abbreviation of the ship in the foreground and the receding diagonal of the distant warehouses would all be highly unusual in a Cézanne. Yet the ochres and reds of the buildings, the 'unfinished' masts, bridge and deck of the ship, and above all the square, overlapping lozenges of different blues in the water, proudly declare their ancestry in his work. Derain's later Cézannesque productions, however, would lose this earlier work's rather pedestrian understanding of his master's complex colour harmonies.

138 HENRI MATISSE Bathers with a Turtle 1908.
What could possibly be so terrifying about a turtle? Yet the central nude stands frozen and while one of her companions tries to feed the creature, the other looks on, oblivious of everything else. There is something deliberate in this juxtaposition of three such different reactions to that lone, diminutive spot of red. Whatever the answer may be (if there is one), Matisse's Arcadia is not without its disturbing elements. This aspect, coupled with the very rough paint textures and the clear signs of many revisions, all serve to qualify the rich beauty of the colour and the monumental simplicity of the design.

or impurity so that he might progressively inhabit more and more of a promised land of pure colour and simplified forms (*see plate 161*). Derain was not unaware of his friend's direction. Matisse stopped at the village of Cassis in the south of France, where Derain was staying in the summer of 1907, on his way to Italy. Soon after he had left, Derain wrote to Vlaminck: 'He showed me photos of his canvases; they are completely stunning. I believe that he is crossing the threshold of the seventh garden, that of happiness.'[16]

It is true, as Derain had written, that Matisse's principal efforts were now directed towards ideal, imaginary subjects (*see plate 138*). In fact Matisse more or less completely banished disturbing or violent subjects from his repertoire. In an article he wrote, entitled 'Notes of a Painter', published in December 1908, Matisse defended and explained his aims:

What I dream of is an art of balance, of purity and serenity, devoid of troubling or depressing subject matter, an art which could be for every mental worker, for the business man as well as the man of letters, for example, a soothing, calming influence on the mind, something like a good armchair which provides relaxation from mental fatigue.[17]

The armchair reference was perhaps unfortunate; taken out of context it almost suggests that Matisse was seeking a vapid, trite and undemanding kind of painting, as indeed some have charged him with. The allusion, however, has a pedigree that has origins in the writings of Charles Baudelaire (1821–1867) on art, and it would have been picked up by Matisse's first readers. In any case, Matisse had the highest faith in the thera-

peutic value of his painting. Once, in Nice, he went to visit a friend who was ill in bed, with a hammer, some nails and a stack of his canvases under his arm. These he hung around his friend's room, saying, 'These will make you feel better', and promptly left. At the same time it must be said that Matisse himself knew better than anyone that a high price would have to be paid for this kind of conviction. If his painting was to function properly and responsibly as the mental armchair he envisaged in 1908, he would strenuously have to avoid tainting his work with any kind of sentimentality.

In a similar manner, in the poem 'Little Gidding', published as part of the *Four Quartes* in 1943, T. S. Eliot (1888–1965) writes of:

A condition of complete simplicity
(Costing not less than absolutely everything).

Matisse approached that condition, but to avoid being trite, left a record of the cost. Thus, all the qualities he chose to translate into paint – the limpid simplicity of *Arab Café*, the monumentally fragrant *Interior with Aubergines* and the crystalline splendour of *Zorah on the Terrace* (*see plates 151, 152 and 163*) – are qualified in their idealism with profound intellectual rigour. The roughness of the paint textures, and the corrections and reworkings of his thin pigments that are left evident to our eyes in these later works tell as they did in *Blue Nude* (*see plate 150*), of the creative struggle by which such images of tranquillity were given substance. In the same way, Matisse's colours might be sumptuous, yet there is a certain austerity about the way he actually puts them down on the canvas. His subjects might be sensual, yet it is more a cerebral sensuality that he celebrates than any mindless, corporeal hedonism. For Matisse 'the professor' was always too much of a rationalist not to temper the wildest of his highly coloured paintings. The king of the Fauves was also a Cartesian.

NOTES
[1] In Jack D. Flam, Matisse, *The Man and his Art, 1869–1918*, London, 1986, 140.

[2] Ibid.

[3] In Jack D. Flam (ed.), *Matisse on Art*, London, 1973, 53.

[4] Matisse to Signac, 14 July 1905, in P Schneider (ed.), *Henri Matisse, Exposition du Centenaire*, exhibition catalogue, Grand Palais, Paris, 1970, 68.

[5] John Golding, 'Fauvism and the School of Chatou: Post-Impressionism in Crisis', *Proceedings of the British Academy*, LXVI (1980), 99.

[6] Ibid.

[7] Charles Morice, 'Enquête Sur Les Tendances Actuelles Des Arts Plastiques', *Mercure de France*, 56 (1 August 1905), 346.

[8] In Pierre Schneider, *Matisse*, trans. Michael Taylor and Bridget Strevens Romer, London, 1984, 187.

[9] Jack D. Flam (ed.), *Matisse on Art*, op. cit., 58.

[10] Ellen C. Oppler, *Fauvism Re-Examined*, doctoral dissertation, Columbia University, 1969, 335-36.

[11] Pierre Schneider, *Matisse*, op. cit., 214.

[12] Theodore Reff, 'Cézanne and Poussin' in *The Journal of the Warburg and Courtauld Institutes*, XIII (January 1960), 150-174.

[13] George Heard Hamilton, 'Cézanne and his critics', in *Cézanne: The Late Work*, exhibition catalogue, New York, 1977, 140.

[14] In E. C. Oppler, op. cit., 338.

[15] Angus Wilson, *Hemlock and After*, Harmondsworth, 1952, 242.

[16] In Judi Freeman, *The Fauve Landscape*, exhibition catalogue, Royal Academy, London, 1990, 105.

[17] Jack D. Flam (ed.), *Matisse on Art*, op. cit., 38.

139 HENRI MATISSE   The Green Line   1905.
Following the fury that surrounded Woman in a Hat *(see plate 126)*
when it was first exhibited at the Salon d'Automne in 1905, Matisse
quickly painted another portrait of his wife. Not that adverse criticism
alone had prompted him to revise his earlier painting; he was probably a
little dissatisfied with it anyway. For although he had painted it with pure,
bright, complementary colours, there was still, he felt, a further degree of
intensity that it lacked. The Green Line was also painted with pure
complementaries but they were laid down in large, flat areas, not as small,
broken dabs as they had been in the earlier picture. 'A kilo of green is more
green than half a kilo,' he said later, looking back at the Fauve years.
(Raymond Escholier, Henri Matisse, Paris, 1937, 137.)

140 HENRI MATISSE View of Collioure 1905.

*It was canvases like this one that were to earn Matisse the name of Fauve
on his return to Paris in the autumn of 1905. Maurice Denis, painter and
critic, vividly likened his use of pure, bright pigments, laid side by side on
bare, white canvas – totally unmingled – to the livid quiver of forms
beneath the intense glare and heat of the Mediterranean sun. Matisse
himself spoke of liberating the expressive potential of pure colour that had
been left unexplored by artists of the past. Kandinsky saw this and other
paintings Matisse had produced during the summer of 1905 when he
visited Paris in 1906. The experience was to have a decisive influence on
his own development of a purely abstract art.*

141 ANDRÉ DERAIN   Mountains, Collioure   1905.

Once again, Derain's work seems to suffer somewhat when it is compared with the raw power of Matisse's painting. Whatever lengthy meditations Matisse may have made before laying down his roughly textured, burning reds and oranges, the colours he employs seem to express the artist's intuitive, spontaneous response to the scene before him. Derain's landscape, on the other hand, seems calculated. The rhythms of the leaves, for instance, seem repetitive when seen against Matisse's more varied treatment of roof-tiles (see plate 140). But as Dogberry said in Much Ado About Nothing: *'Comparisons are odorous.' Derain brought his own inimitable poise and refinement to the fiery heat of Fauvism's crucible.*

142 ANDRÉ DERAIN   L'Estaque   1906.

*On the whole, those painters dubbed Fauve in the critical press were quite
happy with the designation, even though it was not a label of their own
choosing. Nonetheless, there is little that is wild or feral about the clean
precision with which Derain places his colour patches in this landscape.
Each one is separated from its neighbour by a small gap of unpainted
canvas, thus allowing the colours to breathe freely. Without these small
white spaces, the effect of such bright hues, placed together without any
respite, would produce an image of too concentrated an intensity. As it is,
this sunny landscape exudes heat and warmth, without becoming sultry
or oppressive.*

143 ANDRÉ DERAIN   Turning Road, L'Estaque   1906.
Cézanne had often painted at the little village of L'Estaque and one of
his favourite motifs had been a turning road. Thus Derain's canvas
consciously pays homage to the older artist. Yet Cézanne's landscapes were
never populated. Nor did he ever use reds, yellows and oranges so
abundantly, but stuck instead to a palette of greens, blues and ochres.
In this sense, Derain's resolutely unnaturalistic palette looks to another
source – that of Gauguin, some of whose Tahitian paintings he had
seen the previous summer. Gauguin was attracting quite a lot of
attention at the time; later in the year the Salon d'Automne held a large
retrospective exhibition of his work.

144 RAOUL DUFY   Les Affiches à Trouville   1906.

In a lecture given in Paris in 1914, the painter Fernand Léger was to speak approvingly of the way in which the modern advertisement, pasted on to a billboard, had already drastically altered people's everyday visual experience. Its bright colours made the more subtle effects of nature seem dull and tawdry; its brashness was more suited to the dynamic pace of modern life. Eight years before Léger's lecture (and sixty years before the advent of Pop Art) Dufy recognized the crowds bustling past the billboard posters in the Normandy town of Trouville as a lively and eminently suitable subject for a modern painting.

145 RAOUL DUFY   Fête Nautique   1906.

In the end, however, whether filing past advertisements, or as here, dressed up to enjoy a party at a regatta, Dufy's crowds recall the urban life and leisure favoured as subjects by the Impressionists more than they anticipate Léger's radical modernist stance, let alone that of Andy Warhol. In any case, the somewhat dulled tones of Les Affiches à Trouville (see plate 144) hardly match the intense, bold colours employed by Matisse, Derain or Vlaminck in paintings produced at the same date. Nevertheless, when the sun was out, catching the colours of bunting and bright costumes as it does here, Dufy did paint, as it were, straight from the tube.

146 ALBERT MARQUET   Le 14 Juillet au Havre   1906.
Like his friend Dufy (see plate 144), Marquet would only turn to really
bright tones when the occasion permitted; Matisse, Derain and Vlaminck
used this kind of colour for its own sake, irrespective of their subject or the
state of the weather. Marquet left his blues, reds and whites unmixed only
when sanctioned by the flags raised over the streets for the Bastille Day
celebrations in his native Le Havre. But if Marquet's Fauvism thus defines
itself as closer to Impressionism and less radical than that of some of his
colleagues, this conservatism also enabled him to develop in his painting a
subtlety and nuance of tone that was unmatched by them.

147   ANDRÉ DERAIN   La Danse   1906.

*In Bonheur de Vivre, Matisse's bathers recline, embrace, play the flute
and pick flowers. Such energetic pursuits as shepherding and dancing are
relegated to the background. Everything is described, however, with a
languorous grace beneath a vault of sinuous trees. Forms are flat; colour
is unnaturalistic. Something of this sinuosity, flatness and arbitrary
colouring also inform Derain's large decorative canvas; features that
suggest a common source in Gauguin's Tahitian mythologies.
Nevertheless, Matisse's line, for all its concise simplicity, still follows
traditional European canons of realism; Derain's painting, its parrot
and snake deliberately out of scale, suggests that he had been looking at
other, more 'primitive', sources.*

148 KEES VAN DONGEN Modjesko, Soprano Singer 1908.
*More a friend of Picasso (who kept aloof from the Fauves) than a follower
of Matisse and Derain, Van Dongen really only stood on the edges of
Fauvism. His preference for subjects taken from the café-cabaret and the
circus placed him somewhat apart – Fauvism's essential subject being the
landscape – closer to artists like Degas, Picasso and Toulouse-Lautrec. It
was Matisse, however, who remembered seeing him chase after the dancers
at one of the Paris cabarets, trying to draw them at the same time.*

149   ANDRÉ DERAIN   Three Bathers   1907.
Where Matisse's Blue Nude *managed to mediate between the decorative
and the sculptural in true Cézannesque fashion (see plate 150), Derain's*
Three Bathers, *equally indebted to Cézanne, is more one-sided in its
interpretation. Derain has avoided the decorative. He has hewn his
bathers out of colour as hard and as enduring as rock. Matisse's use of
more translucent colour, and his less definite outlines, lend his figure a
dynamic agitation that Derain's bathers, described in more pasty and
opaque hues, will never achieve. At the time, however, Derain's more solid
and sculptural reprise of Cézanne's favourite subject proved the more
influential.*

150   HENRI MATISSE   Blue Nude (Souvenir de Biskra)   1907.
*Matisse began this painting shortly after Cézanne's death late in 1906.
It was presumably intended as a tribute. Matisse had bought Cézanne's*
Trois Baigneuses *(see plate 115) in 1899; the seven years that he had
been exposed to its rough charms paid dividends here as he described his
bony, knotty Venus – her rib-cage visible between her breasts. There is
even something slightly melancholy about her: all those blues, the
downward glance. Yet some of the blue spills out of her to float as an aura
into the surrounding space and this, together with the insistent connection
made between hip and palm-frond, suggests that she also partakes of
nature's evident fertility.*

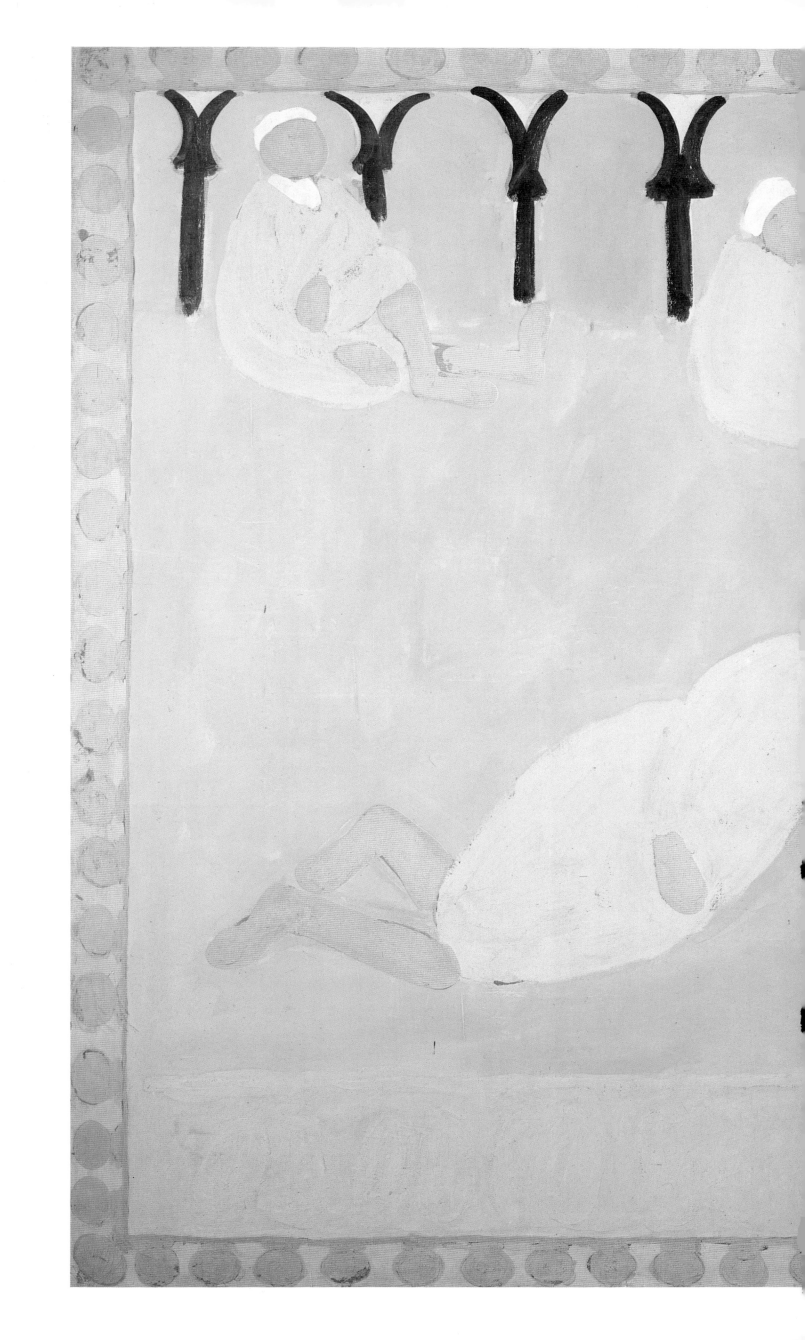

Henri-Matisse

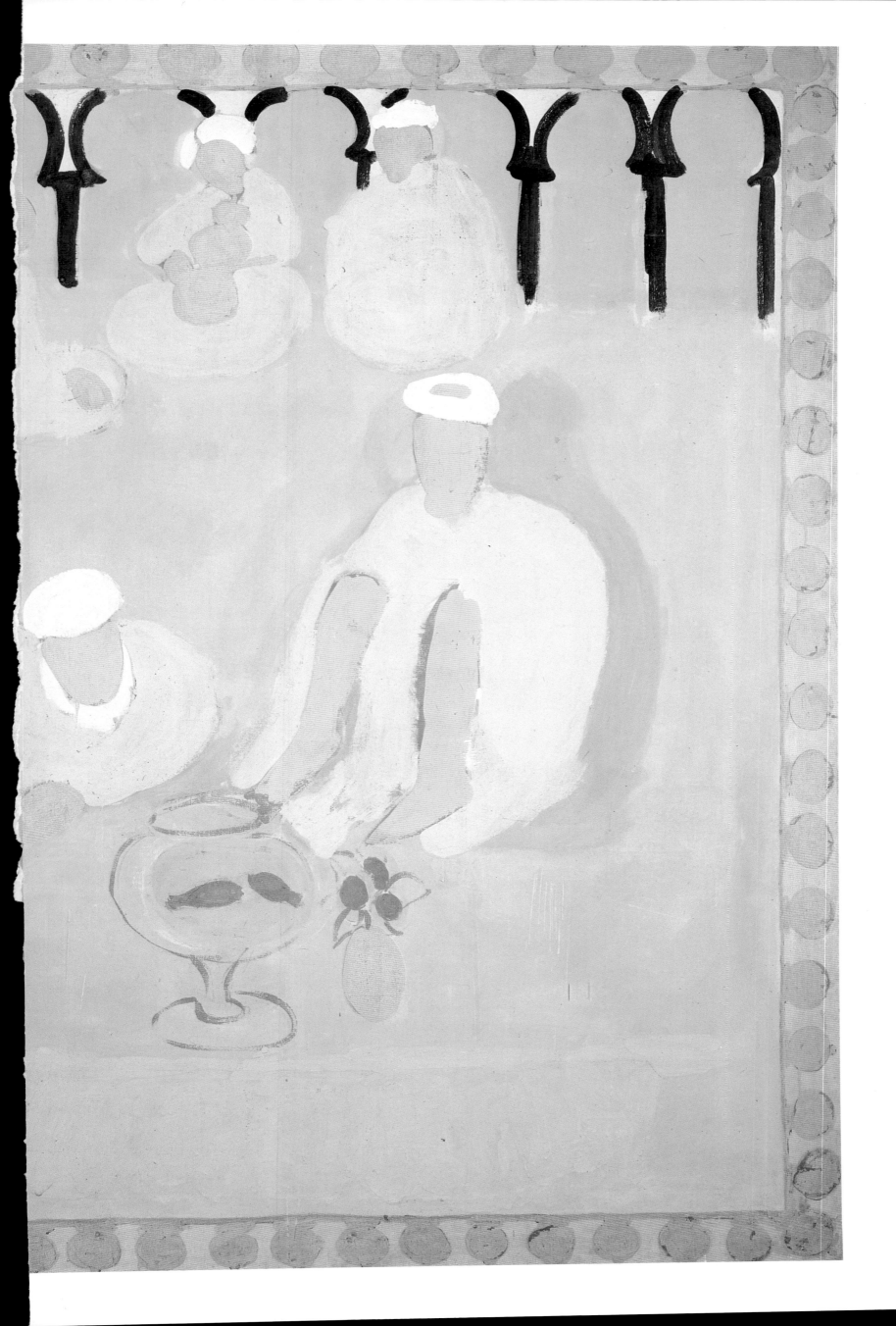

152 HENRI MATISSE Interior with Aubergines 1911.
There is something brilliant about the way the subdued blue-mauve groups of dots react so strongly with the brown of floor and wall. They seem to have been released from the flower-patterned cloth hanging on the screen and, like a perfume, fill the whole room (Matisse's studio). They almost break out of the frame. They also acquire an additional, hallucinatory quality if we focus on the still-life and allow them to hover in our peripheral vision. Fortunately, however, buttressed and controlled by the network of right angles and straight lines, these fragrant blues are prevented from becoming sentimental. In a picture with only a small vase of 'real' flowers and a slightly larger piece of floral cloth, it is still unusual to be reminded so strongly of their scent.

151 HENRI MATISSE Arab Café 1913.
'It must be difficult for them to conceive of the turbulent minds of the Christians and that restlessness of ours which urges us on to novelties. We notice a thousand things which are lacking with these people. Their ignorance produces their calm and their happiness; but we ourselves, are we at the summit of what a more advanced civilization can produce? They are closer to nature in a thousand ways: their dress, the form of their shoes. And so beauty has a share in everything that they make. As for us, in our corsets, our tight shoes, our ridiculous pinching clothes, we are pitiful! The graces exact vengeance for our science.' (Entry for 27 April 1832, Tangiers, The Journal of Eugène Delacroix, trans. Walter Pach, New York, 1948, 122.)

153   ANDRÉ DERAIN   The Pool of London   1906.
In some of his other London pictures, Derain followed the river further to the east: Tower Bridge is visible in the background here. Monet had not travelled this far, nor had he painted the busy commercial life of the river that Derain describes in this picture – with its cranes, smoke and dockers. Thus Derain was showing himself to be independent of his illustrious predecessor. At the same time it is intriguing to note that Derain uses his brightest, most unrelenting palette when he tackles a motif that Monet had painted before him, as in Charing Cross Bridge, London (see plate 134). Here, without that unseen challenge, he adapts its pure reds, greens and blues most cleverly to describe a grey, heavily overcast day.

154   MAURICE DE VLAMINCK   Locks at Bougival   1908.

This work is cleverly executed. Although grass, water, towpath, clouds and sky are all very freely painted, there is nothing particularly 'wild' in their coloration. It is against this rather conventional background that the reds of the trees, both near and far, and the roofs on the far side, find their startling force and power. It is this red, in fact, that structures and organizes the whole canvas. To the left a little red-hulled steamboat can be seen slowly rising in the lock, which is itself faintly traced in the same red. To the far right stands a red bollard. Despite the strong recessional pull of the composition as the river, trees and foreground retreat back into space, the reds come quickly and loudly forward towards the spectator.

155 MAURICE DE VLAMINCK   Houses and Trees   1906.
Vlaminck painted this landscape in the village where Renoir had painted
his Luncheon of the Boating Party (see plate 62) some twenty years or
so earlier. Many of the Fauves returned to places where the Impressionists
had been painting in the 1870s and 1880s; they emulated their
predecessors' rapidly recorded responses to the scene before them, but
armed with a knowledge of Post-Impressionist colour – hence the presence
of such bold, bright reds and oranges. Matisse had first used these reds
beneath the southern sun where his departure from realism might be
justified, or at least partially explained by the need to describe the intense
glare of the light. Vlaminck has here transposed them to the greyer
skies of the north.

157 GEORGES BRAQUE   Landscape at La Ciotat   1907.
After his initiation into Fauvism in the summer of 1906, when he was
painting with Friesz in Antwerp, Braque soon decided to tighten and
strengthen the structure of his compositions. His concern was felt by all the
Fauves: having first released the fire of pure colour, the next step was to
harness its power. For most of the Fauves, including Braque, this was soon
to prove an uncongenial path; but here, Braque organizes his canvas in a
number of different ways. The brilliant yellows and greens of the rocks and
foliage, all encased in prussian blue, spill and bleed into one another. They
create a sense of homogeneity as our eye travels up the canvas.

156 OTHON FRIESZ La Ciotat 1907.
Though his name is not instantly recognizable today, Friesz was to become one of the most famous painters of his generation. He cleverly integrated avant-garde sympathies with establishment success. In 1934 Raoul Dufy described him as: 'the most gifted painter of our generation'. (M. Gauthier, Othon Friesz, Paris, 1957, 125.) In the paintings Friesz made in 1907 at La Ciotat in the south of France, he fully embraced a Fauvist idiom, though he never broached the large, flat areas of colour developed by Matisse and Derain. Here the bold use of a red contour for the mountain and the exciting abbreviations of his calligraphic brushwork testify to his enthusiastic appropriation of some of Fauvism's innovations.

158 GEORGES BRAQUE Viaduct at L'Estaque 1907–08.
The reduction of Braque's palette to greens, yellows and blues, with the occasional touch of red, together with the motif itself, makes this picture a deliberate act of homage to Cézanne (see plate 118). To a certain extent Braque has simplified, even schematized, Cézanne's techniques here: the way in which he rigidly encases his forms with a blue contour, for instance, the homogeneity of the brushwork, or the rather obvious use of the trees to frame the view. Braque needed to find a way of controlling the brightness of the Fauve palette: Cézanne provided him with the perfect example.

159 ANDRÉ DERAIN Cadaquès I 1910.
In 1925 Matisse said: 'Cézanne, you see, is a sort of God of painting. Dangerous, his influence? So what? Too bad for those without the strength to survive it.' (Jack D. Flam, Matisse on Art, London, 1973, 55.) This rather haughty remark was certainly not directed at Derain; it probably reveals the difficulties Matisse himself encountered at certain points in his career as he struggled to survive this god's influence. Nevertheless, Derain's prolonged, concentrated study of Cézanne's work from 1907 to 1910 does seem to have stifled the creative energies he had displayed during the Fauve years. This canvas seems rather an insipid offspring of a Cézanne such as Gardanne (see plate 176).

160 OTHON FRIESZ Travail à L'Automne 1908.
Louis Vauxcelles, the critic who had baptized the Fauves three years before in 1905, described this painting – Friesz's first major figurative piece, exhibited at the 1908 Salon des Indépendants – as belonging to the essential French classical tradition. He also admitted Cézanne to this tradition. Cézanne, it must be said, rarely painted subjects extolling the virtues of agricultural labour. His peasant types, his Card Players, for instance (see plate 122), certainly do not move with the same nervous energy that Friesz has given to his workers. Friesz's composition does recall, however, certain aspects of Cézanne's final Bathers pictures such as Les Grandes Baigneuses (see plate 125): note the framing vault of trees in the foreground, for instance, beneath which all the figures are arranged.

169

161 HENRI MATISSE La Danse II 1909–10.

It seems most appropriate to quote a line here from Yeats's poem 'Among Schoolchildren': 'How can we know the dancer from the dance?' For in this huge decorative panel, painted by Matisse for his wealthy Russian patron Sergei Shchukin, all notions of individuality are lost. As these mythic, prehistoric dancers whirl round and round, their bodies are stretched taut with curved distortions; every other consideration besides the exclusive, collective concentration upon what will become a trance-like, essential rhythm are completely ignored. They have not yet quite reached that stage; the outstretched hands of two of the dancers are about to complete the circle.

162 AUGUSTE RODIN Dancing Figure 1905.

Late in life, Rodin (1840-1917) became friends with the famous Parisian dancers, Isadora Duncan and Loïe Fuller. It was they, initially, who inspired him to make a series of drawings of single dancing figures. Rodin has reduced the human form to the simplest of curving arabesques, in-filling these with the barest of colour washes. On occasion, this wash runs over the edge of the pencil line – but the effect is far from slapdash. In fact, these watercolours of dancers by Rodin provide one of the very few precedents for the simplicity, freedom and grace found in Matisse's Shchukin dancers.

163   HENRI MATISSE   Zorah on the Terrace   1912.
Eighty years after Delacroix, Matisse too travelled to Morocco. Zorah's
slippers seem pretty conclusive proof that Matisse had also read
Delacroix's diary entry for 27 April 1832 – quite possible as it had been
published in 1893. And the goldfish provide further evidence. Matisse
noticed how the Moroccans would stare at the goldfish for hours, as they
relaxed and drank their coffee and as the fish interminably circled their
bowl (see plate 151). These fish became for Matisse symbols for an ideal,
meditative tranquillity – precisely the qualities of calm and happiness that
Delacroix had so admired in the Moroccans. And Matisse has contained
all this richness, of light and of patterned cloth – but really of a way of life
– within a sharp and austere geometric scaffold.

Chapter 4

New Geometries

One of the many portraits Henri Matisse (1869–1954) painted of his daughter Marguerite now hangs in the Musée Picasso, Paris, close to the Place des Vosges. Matisse had given it to Pablo Picasso (1881–1973) in 1907, in exchange for one of the Spanish painter's works, in what must have been some sort of ceremony to mark their mutual respect. The Matisse portrait is in good condition, apparently unscathed by the fact that Picasso and his friends used to use it as a dartboard. That, anyway, is the story recounted by the poet and critic André Salmon (1881–1969). It is most probably untrue.[1] A friend of Picasso, Salmon was a vigorous defender of his painting in the Parisian press, often at others' expense, and at Matisse's in particular. Any darts that punctured the surface of Matisse's canvas would probably have been of a verbal variety. Salmon's story, however, is a dramatic, if fictional illustration of the intense rivalry that was to characterize the relationship between these two giants of twentieth-century painting.

As personalities, they could hardly have been more different. If Matisse was 'the professor', dignified and reasonable in his approach to his craft, there seemed always to be something demonic and aggressive about Picasso's creative spirit (*see plate 165*). For example, the female nude was a central subject for both artists. Yet for all the voluptuousness of Matisse's figures, his attitude to them seems almost chaste. For Picasso, on the other hand, to paint them was comparable to, even an extension of an essentially sexual act. The American expatriate Leo Stein (1872–1947), was later to recount:

One could not see Picasso without getting an indelible impression. His short, solid but somehow graceful figure. His firm head with hair falling forward, careless but not slovenly, emphasized his extraordinary seeing eyes. I used to say that when Picasso looked at a drawing or a print, I was surprised that anything was left on the paper, so absorbing was his gaze. He spoke little and seemed neither remote nor intimate – just quite completely

there . . . He seemed more real than most people while doing nothing about it . . . The homes, persons and minds of Picasso and Matisse were extreme contrasts. Matisse – bearded, but with propriety; spectacled neatly; intelligent; freely spoken, but a little shy in an immaculate room, a place for everything and everything in its place, both within his head and without. Picasso – with nothing to say except an occasional sparkle, his work developing with no plan, but with the immediate outpourings of an intuition which kept on to exhaustion after which there was nothing till another came.[2]

165   Photograph of Picasso in his studio, Paris, 1916.

164   GEORGES BRAQUE   The Portugese   1911.
In this painting the Portuguese man of the title is playing a guitar in a café. The figure, objects and the space they inhabit, however, have largely been fractured and shattered, only to be reconstructed again on a geometric scaffold. A few references or clues to the world of appearances remain: a curtain and cord, the hole of a guitar, and the guitar strings, which also stand for the man's hands, eyes and moustache. If in the earlier still-life Violon et Cruche *(see plate 196) it seems as though Braque might possibly have painted his subject from life, here he has clearly conceived of painting as a type of sign language.*

It was in Paris early in 1906, at Leo and Gertude Stein's flat at 27 rue de Fleurus on the Left Bank, that Picasso and Matisse met for the first time. Right from the start they seemed to see each other as rivals – in the first place for the Steins' patronage, and only a little later for the leadership of the Parisian avant garde. Matisse was ten years older than Picasso, and by 1907 he had occupied this position of leader for over two years. He had painted his *Blue Nude (see plate 150)* in 1907 – a pictorial revision, inspired by Paul Cézanne (1839–1906), of the pastoral ideal he had attempted to realize one year earlier in the *Bonheur de Vivre (see plate 135)*. It was from this base that Matisse was to develop the refined

166 PABLO PICASSO La Vie 1903.
As the title (meaning Life) suggests, Picasso has presented us with an allegory. A young naked couple stand on the left. The man conspicuously points to a clothed, elder woman holding a sleeping baby on the right. Perhaps the man in the foreground is indicating that if the two produce a child (the position of the woman's legs suggest that this is her desire), her wish for fulfilment in childbirth will end in loneliness – a fate that she is reluctant to contemplate. Other, more autobiographical, interpretations are possible: the man's face resembles that of a friend of Picasso who committed suicide at about the same time.

decorative richness of subsequent paintings such as *Bathers with a Turtle, Zorah on the Terrace,* and *Arab Café (see plates 138, 163 and 151)*. But it was in the same year, and from a similar starting point, that Picasso was to evolve in a completely different direction. He, too, was to learn much from Cézanne's legacy, but he would apply the master's lessons to create works that were diametrically opposed to Matisse's. The result was to be a style called Cubism.

Cubism would isolate Matisse with his decorative concerns and would establish Picasso as the undisputed master of the Parisian avant garde. It would also to bring to an end traditions of European painting that had existed for five hundred years, and would itself become the principal bedrock for many subsequent innovations in twentieth-century art, architecture and design. Even looking back today at the first Cubist paintings, they still seem modern; yet at the time they were painted, before the First World War, the car was only just beginning to replace the horse. More so than any other contemporary movement in the visual arts, Cubism managed categorically to separate the nineteenth century from the twentieth.

Rope and Paraffin

Pablo Picasso was born in 1881 in Malaga, Spain. From an early age he was taught drawing and painting by his father, who was himself an art teacher. He displayed uncommonly precocious talent. In 1901, at the age of twenty, he settled in Paris, living in a strange building known as the 'Bateau Lavoir' in the rue Ravignan in Montmartre. For the next few years he rummaged around and experimented with the various styles and subjects of his contemporaries, influenced in particular by the work of Henri de Toulouse-Lautrec (1864–1901), Edvard Munch (1863–1944) and Vincent van Gogh (1853–1890). A cold, pale blue dominates the majority of his paintings from this period, and he tends to depict melancholy subjects that focus on the misery and suffering of human existence *(see plate 166)*.

By 1905 Picasso had changed tack; leaving behind the morbid blues of the preceding years, he seemed now to prefer taking rose or pink as the dominant hue. His works lightened in mood accordingly, and though these pictures of acrobats and other circus performers still dealt with those dwelling on the margins of life, the figures are described with a calm dignity rather than with the sometimes heavy-handed morbidity of the earlier Blue period *(see plate 181)*. Picasso and his friends had begun to frequent the Montmartrois Cirque Médrano, following the example of others like Georges Seurat (1859–1891) and Lautrec before them *(see plate 167)*. Much of the spirit of the circus was to infect Picasso's behaviour, as years later Gertrude Stein (1874–1946) recorded: according to her account a young German named Wilhelm Uhde (1848–1911), a friend of Picasso, 'kept a kind of private art shop. It was here that Picasso and Braque went to see him in their newest and roughest clothes and in their best Cirque Médrano fashion kept up a constant fire of introducing each other to him and asking each other to introduce each other.'[3] The game presumably went on for hours. As part of this spillage of the absurd and slapstick into his everyday life, Picasso also began to dress in circus fashion. Gertrude Stein

167 MARIE LAURENCIN *Group of Artists* 1908.
Laurencin paints a charming, deliberately naïve memorial to the early years of Cubism. A rather perplexed Guillaume Apollinaire (1880–1914), poet and one of the first champions of Cubism in the Parisian press, sits in the centre holding a book. Picasso is seen in profile to the left, painted in a way that is reminiscent of some of the heads in his own Demoiselles d'Avignon (see plate 194). To the right, his mistress Fernande Olivier looks out coyly. Apollinaire's mistress, Laurencin herself, presides over the whole group, holding a simple flower.

again records him saying, looking back on the 'Bateau Lavoir' days: 'You have no idea how hard it was and expensive it was in those days to find English tweed or a French imitation that would look rough enough and dirty enough.'[4] This was more than just a young man's posturing. For much of the wit and fantasy of the make-believe world of circus would later inform the ingenious and intelligent lampoons of his later Cubist paintings. Some acquaintance with this particular strain of humour is essential if one is to grasp the playful nature of what is at the same time a highly intellectual and demanding style of painting (*see plates 184, 185 and 186*).

Meanwhile Picasso's painting was about to undergo another fundamental transformation. In 1906, still within what is generally called his Rose or Pink period, and in line also with other contemporary developments, Picasso began to evolve a singular, massive, but unmistakably classical style (*see plate 183*). It was under this particular aegis that at the beginning of the year he started to work on a portrait of his main patron, Gertrude Stein (*see plate 182*). Both sitter and artist endured over eighty sittings in the early months, and yet Picasso put the unfinished portrait aside, unable to pinpoint or remedy his dissatisfactions with it, apart from painting out the head. In May, shortly before leaving Paris for a holiday, he saw an exhibition at the Louvre of primitive Iberian sculpture. It was under the influence of these sculptures that Picasso repainted the head and hands of the portrait on his return to Paris in August.

The question of who it was among the avant garde that first realized the pictorial potential of primitive sculpture has never been proved. André Derain (1880–1954), Maurice de Vlaminck (1876–1858), Henri Matisse, Georges Braque

(1882–1963) and Picasso himself have all been credited with being the first to collect it, though in fairness it must be said that the discovery was made by one of the previous generation: Paul Gauguin (1848–1903). In any case, all of the above are certainly known to have been collecting primitive sculpture by at least the beginning of 1907. And for Picasso the revelation was enormous: here was an art that was powerfully expressive of feeling and emotion, yet one that paid little or no heed to any traditional doctrine of realism.

Picasso's thinking was also just beginning to be affected by Cézanne's painting. Possibly stimulated by Matisse's *Blue Nude (see plate 150)*, he too decided in the first months of 1907 to produce a large, figurative work of nude figures inspired by Cézanne's late Bathers paintings. Seventeen preparatory sketches survive for his *Demoiselles d'Avignon (see plate 168)*. From these it is clear that the finished piece – on one level at least – was going to comment somewhat ironically on the idealized setting Cézanne had given his bathers to inhabit. Instead of being figures that occupy a timeless, fertile landscape, Picasso's bathers, the 'demoiselles', are a group of prostitutes in a brothel. As the number of sketches increased, however, Picasso exchanged the Cézannesque idiom of this early notation for one that owed more to the Iberian sculpture he had used as inspiration in the portrait of Gertrude Stein. It was in this style that he painted the first version of the final canvas in May.

At this point he was to assimilate another jolt from the primitive; this time from the African sculpture he saw at the

168 PABLO PICASSO *Study for Les Demoiselles d'Avignon* 1907.
This early study for Picasso's seminal painting blatantly reveals its initial derivation from Cézanne. Firstly, in the nervous repetition of small arabesque lines which build up the bodies of the figures (see also plate 114), and then in two specific borrowings. The crouching nude in the bottom right-hand corner originates in one of the bathers in the Cézanne painting owned by Matisse (see plate 115). Above her, the nude with raised arms adopts a pose often employed by Cézanne. The two men who invade the brothel here were to be removed in the artist's final version of the picture.

Ethnographic Museum at the Trocadéro in Paris. In 1937 Christian Zervos, the first of Picasso's myriad biographers, wrote: 'Thirty years later Picasso still speaks with profound emotion of the shock he received that day upon seeing the African sculpture.'[5] In July he returned to his monumental canvas and repainted the two figures to the far right-hand side of the picture (see plate 194).

Even more than the Iberian sculpture he admired, the African pieces he saw rejected cherished European notions of realism that avant-garde artists since the Impressionists had been questioning and harrying but had never quite completely abandoned (see plate 170). According to André Salmon, Picasso later described this sculpture as 'reasonable';[6] its anonymous makers had carved the wood in order to express

169 JEAN-AUGUSTE-DOMINIQUE INGRES Le Bain Turc 1862.

This Turkish brothel scene was painted by Ingres (1780–1867) when he was in his eighties. There is something rather excessive about this mountainous, teeming pile of immaculate young bodies, but at the same time Ingres tempers his octogenarian fantasies by depicting his prostitutes with cold sensuality. Each of those too-rounded hips and provocative, outwardly thrust breasts is encased by a fine contour. There is only the subtlest, finest modelling on their faultless, pneumatic flesh. But this is a pornographic kind of perfection.

their experience of the world – not according to what the eye could see, but as the mind apprehended it. They had depicted the human form as they understood it, not as it appears. In the end, it was more a conceptual than a perceptual art.

The striated masks and violently extreme formal distortions in the two right-hand figures of Picasso's painting heralded the eruption of such ideas in the history of modern European art. Moreover, the squatting figure in the corner shows us her back at the same time as she faces us, resting her chin in her hand. Above her, her partner's breasts seem modelled as concave rather than convex. Everywhere, in fact, traditional notions of representation have been quite blatantly, almost playfully subverted. Picasso's demoiselles confront the viewer in a compressed and claustrophobic space. There has been no attempt to situate them in a traditional three-dimensional box. The glacial blue and white draperies slice across this flattened stage set, while the plush red curtains to the left, similarly sharp and angular, are deprived of any of their usual textured softness.

All these subversions or distortions were not simply made for their own sake, but relate to Picasso's expressive treatment of his theme. It is as though the seductiveness of flesh and the caress of velvet and silk, all the usual enticements of the brothel (see plate 169), have been peeled away. And by stripping the image of its sensual camouflage, Picasso exposes, to put it mildly, the raw and aggressive nature of its sexual func-

tion. Nothing escapes this terrible revelation. The spectator would cut himself as deeply on the melon in the foreground as on one of the demoiselles' razored elbows. For the blank, listless expressions of the two central nudes, staring directly out at us, force us into the position of the prospective client reviewing the merchandise. All the formal distortions seem close to a portrayal of the client's or the viewer's violent imagination where both viewer and subjects become sexual predators. As one of Picasso's friends said on first seeing the picture late in 1907: 'You paint as if you wanted to force us to eat rope or drink paraffin.'[7] The friend was Georges Braque, who had been introduced to Picasso by the poet and critic Guillaume Apollinaire (1880–1914). Recently involved in the Fauve group headed by Matisse, Braque had begun, by the summer of 1907, to dissociate his work from that of the Fauves – and their uninhibited enjoyment of colour. Under the influence of Cézanne, he had been trying independently to formulate a more disciplined style. It was at this point in his development that he first met Picasso, that he saw and was so shocked by the *Demoiselles d'Avignon*. Cubism was to be their collaborative creation.

The Path to Cubism

Most writers on Cubism have argued that the *Demoiselles d'Avignon* is not a fully fledged Cubist painting. Its expressive subject matter and bright colouring have separated it from what are called Cubist works – more restrained both in theme and colour. But as Braque studied some of the innovatory aspects of Cézanne, and Picasso was willing to flout pictorial convention, the combined forces of the two would shortly bring about its birth. Braque responded immediately to the *Demoiselles* with a large female nude, in which he filtered into a Cézannesque mould some of its radical stylistic mutations but none of its thematic violence. In fact, it was Braque's work that first attracted the analogy with cubes. In the summer of 1908 Braque had gone back to L'Estaque, Cézanne's country, to paint landscapes (*see plates 171 and 172*). On his return to Paris that autumn some of the paintings he had produced were refused entry at the Salon d'Automne; Matisse, who was serving that year on the selection committee, was behind the decision. In protest Braque withdrew all his works; he exhibited them at the gallery of a private dealer, Daniel-Henry Kahnweiler, in the rue Vignon, where he had been selling his work since 1907. Louis Vauxcelles (b. 1870), who christened the Fauves three years before, gave the show a short notice in *Gil Blas*: 'He constructs deformed metallic ·men, terribly simplified. He despises form, reduces everything, places and figures and houses, to geometrical schemas, to cubes. Let us not make fun of him, since he is honest. And let us wait.'[8] Immediately below Vauxcelles's review, by a coincidence so symbolic that it seems to have been fated, there was an article on Wilbur Wright, one of the Wright Brothers, entitled 'The Conquest of the Air' (*see also plate 17*): the simultaneous announcement of profound cultural and technological change. Picasso did not miss the point; he was later to use 'Wilbur' as a nickname for Braque. For the moment, however, the two pursued separate paths; they only really started to work closely together early in 1909. In 1908 Braque continued to extend Cézanne's developments in land-

170   Dan ceremonial mask, Ivory Coast, late nineteenth century.

scape (*see plate 195*). Picasso, meanwhile, in another extraordinary effort, produced a second massive figurative piece which shows that he too had assimilated some of Cézanne's lessons (*see plate 187*). He retained the thematic boldness of *Les Demoiselles*, however, in this new commentary on Cézanne's Bathers pictures. The historian Leo Steinberg has since memorably described the picture as a kind of creation myth. Noting the nominal differentiation in gender between the right- and left-hand figures, male and female respectively, and the way in which they both seem derived, or even in the process of evolving from the more incohate, central figure, Steinberg describes the picture as 'a visualization of those irrepressible forces through which the human condition is polarized';[9] in other words, of the original moment of a natural separation of the sexes, as Steinberg goes on to explain:

The whole story is given. It begins in the subhuman clod at center – primitive and inert, barely evolved from the bedrock behind, a figure that seems less a bathing companion than an interior condition personified in a preconscious hominid, the reserved matrix whence humanity sunders forth, the he and the she of it.

While the painting does in fact owe much to Cézanne, Picasso has relocated the master's bathers in his own version of Genesis. As Steinberg colourfully put it: 'Where Cézanne's Arcadians sport under open skies in agreeable weather, Picasso finds encaved sleepers toiling in sunless heat . . . In *Three Women*, the pleating of rigid flesh materializes like a terrain under geological pressure.'[10] Picasso probably found the more visionary among Cézanne's later works just as stimulating in their expression of vast, inhuman but natural forces as

171 GEORGES BRAQUE   Houses at L'Estaque   1908.
This landscape was painted during the summer of 1908 while Braque continued to study the work of Cézanne. It was one of the paintings rejected by Matisse from the Salon d'Automne later that year, and which was subsequently dubbed 'Cubist' in the Parisian press. Braque flattens the illusion of space by leaving out the sky. The walls and roofs are not modelled according to a consistent light source: shadows fall across their planar surfaces somewhat arbitrarily; their edges, sharply defined in places, fade out in others, so that the plane of wall or roof bleeds into its neighbour. Despite all these liberties, the image is not too dissimilar to a photograph taken of the same scene.

the Bathers pictures themselves – especially such landscapes as the late views of Mont Sainte-Victoire. Whatever the case, he has here adopted Cézanne's narrow tonal range and shallow illusion of space, and he continued these researches the following year (*see plates 173 and 188*).

A Mirror Held up to Nature

It was in 1909 that the close association between Picasso and Braque began, a working relationship that was to last until the outbreak of war in 1914. 'We saw each other every day and talked a lot and things were said between us that will never be repeated . . . We were like two mountain climbers roped together,' Braque said of these years. Picasso is quoted as saying: 'Either I went to Braque's studio or Braque came to mine. Each of us had to see what the other had done during the day.'[11] The two men made a well-balanced team. As Wilhelm Uhde recorded: 'Braque's temperament was limpid,

precise and bourgeois; Picasso's sombre, excessive and revolutionary.'[12]

It is worth considering at this point exactly what Braque and Picasso had learned from Cézanne. We have already seen how Cézanne's first followers in the 1890s – the Nabis – saw him as a decorative painter. By 1905 or so this view had altered so that he was seen in more classical terms, and at the same time as an artist who mediated between a flat, two-dimensional decorative style and more traditional, three-dimensional, volumetric concerns.

Thus, in a late still-life by Cézanne. *Still-life with Curtain (see plate 174)*, for example, we find that the edge of a table-top has been distorted. Its leading edge has not only been broken but missed out altogether – below the central plate, towards the left. In the right-hand half of the painting the flat surface of the table appears to have been tipped up somewhat, so that instead of receding easily back into an imaginary three-dimensional space, it seems to be making an effort to align itself with the flat surface of the canvas. Cézanne made these sorts of adjustments because he was combining information about his objects taken from a number of different viewpoints. The painting thus records views of the objects taken at different moments in time and from separate positions in space; yet these various perspectives are synchronized and ordered. Spatial relationships are still clearly described but we understand them, rather than feel them as immediately related to optical perception. Cézanne himself said: 'There are two things in the painter, the eye and the mind; each of them should aid the other. It is necessary to work at their mutual development, in the eye by looking at nature, in the mind by the logic of organised sensations.'[13] Cézanne's very last works were, it seemed, based as much on theory as on observation. Thus, in a watercolour such as *The Forest – The Park at*

172   Photograph by Daniel-Henry Kahnweiler of the motif of Braque's *Houses at L'Estaque (see plate 171)*.

Château Noir (see plate 203), Cézanne's colour modulations, which veered towards the abstract whilst to some extent being independent of the senses and not literally descriptive, were yet expository metaphors for his sensations. In the end, Cézanne's art provided Picasso and Braque with the foundations on which to create a new type of painting that was both representational and non-illusionistic.

The roughness of Cézanne's surface textures and his lack of conventional finish were also important components of this achievement. That, anyway, is what Braque thought:

When Veronese paints two apples, it is beautiful, very beautiful if you wish. But for me it's theater, it's pompous. It took many years, even centuries, for this theatrical spirit to be eliminated. Cézanne gave it the coup de grâce. He swept painting clear of the idea of mastery.[14]

It is this lack of theatre, pomposity, or mastery which makes it impossible for the viewer in front of a Cézanne to forget that he is looking at a picture, not an illusion. This idea of the dignity of the work of art, its right to exist on its own without reference to visual reality, was forcefully expressed by Braque in relation to his own work:

I couldn't portray a woman in all her natural loveliness . . . I haven't the skill. No one has. I must, therefore, create a new sort of beauty, the beauty that appears to me in terms of volume, of line, of mass, of weight . . . I want to expose the Absolute, and not merely the factitious woman.[15]

Here we can see how Braque, having recognized one of the implications latent in Cézanne's work, has extended it for new purposes. Cézanne claimed that art should be a harmony parallel to nature that involved the interaction of eye and mind; Braque claims a greater status for the work of art – one fiercely independent of visual sensations and firmly rooted in the mind. For the next four years Picasso and Braque pursued such ideas with wit, invention and intellectual rigour. They limited their subjects to the studio, the café and the occasional portrait, and their palette to a narrow range of earth tones so as to be free to explore such ideas without other interference.

In *Violon et Cruche (see plate 196)* it is as though Braque has taken a traditional view of his objects, and then shattered this mirror held up to nature – only to reconstitute its fragmented shards arbitrarily on the flat picture surface. Edges are broken, light and shade hopelessly inconsistent. In fact, it seems as though the objects have been broken down into numerous dark and light planes that lie at a bewildering number of different angles. At times the violin and pitcher seem to bleed into the surrounding space that would normally separate them but which here seems as present and as tactile as the objects themselves. If Cézanne had sometimes combined in his still-lifes information taken from three or four different viewpoints, Braque has increased this to such a pitch that the very integrity of his objects is threatened.

The multiplicity of viewpoints in such early Cubist works was described by the critics in purely temporal terms. In traditional perspective, the position of each object in a painting stands in a fixed relation to every other and to the viewer – the painting thus also describing one moment in time. Picasso and Braque shattered this traditional idea of unity by combining in one picture views of an object taken from a

173 PABLO PICASSO Factory at Horta de Ebro 1909.
Painted in the summer of 1909, during which Picasso continued his pursuit and development of Cézanne's legacy, this landscape is dominated by the tall chimney in the centre. We look down its diamond-shaped aperture, yet straight ahead at its shaft. Two views are thus combined into one image. At the same time, the strong contrasts of light and shade employed by Picasso model this feature in such a way that it seems closer to us than its distant position in the landscape would suggest. It is in ways like these that Picasso confuses our expectations, causing the elements of his landscape to oscillate between flatness and depth.

multitude of different angles. In this way, they were giving the viewer a pictorial account of how one's knowledge of an object is built up through the passage of time. Cubism was thus a highly realistic art but one that broke with established methods of representation.

Picasso and Braque certainly needed critics to give this kind of reasoned explanation of their experiments if the public were to understand them. During the years of their close, almost daily collaboration, however, Picasso and Braque rarely exhibited their paintings. When they did, they avoided the two large avant-garde salons, the Indépendants and the Salon d'Automne, choosing instead to show their work at small, private galleries like Kahnweiler's. Through the patronage of the Steins, they also succeeded in finding a modest but faithful number of private collectors to buy their work.

Not being compelled to sell their wares in the largest (and hence more conservative) markets gave them an independence that was to have an important bearing on their development, enabling them to refine and pursue the experimental nature of their early Cubist paintings. In *Violon et Cruche* Braque had included at the top of the picture an illusionistically painted nail, which holds some papers to the wall and even casts a shadow on it *(see plate 196)*. It is the only part of the painting where Braque has retained a traditional method of representation, one that is brilliantly and categorically subverted by the rest of the work. This blatant juxtaposition of two opposed systems of representation, however, also indicates the artifice of all such systems, whether based on a fixed, static view of nature or one that understands a variety of viewpoints. As Picasso was later to say: 'We all know that

Art is not truth. Art is a lie that makes us realize truth.'[16] From the hints implied by Braque's nail, Picasso and Braque developed Cubism as an investigation into the nature of art itself and its relation to external reality. It was an investigation conducted, to use Gertrude Stein's phrase, 'in their best Cirque Médrano fashion' (see plates 164 and 189).

Picasso's *Still-Life with Chair Caning* (see plate 190) continued the attack on the illusionistic tradition in a more radical but similarly intellectually playful manner. The subject, a still-life, could hardly be more neutral. Picasso, however, is not attacking or examining the idea that the painter should describe nature but rather the way in which nature is described. Firstly, he rejects traditional notions of pictorial space. Since the development in the Renaissance of fixed-point perspective, pictorial space had acted like a three-dimensional box within which the protagonists of a picture – figures, landscape elements or still-life objects – took their places. Here, though, the viewer need not imagine three-dimensional space, for the glass, pipe and newspaper are firmly stuck on to the two-dimensional surface of the picture.

Picasso also rejects the painter's traditional materials. He has represented the chair in his still-life with a piece of fabric printed in the pattern of chair caning; he has simply cut it out and stuck it on to the canvas. While this piece of fabric retains some sort of illusionistic function, that sense seems simultaneously to be denied: both because it is surrounded by blatantly non-illusionistic forms and also because it is machine-made. Picasso, then, also seems to be questioning the belief that a painting should display the manual skill of the artist. The coil of rope also participates in this questioning

174 PAUL CÉZANNE Still-Life with Curtain 1898–99.
The curled lip of the jug is described with small touches of blue, green and yellow; the napkin has been treated in the same way. It is not modelled with a crude combination of black, white and grey, but with a mixture of blues, greens and yellows which not only serve to indicate its complex folds and pleats, but also relate to other areas of the canvas – the greens in the curtain, the yellows in the table, the blues in the shadows. It is by this subtle use of colour that Cézanne manages to forge a strong, organic cohesion between the disparate objects of this still-life. If Picasso and Braque ignored Cézanne's colouristic virtuosity, they explored other facets inherent in his achievements.

acting as it does as an ironic substitute for the easel picture's traditionally gilt frame. Materials from the real world have been introduced into the world of painting, highlighting its artificiality and attempting to blur the distinctions usually made between the two spheres.

For all its radical elements, however, Picasso is still describing the real world – chair, table, glass and pipe. In this sense his picture functions in a very traditional manner. For Cubism was never an abstract art. Its neatness was that it remained descriptive of visual reality without limiting itself to the imitation of appearances.

Collage, which took materials from the everyday world and repositioned them in the realm of art, was the inevitable climax of the prolonged dissection by Picasso and Braque of painting's traditional function as a description of nature (see plates 191 and 192). It reached its apogee, perhaps, when one of their followers, a Spanish painter named Juan Gris (1887–1927), painted a Cubist rendition of a bathroom. When he reached that part of his composition where the bathroom mirror was to stand, he simply stuck a piece of a real mirror on to his canvas – what seems now a particularly clever attack on illusionism.

A New Movement

Juan Gris had been living close to Picasso in Montmartre since 1906 but he only began to paint seriously in 1911 (see plate 175). He quickly assimilated the pictorial language Picasso and Braque had been formulating over the previous two years – the fragmentation of planes, collage and the like – to produce his own Cubist paintings. These are immediately distinguishable from those of both Picasso and Braque by the austere clarity of their composition and the smoother texture of their surface (see plates 197 and 198). The rough edges and gritty feel of the forms produced by Picasso and Braque (coarse like the tweed fabrics they liked to wear) seem to speak of the intuitive rush of inspiration, as yet another traditionally cherished tenet of illusionism fell under their experimental probing. Their works, like Cézanne's before them, spurn the varnished patina of paintings that were polished to a high degree of finish (see plate 176). Gris, on the other hand, enjoyed giving his works the pristine quality of a fully resolved, irrefutable geometrical formula.

These three central protagonists inspired others to follow and in 1911 the Cubist movement emerged into the public domain at both the Salon des Indépendants, where all their works were hung together in room 41, and at the Salon d'Automne. It was only at this point that the term 'Cubism' began to be widely used in the press. Cubism was to reach its zenith in October the following year, at the Section d'Or exhibition at the Galerie de la Boëtie in Paris. Gris took part in this exhibition, but characteristically, both Picasso and Braque abstained. Thus, Cubism's public image was first defined by painters such as Albert Gleizes (1881–1953), whose conversion to a Cubist style now reveals itself to have been rather superficial (see plate 200).

Meanwhile, two other painters, independently of Picasso and Braque, had also been making significant advances as a result of their study of Cézanne: Robert Delaunay (1885–1941) and Fernand Léger (1881–1955). The two were

175 JUAN GRIS Portrait of Picasso 1912.

friends, and would have been aware of what Picasso and Braque had embarked upon as early as 1910 when Léger first met Picasso. Léger, however, had already been applying some of Cézanne's spatial ambiguities in his own large works such as *Nus dans un Paysage (see plate 199)*. In a manner comparable to that of Picasso and Braque in their paintings of 1908 and 1909, Léger attempted to depict his giant, heroic wood-cutters within a compressed space that hovers between flatness and recession. He emphasized this two-dimensional element in *La Noce (see plate 177)*, a painting he produced the following year as a wedding present for André Salmon. Here we are permitted, through the gaps in the diaphonous, iridescent clouds, to view Léger's characteristically tubular figures as they bustle above distant scenes of streets and houses. Léger's robust formal language shows itself capable of tender inflection in this peculiarly poetic and affectionate portrait of city life. His enthusiasm for the changes brought by modern technology to every sphere of life was complete, untainted by forebodings that increasing mechanization was in any way detrimental to human life. He expressed this optimism in a lecture he gave in Paris in June 1914:

The breaks with the past that have occurred in our visual world are innumerable. I will choose the most striking. The advertisement hoarding, which brutally cuts across a landscape in obedience to the dictates of modern commerce, is one of the things that have aroused most fury among men of so-called good taste . . . And yet that yellow or red billboard, shouting in a timid landscape, is the finest of possible reasons for the new painting . . . Now the railway trains and automobiles, with their plumes of smoke or

dust, take all the dynamic quality for themselves, and the landscape becomes secondary and derivative.[17]

For Léger, the changes in the visual world brought about by the billboard demanded similar transformations in that of painting. It too would have to emulate the dynamism of the railway train. In the same way that the bold colour and furious energy of these modern phenomena placed the subtleties of nature's own palette at a disadvantage, so any modern painting would overcome the timidities of the past by the power of its formal language, and above all, he argued, by contrast. By 1913 Léger had evolved a range of simple, fundamental pictorial contrasts with which he would celebrate the newness of the modern visual world. For the most part he chose subjects directly related to this theme – machine-like leviathans, for instance, working as heroically in the new factories as his massive, rural woodcutters had done four years earlier *(see plates 7 and 177)*. Despite all this mechanization,

176 PAUL CÉZANNE Gardanne 1885–86.
Cézanne evidently left this landscape unfinished, unhappy that once again he was unable to translate his sensations into paint. Yet this shortcoming was to be Braque's and Picasso's gain. It is easy to spot the beginnings here of the geometric scaffold on which Braque would later arrange his fragmented Cubist images. The textural discrepancies between the parts of the canvas Cézanne managed to cover with paint and those which he left bare, were also reflected in the Cubist masters' paintings. Braque's The Portugese *(see plate 164), like Cézanne's landscape here – though less recognizable and more abstract – is most densely painted towards the centre of the canvas, fading out somewhat towards the edges.*

177 FERNAND LÉGER La Noce 1911–12.
In the same way that Cézanne rarely painted a white napkin with only black, white and grey, so in this wedding picture Léger's clouds – generally thought of as grey – are delicately tinged with colour. Their subtle, rainbowed hues are picked up and intensified in the brasher costumes of the city dwellers that we can glimpse through the gaps. However, such understated correspondances are not so strongly felt as the contrast between the pale, soft amorphousness of the clouds and the steely greys of the figures and cityscape below. For Léger has constructed this image using a wide vocabulary of essential, pictorial contrasts.

however, Léger would sometimes rework subjects from an older period in this modern, epic idiom *(see plate 201)*.

As yet none of the Cubists had really applied themselves to the legacy of Cézanne's colour. The rigours of the Cubist experiment had been such that, initially anyway, colour had been strictly limited to a narrow range of earthy hues. After the first few years Picasso and Braque had made a concerted effort to reintroduce colour into their painting, a procedure much facilitated by the use of collage *(see plates 191 and 192)*. The true inheritor of Cézanne's advances in this field, however, was Léger's friend Robert Delaunay.

Delaunay had exhibited alongside the other Cubists in the infamous room 41 at the Indépendants in 1911. But the path he chose to pursue at that point was to take him in a slightly different direction from his colleagues. It would soon lead him to a completely abstract painting and hence to the very opposite of Cubist endeavours *(see plate 204)*. Back in 1907, a large exhibition of Cézanne's watercolours had been mounted at the gallery of Bernheim-Jeune. It was the first comprehensive

showing these works had received. Other exhibitions followed, and by 1914 Guillaume Apollinaire, the Cubists' essential champion in the Parisian press, singled them out as the single most important influence on contemporary artists. The eulogy was in fact a little belated, for Delaunay had painted a number of works two years before that parade quite obviously their debt to Cézanne's later watercolour technique. And indeed he was later to remark of them: 'What a remarkable limpidity, tending to become a supernatural beauty beyond anything previously seen.'[18] Delaunay's series of paintings entitled *Fenêtre*, ostensibly views of Paris seen through the refracting lens of a window, reveal too that the artist's verbal responses to the lyrical, poetic and above all abstract qualities of Cézanne's watercolours were also translated into paint *(see plates 202 and 203)*. Apollinaire surely chose the correct word when he described such works as 'Orphic'.

By this stage Cézanne's reputation was secure. Certainly it did not need defending. Since his death in 1906 his stature had been growing steadily, almost exponentially in the critical press; his influence on vast numbers of younger painters had already reached epidemic proportions. Writers and artists argued heatedly amongst themselves as to who was the true inheritor of Cézanne's legacy. But when Delaunay produced *La Ville de Paris* in 1912 *(see plate 178)*, he painted it as a strange sort of sympathetic act, identifying himself with the neglect and ridicule Cézanne had suffered when he was alive.

Cézanne's long friendship with Zola had ended when the latter's novel *L'Oeuvre* was published in 1886. The central figure in the book, the artist Claude Lantier, eventually commits suicide, unable to complete the massive, figurative work he has been working on for many years. Zola had modelled Lantier on Cézanne, amongst others. Cézanne, who was only too painfully aware of his inability to bring his own paintings to the level of finish he desired, found this more or less explicit and public indictment of his efforts by his oldest and closest friend too much to bear. The two men never spoke again. During the course of the novel, Zola had described at length the subject of the great work that Lantier was fated never to finish. The picture was to depict three monumental female nudes, modern versions of the Three Graces, standing before a panoramic view of the city of Paris.

This is the scene Delaunay has painted in his *La Ville de Paris* *(see plate 178)*. In one sense it may seem rather a boastful subject to choose, as though Delaunay might be claiming that he was able to finish something that – according to Zola at least – Cézanne was unable to complete. In any case, the painting was a large and public bid, on Delaunay's part, to identify himself as Cézanne's heir. And, certainly, this work and Delaunay's subsequent abstract paintings are among the purest of Cézanne's pictorial descendants. Beside them Denis's *Hommage à Cézanne* *(see plate 124)*, which was painted only twelve years earlier and which inaugurated Cézanne's apotheosis within the avant garde, looks curiously dated.

Cubism Politicized

Leger was not alone in his optimism for modern technology. Similar ideas had been voiced in the very first years of the new century by the French Naturist poets, by the distinguished writer and critic Octave Mirbeau (1850–1917) and, slightly later, by Guillaume Apollinaire. The fiercest, most violent expression of such ideas, however, was to be articulated by an Italian group of artists called the Futurists.

Futurism was a movement created not in the studio nor in the café, but in the press, when the first Futurist manifesto (there were subsequently to be many others) was published on the front page of *Le Figaro* on 20 February 1909. Its author was the Italian poet, dramatist and expert publicist Filippo Marinetti (1876–1944). His eulogy to modernity was forceful and uncompromising:

We declare that the splendour of the world has been increased by a new beauty: the beauty of speed. A racing car, its body ornamented by great pipes that resemble snakes with explosive breath . . . a screaming automobile that seems to run on grapeshot, is more beautiful than the *Winged Victory of Samothrace* . . . We want to glorify war – the world's only hygiene – militarism, patriotism, the destructive act of the anarchists, the beautiful ideas for which one dies, and contempt for women. We want to destroy museums, libraries, and academies of all kinds, and to make war on moralism, feminism . . . We shall sing the nocturnal, vibrating incandescence of arsenals and shipyards, ablaze with violent electric moons, the voracious stations devouring their smoking serpents . . . the broadbreasted locomotives that paw the ground of their rails like enormous horses of steel harnessed in tubes. . . .[19]

It is stirring stuff, and there is a lot more in the same vein. Léger's address to the same ideals, made some five years later, seems reasonable and almost tame in comparison. Marinetti's use of the word 'we', however, was not a little misleading, for at the time there was no Futurist group. Nonetheless, his rhetoric quickly attracted the attention of five young Italian painters, who confirmed their commitment by putting their names to a virtual replica of the *Figaro* manifesto, published in Italy in February 1910: Umberto Boccioni (1882–1916),

Giacomo Balla (1871–1958), Luigi Russolo (1885–1947), Gino Severini (1883–1966) and Carlo Carrà (1881–1966). Marinetti's first manifesto, then, bold and conspicuous on the front page of *Le Figaro*, was really, at this stage, more of an advertisement for recruits for an as yet non-existent movement than an accurate statement of collective aims. Even Citizen Kane showed no better understanding of the potential of media manipulation.

Two months after the second manifesto had been signed and published, Boccioni published his own *Technical Manifesto of Futurist Painting* in which he attempted to set out in slightly greater detail the aims of the newly formed group:

We want to re-enter life. That the science of today should deny its past corresponds to the material needs of our time. In the same way art, denying its past, must correspond to the intellectual needs of our time.[20]

Italy had remained more or less completely oblivious to the cultural developments and innovations of nineteenth-century France. This was partly because for most of that century her energies had been directed to the more pressing problem of political unification: Italy had only become a unified nation

178 ROBERT DELAUNAY La Ville de Paris 1912.
In this massive painting, Delaunay self-consciously attempts to rewrite literary history. But he is doing more than completing the painting that caused the death of Zola's fictional artist Claude Lantier. A fragmented Eiffel Tower appears to the right of the third nude; to the left, the prow of a sailing ship can be seen against an embankment: these details deliberately recall 'Le Douanier' Rousseau's Self-Portrait–Paysage (see plate 184). Rousseau died two years before Delaunay painted this picture. Thus, it can be seen as a posthumous tribute both to his friend Rousseau and to his major inspiration Cézanne, on whom Zola had based Claude Lantier.

179   Photograph of Luigi Russolo with Noise Intoners.
In this strange image Russolo appears on the left, with his assistant Ugo
Piatti on the right. When Russolo performed some of his Futurist music
outside the Coliseum in London in 1914, with the aid of these intoners,
the poster advertising the event listed the wide range of noise machines
that would be employed. These included: 'Buzzers, Exploders, Thunderers,
Whistlers, Murmurers, Gurglers, Rattlers, Cracklers [and] Roarers'. (In
Caroline Tisdall and Angelo Bozzolla, Futurism, *London, 1977, 105.)*

state in 1861. At the same time, the extraordinary riches of
her ancient cultural history had seemed to hamper the assimilation of all the more modern tendencies that had grown so
fruitfully in France. The vehemence of the Futurists' rejection
of the past, as Boccioni expressed it in 1910, was in large part
motivated by the desire to rid themselves of the stultifying
burden of tradition. They were not the first to feel its weight.
Earlier in the nineteenth century many of the English
Romantic poets had enjoyed the overwhelming sensations
induced in them as they contemplated the remains of Rome's
glorious past. Later in the twentieth century, the psychologist
Carl Gustav Jung (1875–1961) was to explain that his decision never to visit Rome was made because he felt that his
sensibility would not be able to withstand the power of that
city's history, still living as a smouldering presence in the
stone of the Pantheon, Forum and Colosseum.

As if turning their backs on those monuments' static solidity, the Futurists defined the essential condition both of the
modern world and of their paintings as dynamic. Boccioni
stated in his *Technical Manifesto*:

We proclaim . . . that universal dynamism must be rendered as dynamic
sensation; that movement and light destroy the substance of objects . . .
Our bodies enter into the sofas on which we sit, and the sofa enters into
us, as also the tram that runs between the houses enters into them, and
they in turn hurl themselves on to it and fuse with it .[21]

In other words, the new speed and energy with which modern
technology had transformed older methods of travel and com-
munication should be translated into painting in terms of a
dynamic interaction of all its constituent parts (*see plate 208*).

Initially, however, it seemed that the Futurists' formal language lagged behind the radical modernism of their rhetoric.
In 1910 they were all working for the most part in an adapted
divisionist manner. So in 1911, Marinetti, who had inherited

an enormous fortune from his parents, financed a trip to Paris
for Boccioni, Russolo and Carrà, where they would be able to
study the most advanced French painting. It was Severini
who, having already lived there, had suggested that such a
trip would be the best way of developing a style of painting
appropriate to their revolutionary aims. He showed his colleagues the recent paintings of Picasso and Braque, and the
group rapidly added a Cubist idiom to their earlier divisionist
leanings (*see plates 205, 206 and 207*).

At this point Marinetti, with his brilliant understanding of
the value of publicity, stepped in to broadcast the Futurists'
work throughout Europe: '[Under] Marinetti's auspices, the
presentation of culture was for the first time handled as if it
were a political campaign.'[22] An exhibition was hastily organized at the Bernheim-Jeune gallery in Paris in February
1912, and it later travelled to London, Berlin, Brussels,
Hamburg, Amsterdam, Munich, Vienna, Budapest and
numerous other European cities (*see plate 180*). The exhibition was always accompanied by lectures and marked by
the publication of books and articles.

Futurism was only in part a movement represented by
painters; in fact, it encompassed a variety of manifestations in
different media. The Futurists were determined to inject their
revolutionary ideals into every cultural sphere – music, literature, architecture, sculpture, photography and cinema as
much as painting (*see plate 179*). To this end Marinetti used
every possible means to generate publicity. He lavished his
fortune on the publication of books, leaflets, magazines and
manifestoes, many of which he arranged to have distributed
free of charge wherever the next Futurist exhibition was to
take place. One of his most successful and influential innova-

180   GIACOMO BALLA   Leash in Motion   1912.
A literal, humorous illustration of the Futurists' ideological commitment to
what they described as the essential condition of modern life: 'dynamism'.
Indeed, 'A diminutive daschund trotting along in a flurry of scampering
legs and wagging his tail next to the feminine swirls of his mistress's skirts
and dainty boots, . . . comes close to being a kitsch symbol for the Futurist
principle of paths of movement.' (Caroline Tisdall and Angelo Bozzolla,
Futurism, *London, 1977, 64.)*

tions was the 'Futurist Evening'. Usually held in an urban theatre or music hall, a Futurist Evening comprised a mixture of theatre, concert, political assembly and, if all went according to plan, a riot. For success meant derision, insults and pandemonium rather than applause. The subsequent attention these evenings attracted in the press, however, only made them increasingly popular. The occasional charges of obscenity and public disorder that were brought against Marinetti and others as a result of such exploits were likewise turned to good account.

Thus far, Futurism's political programme had generally limited itself to an impassioned rejection of past traditions, seeking instead to embrace whole-heartedly modernity in all its different manifestations (*see plate 209*). But as Europe drifted closer and closer to war, the Futurists became more specific about their goals. They believed that Italy should intervene, militarily if necessary, in the growing antagonisms between France and Germany that were threatening to engulf the whole continent in hostilities (*see plate 210*). In the first manifesto in 1909, Marinetti had written: 'We want to glorify war – the world's only hygiene . . . .' But his faith in the purgative benefits of destruction was to prove misplaced. Futurism effectively came to an end with the outbreak of war in 1914. Boccioni, its leading painter, was killed in 1916, and Marinetti, through his friendship with Mussolini (1883–1945), increasingly directed his efforts towards the promotion of Fascism. The rest of the group turned away from the public platforms they had occupied for the past four years and returned to the privacy of the studio, to more traditional methods of work.

NOTES

[1] André Salmon, *Souvenirs*, cited and discussed in Ellen C. Oppler, *Fauvism Re-examined*, doctoral dissertation, Columbia University, 1969, 152.

[2] Leo Stein, *Appreciation: Painting, Poetry and Prose*, New York, 1947, in *Four Americans in Paris*, exhibition catalogue, New York, 1970, 96–97.

[3] Gertrude Stein, *The Autobiography of Alice B. Toklas*, London, 1933, 106.

[4] Ibid, 55.

[5] In William Rubin, 'Pablo and Georges and Leo and Bill', in *Art in America*, 67 (March–April 1979), 144.

[6] André Salmon, *La Jeune peinture française*, Paris, 1912, in Edward F. Fry, *Cubism*, London, 1966, 82.

[7] In William Rubin, 'Cézannisme and the Beginnings of Cubism', in *Cézanne: The Late Work*, exhibition catalogue, New York, 1977, 196.

[8] Louis Vauxcelles, *Gil Blas*, 14 November 1908, in Edward F. Fry, op. cit., 50. There is also a story that it was Matisse who described Braque's entries to the Salon d'Automne that year as being made up entirely of 'cubes'.

[9] Leo Steinberg, 'Resisting Cézanne: Picasso's "Three Women"', in *Art in America*, 66 (November–December 1978), 123, 120.

[10] Ibid, 118.

[11] Dora Vallier, 'Braque, la peinture et nous', in *Cahiers d'Art*, October 1954, 14, and Françoise Gilot and Carleton Lake, *Life with Picasso*, New York 1964, 14. Both cited in William Rubin, 'Pablo and Georges and Leo and Bill', op. cit., 127.

[12] Wilhelm Uhde, *Picasso et la Tradition Française*, in John Golding, *Cubism: A History and An Analysis*, London 1959, 32.

[13] Emile Bernard, 'Paul Cézanne', in *L'Occident*, (July 1904), in P. M. Doran (ed.), *Conversations avec Cézanne*, Paris, 1978, 36.

[14] Cited in William Rubin, 'Cézannisme and the Beginnings of Cubism', op. cit., 167.

[15] In Gelett Burgess, 'The Wild Men of Paris', in *The Architectural Record*, (May 1910), 405.

[16] Picasso, statement, 1923, in Alfred H. Barr Jr, *Picasso: Fifty Years of his Art*, New York, 1946, 270.

[17] Fernand Léger, 'Les Réalisations picturales actuelles', in *Soirées de Paris*, 15 June 1914. In Edward F. Fry, op. cit., 136.

[18] Pierre Francastel and Guy Habasque (eds.), *Du cubisme à l'art abstrait*, Paris, 1957, 58.

[19] In Norbert Lynton, 'Futurism', in Nikos Stangos (ed.), *Concepts of Modern Art*, London, 1985, 97–98.

[20] Ibid, 99.

[21] Ibid.

[22] Caroline Tisdall and Angelo Bozzolla, *Futurism*, London, 1977, 9.

181 PABLO PICASSO   Family of Saltimbanques   1905.
In this huge canvas – measuring 6 by 4 feet – Picasso has abandoned
the allegorical tone of his earlier work (see plate 166). Indeed, no
psychological or narrative thread seems to connect the figures. However, he
lends these circus performers a certain restrained romantic melancholy.
The German poet Rainer Maria Rilke (1875–1926), who met Picasso in
1905, composed the fifth of his 'Duino Elegies' with this picture in mind:
'But tell me, who are they, these acrobats, even a little more fleeting than
we ourselves – so urgently, ever since childhood, wrung by an (oh, for the
sake of whom?) never-contented will? That keeps on wringing them,
bending them, slinging them, swinging them, throwing them and catching
them back. . . .' (Translated by J. B. Leishman and Stephen Spender,
cited in Alfred H. Barr Jr, Picasso: Fifty Years of his Art, *New York,*
1946, 37.)

182 PABLO PICASSO   Portrait of Gertrude Stein   1906.
*Picasso's resolute independence from fashion is well illustrated here. For
this portrait was painted in the same year that many of the Parisian avant
garde were brightening their palettes with all the burning extremes of
Fauve colour. The composition of the figure owes something to Cézanne,
and in particular to his Portrait of Madame Cézanne (see plate 98),
which was owned at the time by Gertrude and Leo Stein. When Picasso
came to repaint the head and hands, he did so without referring to his
model; the broad, severely drawn features, modified here to the realistic
demands of portraiture, reveal the influence of primitive Iberian sculpture.*

183 PABLO PICASSO   Two Nudes   1906.
*One of this pair of solid, squat women appears to be ushering the other
through a thick, heavy curtain into an unseen room beyond. The angled
head, enquiring expression and pointing finger seem to speak of a dialogue
to which we, as spectators, are not privy. At the same time, however, these
could be two different views of the same woman. Picasso's reduced palette
of ochres and burnt reds lends flesh and drapery alike the rough texture
and colour of old terracotta or sandstone. Massive and monochrome, these
women belong to another, more ancient race than our own.*

184 HENRI ROUSSEAU Self-Portrait–Paysage 1890.

185 HENRI ROUSSEAU The Sleeping Gypsy 1897.

Henri 'Le Douanier' Rousseau (1844–1910), so-named because his real profession was that of a municipal customs officer, first had a painting exhibited at the official Salon in 1885. The canvas was slashed, and thereafter he always showed his work at the Salon des Indépendants. Picasso's interest in the circus and in primitive art attracted him to Rousseau's brightly coloured, meticulously finished, child-like and naïve paintings. Rousseau, living in a tiny one-room apartment in Montmartre and for years considered something of a harmless joke in the art world, was glad to find someone with a serious interest in his work. He is reported to have said to Picasso: 'We are the only great contemporary artists. I in the modern manner, you in the Egyptian.'(George Heard Hamilton, Painting and Sculpture in Europe, 1880–1940, Harmondsworth, 1981, 223.) He was introduced to Picasso's circle of friends, and his adoption by this group of younger artists, poets and writers culminated in a famous banquet given in his honour in Picasso's studio in 1908. Rousseau considered his invention of the 'portrait–paysage' – that is, an amalgam of portrait and landscape – one of his most significant innovations. In the Self-Portrait–Paysage, Rousseau hovers slightly above the ground in front of a fanciful Parisian setting. The boat and waterway refer to his profession; the names of his two wives are inscribed on his palette. In the landscape behind he singles out the Eiffel Tower and a balloon, imagery that was to become central to a number of the Cubists, especially Robert Delaunay (see plate 202). In others of his works, Rousseau creates static, crisp scenes with a peculiar, mysterious power. Both the dark lushness of The Snake Charmer, which was commissioned by Delaunay's mother, and the potential savagery of The Sleeping Gypsy, seem to reside in a world of dreams.

186 HENRI ROUSSEAU The Snake Charmer 1907.

187 PABLO PICASSO   Three Women   1908.
Alice B. Toklas, the companion of Gertrude Stein, saw this painting in
Picasso's studio soon after it was finished. Gertrude Stein records her
impressions: '. . . frightening . . . I felt that there was something painful
and beautiful there, and oppressive but imprisoned.' (Gertrude Stein,
The Autobiography of Alice B. Toklas, *New York, 1933, 22.) Toklas's*
description is a revealing one. For there is a sense that these bodies
are trying, with enormous effort, to extricate themselves from their
surroundings. The figure to the right has succeeded but her limbs remain
heavy, while the one to the left flexes her new-born muscles with more
defined vigour. The third central figure remains the least developed.

188 PABLO PICASSO   Tables and Loaves and Bowl of Fruit
1909.
The shiny, highly polished surfaces of drapery and fruit in this imposing
still-life indicate the influence of 'Le Douanier' Rousseau (see plates
184–186). More than that, however, Picasso is looking to Cézanne. The
high viewpoint, the broken edge of the table, indeed the subject itself all
reveal his overriding influence. Probably following Braque's example, and
after the immense creative effort of the Demoiselles d'Avignon *(see*
plate 194), Picasso chose to consolidate the advances he had made during
the previous two years by submitting himself to the discipline of working
under Cézanne's aegis.

190 PABLO PICASSO Still-Life with Chair Caning 1912.
'The word Journal which starts off so securely as painted letters on painted paper begins to slip off into space by the time it reaches u, is partly eclipsed by the pipestem, and dies obscurely in the shadow of the cubist goblet.' (Alfred H. Barr Jr, Picasso: Fifty Years of his Art, New York, 1946, 79.) Picasso and Braque started to introduce lettering into their Cubist works in about 1911. It was particularly useful because it could be used to refer, as it does here, to something as concrete as a newspaper. At the same time lettering was completely flat, and thus highlighted the attenuated illusionism of everything else described in the painting.

189 PABLO PICASSO The Poet 1911.
Picasso and Braque brought Cubism to the verge of abstraction when they were working together in Céret during the summer of 1911; Picasso's poet is a pipe smoker, as the rack of pipes in the top right-hand corner indicates, but other recognizable features are very difficult to identify. Picasso and Braque, however, always recoiled from a purely abstract art. It was this situation which led them to experiment with lettering, and later with collage, for they saw this as a way of retaining clear reference to the outside world whilst not resorting to naturalistic description.

191 GEORGES BRAQUE   Still-Life with Playing Cards   1913.
*The grain of the wood of the table here has been described by dragging a
house decorator's comb through wet paint. Braque had been trained as
a house painter before he decided to become an artist. It was he who first
took this everyday technique from the world of the interior decorator and
used it in the realm of the fine arts. It was the kind of witty, subversive joke
on traditional conventions of illusionism that so appealed to Picasso and
Braque, for with this technique the artist could describe both the texture
and colour of a wooden table without resorting to established techniques of
representation.*

192 PABLO PICASSO Glass and Bottle of Suze 1912–13.

Pieces of actual newspaper, coloured paper and patterned wallpaper
have been employed by Picasso in this painting to describe – in a highly
simplified and artificial manner – the bottle and glass that stand on the
table. Picasso began to introduce collage elements into his still-life
compositions in 1912 – with an increasing sophistication. Newspaper here
represents both the thick glass of the goblet, and, when delicately shaded,
the refracting glass of the bottle neck. Elsewhere it merely fills in the
surrounding space. Yet while Picasso's game never allows the newspaper to
signify itself, the wallpaper is doing exactly and only that.

193   PABLO PICASSO   Woman with a Fan   1908.
As though in partial retreat, after all the experimental excesses of Les
Demoiselles d'Avignon, *Picasso painted this nude study the following
year. While the 'demoiselles' paraded their nakedness without shame,
this is a modest nude; she avoids direct eye contact with the viewer, and
though one breast is exposed, she hides her sex with the fan in her right
hand. Again, however, the viewer is forced into the position of a voyeur.
Her hunched right shoulder is joined to her left arm with a sweeping arc, a
graphic indication, perhaps, of the unseen tensions that lie behind this
figure's diffidence.*

194   PABLO PICASSO   Les Demoiselles d'Avignon   1907.
*By removing the two men that he had included in the study, Picasso has
redirected the force of these women's cutting sexual aggression. Now it is
directed outwards at the spectator rather than being kept more decorously
within the narrative of the work itself. Picasso's painting has undergone an
extraordinary transformation: from the choked melancholy of* La Vie *(see
plate 166) and the classical restraint of* Two Nudes *(see plate 183) has
emerged this eruption of stylistic and thematic violence. Braque called this
painting the 'bordello philosophique' (Edward F. Fry,* Cubism,
*London, 1966, 82), for its spatial and formal innovations were to be
crucial in his and Picasso's evolution of Cubism's more intellectual rigours.*

195 GEORGES BRAQUE Normandy Port 1909.
This was one of the first landscapes that Braque composed entirely in the studio. His drastic reorganization of the harbour scene into a number of interlocking facets or planes was at this stage easier to achieve from memory, away from the motif, than it was when confronted by the scene itself. The sea, harbour wall, lighthouse and boats are here all subjected to the same treatment – converted into a system of parallel faceting. In this way, the traditional methods of modelling and perspective are deliberately subverted. It is as though the information about a landscape – or anything else for that matter – that such methods could impart was no longer felt to be sufficient. The perception of nature was now more complex.

196 GEORGES BRAQUE Violon et Cruche 1910.
For all the fragmentation of space and object into a multitude of interpenetrating, angular planes, everything here remains easily recognizable. Violin, jug, table, paper, even the dado on the back wall: all remain quite familiar. The top corner of a sheet of paper has been folded over and its pointed tip casts a shadow on the rest of the page. This shadow and the orientation of the page indicate that it is receding diagonally into space. Elsewhere, however, the set of spatial coordinates that this detail establishes for our eye are contradicted. By the time the eye reaches the violin, any notion of a stable illusion of space is irrevocably lost as its wooden body is apparently squashed flat on to the surface of the canvas.

197 JUAN GRIS   Bottle of Rum and Newspaper   1914.
*Juan Gris recapitulated and purified most of the innovations of Picasso
and Braque in works of an absolute mathematical clarity. There is a
certain precision in this still-life about the way Gris turns his bottle, so
that it is seen from a high, angled viewpoint, which is both calm and
utterly logical. Part of it is shaded in pencil, part represented by a piece of
coloured paper stuck on to the surface of the picture. Real labels have also
been glued into place; naturally they remain flat while the body and neck
of the bottle are described, albeit allusively, in a three-dimensional space.
Paint has been scraped away to denote the space surrounding the table
and to add a further textural richness to this immaculate image.*

198 JUAN GRIS   Glass of Beer and Playing Cards   1913.
*Within a neat and exact linear grid, the glass of beer and playing cards
are systematically viewed from different angles. Each segment is also
rendered in a different manner. Thus, the left profile of the glass is
naturalistically painted in oil, while to its right, its opposite profile has
slipped a couple of inches downwards and is depicted simply as a light
contour on a dark background. Moreover, as a shadow falls across its
pattern, the wallpaper above is realistically described; to the extreme
left, however, this same pattern turns out merely to be printed paper
stuck on to the canvas.*

199 FERNAND LÉGER Nus dans un Paysage 1909–11.
'The woodcutters bear the trace of the blows their axes make on the trees, and their colouring shares in the greenish light that filters down through the branches.' So Apollinaire described this large painting by Léger when it was exhibited at the 1911 Indépendants. (In G. Banquier, Fernand Léger: Vivre dans Le Vrai, Paris, 1987, 38.) Tonally, texturally or formally there is indeed little difference between tree and man. Like Cézanne's late Bathers pictures, Léger's woodmen are very much part of the landscape they inhabit. But if Léger's tubular idiom was new, the theme he chose to illustrate was an ancient one.

200 ALBERT GLEIZES Man on a Balcony 1912.
Gleizes will probably always remain better known for his book on Cubism than for his paintings in that style: Du Cubisme, which Gleizes co-wrote with Albert Metzinger (1883–1956), was published in Paris in 1912 and was the first book on the subject. As a painter, however, Gleizes revealed a rather superficial understanding of the truly revolutionary aspects of Cubism. In this portrait, he has simply overlaid a traditionally modelled figure set in a perspectival space with a sort of transparent Cubist grid. The image lacks any of the subversive questioning present in the work of Picasso, Braque and Gris.

201　FERNAND LÉGER　Le Réveil Matin　1914.
*With a painterly vocabulary comprising a handful of colours and basic
geometric shapes, Léger has managed to describe a figure yawning and
stretching as it is wrenched from sleep by the alarm clock that appears in
the bottom right-hand corner. The colours he employs are roughly applied,
sometimes leaving the geometric compartments they fill bare at the edges,
at others spilling over the incisive black outlines. Although the figure is
reduced to a series of sharply drawn, roughly modelled cylinders, however,
a feeling of massive solidity still exudes from the image.*

202 ROBERT DELAUNAY Fenêtre 1912.

203 PAUL CÉZANNE The Forest – The Park at Château Noir
1900–04.

*The source of Delaunay's painting – one of a series he based on the view
from his window – lies obviously in the late watercolour work of Cézanne.
Converting the subtleties of Cézanne's overlapping strokes of watercolour
into the more opaque medium of oil, Delaunay places the Eiffel Tower at
the centre of his composition. Curling arcs, seemingly born from its flanks,
simultaneously suggest gauze or lace curtains interposing themselves
between the tower and our gaze. Between these two planes, the
interpenetrating lozenges of colour describe a third layer – the light – in
this dazzling, virtuoso amalgam of transparencies. Yet, distilling the
abstract beauty from Cézanne's translucent touches of colour, Delaunay
all but loses sight of his subject. For even as the eye discovers these layers
and locates them in optical experience, Delaunay's colours begin to lose
strength as realistic analogies. They begin instead to speak their own
musical, abstract language. Delaunay titled this painting Fenêtre,
meaning Window, but this is more than just a denotative label. Since the
invention of perspective, the picture had been intended to act as a window
on to nature; the title here draws attention to this convention, but the
abstract power of the colours, irrespective of their realistic function,
simultaneously points also to its inevitable, imminent redundancy.*

204 ROBERT DELAUNAY Sun Disks 1912–13.
It did not take Delaunay long to relinquish his already tenuous hold on earthly things and to explore a purely abstract world of colour. He believed that line inhibited the full, expressive potential of colour, and banished it in so far as he then constructed his paintings using only circular forms. He thus also relinquished any connection he had with Cubism – still visible in the angular grids employed in the Fenêtre series (see plate 202). Cubism, in any case, was always concerned with balancing the realistic with the abstract. Delaunay's more lyrical temperament was not satisfied by that kind of intellectual fastidiousness.

205 UMBERTO BOCCIONI The Street Enters the House 1911.
A woman with her back to us leans over a balcony looking at a
tumultuous, dizzying view of houses, building site and street. Boccioni's
adoption of the Cubists' use of a multitude of different perspectives is clear,
applied here to an exhilarating, urban panorama. A tiny Pegasus appears
on the woman's rump, a literal illustration of the kind of perceptual
simultaneity Boccioni described in his Technical Manifesto: 'How often
have we seen upon the cheek of the person with whom we are talking the
horse which passes at the end of the street.' (In Caroline Tisdall and
Angelo Bozzolla, Futurism, London, 1977, 43.)

207 GINO SEVERINI Dynamism of Forms – Light in Space
1912.
Of all the Futurists, Severini stayed in Paris for the longest time. His more
extensive exposure to contemporary avant-garde French painting can be
seen in a painting such as this. Where most of his companions were happy
quickly to assimilate a rudimentary Cubist vocabulary in order to express
their modernist ideology of dynamism and energy, Severini reveals here
that he has been looking hard at the paintings of Robert Delaunay, and
in particular at his Fenêtre series. In fact, Dynamism of Forms contains
none of the political attitudinizing of much other Futurist work. Rather
it seems to present an abstracted image of the movement of light.

206 GIACOMO BALLA Flight of Swifts 1913.
*Balla was always interested in finding painterly forms for the purely
optical manifestations of movement. At the same time his delight in
producing images that described movement in the animal kingdom
differentiates him from the other Futurists, whose work was characterized
by a love of urban or mechanical subjects. Here Balla's description of
the swifts' bodies is subordinated to his concentration on the imaginary
lines traced in the air by their flight. These make pleasing, energetic arcs
across the canvas, but it is difficult not to wonder whether painting was
the most appropriate medium for this subject. Some form of photography
might have been more suitable.*

208 UMBERTO BOCCIONI The City Rises 1910.
A terrifying horse charges into a busy building site, far too powerful for the construction workers to hold back. In fact it is seen twice. Originally intended to form part of a triptych celebrating the progress of modern industry with the horse as the symbol of energy and dynamism, this painting was described by Boccioni himself when he wrote to a friend: 'I was after a large synthesis of work, light and movement. It is done without any modelling and all the mastery of skill is sacrificed for the sake of the highest emotion.' (G. Verzotti, Boccioni: Catalogo completo, Florence, 1989, cat. no. 90.) *Within a year, however, he would couch his visions of modernity in a Cubist, not a divisionist idiom.*

209 LUIGI RUSSOLO Rebellion 1911–12.
Bursting with forceful energy, the crowd presses forward, their momentum literally causing the composition to divide, the houses in the street to collapse. It would be difficult to get much more literal. But Russolo's most significant contribution to Futurism was his music, not his painting. In fact, with the exception of Boccioni and Carrà, the movement itself did not contribute much that was original or influential in the realm of painting. It was their performances and their exploitation of the media that would have the greatest influence on later generations.

210 CARLO CARRÀ Interventionist Manifesto 1914.
Carrà evidently learnt a great deal from his trip to Paris in 1912 and especially from the collages of Picasso and Braque. The spiralling composition here, however, has no precedent in the work of the two Cubists. In a letter to Severini, Carrà described this tiny collage as, 'the plastic abstraction of civil tumult'. (In Caroline Tisdall and Angelo Bozzolla, Futurism, London, 1977, 187.) At the centre of the spiral, the clipped newspaper cuttings exhort Italy's airmen to step forward to fight, and this appeal is supported by a chorus of 'E Viva', written out in white on the outer spirals. The straight diagonals that cut across this spiral contain references to poetry – 'La Rosa' by Apollinaire and Marinetti's 'Zang Tumb Tuum'.

Chapter 5

Developments in Germany

In his introduction to the second Post-Impressionist exhibition in 1912 Roger Fry declared: 'Post-Impressionist schools are flourishing, one might almost say raging, in Switzerland, Austro-Hungary and most of all in Germany.'

It is interesting that Fry should have singled out Germany as a particular stronghold of the new art. The German artists of that avant-garde generation, or, to give them the name they adopted for themselves, the Expressionists, were in fact not represented at either of Fry's epoch-making exhibitions in 1910 and 1912. And, indeed, although even the poet Rupert Brooke (1887–1915) was aware of their existence, referring in a review of the second exhibition to 'Die Wilden' and 'Die Expressionisten', he cannot have experienced much, if any of their work at first hand. Furthermore, while he might express a fashionable regret at the absence at the show of 'Pechstein of Berlin', he fails to mention any of the German's contemporaries who might today be considered to have been more important.

Fry's statement might have seemed to the British public simply to confirm the suspected artistic and social anarchy that appeared to be riding roughshod over the entire Continent. To the artists of the German avant garde, however, his emphatic view of their position would have come as no surprise.

Since the 1880s German art had been in a state of some turmoil. It was at that date that the various rebel art factions – the 'Secessions' – first came into existence, and subsequently gave individual character to the art worlds of Munich, Vienna and Berlin.

In Germany during the 1880s the Romantic tradition held sway and the only diversity in German painting was between the heroic and the modern. Just as elsewhere in Europe, history painting was considered the ultimate art form. But in common with many of their European cousins, German

211 ERNST LUDWIG KIRCHNER Self-Portrait with Model 1910.

In this painting Kirchner displays a new self-confidence and an alarming new style that he had developed by combining the colour of Matisse, the stylization of primitive art and the Vienna Secession, and the figure composition of Munch. With broad brushstrokes, applied no doubt with the very brush the artist is holding in the portrait, Kirchner covers his canvas with contrasting strokes of colour which emphasize the coolness of the light blue slip worn by his model. This was quite probably Kirchner's current lover. The pose of the artist and his informal dress also reveal the bohemian conditions in which the painters of Die Brücke were working.

artists at this time had fallen under the spell of the French, although initially it was not to the Impressionists that they looked, but to the Barbizon painters: Jean-Baptiste Camille Corot (1796–1875), Jean-François Millet (1814–1875) and Narcisso Diaz de la Peña (1808–1876) and the omnipresent Jules Bastien-Lepage (1848–1884). The Berlin, Weimar and Dresden Academies were immensely powerful, however, and had openly declared themselves against the younger generation of *plein-air* painters. Thus, French Impressionism, known in Germany from the late 1880s chiefly through the works of Edouard Manet (1832–1883), Claude Monet (1840–1926) and Pierre Auguste Renoir (1841–1919), did not have any direct effect upon German painters until the early 1890s; it was subordinated to the earlier French schools and to the Hague painters typified by Josef Israels (1824–1911). When the change did come, however, it was as a direct result of the impact of the Impressionists upon a small group of young German artists.

In 1889 the German painter Max Liebermann (1847–1935) exhibited work at the Paris International Exhibition. German artists had officially been discouraged from taking part in this fair, because it was seen by the Kaiser as a glorification of the regicidal revolution of 1789. Liebermann, however, took no notice of the official line and, along with a few others, submitted work. It was well received. Encouraged by his success and spurred on by the recent inspiration of Impressionism, Liebermann founded the Alliance of Eleven in February that same year. This society of independent artists was the first step towards the birth of Expressionism.

Liebermann had studied at the Weimar Academy from 1868 to 1873, before visiting France in 1874. Here he had seen a variety of French art but had been more taken with the work of the Barbizon painters than with that of Manet and Edgar Degas (1834–1917). On his return to Germany in 1878, however, he was hailed by his contemporaries as the herald of Impressionism. At the time two other German painters were also described as Impressionists: Lovis Corinth (1858–1925) and Max Slevogt (1868–1932). Both had studied in Munich and later in Paris, Corinth under Adolphe Bouguereau (1825–1905) and Slevogt at the Académie Julian. But on their return they had both fallen under the spell of the naturalist style of Franz von Lenbach (1836–1904), arguably the most important German painter of his generation, who favoured a dark, Dutch palette. Holland was at this period regarded as a sort of 'little Germany' and the Dutch painters of the seventeenth century were held in the highest regard.

Thus, despite the natural empathy of his two colleagues, it was Liebermann alone who made the crucial first move in 1889.

Three years later, in 1892, the Norwegian artist Edvard Munch (1863–1944) was invited to exhibit with the Verein Berlin Kunstler, which had grown out of Liebermann's Alliance of Eleven and which now specialized in the exhibition of realist and Impressionist pictures. The show ran for only one week and, after a heated debate in the council of the Kunstler, Munch was requested to withdraw his works, which were considered an insult. The suppression of Munch, commonly regarded as the leader of the young avant garde, outraged the younger generation and provided the spark for a bright flame. The younger artists of the society sprang to revolt, with Max Liebermann, at the ripe age of forty-two, at their head. Corinth invited Liebermann to join the artists of the Munich Secession, a society of similarly disaffected young artists that had formed earlier in 1892. The Secession had been the brainchild of the painter Franz von Stuck

212 MAX LIEBERMANN   The Parrot Walk   1902.
In this painting of the gardens of Amsterdam Zoo Liebermann is shown at the height of his Impressionist style – for which he became so renowned in the Germany of the 1890s. With its smartly dressed woman and sweet children, it represents the gentler side of German art. It is also a good illustration of the speed with which the avant-garde tendencies developing in Europe took hold in Germany. For this work was among those exhibited at the 1903 exhibition of the Berlin Secession, the breakaway group which Liebermann himself had founded in 1898 as a result of his frustration with the German academic tradition, yet which was already regarded as a bastion of conservatism by the time his work was shown.

(1863–1928). Deeply impressed by the French Symbolist painters, and in particular by Puvis de Chavannes (1824–1898), von Stuck had combined their ethereal qualities with the heroic subject matter favoured by the German classicizing painters of earlier in the century. He had formed the Secession as the Association of Artists, specifically to counter what he saw as the stifling power of von Lenbach and his Dutch gloom.

Corinth and Liebermann had known of each other's work since the late 1870s when both had been painting religious subjects in a naturalist style. Now they once again found themselves united. It should be stressed, however, that their art cannot be said to have been revolutionary in appearance at this stage. Although Liebermann was beginning to look to a brighter palette, Corinth's canvases of interiors and portraits were still very much in the style of the Hague school painter Josef Israels. It is interesting to note, however, that Israels had influenced the early work of Vincent van Gogh (1853–1890) and that he had also accepted the new Secession group's somewhat surprising invitation to join them in Munich. It is hard in retrospect to relate Liebermann's work to his admiration for that of Munch, although undoubtedly such an admiration was quite genuine. In his *Parrot Walk* of 1902 (*see plate 212*) it is impossible to detect any of the intense feeling and inner anxiety found in similar street scenes by Munch (*see plate 224*), but the picture does, on the other hand, betray some progress towards a real interest in Impressionism. Corinth, similarly, worked in a dark palette and *intimiste* style reminiscent of Manet or Degas (*see plate 225*) and at best of Edouard Vuillard (1868–1940), as seen in his *Portrait of Conrad Ansorge* (*see plate 213*) painted in 1904, although the essence of his style is still realist. It was not until 1905 that he began to work in a looser style, evidently influenced by Liebermann, and clearly discernible in his *Childhood of Zeus* (*see plate 226*).

Max Slevogt was with Corinth in Munich from 1890. He also gradually moved away from his dark palette of the 1880s, taking up the brighter colour and looser brushstrokes of the Impressionists. His *Don Giovanni* painting (*see plate 214*), executed in 1901, bears witness to this. By now, however, he had moved to Berlin. For if Munich provided the model for the revolutionary art movements of the pre-war years, it was in Dresden and Berlin that they were first to be realized. It was to Berlin that Munch had first been attracted in 1892, and having outraged the critics and conservative elements there, he had acted like a magnet for younger artists desperately looking for a new direction. While the Parisian avant garde had not welcomed him, Berlin's young artists extended their hands to Munch, and his influence on the style of the generation of artists then about to graduate is evident in countless of their canvases dating from the first two decades of the century.

Another foreigner whose work was to have a profound effect on the future Expressionists was the Swiss artist Ferdinand Hodler (1853–1918). By the end of the 1880s Hodler, who had first made his reputation as a realist, was turning to Symbolism. He evolved a theory of artistic harmony which he called Eurythmy: 'An inter-relationship of the harmony of the form–rhythm of nature with the rhythm of emotion'.[1]

His theory, which in many ways can be seen as paralleling Matisse's ideas on life's natural rhythm, is perhaps best exemplified in his painting *Night* of 1891 (*see plate 227*), in

213 LOVIS CORINTH Portrait of Conrad Ansorge 1904.
In this slightly later portrait by Corinth we can see the artist moving towards a looser technique and brighter palette, although he still confines himself within the realm of realism. Such paintings serve to demonstrate that while Corinth might appear to have been somewhat radical in his actions – including the establishment of the Munich Secession in 1892, for instance – in his painting he was still locked in a tired academic tradition. It was not until after 1905 that he was able to exploit fully the new techniques brought to Germany by Liebermann.

which he attempts to represent the various experiences of sleep – dreams, nightmares, love and rest – according to his theory of Eurythmy. The painting was shown in Paris in 1891 and found immediate favour with the arch-Symbolist Puvis de Chavannes. From 1892 onwards Hodler became increasingly involved with the Secession groups in Munich and later in Berlin, and his exhibits at their shows in 1894 and 1897 were highly praised by the younger artists. Hodler later went on to paint empty landscapes such as his *Schynige Platte* (*see plate 228*), in a unique style which blends the technique of Paul Cézanne (1839–1906) with the feeling of the Symbolists. Thus, it was through the work of two foreigners, Munch and Hodler, that the German avant garde was given an indication of the way in which they might adapt the northern tradition to embrace the formal breakthroughs taking place in France.

The Munich Secession set the ball rolling. In 1893 the Dresden Secession was formed under Gotthardt Kühl (1850–1915), and in 1897 that at Vienna under the Jugendstil painter Gustav Klimt (1862–1918). These were swiftly followed in 1898 by the Berlin Secession under Liebermann. The specific aim of the Berlin group was to show all the art that was considered by the establishment to be immoral: van Gogh, Cézanne and Gauguin, Hodler, Monet, Camille Pissarro (1830–1903), Félix Vallotton (1865–1925), James McNeill Whistler (1834–1903) and Auguste Rodin (1840–1917) were all represented. Berlin was fast becoming an art centre with which to reckon.

Unlike France, however, Germany did not have one natural, traditional national capital in which to concentrate all its artistic activity during the early years of the twentieth century; it had been divided into a number of small states and principalities for several hundreds of years. But if in geographical location the German artists lacked a sense of unity, their struggle was made all the more powerful by that which did unite them: the Northern Romantic tradition. During the 1890s and early 1900s a number of artistic centres and colonies (*Gemeinschaft*) sprang up all over Germany, united by this common spirit. In 1894 the Munich Secession had spawned the breakaway artists' colony of Neu-Dachau on the Dachauer Moor; their subject matter was bleak and their palette muted. A second such group called the *Scholle*, meaning the Clod, had emerged in 1899. It was, however, at Worpswede, twenty miles from Bremen, that perhaps the most important colony evolved.

The idea of establishing a colony here had first been raised in 1884 by the painter Fritz Mackensen (1866–1953), but it was not until 1889 when Otto Modersohn (1865–1943), his contemporary at the Düsseldorf Academy, came here that the idea began to bear fruit. Reflecting the ideals of the Pont-Aven painters in France, the Worpswede artists attempted to escape from the modern world to a state of natural grace embodied by the peasant farmers of the Bremen countryside. Modersohn encapsulated the feeling for which they were striving in his touching image of a *Worpswede Peasant Girl under a Willow Tree* of 1895 (*see plate 215*). In 1898 they were joined by the young painter Paula Becker

214 MAX SLEVOGT The Champagne Aria from *Don Giovanni* 1901.

Together with Corinth and Liebermann Slevogt formed a triumvirate: the three German artists who stood in the vanguard of art in Germany during the 1880s and 1890s, painting in a manner informed by Impressionism. In this picture, one of several images painted by Slevogt of the renowned Portuguese baritone Francesco d'Andrade, the artist surpasses his two contemporaries – in his choice of viewpoint and of subject matter, as well as in the looseness of his style. In both the former he recalls pictures by Edgar Degas that he would undoubtedly have seen while a student at the Académie Julian in Paris in 1889.

(1876–1907), who had trained in Berlin during the previous two years. At this stage all three artists were still painting in a realist style, although they did approach the landscape tradition with a new vitality. Their exhibitions at the Kunsthalle in Berlin in 1894 and at the Munich Glasspalast the following year brought them considerable fame. It was Paula Becker, however, having in 1901 married Modersohn and taken the name Modersohn-Becker, who achieved artistic immortality for the group. Along with Munch it was she who was instrumental in making comprehensible to German artists the ideas and achievements of the French avant garde. On her first visit to Paris in 1900, she saw paintings by Cézanne hung at Ambroise Vollard's (1868–1939) gallery and on her return to Germany she effected a complete change of technique. From that date onwards she looked increasingly to France, visiting Paris again in 1903, 1905 and 1906, and each time returning with something new – lessons learnt from van Gogh, Gauguin and the Fauves. Quite suddenly things started to make sense.

As early as 1899 Modersohn-Becker had declared: 'To employ the closest observation in seeking the greatest simplicity is the source of greatness.'[2] The great Austrian poet

215 OTTO MODERSOHN Worpswede Peasant Girl under a Willow Tree 1895.

This picture of a young peasant girl leaning against the trunk of an old willow tree was painted by Modersohn in Worpswede near Bremen, where he had established an artists' colony in 1889. The painting seems to sum up everything that Modersohn and his friend the painter Fritz Mackensen hoped to achieve in their rural retreat. They believed in the purity and innocence of the country people, and this fresh-faced girl must have seemed to be the embodiment of such virtues. In its composition the picture appears to echo the work of van Gogh and Gauguin, although, somewhat curiously, Modersohn had probably not seen the work of either artist at this time.

Rainer-Maria Rilke (1875–1926) had been visiting the artists for some years when he wrote an essay on life at Worpswede. It was in that essay that he observed: 'The language was new, the expression unusual, the contrasts resounded together like gold and grass.'[3]

Shaped by the artistic vocabulary of Gauguin, it is that synthesis that we see in Paula Modersohn-Becker's portrait of Rilke's wife (*see plate 229*), painted in 1905. For the first time a German artist manages to marry naturalism of subject with a new and exciting technique, whilst maintaining the traditional notion of the Ideal which had pervaded German culture since the Romantic period. This alliance was consummated the following year in Modersohn-Becker's powerful *Reclining Mother and Child* (*see plate 230*). This picture now takes on a bitter poignancy as it was only a year later that she herself was to tragically die in childbirth. Her achievement, however, could not be undone and undoubtedly she profoundly influenced the development of Expressionism.

At the same time that Paula Moderschn-Becker was making her influential discoveries at Worpswede, another German artist was taking tentative steps in a similar direction in his studio on the small Baltic island of Alsen.

Emil Nolde (1867–1956) occupies an interesting position in early twentieth-century German art. He seems always to be present at the moment of breakthrough, and yet never quite commits himself to one particular movement. His own style is far too personal to be dominated by the needs of a group. Nolde, born Emil Hansen, came from a simple farming family in the town of Nolde in the bleak countryside of Schleswig. The profound religiosity of his parents not only conditioned his upbringing but indeed never left Nolde; all his paintings contain a pronounced spiritual element. In 1890 the young Nolde was apprenticed as a draughtsman at a Berlin furniture factory and from 1892 to 1898 he taught draughtsmanship at St Gallen in Switzerland. It was here that he first saw the work of Ferdinand Hodler and another Swiss Symbolist painter Arnold Böcklin (1827–1901).

Impressed by their vision, Nolde decided to take up painting and, having been turned down by the Munich Academy, went to study for a year in Dachau, where there had been an artists' colony since 1894. Between 1898 and 1899 he worked with the landscape painter Adolf Hölzel (1853–1934) in Munich and Dachau and in 1899, at the age of thirty-two, Nolde travelled to Paris. He spent nine months there, studying at the Académie Julian and assimilating the new artistic currents then pervading the city. Between 1900 and 1903 he travelled between Schleswig, Denmark and Berlin, before finally settling in Alsen.

By this time Nolde had decided to reject Impressionism. Instead he began to produce empty landscapes in the style of *Moonlit Night* (*see plate 217*) which recall the pale grey and yellow tonalities of the Dresden school and which in feeling suggest the seminal introspective spirituality of such Northern Romantics as Caspar David Friedrich (1774–1840). However, the wide range of work that Nolde had seen in Paris had made a deep impression upon him and by 1904 he was painting in a brighter palette (*see plate 233*) that betrays the influence of Gauguin, van Gogh and Munch, whom he later admitted: 'Inspired me with admiration and love'.[4]

With this new vision pervading his work, it is perhaps not surprising to learn that Nolde was invited two years later in

1906 to join a group of young artists working in Dresden, who shared a common artistic inspiration and to a certain extent the same ideologies.

A New Truth

If the foundations for German modernism had been laid by Modersohn-Becker and Nolde, chiefly inspired by the French and by Munch, then the bricks and mortar were provided by this group – Die Brücke, meaning the Bridge – between 1905 and 1913. Its chief members were Ernst Ludwig Kirchner (1880–1938), Eric Heckel (1883–1970), Karl Schmidt-Rottluff (1884–1976), Max Pechstein (1881–1955), Otto Mueller (1874–1930) and, briefly, Nolde himself. All of these artists were important in their own right. However, before we examine the work of each of them, we should take a brief overview of the birth and development of the group itself.

Die Brücke was officially inaugurated in Dresden in 1905, although its origins go back as far as 1901. It was during that year that Heckel encountered Schmidt-Rottluff at a meeting of the literary society of their school in Chemnitz, near Dresden.

216 ERIC HECKEL Nietzsche 1905.
This moody woodcut of Friedrich Nietzsche is testimony to the reverence in which the artists of Die Brücke held the great German philospher. Eric Heckel was the writer's chief apologist within the group and thus this image can also be seen as the pupil paying homage to his master. The artists of Die Brücke had inscribed Nietzsche's dictum 'I hate the plebian crowd' in their visitors book. Moreover, it was through his writings that the character of the group's painting, with its emphasis on freedom and sexuality, took its form. Here, occupying the entire picture area, bristling with moustaches and staring wildly into space, the master seems every inch the superman of his literary creation Zarathustra.

217 EMIL NOLDE Moonlit Night 1903.
Nolde's earliest style of painting was heavily influenced by the painting of the Dachau artists' colony and in particular by that of Adolf Hölzel with whom he worked from 1898 to 1899. In this cool, tonal landscape, the spectator looks down upon a farmhouse that recalls Nolde's childhood, beside the bend in a river; it is painted in the grey and yellow palette favoured by the Dachau painters. The title seems misleading, as the moon itself is hidden behind cloud. Yet the scene is still moonlit, charged with a sense of mystery fully in-keeping with the Northern Romantic tradition that the artist was later to do so much to revive.

When, in 1904, Heckel went to Dresden to study architecture at the Technische Hochschule, Schmidt-Rottluff was quick to follow him. By this time Kirchner and fellow artist Fritz Bleyl (b. 1881) had been studying at the Hochschule in Dresden for some two years, having met there in 1902. It would only be a matter of time before Heckel and Kirchner met.

Kirchner's first impression of Heckel was of a young man ascending the stairs to his apartment, reciting lines from Nietzsche's *Thus Spake Zarathustra* (written between 1883 and 1892). Indeed, Heckel was primarily a literary animal; he later admitted that at first he had been unable to decide whether he wanted to be an artist or a writer, and his choice of author on this occasion was highly significant. The four young students – Kirchner, the eldest, was only twenty-five – quickly became friends.

It soon became obvious that they all shared a desire to become artists rather than architects, and on 7 June 1905 they announced the formation of Die Brücke. Their particular group would differ from others like it by being open to all-comers – artists and lay people alike. In fact, anyone who was sufficiently interested to pay the modest subscription could join. In return lay members would receive an annual collection of prints. Sixty-eight people would eventually join in this way.

Unlike their French predeccesors, the artists of Die Brücke were united not only in the art they produced but in the ideology which shaped it as well. Thus, at the suggestion of Heckel and Schmidt-Rottluff, they chose a name for themselves that was taken from Nietzsche: 'Man is a rope, tied between beast and Higher Man – a rope over an abyss . . . What is great in man is that he is a bridge and not an end.'[5]

The four young men now began to draw, paint and carve incessantly. Kirchner described the atmosphere:

The first thing for the artists was free drawing from the free human body in the freedom of nature. It started in Kirchner's studio as a matter of convenience. We drew and painted. Hundreds of drawings a day, with talk and fooling in between, the artists joining the models before the easel and vice-versa . . . The studio became the home of the people who were being drawn, they learned from the artists and the painters from them. . . . [6]

They wanted to build something akin to the artistic communities of Pont-Aven and Worpswede. At the same time, however, they were searching for a greater sense of purpose and a surer sense of freedom, characteristics that they believed were intrinsically German. Kirchner was later to describe this driving force as: 'A naïve and pure compulsion to bring art and life together in harmony'.[7]

Under the guidance of Heckel, they looked to Nietzsche for their spiritual inspiration. For they now appeared to embody the aims of his creation, Zarathustra:

Zarathustra gazed into the forest and the stillness, in surprise he gazed into himself. Then he arose quickly, like a seafarer who suddenly sees land, and rejoiced: for he beheld a new truth. And then he spoke to his heart thus: 'A light has dawned for me . . . I need living companions who follow me because they want to follow themselves – and who want to go where I want to go . . . The creator seeks fellow creators, those who inscribe new values on new tables . . . They will be called destroyers and despisers of good and evil. But they are harvesters and rejoicers.'[8]

In 1906, a year after the group had been founded, Kirchner composed Die Brücke's manifesto. He produced a woodcut which combined a representation of a bridge spanning a river between two trees with the text of the manifesto itself (*see page 424*). The bridge, of course, was that of the group's name; it was described in the Jugendstil style popular in Vienna and Munich at the time, and was purely decorative in intention. In the text to the right, however, there is evidence of a very different culture (*see plate 218*). Unsurprisingly, the sentiments expressed are deeply rooted in Nietzsche, indeed it might have been written by the man himself:

Believing in development and in a new generation both of those who create and of those who enjoy, we call all young people together, and as young people who carry the future in us we want to wrest freedom for our gestures and for our lives from the older, comfortably established forces. We claim as our own everyone who reproduces directly and without falsification whatever it is that drives him to create.[9]

While they looked to Nietzsche for theory, for the content and style of their new art the artists of Die Brücke explored more tangible sources. The Old Masters provided a rich fund of inspiration, most notably in the prints of Lucas Cranach (1472–1553) and Albrecht Dürer (1471–1528) which were housed in the Kupferstich-Kabinett in Dresden where, from 1900 onwards, it was also possible to see the graphic works of Henri de Toulouse-Lautrec (1864–1901). The Dresden Ethnographical Museum housed an extensive collection of tribal art and Kirchner in particular spent many hours there, studying the art of Oceania, and more specifically that of the Palau Islands. From 1905 onwards temporary exhibitions by

218   ERNST LUDWIG KIRCHNER   Die Brücke Manifesto   1906. *Kirchner's woodcut for the manifesto of Die Brücke reveals certain clues about the nature of the group's art. The manifesto is not merely intended to be read. It is intended to be looked at, and carefully scrutinized so that the spectator realizes that the group is telling him about themselves not only through the written word but also by the very means in which that word is presented. The actual typeface of the manifesto reveals the influence of the primitivism of Oceanic tribal art that was to become so crucial to Kirchner's art; by this time he had studied it in the Dresden Ethnographical Museum.*

modern artists became a third source. In November 1905 the Gallery Arnold held a van Gogh show featuring fifty of his paintings and the following year a similar exhibition which focused on Munch, displaying twenty works. Also in 1906 the Gallery Arnold mounted a mixed exhibition of French painting including such artists as the divisionists Georges Seurat (1859–1891), Henri-Edmond Cross (1856–1910) and Paul Signac (1863–1935), alongside Emile Bernard (1868–1941) and Paul Gauguin and the Nabis Félix Vallotton, Edouard Vuillard (1868–1940), Pierre Bonnard (1867–1947) and Maurice Denis (1870–1943). The artists of the Vienna Secession – Gustav Klimt and Carl Moll – were shown in 1907, and in 1908 there was another van Gogh exhibition (one hundred works this time), and a Fauve show.

It was the sixteenth-century German woodcut tradition that the young Die Brücke artists drew from the Old Masters. Nevertheless, they were also fascinated by the primitive shapes and natural organic forms of tribal art and their palette was informed by van Gogh, the Fauves and Munch – at times blisteringly bright, at others cooly melancholy.

These were years of self-discovery. The group worked in a studio Heckel had found in a butcher's shop in Berliner Strasse in the seediest part of Dresden, the most intense period of work lasting from 1905 to 1909. Nolde, now painting in a manner close to van Gogh's (see plate 23), and Pechstein, a student at the Dresden Academy, were invited to join the group in 1906.

Die Brücke only existed as a coherent entity until 1910. It was during that year that the group moved to Berlin. Nolde had already left in 1908, for he saw that the others' work was already drifting away from the level that would be acceptable to the Berlin Secession. The rest of the group submitted work to the Berlin Secession when they arrived, however, but it was rejected. They founded the Neue Sezession in reaction, but this was the beginning of the end. While Heckel, Pechstein and Kirchner continued to paint together, particularly in the open air at Moritzburg, it became clear to each of them that they had come so far as individuals during the previous five years that their work could no longer be classified collectively. The actual fragmentation did not begin until 1911, however, first to go being Pechstein. In May 1913 the group carried out its last united action, printing formal cards to announce its own demise.

Die Brücke disbanded on a high note. In 1912 their work was hung in triumph at the Cologne Sonderbund exhibition. In the course of just seven years these few artists had succeeded in changing not only the face of German art but the way in which art was regarded in that country. The work of each of the leading lights of the group, therefore, deserves individual scrutiny.

Leaves of Grass

Ernst Ludwig Kirchner is generally considered to have been the artistic driving force behind Die Brücke. He was the son of a middle-class chemical engineer and was brought up as a strict Protestant – a result, as he later described it, of 'the dark heritage of fanaticism in the generation of Brandenburg ministers on my father's side'.[10] As a young man he was tall and slim in appearance and in character obsessive to the point of paranoia, in particular as far as his work was concerned. His output even then was prolific.

As has already been mentioned, Kirchner had studied architecture in Dresden, before in 1903 moving briefly to Munich where he studied for a year at the school of von Debschitz and Obrist, and was exposed to the excesses of the popular Jugendstil style of decoration. It was while in Munich that Kirchner began to visit museums and exhibitions and developed his interest in fine art. One show which did not impress him, but which had a momentous effect on his life

was the Munich Secession exhibition of 1903. He later recalled the occasion:

In 1900 [sic] I had the bold idea of renewing German art . . . it came to me at an exhibition of the Munich Secession, in Munich where the pictures made the deepest impression on me because of the insignificance of their colour and execution and because of the total lack of public interest. Indoors these pale, bloodless, lifeless slices of studio bacon; outdoors colourful, flowing, real life in sunshine and excitement.[11]

Kirchner found the colour and real life he sought during the same year at another Munich exhibition: the show organized by the Phalanx group of artists under the Russian expatriate artist Wassily Kandinsky (1866–1944). An exhibition of contemporary French and Belgian painting, it included works by Signac, Lautrec, Vallotton and, importantly, van Gogh:

An exhibition of French Neo-Impressionists caught my attention: I found the drawing weak, but I studied the theory of colour based on optics and came to the opposite conclusion, namely that non-complementary colours and the complementaries themselves should be generated by the eye, in line with Goethe's theory.[12]

The juxtaposition of two such contrasting exhibitions persuaded the precocious twenty-three-year-old Kirchner that German art was dead and in need of revitalization. And he believed that he was the man for the job. Instead of joining Kandinsky, however, as other artists might have done, Kirchner set out to accomplish the task on his own. He returned to Dresden to take his final exams at the Hochschule and then decided to give up architecture to become a painter.

In his early work Kirchner's style was closest to van Gogh's; he used quick brushstrokes, heavy impasto and bright colour to create images, such as his Woman in a Birch Wood (see plate 231), which contrasted blatantly with the dull tonalities he was protesting against.

Between 1906 and 1908 Kirchner's work took on an increased heaviness, yet at the same time was moving steadily towards the spareness of line and two-dimensional quality that were to become his trademark. In September 1908 he saw an exhibition of work by the Fauves in Dresden and was particularly attracted by Matisse's paintings; indeed, the Frenchman's influence is clearly discernible in Kirchner's own painting Doris with a Ruff (see plate 238) which dates from this time. The heavy technique of this picture, however, still betrays both his admiration of van Gogh and the lasting power of Munch, echoes of whose style can be detected throughout Kirchner's entire career. By the time Kirchner painted Girl under an Umbrella the following year (see plate 239), the impact of Matisse had become more apparent, and it was in this style that he continued to paint until 1910.

Kirchner's mature work dates from 1910 onwards. He abandons Matisse and van Gogh and creates a style of his own founded upon the combination of an assuredness of handling, his extensive study of primitive art and his regard for the German Old Masters. Possibly the first painting to exemplify this new confidence is his Self-Portrait with Model (see plate 211). Here Kirchner uses the vibrant colours of the Fauves to quite different effect, for he forges an eclectic style with many facets: an angularity derived from tribal art; a stylization and figural elongation which may owe something to his exposure to Klimt's work at the Vienna Secession show of 1907; the figure grouping of Munch; and a technique evidently developing out of his rediscovery of the carving process involved in woodblock printing. The cumulative effect is disturbing.

The painting also provides a commentary upon the way of life enjoyed by the artists of Die Brücke. The model, a tawdry-looking girl in bright orange stockings and a cheap blue slip, sits apprehensively behind the artist, who himself wears nothing but a brilliantly striped dressing-gown, or might it be a coat? First-hand accounts confirm that this was how Kirchner lived and worked. One of the key tenets of the group was freedom, and this freedom was not only artistic but social, moral and sexual.

As early as 1905 Kirchner had produced a number of sexually explicit woodblock illustrations to the *1001 Nights*, and every summer he would desert Dresden, retreating to the unspoilt beauty of Fehmarn, an island in the Baltic, in order to paint nudes in the open air. In 1910 Kirchner, Heckel and Pechstein went to paint together in the quiet countryside surrounding the lakes at Moritzburg; they took with them two sisters from Dresden, and as Pechstein recalls: 'We lived in complete harmony, we worked and we went swimming. If we

219 ERNST KIRCHNER   Women at Potsdammer Platz   1914.
In this heavily worked woodcut we can see the darker side of Kirchner's art. Here he chooses to describe two 'ladies of the night', who stand in the lamplight at ten o'clock on a chilly winter evening waiting for a client. He is hurrying across the street towards their symbolic black circular island; he wears the bowler hat of what Kirchner considered the irresponsible, hypocritical bourgeois. The man takes a tentative step into the circle of light surrounding the women; they appear, meanwhile, to rise out of it as if above an abyss. It is an image of urban savagery, made all the more powerful by the primitive style in which Kirchner portrays his victims.

needed a male model to set off the girls, one of us would leap into the breach.'[13] The resulting canvases of nudes frolicking in landscapes, often painted with no little degree of sexual frankness, can be seen as the manifestation of a desire to escape to a primitive naturalism that is reminiscent of the sentiments of Gauguin. At the same time, and on another level, this was yet one more way of liberating themselves from the stifled world of Wilhelmian Germany, the repressive moral standards of which seemed anathema both to the artists' desire for a new society and their confirmed faith in Nietzsche. For the philosopher had written:

This aphrodisiac bliss (physiologically: the creative instinct of the artist and the distribution of semen in his blood). The demand for art and beauty is an indirect demand for the ecstasies of sexuality communicated to the brain.[14]

At the same time, in Vienna, the young artist Egon Schiele (1890–1918) was also producing work that displayed unreservedly this new sexual freedom. Indeed, his depictions of himself and his models, in a style derived from the Jugendstil painter Gustav Klimt, were so frank that in 1912 Schiele was arrested on a charge of pornography (*see plate 237*). For Kirchner, however, it was his commitment to Nietzschean philosophy that justified the overt sexuality of his art, and this was further qualified by his love for the poetry of the American Walt Whitman. Kirchner later wrote of his years in Dresden: 'That great poet Walt Whitman was responsible for my outlook on life. During my dismal days of want and hunger in Dresden his *Leaves of Grass* was and still is my comfort and encouragement.'[15] Whitman, who had died in 1892, had sought in his poetry to unite art and life by encouraging the exploration of the inner self – in just the same way as the new generation of German artists were in around 1910. His work was widely read in Germany, largely as a result of his having been equated with Nietzsche's 'New Man' by the influential Berlin intellectual Johannes Schlaf, who had translated *Leaves of Grass* into German in 1907.

Kirchner's *Figures Walking into the Sea* (*see plate 236*), which he painted in 1912, seems to capture the feeling of joyful, innocent sexual freedom inherent in both Nietzsche and Whitman. It might almost serve obliquely to illustrate Whitman's verse:

Which of the young men does she like the best?
Ah the homeliest of them is beautiful to her . . .
Dancing and laughing along the beach came the twenty-ninth bather,
the rest did not see her, but she saw them and loved them . . .
An unseen hand also passed over their bodies,
It descended tremblingly from their temples and ribs.[16]

or:

To be surrounded by beautiful, curious breathing laughing flesh is enough . . .
I do not ask any more delight . . . I swim in it as in a sea.[17]

Nevertheless, Kirchner's interest in sexuality also drew him – as it had Lautrec – to the seedier side of society, and he produced numerous images of prostitutes. His concern with their relationship to men is well demonstrated in his woodcut of 1914 (*see plate 219*) which shows two such women standing on what might be a traffic island in Potsdamer Platz, but which is in reality a graphic element emphasizing their isolation from the world around them as they are approached by a client. Here Kirchner's work in woodcut, a medium with which he had been experimenting for the previous ten years, has reached its zenith. He is able to unite the stark line of the primitive with the chiaroscuro of Rembrandt (1606–1669) – whose work he could see in the Kupferstich-Kabinett – and the confrontational figure grouping that he continued to borrow from Munch.

In 1913, with the dissolution of Die Brücke, Kirchner moved to Berlin. He was conscripted into the army at the outbreak of war but was discharged in 1915 after a nervous breakdown (*see plate 250*).

Natural Order

If Kirchner was the practical leader of Die Brücke, then Erich Heckel was undoubtedly the theorist. Born in Dobeln in Saxony in 1883, Heckel was educated at the Gymnasium in Chemnitz and it was here, at the age of eighteen, that he met his future artistic colleague Karl Schmidt-Rottluff. United by an interest in literature, the two boys immediately became firm friends. Although possessed of a sound self-confidence, Heckel was a quiet boy and was teased by his fellow pupils for his intensity. His tutor at the Hochschule in Dresden, where he studied architecture, later recalled the prolonged study that Heckel would bestow on any one particular object:

I found him in front of Grünewald's Pietà, which was still in the Stiftskirche in Aschaffenburg at that time, and with the greatest of care he had copied the hands that are movingly wrung over the dead body into his sketchbook, which was three times the size of any of ours.[18]

Unlike Kirchner, when Heckel graduated from the Hochschule, he entered an architectural practice, though at the same time becoming one of the founder members of Die Brücke. In fact it was Heckel, more than any other, who was responsible for organizing the group. He took charge of their finances and found them the butcher's shop studio where they first painted. And it was he who recruited Max Pechstein in 1906, before disappearing to the countryside with Schmidt-Rottluff to paint.

While still employed as an architect between 1905 and 1907, Heckel produced works, such as his *Brickworks* (*see plate 232*) in a style similar to van Gogh's, using heavy impasto and tactile knobs of paint squeezed straight from the tube on to the canvas. Kirchner and Nolde were painting in the same mould at the time. Having seen the Fauve show in September 1908 – after his short sojourn in the country – Heckel began to turn away from the impasto inspired by van Gogh in favour of the softer, more lyrical style of *Village Dance* (*see plate 220*), which is more reminiscent of the 1906 work of Albert Marquet (1875–1947) and Raoul Dufy (1877–1953). During that year he also admitted a liking for Gauguin, a sentiment he shared with Pechstein.

In 1909 Heckel travelled to Italy, where he was particularly attracted by Etruscan art. When he returned to Germany later in the year the flavour of this European primitivism became evident in his painting, along with a brighter palette. His *Nude on a Sofa* (*see plate 235*) combines these characteristics

with a new two-dimensionality that relates the painting to the work of Matisse.

During 1910 Heckel underwent something of a spiritual awakening. The man whom Kirchner first remembered reciting Nietzsche and who was responsible for introducing the literary backbone to Die Brücke in its infancy now abandoned conventional religion in favour of the Nietzschean moral ethic which had always underlain his thought. It was not in Nietzsche himself that Heckel discovered this new faith, however, but in the work of Fyodor Dostoevsky (1821–1881); and he encapsulated his ideas in *Two Men at a Table* (*see plate 249*), a painting that describes a scene from the Russian author's novel *The Idiot*. This belief in the natural power of man also imbues Heckel's landscapes, culminating in 1913 in the crystalline masterpiece *Glassy Day* (*see plate 234*) in which the artist seems to express his growing wonder at the natural order of nature.

Total Accord

Three other artists deserve mention before we look at the career of the third great name associated with Die Brücke. Karl Schmidt-Rottluff, temperamentally withdrawn and introverted, was the youngest of the artists of Die Brücke, but nevertheless a key figure in the development of the group. A schoolboy friend of Heckel, he was almost as passionate as the older boy about literature and in particular about Nietzsche. It was also he who had written to Nolde in 1906,

220 ERIC HECKEL Village Dance 1908.
During the course of one year Heckel has made a quantum leap in his art. In this description of a dance in a village hall he has left behind the laboured intensity of his Brickworks (see plate 232); now his composition has been carefully thought out and his application of paint is sparing. A solitary couple turn on the dance floor while all the village women sit around. The scene is as primitive a ritual as one might see on a Polynesian island and, as such, is a subject that would rate highly in the canon of Die Brücke. The framing curtain and bold outlines suggest that Heckel had been studying not only the work of Gauguin but also that of Matisse.

221 KARL SCHMIDT-ROTTLUFF Two Female Nudes 1911.
It is in relief sculpture that Schmidt-Rottluff really stands out from the other Die Brücke artists. In this strange piece he explores the common theme of the nude in a landscape in a very different way. Two girls are described. Yet we see neither of their faces. Instead we are presented with a mass of interlinked limbs, such that it is at first difficult to make out just what belongs to whom. On deeper scrutiny, however, we begin to see that the figure on the left is in fact bending forward, legs apart, her right hand on her hip, her left hand on the ground. The mass of her hair at the top of the image is picked up by the black triangle of her pubic hair below. The figure on the right is shown half-kneeling on her left leg, her right interlocking with that of her neighbour. Three-dimensional form has been distilled here into an almost abstract pattern.

inviting him to join the group. While in his painting he displays an interest in van Gogh and Munch (*see plate 241*), it is as a sculptor that Schmidt-Rottluff is of most interest. His *Two Female Nudes* of 1911 (*see plate 221*) is an extraordinary image which seems to recall, perhaps more than any other work of the group, the primitive paintings and carvings of the Palau islanders (on display in the Dresden museum), and which simultaneously anticipates the artist's move towards abstraction which occurred after 1912.

Max Pechstein had begun his artistic career studying decorative painting, before deciding to go to the Dresden Kunstgewerbeschule in 1900. In 1902 he transferred to the Dresden Academy of Fine Arts. He left four years later in 1906 and it was during this year that he was recruited to Die Brücke by Heckel, at a point when he was enraged about not having been allowed to put the finishing touches to a mural at the third German Arts and Crafts exhibition:

I gave furious vent to my feelings. Suddenly there was someone at my side, seconding my vituperations. It was Erich Heckel, who was still working for Kreis at that time. Joyfully we discovered our total accord in the drive towards liberation, an art which charged forwards, unimpeded by conventions. And that was how I joined Die Brücke.[19]

Pechstein travelled extensively and it was this aspect of his life that was to prove important to Die Brücke. He became, as it were, the broadcaster abroad of artistic developments inside Germany. It seems rather less surprising in the light of this knowledge that it should have been Pechstein and not

Kirchner or Heckel whose absence Rupert Brooke should have regretted at Roger Fry's second Post-Impressionist exhibition in London in 1912.

Pechstein was in Italy in 1907, before moving on in December of that year to Paris, where he showed three pictures at the Salon des Indépendants. He also met Kees van Dongen (1877–1968), Henri Manguin (1874–1949) – and possibly Matisse, which would have given the German avant-garde group direct contact with one of their acknowledged masters. Such was the effect of this four-month trip that between 1908 and 1909 Pechstein began to develop what might be described as the 'German-Fauve' style (*see plate 240*).

Pechstein was the quickest of all Die Brücke's artists to adopt other styles. He saw the work of Gauguin in Dresden in 1910 and after this date combines his reliance on Matisse – seen in *Under the Trees* (*see plate 292*) – with something of the Tahitian exile's style. In some cases he even makes literal transcriptions of Gauguin's forms, although such a move might be seen as an attempt to subvert the traditional, and Pechstein was never quite as radical as either Kirchner or Heckel. Indeed, when they abandoned the Neue Sezession in 1912 he chose to remain.

Otto Mueller (1874–1930) was a late recruit to Die Brücke. Some six years older than Kirchner, he joined the group in 1910 having had his work rejected by the Berlin Secession. Mueller had studied lithography in Gorlitz before progressing to the Dresden Academy in 1894, and had been working in Dresden independently of any of Die Brücke's activities since 1899. Although his palette does not perhaps reflect that prevalent amongst the group, the angularity of his elongated figures (*see plate 243*) suggests both his somewhat romantic, Gauguinesque desire for a primitive lifestyle and the combined influences on his work of tribal art and the work of Kirchner.

Problematic Faith

It is impossible to categorize Emil Nolde simply as a member of Die Brücke. He was a member of the group for only a few months between 1906 and 1907. Moreover, the scope of his achievement is on an altogether more monumental level. It was in 1906, shortly before he accepted their invitation to join the group, that Nolde first came across the work of Die Brücke – in the collection of the Hamburg collector judge Gustav Schiefler. While Kirchner and Heckel received from Nolde a sound instruction in the techniques of surface engraving which was to stand them in good stead throughout their careers, it is hard to imagine what Nolde got from his involvement with the group. The most obvious effect on his art was that he developed a preoccupation with sensuality. He sustained this even after his departure from the group and indeed it can still be seen in his frenzied *Dance around the Golden Calf* (*see plate 245*).

Nolde's autobiography also reveals an interest in the work of Nietzsche which would appear to link him spiritually with Heckel. Nolde remained devoutly Christian throughout his life, however, and his use of Nietzschean theory has a more sinister side. He directs Nietzsche's anti-Christian ideas against the Jews in a fervent anti-Semitism which appears repeatedly in his work. In his *Last Supper* (*see plate 244*), for instance, Nolde depicts even the disciples as the ugly stereo-

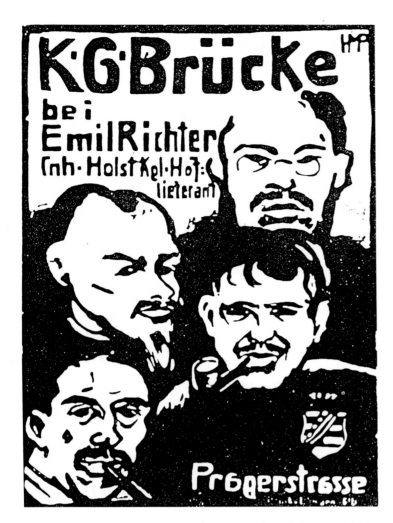

222 MAX PECHSTEIN Poster for Die Brücke exhibition 1909.
Here is a rare image of the artists of Die Brücke executed at the height of their activity in 1909. Apart from Kirchner's retrospective group portrait painted in 1926, this is the only reliable artistic portrait we have of the four artists. Here are Ernst Ludwig Kirchner, Eric Heckel, Karl Schmidt-Rottluff and Max Pechstein himself, depicted in stark outline, almost as caricatures. It is an arresting image and must certainly have attracted attention when posted around Dresden to advertise their exhibition at Emil Richter's gallery in Dresden.

types favoured by the future Nazis. It is perhaps ironic that his work should have featured in Hitler's notorious exhibition of degenerate art held in 1937.

It is in Nolde's approach to religious subject matter that we can find the essential reason for his break with Die Brücke. Having attempted a few genuinely sensual canvases, he grew scornful of such depravities, seeing them as directly opposed to the religion of his youth. He was determined to turn them against their inventors and, using a Fauve palette and subject matter that would have been favoured by Die Brücke, he produced such images as the *Dance around the Golden Calf* (*see plate 245*), which portray sybaritic indulgence as wasteful and decadent. In Nolde's religious subjects he emphasizes not the divine aspect of religion but that ecstatic, charismatic devotion which equates the religious experience with the sexual and which he had first encountered as a child. He later admitted:

After school . . . I lay down with my back pressed to the ground and my eyes closed, with my arms stretched out stiffly. And then I thought, 'So lay your Saviour Jesus Christ when the men and women took Him down from the cross.' And then I turned myself over, dreaming with problematic faith that the whole wide, round, wonderful earth was my beloved.[20]

In 1909 Nolde attempted to form his own artistic group comprising Munch, Matisse and Schmidt-Rottluff, but it came to nothing. His work by this stage had become almost entirely concerned with religious themes, apart from the paintings he produced during the winter of 1910–11, which depict scenes in the cafés and restaurants of Hamburg. The following year Nolde resumed his religious theme, beginning work on a major series of paintings following the life of Christ. Once again colour is used to convey emotion here, and it is to the legacy of the Fauves that Nolde turns.

It is interesting that Nolde's own religious revival should have coincided with a similar more general revival in Germany as a whole. This manifested itself in literature in the writings of Wilhelm Worringer, who in 1910 published his essay 'Form Problems of the Gothic'.

Formally, Nolde's art becomes more complex at about this time. In 1911 he visited the Belgian painter James Ensor (1860–1949) in Ostend and was impressed by the way he used masks from Africa and Oceania as models for the hideous faces that featured in his pictures. On his return to Germany Nolde began work on his great *Crucifixion* (*see plate 246*) in which he combined a number of references: while the basic concept of the triptych and its overall composition are based on Mathias Grünewald's magnificent and quintessentially German Isenheim Altarpiece painted in 1515 at Colmar, the facial types bear more than a passing resemblance to those Nolde had featured in his *Masks* (*see plate 247*) the previous year – painted after his meeting with Ensor. The figures themselves seem to combine the attenuated forms of the sixteenth century with those of Kirchner, and the whole canvas is painted in a manner and palette that have roots in Munch and the Fauves.

The effect of Nolde's eclecticism is to create a terrifying image. It is just possible that Nolde might have been using primitive masks as models in an attempt to portray what he saw as the natural primitivism of the Jewish people, clouded as his vision was by religious zeal. What is certain is that Nolde was increasingly fascinated by primitive art. In 1912 he began a book on the subject, writing: 'The absolute originality, the intense, often grotesque expression . . . may well be what gives us pleasure.'[21]

Whatever sinister prejudices he may have embraced, Nolde had succeeded in revitalizing the indigenous German art tradition. The fact that France had proved such a disappointment, however, seemed a lasting regret to him: 'Paris had given me so little, and yet I had hoped for so much.'[22]

In 1913 Nolde left Germany on a voyage of discovery. As part of a German Imperial Colonial Office expedition to New Guinea, he was to further his study of primitive art. Unfortunately, he was forced to return to Germany after the outbreak of the First World War, but the paintings he produced on that trip, *Tropical Sun* (*see plate 248*) for instance, confirm his confident and dramatic colour sense and his unresolved search for the inner self of the artist. Towards the end of his life he wrote:

What the artist learns matters little. What he himself discovers has a real worth for him, and gives him the necessary incitement to work. When such creative activity ceases, when there are no more difficulties or problems, external or internal, to solve, then the fire is quickly extinguished . . . An ability to learn was never a sign of genius.[23]

223 MATTHIAS GRÜNEWALD Isenheim Altarpiece 1510–15. *Matthias Grünewald was a contemporary of Dürer and a devout follower of the Lutheran faith. As such he provided a superb model for Emil Nolde hundreds of years later. Indeed Nolde chose to base the composition and concept of his Life of Christ triptych (see plate 246) on Grünewald's Isenheim Altarpiece, a work that had been commissioned in 1515 for the hospital for skin diseases in Isenheim. Grünewald's Christ has a terrible, deathly intensity about Him; the essentially northern religious character of this must have appealed to Nolde.*

The Neue Sezession

While the artists of Die Brücke had been pushing the boundaries of German art forever further outwards, the Berlin Secession, founded in 1898 by Max Liebermann, had continued to function. Although it numbered among its members Matisse, Munch and Nolde, it had by now become a more or less conservative body. In 1910 eighty-nine paintings were rejected, constituting the work of twenty-seven artists. Nolde who, with some other members of Die Brücke, was among the number, deliberately engineered a crisis within the Secession; he published a letter in which he publicly attacked Liebermann. Nolde was consequently asked to resign from the Berlin Secession and when he did so he laid the foundations for the formation of the Neue Sezession, a breakaway group of so-called younger artists, under the presidency of Max Pechstein.

The Neue Sezession gave Die Brücke a higher international profile and served, for the time being at least, to unite the diverse artistic centres of Dresden, Munich, Berlin and Prague. Here it was that Expressionism was born. The introduction to the catalogue of the third Neue Sezession exhibition in the Spring of 1911 could be describing one of a number of avant-garde groups working in Europe during the first years of this century. Unlike the Impressionists we are told that the new generation of artists:

No longer want to reproduce nature in each of its transient manifestations. Rather they condense their personal sensations of an object, they compress them into a characteristic expression, in such a way that the expression of their personal sensations is strong enough to produce a wall painting. A coloured decoration.[24]

Herein lies the only genuine similarity between the early Expressionists and the Fauves. As the third Neue Sezession show opened, the Berlin Secession was showing paintings by the Fauves which it labelled 'expressionist'. Here the resemblance ends. The German experiment which took place between 1905 and 1913 employed Fauve colour and technique as a means to an end. Just as Munch had looked to Gauguin to find the means with which to explore his own inner complexities, so Kirchner, Heckel and their associates, with the possible exception of Nolde, looked initially to Matisse, André Derain (1880–1954) and also to Munch himself for the means with which to confront basic needs for self-examination. The French were still held in the thrall of a tradition of realism which the Germans had only inherited third-hand. As such, it was a tradition destined to be subjugated by the overwhelming power of northern spirituality.

NOTES.

[1] F. Hodler, in H. Muhlestein, *Ferdinand Hodler*, Weimar, 1914, 259.

[2] P. Modersohn-Becker, Diary entry 25 Feb 1903, in Paula Modersohn-Becker. *Briefe und Tagebuchblatter*, Munich, 1957.

[3] R-M. Rilke, *Worpswede Monographie* 1903, 54.

[4] Emil Nolde, *Jahre der Kampfe*, 1967,

[5] Friedrich Nietzsche, *Thus Spake Zarathustra*, the prologue, trans. R.J. Holingdale, London, 1961.

[6] Ernst Ludwig Kirchner, diary 1923, see D.E. Gordon, *Kirchner*, Munich, 1968.

[7] Ibid.

[8] Friedrich Nietzsche, op. cit., the prologue, part 9.

[9] E.L. Kirchner, *Die Brücke manifesto*, Dresden, 1906.

[10] Ernst Ludwig Kirchner, letter to Conrad Valentin, in April 1937, in Wolf-Dieter Dube, *The Expressionists*, London, 1972, 38.

[11] Ibid.

[12] Ibid.

[13] Max Pechstein, quoted in Harald Osborn *Max Pechstein*, Berlin, 1922.

[14] Friedrich Nietzsche, *The Will to Power*, Bonn, 1878, 424.

[15] Ernst Ludwig Kirchner, letter to Conrad, in Dube, op. cit.

[16] Walt Whitman, 'Song of Myself', verse 11, in *Leaves of Grass*, New York, 1855.

[17] Walt Whitman, 'I Sing the Body Electric', verse 4, in *Leaves of Grass*, New York, 1855.

[18] Fritz Schumaker, quoted in Dube, op. cit., 52.

[19] Max Pechstein, in Osborn, op. cit.

[20] Emil Nolde, op. cit.

[21] Emil Nolde, *Kunstausserungen der Naturvolker,* 1912.

[22] Emil Nolde, in Herbert Read, *Art Now*, London, 1960.

[23] Emil Nolde, *Kunstausserungen der Naturvolker*, op. cit.

[24] Max Raphael, catalogue introduction to the third exhibition of the Neue Sezession, 1911.

224 EDVARD MUNCH Evening on Karl Johan Street 1892.
*It seems curious that while Liebermann continued to paint in the
Impressionist style of his* Parrot Walk *(see plate 212), he was also able
to admire the work of the Norwegian artist Edvard Munch. Indeed he went
so far as to invite Munch to exhibit in Berlin in the year that this work was
painted. Munch was an important influence on German art throughout
the first decade of the twentieth century and this picture, with its hollow,
staring faces and eerie palette, forms a valuable bridge between the intense
Impressionism of Liebermann and the unsettling spirituality of Kirchner,
who knew this painting well.*

226 LOVIS CORINTH The Childhood of Zeus 1905.
*It should be noted, here, that while the artist displays an unprecedented
freedom and lightness in his 'Impressionist' approach to the picture
surface, the subject matter he has chosen still remains within the
boundaries prescribed as appropriate by the Academy. Nevertheless,
in this frenzied scene of Dionysian revelry, Corinth has unwittingly set
a precedent for the future; an unbridled sensuality fills the picture here
as it will again in the work of the Expressionists.*

225 LOVIS CORINTH Self-Portrait with Model 1901.
*Along with Liebermann, Corinth was regarded as one of the major artists
of the German Impressionist movement of the 1890s. This picture of
the artist with his gypsy model is painted in a style derived from that of
the German naturalist painter Franz von Lenbach, by whom Corinth was
heavily influenced. The artist is presented as an heroic figure. Moreover,
the dark palette and moody feeling, together with the actual physical
appearance of Corinth himself, suggest similar portraits by Corinth's own
great hero Rembrandt.*

228 FERDINAND HODLER Schynige Platte 1909.
*Hodler turned to landscapes in his later work. Always empty, devoid of the
human figure, these monumental images seem to point to a pantheistic
Symbolism in the manner of Cézanne and Munch; the artist seems to have
imbued the landscape itself with a timeless spirituality. It was these
powerful works, as much as his figurative Symbolist paintings, epitomized
by* Night *(see plate 227), that caused a stir among the younger
generation of German painters when they were exhibited at the Berlin
Secession. They also contributed to the revival of the Romantic spirit in
German art.*

227 FERDINAND HODLER Night 1890.
Generally regarded as Hodler's masterpiece, Night *had an immense
impact upon German art during the early twentieth century. Having first
painted pictures for the tourists in his home town of Bern, Hodler had
studied at Geneva before visiting Paris in 1881. He was initially
influenced by Corot and Courbet, but by the date of this painting he had
succumbed to the ideas of the Symbolists and had begun to paint in a style
similar to that of Puvis de Chavannes. Through his theory of Eurythmy,
Hodler attempted to portray in this work – and in its companion piece*
Day, *which he painted in 1900 – all the events of a single night. From the
left we can see sleep, rest, death, love and nightmare.*

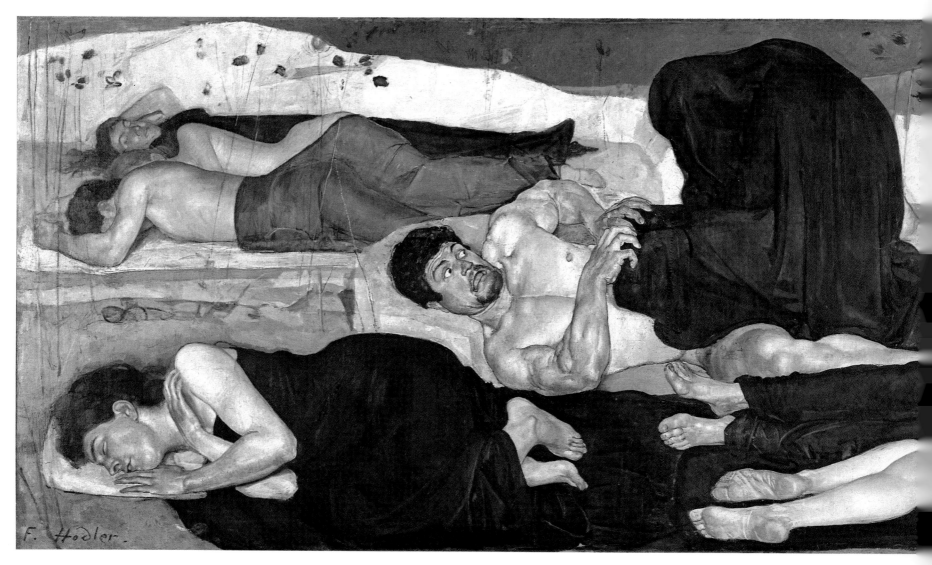

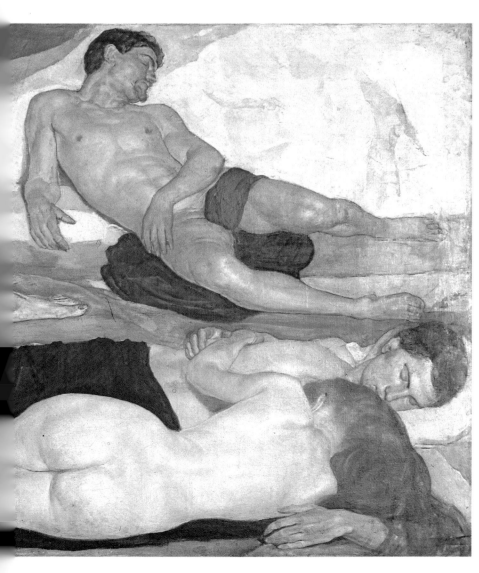

230 PAULA MODERSOHN-BECKER Reclining Mother and Child 1906.

In the space of only one year Paula Modersohn-Becker transformed the largely naturalist style of her painting – seen in her portrait of Clara Rilke (see plate 229) – moving on to develop the sculptural monumentality of her Reclining Mother and Child. Gauguin's influence seems stronger than ever in this image where the artist sacrifices colour in the interest of purity of form. The mother appears to have been sculpted from a block of coloured marble in a style far ahead of its time; Paula herself called it her 'great easiness of form'. Throughout her tragically short career Paula was preoccupied with the mother and child theme; this makes it all the more poignant that she should have died in childbirth just one year after this picture was painted.

229 PAULA MODERSOHN-BECKER Portrait of Clara Rilke-Westhof 1905.

In 1898 Modersohn and Mackensen were joined at Worpswede by the artist Paula Becker. Three years later she and Modersohn were married, Paula adding her husband's name to her own in the fashion of the time. A frequent visitor to the colony was the Austrian poet Rainer-Maria Rilke, who expostulated to the artists his Symbolist theories of the pantheistic presence in nature. His wife Clara came with him, and it was she whom Paula Becker chose to paint. In its heavy outlines and simple planes of colour, the portrait shows Paula's first tentative response to the work of Gauguin, which she had seen on her trips to Paris in 1900 and 1903.

231 ERNST LUDWIG KIRCHNER Woman in a Birch Wood 1906.

In 1903 Kirchner attended two exhibitions in Munich which profoundly changed his life. The first, of contemporary German paintings in the style of the Dachau school, he found bland and lifeless. The second captivated him. One of the artists featured in the show was Vincent van Gogh, and from that moment onwards Kirchner abandoned pale tonalities in favour of untarnished primary colours and bold, fat brushstrokes – the characteristics that had so affected him. The similarity with Nolde's work of the same date is striking; surely the two artists must have been looking to the same source for inspiration and guidance.

232 ERIC HECKEL Brickworks 1907.
*In 1907, like Kirchner and Nolde, Heckel was still painting in a style
redolent of van Gogh, whom he had emulated since 1905. Here his
untutored hand has squeezed such quantities of paint straight out of the
tube on to the canvas that the whole picture seems to move before our eyes
in a great sea of green and blue. The paint has been so heavily worked
that it seems to bear testimony to Heckel's much reported capacity for
concentration. The brickworks itself seems to throb with activity through
the heat of its intense redness, while strokes of red vie for prominent
positions amidst the yellow, blue and green in the rainbow sky above.*

233 EMIL NOLDE In the Corn 1906.
*In this painting, executed just before Nolde was invited to join Die Brücke
in Dresden, we see the artist at the height of his first stylistic phase. While
in Paris in 1899 Nolde had seen the work of van Gogh; despite his later
protestations that Paris had had no effect upon his art, it is clear that he
never lost touch with the legacy of that trip. The bold dashes of thick paint
and bright yellow and blue colours in this painting are both strongly
evocative of the work of the Dutch master. It is interesting too, in the
light of his future work, that Nolde moves away in this painting from an
empty landscape to include figures; this bears witness once again to the
influence of his contemporaries in France.*

234 ERIC HECKEL   Glassy Day   1913.
*Heckel's art can be considered to have reached a climax in this
extraordinary canvas, in which he takes the classic Die Brücke motif of a
nude in a landscape and transforms it almost to the point of abstraction.
The surface of the water beside the standing nude is glassy, as indeed is the
sky which it reflects; the clouds that appear to speed across that sky seem
no more than two pieces of crystal. The rock formations on the left,
together with the full stomach and breasts of the girl, provide some relief
from this angularity. Both signify, in Heckel's ideal of the perfectly
harmonious mystery of nature, the means of regeneration and growth.*

235 ERIC HECKEL   Nude on a Sofa   1909.
*This image of ennui is one of the last Heckel executed before he moved
on to concentrate on subjects of deeper philosophical significance in 1910.
Here we see a young model, exhausted after a day's posing in the studio,
reclining on a sofa. The whole scene is worthy of Matisse, Manguin,
van Dongen or Camoin, all of whose paintings of similar subjects it
immediately calls to mind. This is Heckel at his most lyrical, apparently
as relaxed himself as the girl he describes. As his choice of subject matter
changed, his style would develop a new angularity and his work would
never again recapture the innocence of this vision.*

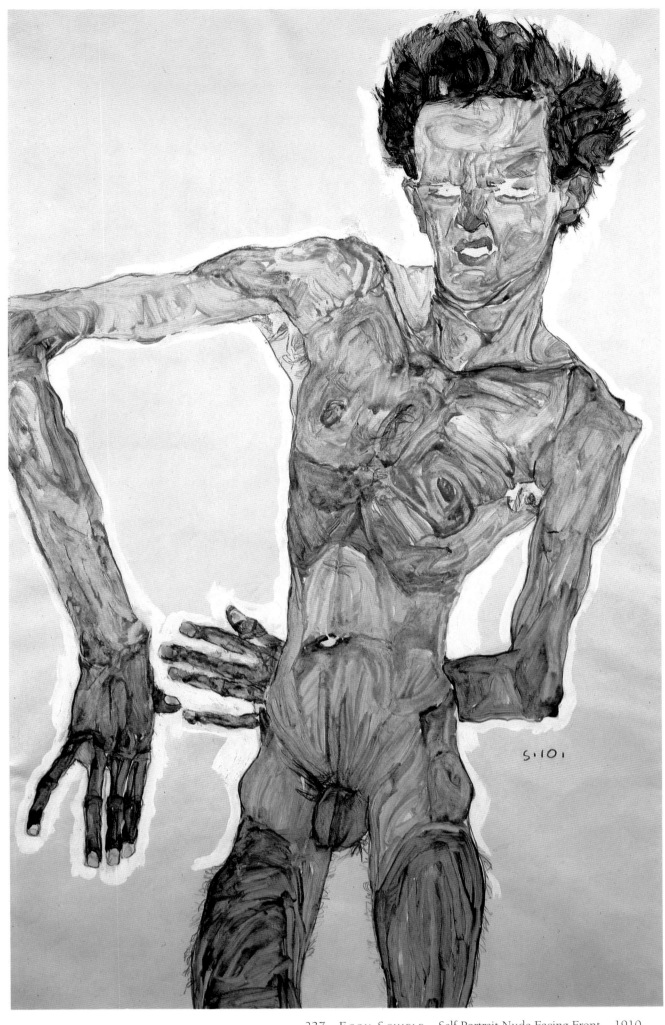

237 EGON SCHIELE Self-Portrait Nude Facing Front 1910.
Schiele painted this self-portrait in 1910 when he was twenty years old. It is typical of his frank approach to his own sexuality, an attitude that permeated his entire short output. Stylistically the picture shows the influence of the Jugendstil painter Gustav Klimt, one of the founders of the Vienna Secession in 1898; it also bears comparisons with the work of Oskar Kokoschka. Schiele's painting cannot be said, however, to have belonged to any one particular school. In contrast to the work of other Die Brücke artists, the sexual content of Schiele's work was the result of his interest in the writings of Sigmund Freud. He was even more blatant in his depiction of sexual activity than Kirchner, and pursued some images to the point of pornography. Indeed, he was arrested on a pornography charge in 1912.

236 ERNST LUDWIG KIRCHNER Figures Walking into the Sea
1912.
Every summer Kirchner left Dresden to paint in the country. He did this primarily to be able to paint nudes in the landscape. In such works as this he was able to achieve something of the natural primitivism for which he yearned and which he visualized in the writings of the poet Walt Whitman. Here, below a lighthouse, a man and woman join hands and stroll out into the sea, quite naked, very much at ease and perfectly contented. On the shore lies another figure, of uncertain sex, head on hand. It is hard to gauge the reaction of this third party to the scene, but if, like Kirchner, we believe Whitman, then it is surely one of serenity.

238 ERNST LUDWIG KIRCHNER   Doris with a Ruff   1908–09.
*In this unsigned and undated portrait Kirchner seems uncertain about
precisely the direction in which his art should be developing. Doris seems
to engage us with the hollow stare of a Munch figure, while at the same
time she appears to owe something to Matisse, whose influence is obvious
in much of Kirchner's work of this period. It is a stark, unforgiving image
which, if nothing else, marks Kirchner's abandonment of the wild
brushstrokes that characterized his early canvases inspired by van Gogh.
He has moved towards a more measured application of paint which
may even suggest that he had been taking note of the achievements of
the divisionists.*

239 ERNST LUDWIG KIRCHNER   Girl under an Umbrella
1909.
*This intimate canvas, painted by Kirchner in the year after the Fauve
exhibition in Dresden, shows how deeply the artist was impressed by what
he had seen there. The picture is comparable with Matisse's Blue Nude of
1907 (see plate 150) with which it has much in common. In composition
Kirchner's painting is almost an exact mirror image of the Matisse. In
colour, too, the artists share a taste for the unnatural. Kirchner's nude has
an almost entirely two-dimensional quality, however, and the brushstrokes
with which the artist depicts her umbrella are wild in comparison with
those employed by the Frenchman.*

240 MAX PECHSTEIN   Before the Storm   1910.
*Here is the great publicist of Die Brücke at his most painterly. While the
subject is Impressionist and the handling close to van Gogh and Munch,
the great swathes of the fields and the mass of trees suggest that Pechstein
was more concerned with the importance of formal composition than with
the accurate representation of reality. It is a deeply intense image and
was painted during the course of a year that Pechstein spent first with
Kirchner at Moritzburg and latterly with Schmidt-Rottluff at Dangast.
In its wild brushstrokes and impasto it can be said to have been one of
Pechstein's winter paintings. For in the summer, when he went to the
Baltic, everything about his art underwent a complete change.*

241 KARL SCHMIDT-ROTTLUFF Norwegian Landscape 1911.
The youngest of the artists of Die Brücke, Schmidt-Rottluff was even more
withdrawn than Heckel. He is drawn in his painting to those two other
great introverted geniuses of northern avant-garde painting at the turn of
the century: van Gogh and Munch. This Norwegian landscape, painted in
the country of one of his mentors in 1911, is a typical example. In his low
viewpoint, elongated shadows and boldly painted buildings which seem
almost to shimmer, Schmidt-Rottluff is close to Munch. His choice of
colour is another point of contact; he uses the same blood-red backdrop
and heavy black and blue shadows as Munch had used in his early work.
In his line, however, he is not so precise as the Norwegian and it is here
that the influence of van Gogh comes into play.

242 MAX PECHSTEIN Under the Trees 1911.
Pechstein reserved one style for winter (see plate 240) and quite another
for summer. This study of four models frolicking under the trees is an
example of his warm-weather approach. While his winter paintings reflect
the bone-chilling Angst and northern temperament of van Gogh, those of
the summer recall the fresh sunny palette of Matisse and the Fauves. In
essence this scene might easily be an adjunct to Derain's bacchic Dance of
1906 (see plate 147) or Matisse's Bonheur de Vivre (see plate 135)
of a year earlier.

243 OTTO MUELLER Three Nudes before a Mirror 1912.
Mueller joined the ranks of Die Brücke in a fit of pique in 1910 at the
advanced age of forty-three, having had his work rejected by the Berlin
Secession. He was never suited temperamentally to the excesses of
Kirchner and Heckel and his paintings often look strained or contrived. As
much may be said of this painting in which, despite presenting his figures
with an interesting angularity, Mueller has failed to achieve the harmony
of form and colour that would have characterized the work of his
colleagues. He has limited himself to a muted palette that is simply not
suited to the superbly sensual subject of three young girls preoccupied
by their reactions to their own reflections.

244 EMIL NOLDE   Last Supper   1909.

From 1908 onwards Nolde tended increasingly to chose subjects of
a religious nature. That these were ultimately inspired by his powerful
recollections of his own strict Protestant childhood is beyond doubt.
However, in the form they took, they were far removed from the Lutheran
traditions of his youth. In this depiction of the Last Supper Nolde does
not show us the traditional view of a table with Christ surrounded by his
dutiful disciples. Instead this is a ghastly parody of the familiar scene, in
which the hideous-faced disciples encroach upon the central figure of
Christ. His face alone is depicted with something resembling dignity.

245 EMIL NOLDE   Dance around the Golden Calf   1910.

The disturbing trait of anti-Semitism first glimpsed in Nolde's Last
Supper (see plate 244) resurfaces here in his depiction of the adoration
of the Golden Calf. Were it not for the title of the painting, this might be a
simple celebratory dance of joy, as innocent and wonderful as any of those
depicted by Matisse, his fellow Fauves or the painters of Die Brücke.
However, in Heckel's eyes such a dance must be tainted with sin, and
thus he presents us with the spectacle, not of some golden age, but rather
of a godless age in which the Jews become no more than evil savages.

246 EMIL NOLDE Crucifixion 1912.
*Perhaps this massive Crucifixion, which he painted between 1911 and
1912, is Nolde's masterpiece. Modelled on Grünewald's Isenheim
Altarpiece (see plate 223), it brings a new and disturbing dimension
to the depiction of religious subject matter. Christ hangs in the centre.
His face and those of the people who surround him are no more than
masks, the feature of Ensor's work that had so fascinated Heckel. The
Nativity and episodes from Christ's early life are illustrated to his left
and on the right we are shown the Resurrection. While Christ crucified
is portrayed as a goggle-eyed charismatic, there He is a body cloaked
in flame. Where others have failed, Heckel succeeds in translating the
passion of his faith into visual terminology.*

248 EMIL NOLDE Tropical Sun 1914.
This picture was painted by Nolde in New Guinea at the outbreak of the First World War; it is one of the few canvases Nolde painted during his abortive colonial expedition in 1913 before being obliged by the outbreak of war to return to Europe. Although it represents the final failure of his desire to discover for himself a primitive world of art that he might use in his own painting, with its deep reds, greens and blacks it affirms the confident new tonality with which Nolde was working by this date. Its subject matter seems to provide a commentary on the demise of the world as it was then known.

247 EMIL NOLDE Masks III 1911.
Heckel's trip to Ostend in 1911 to meet the painter James Ensor was to have a long-lasting effect on his art. In superficial terms he borrowed Ensor's technique of using primitive masks as faces in his paintings. The Belgian had combined this device with the subject matter of Bosch and Breughel, the technique of the early French Impressionists and the fashions of his own twentieth-century world to produce paintings, often religious in theme, that are suggestive of a devastating and surreal terror. Heckel was impressed by these images; he had himself been attempting to find the means by which he could express his own religious emotions. This painting of masks is a tentative attempt to emulate the style which was to shape his future work.

249 ERIC HECKEL   Two Men at a Table   1912.
In 1910 Heckel found in the works of Dostoyevsky a Nietzschean form of
philosophy that would influence his art for the rest of his career. This
picture serves as an illustration of that philosophy, depicting, as it does,
the climactic scene from Dostoyevsky's novel The Idiot. *Prince Myshkin*
sits on the left of the table, the embodiment of the idiot-savant of the title,
facing his prospective assassin Rogozhin, who reaches for the knife on
the table. The knife itself points at a painting of the dead Christ,
simultaneously pointing out and paralleling Myshkin's own attitude of
self-sacrifice.

250 ERNST LUDWIG KIRCHNER   Self-Portrait as a Soldier
1915.
The war spelt the end of an era for the young generation of German
painters working during the first decade of the twentieth century. Eric
Heckel volunteered for the Red Cross and became a medical orderly in
Flanders, where he met Ensor. Otto Mueller was conscripted into the army
as was Pechstein, although the latter managed to realize his ambition of
visiting the Palau Islands beforehand. Kirchner enlisted too, in the 75th
regiment of artillery. This is the drab uniform in which he depicts himself
in this self-portrait. He is horribly mutilated, his right hand severed: here
is the frustrated artist who cannot paint, the presence of the nude model
seeming merely to mock his tragedy. In the year that this picture was
painted Kirchner was invalided out of the army having suffered an acute
mental breakdown.

Chapter 6

Towards Abstraction

When Henri Matisse (1869–1954) expressed a belief in the healing powers of his paintings to his friend in Nice or likened his aspirations for them to a mental armchair, it is obvious that behind such statements lay some sort of faith in the therapeutic value of art. He would later to go so far as to say: 'All art worthy of the name is religious.'[1] Matisse's faith might have been exalted, or perhaps merely foolish, but ever since Friedrich Nietzsche (1844–1900) had proclaimed the death of God, numerous artists had felt compelled somehow to fill the role of the priest; the philosophical scepticism of the nineteenth century had rendered it increasingly irrelevant. Matisse's espousal of this role was characteristically circumspect. Asked if he believed in God, he replied: 'Yes, when I work . . . I then find myself thwarted of the profit of the experience that should be the reward for my effort.'[2] This is the expression of a very qualified belief – one that he could endorse only during the 'furore' of creation. Perhaps it was only then that all parts of the personality – reason, instinct, spirit – were totally engaged, leaving no room for doubt. It was the fullest moment. Matisse confessed, however, that he would be left frustrated, for once creation was finished, God would vanish. Of course this vanishing was also the spur for further creation – thus we are the richer for his doubts.

In a more unequivocal vein, the Dutch artist Vincent van Gogh (1853–1890) had repeatedly described his endeavours in religious terms – as though painting could and should offer the spectator cogent messages of succour and consolation, ecstasy and hope. Van Gogh's nationality was telling in this respect because it was outside France, in fact, that such a renewed, spiritual function for art was most consciously and deliberately entertained. As Robert Rosenblum has written:

German artists, in particular, seemed to feel the oppression and hypocrisy of the middle-class materialism that dominated Europe on the eve of the First World War and some of them reached extraordinary extremes in their

search for a state of being that could unite them most closely with the primal truths of the natural and the supernatural.[3]

For if the weight of their strong native heritage of rationalism and classicism constrained French artists from holding such beliefs, German artists could look back to more mystical and romantic traditions, represented by artists like Albrecht Altdorfer (c. 1480–1538), Albrecht Dürer (1471–1528), Caspar David Friedrich (1774–1840) and Philip Otto Runge (1777–1810). Thus Emil Nolde (1867–1956), briefly associated with the artists of Die Brücke in Dresden and Berlin, had constructed a specifically Christian programme in many of his paintings, seeking to revive the expressive fervour of the art of Matthias Grünewald (c. 1470/80–1528). It was in Munich, however, in the work of the artists of the Blaue Reiter group, meaning Blue Rider, that such Germanic or northern European traditions were to undergo their fullest revival.

The Blaue Reiter had a very short collective history. Two exhibitions were mounted in Munich in 1911 and 1912, and an important book was produced entitled the *Blaue Reiter Almanac*. But the group had ceased to function before its members were either killed or dispersed in the First World War. The first exhibition opened in Munich in December 1911 and ran into January 1912; it comprised paintings by the twelve artists involved, together with work by Robert Delaunay (1885–1941) and Henri Rousseau (1844–1910). Subsequently the show travelled to Cologne and Moscow, and also to Berlin where it found exhibition space at the newly opened Der Sturm gallery owned by Herwarth Walden. Here the work of the Munich artists was hung alongside paintings by the Viennese-born artist and dramatist Oskar Kokoschka (1886–1980) (see plates 292 and 293). The second exhibition ran from February to April 1912 and comprised only prints, drawings and watercolours. A much larger number of artists had their work shown this time: many Die Brücke artists exhibited, as did a number of foreign artists including Pablo Picasso (1881–1973), Maurice de Vlaminck (1876–1958), Georges Braque (1882–1963), Delaunay, André Derain (1880–1954) and Roger de la Fresnaye (1885–1925).

However, although numerous painters were to be involved in its activities, the Blaue Reiter was really the creation of two men: Wassily Kandinsky (1866–1944) and Franz Marc (1880–1916). It was they who edited the *Blaue Reiter Almanac*: a collection of essays and reproductions of a wide variety of pictures that served to reflect the aims and ideals of

251 ALEXEI VON JAWLENSKY Night in St Prex 1916.
Jawlensky's dark, sombre colours have soaked so far into the canvas that its weave remains visible to the eye. A cypress tree and a path stand out immediately, but all the other forms have lost the characteristic shapes by which we know them during the day. Indeed, the eye has to get used to these subdued tones just as it has to adjust at night, opening the pupil wide to glean any information through the obscurity. These shapes and colours, however, will never resolve themselves into recognizable forms. We are thus left sensing the presence of this landscape without quite being able to see it.

the group. The volume was not confined to the fine arts but also dealt with primitive art, craft and design, music, poetry and drama. Whatever the subject, however, there was an emphasis upon the efforts of artists from different epochs to expand the expressive means at their disposal.

Kandinsky and Marc were both committed, not only to the revival of a spiritual function for their art, but also through that, to the regeneration of society. Choosing 'Blaue Reiter' as the title for their group was a succinct – albeit personal – symbol of their aims. Both men believed that blue was the colour most closely associated with heaven; and while the horse was the symbol of instinctive, intuitive creativity, the rider was the artistic consciousness that gave shape and body to that creative spirit. Marc was to write in the *Almanac* that he wanted: 'To create symbols for [their] own time, symbols that would take their place on the altars of a future spiritual religion'.[4] Kandinsky, in his book *Concerning the Spiritual in Art*, which was published in 1911, was to write:

Art is not a mere purposeless creating of things that dissipate themselves in a void, but a power that has a purpose and must serve the development and refinement of the human soul . . . If art renounces this task, then this gap must remain unfilled, for there is no other power that can replace art . . . The artist must have something to say, for his task is not the mastery of form, but the suitability of that form to its content.[5]

252   W A S S I L Y   K A N D I N S K Y   The Blue Rider   1903.
Originally entitled simply The Rider, *Kandinsky renamed this painting in 1912 following the publication of the* Blaue Reiter Almanac, *the book he produced with Franz Marc. It is unlikely, therefore, that the subject of this oil painting would originally have had quite the significance that its second name later invested in it. Nonetheless, it is a dramatic example of the imaginary, oneiric quality of Kandinsky's early works. The rider races over a grassy hill on some unspecified heroic quest. There is more than a suggestion of courtly romance about this subject, one that Kandinsky captures with a vivid freedom of brushwork and colour.*

Such statements defined the Blaue Reiter's goals as standing in opposition to those celebrated by Fernand Léger (1881–1955) and the Futurists, which glorified the material world of modern industry and the machine. Similarly, their rejection of an art based purely on formal innovation, divorced from inner, spiritual significance, constituted an unspoken attack on the researches of the Cubists, or indeed on any art that was satisfied with the imitation or representation of nature. As Marc was to write in 1912: 'We no longer cling to the reproduction of nature but destroy it, so that the mighty laws which hold sway behind the beautiful exterior can be revealed.'[6] Marc and Kandinsky, however, were unable to carve out for their art a niche that was categorically and completely distinct from other contemporary developments in France and Italy. For, as we shall see, the pictorial language that they and the other Blaue Reiter painters evolved in order to realize their mystical notions was indebted to recent French precedents – most notably those of the Fauves and of Robert Delaunay. Despite the growing nationalistic forces that were shortly to erupt in war between France and Germany, and despite as well these artists' desire to create a kind of painting different in function from that being produced in Paris, Europe was by now too small for them to be able to ignore the stylistic influences of their French counterparts, even if they had wanted to.

A New Harmony

Wassily Kandinsky had been born and raised in Moscow and had initially trained to be a lawyer. But, having belatedly decided to abandon that particular path by turning down a lectureship in law offered to him by a university in Estonia, he arrived in Munich in 1896 to begin a career as a painter. Kandinsky was fortunate in having a rich father who had made a fortune as a tea-merchant; he was given a living allowance which enabled him to pursue his own idiosyncratic interests without worrying about having to sell his work. Thus, having finished his formal education as an artist, he could explore – even in some of his first independent works – painterly traditions that were unlikely to find much commercial success. In particular he could indulge his fascination for the 'primitive', peasant art that he had seen both in his native Russia and more recently in the Bavarian countryside (*see plates 252 and 267*).

In 1908 Kandinsky bought a house in the village of Murnau with his lover, the painter Gabriele Münter (1877–1962); they were to spend every summer there with their friends until 1914, devoting their time to landscape painting. One of the paintings he produced in the winter of 1909 in the nearby village of Kochel reveals that other influences were also affecting his work (*see plate 268*). The high key of the colours and thick swabs of pigment put down from an evidently laden brush, as well as the choice of landscape as a subject instead of a Romantic image, are unmistakable signs of a Fauve influence. Kandinsky had spent about a year in Paris between 1906 and 1907 when he was able to study the work of Matisse, Derain and others of the Fauves at first hand. He also took the opportunity to show his own work at the Salon d'Automne, alongside these and other French painters; he exhibited there from 1905 until 1910. Landscape studies such as this, in which Kandinsky was pushing to an extreme his subjective responses to the scene before him, could justifiably be described as Fauve. More than that, they encouraged him to worry less and less about any kind of accurate depiction of nature. He was later to write:

I was once told about a very famous artist who was quoted as saying: 'In painting take one look at your canvas, half a glance at your palette, and ten at the model.' It sounded very good advice, but I soon discovered that where I was concerned the exact opposite was true. I was looking ten times at the canvas, once at the palette, and giving half a glance at nature. In this way I learned how to fight the canvas, to recognise its capability of with-standing my desire.[7]

Kandinsky was, in fact, hovering on the edge of a purely abstract art. The birth of such an art had really always been inevitable, given the way avant-garde nineteenth-century painting had developed. With its progressively strong emphasis on the emotionally expressive properties of line and colour and its preference for a pictorial equivalent of the artist's subjective sensations in front of the motif rather than his accurate record of nature, any lingering theoretical attachment to ideas of illusionism or representation alone were becoming increasingly hard to justify. As early as 1846 Charles Baudelaire (1821–1867) had written: 'Painting is only interesting by virtue of line and colour.'[8] This statement begs the question: why bother depicting anything at all? In 1890 Maurice Denis (1870–1943) had voiced much the same idea when he wrote: 'Remember that a painting, before it is a warhorse, a female nude or some little genre scene, is primarily a flat surface covered with colours arranged in a certain order.'[9]

Painters were obviously slow to realize the full implications of such remarks, though it is worth remembering that to break away completely from a whole tradition of image-making would be a challenge only the bravest or most foolhardy would be prepared to take. Even the Cubists had recoiled from such a proposition. For, as Kandinsky wrote: 'What is to replace the missing object?'[10] In other words, to what established vocabulary of forms could an artist turn if he decided to banish all vestiges of representation from his repertoire? Quite simply, there was none. This was all uncharted territory to explore.

In this situation, an artist on the brink of such a momentous step would obviously turn to any support that was offered. One of the principal stimuli in Kandinsky's development of a highly expressive art that no longer needed to make any reference to the visual world came through his love of music: 'An artist who sees that the imitation of natural appearances, however artistic, is not for him – the kind of creative artist who wants to, and has to, express his own inner world – sees with envy how naturally and easily such goals can be attained in music, the least material of the arts today.'[11] Kandinsky saw in music an art whose very means were abstract, more or less irrevocably unrelated to natural phemonena; yet which, for this very reason, was profoundly expressive of states of mind and feelings that the more material realms of words or images were too crude to describe. Before it could become the infinitely responsive and subtle instrument that music already was, painting too would have to endeavour to emulate that older art's inherently abstract means (see plate 253).

253   WASSILY KANDINSKY   Impression No. 3 – Concert   1911. *Kandinsky attended a concert of music by Arnold Schoenberg (1874–1951) in Munich in January 1911. This picture was painted shortly afterwards. Kandinsky was particulaly interested by the way Schoenberg constructed his work according to a new twelve-tone scale – a departure from standard practices that he felt was analogous to his own experiments in painting. Schoenberg was later to write an essay for* the Blaue Reiter Almanac. *In this painting, the large black form is a very free representation of a grand piano, the shapes below and to the left the concert-goers. The huge sweep of yellow and the vertical white strips suggest the exhilarating music filling the hall.*

Two other, more painterly experiences were to convince Kandinsky both that it was possible to achieve this state of abstraction in paint and, what is more, that it was absolutely necessary. The first of these had occurred in Moscow in the 1890s, shortly before his departure to Munich, and indeed it may also be counted as one of the decisive events which convinced Kandinsky to give up law and take up painting. As he describes the event in 1913, it also seems to have impressed upon him the emotive powers of the purely abstract qualities of light and colour in a painting. He had gone to see an exhibition of French Impressionist painting and was particularly struck by one of the grainstack canvases (see plate 51) by Claude Monet (1840–1926):

And suddenly for the first time I saw a picture. That it was a haystack [or rather, a grainstack], the catalogue informed me. I didn't recognize it . . . And I noticed with surprise and confusion that the picture not only gripped me, but impressed itself ineradicably upon my memory . . . Painting took on a fairy-tale power and splendor. And, albeit unconsciously, objects were discredited as an essential element within the picture.[12]

Much later, probably around 1908, while he was staying at the house in Murnau, a rather similar thing happened, though this time Kandinsky was fully aware of the implications involved:

It was the hour when dusk draws in. I returned home with my painting box having finished a study, still dreamy and absorbed in the work I had completed, and suddenly saw an indescribably beautiful picture, pervaded by an inner glow. At first, I stopped short and then quickly approached this mysterious picture, on which I could discern only forms and colors and whose content was incomprehensible. At once, I discovered the key to the puzzle: it was a picture I had painted, standing on its side against the wall. The next day, I tried to re-create my impression of the picture from the previous evening by daylight. I only half succeeded, however; even on its side, I constantly recognized objects, and the fine bloom of dusk was missing. Now I could see clearly that objects harmed my pictures.[13]

In fact, developing an abstract art was not quite as easy as the latter story might suggest. Kandinsky was reluctant to banish categorically all references to nature in his pictures. While the spectator will get little reward for looking for any specific narrative meanings in the first paintings Kandinsky made in his new abstract style, hints of vaguely recognizable forms or figures still linger (see plates 269, 270 and 272). However, it was Kandinsky's intention that the spectator slowly feel his or her way into these works, responding intuitively and emotionally to the colours and forms. He wanted the act of looking at a picture to become a meditative experience, rather than a flexing of the muscles of rationality.

Thus, in Composition 6 (see plate 273), Kandinsky presents us with an image of disintegration and collapse, in which all accepted notions of order have lost their validity. It is an apocalyptic image. Nothing is stable here: seething, volatile colour and whip-like lines together form an impression of uncontrollable, undirected energy. Bursts of fiery colour flash out from the predominant blue of the whole. But colour is unrelated to any specific natural forms. It has no defining edges; rather, colours melt and bleed into one another.

Certain recognizable forms suggest themselves: boats, a fish tail, possibly even a sea-monster and some figures. But they are all allusively and equivocally stated. The picture's meaning and power lies instead in the tremendous, even terrifying energies which its lines and colours, basically free from an illusionistic function, unleash upon us. Kandinsky himself wrote:

It is perhaps with envy, or with a sad feeling of sympathy, that we listen to the works of Mozart. They create a welcome pause amidst the storms of our inner life, a vision of consolation and hope, but we hear them like the sounds of another, vanished, and essentially unfamiliar age. Clashing discords, loss of equilibrium, 'principles' overthrown, unexpected drumbeats, great questionings, apparently purposeless strivings, stress and longing (apparently torn apart), chains and fetters broken (which had united many), opposites and contradictions – this is our harmony.[14]

Such material does not seem well suited for visual harmony, and yet Kandinsky has created a very beautiful painting. The two strong diagonal accents do much to hold the composition together, though emotionally they suggest some sort of dynamic force piercing the more opaque turmoil of the rest of the canvas. The iridescent colours express exhilaration and excitement as much as apocalyptic violence. Nevertheless, though the picture might be cathartic, overall it is an image of convulsive and irresistible powers, a painting in which all references to the visual world are engulfed and overwhelmed by the emotionally expressive power of colour and line alone.

Though it looks spontaneous, Composition 6 was in fact the result of a carefully planned series of preparatory sketches in which the effect of each line, colour and form had been calculated and studied. From his very first essays in an abstract manner, Kandinsky had used musical terms as titles for his pictures: Impression, Improvisation and Composition. These he had adopted to help guide his first viewers' responses, indicating that they should react to his works in the same way that they let themselves be moved by the abstract qualities of music. In Concerning the Spiritual in Art, he elucidated the differences he intended by these terms:

1. The direct impression of 'external nature', expressed in linear–painterly form. I call these pictures 'Impressions'.
2. Chiefly unconscious, for the most part suddenly arising expressions of events of an inner character, hence impressions of 'internal nature'. I call this type 'Improvisations'.
3. The expression of feelings that have been forming within me in a similar way (but over a very long period of time), which, after the first preliminary sketches, I have slowly and almost pedantically examined and worked out. This kind of picture I call a 'Composition'. Here, reason, the conscious, the deliberate, and the purposeful play a preponderant role. Except that I always decide in favor of feeling rather than calculation.[15]

Kandinsky's activities in Munich did not revolve entirely around the development of an abstract art. As the quotation above indicates, he was also keen to ensure that this new type of painting was comprehensible to the public. Naturally, painting as radical as this would demand careful explanation, and Kandinsky, committed as he was to an exalted social function for his art, took it upon himself to provide the explanation in books – his Concerning the Spiritual in Art, for instance. The Blaue Reiter exhibitions and the Almanac of 1911–12 were to be the climax of this public involvement in the dynamic cultural life of his adopted city, but Kandinsky's activities in that sphere had begun much earlier. In 1901 he had helped to found Phalanx, a group of Munich artists opposed to the Academy, whose exhibitions also featured the work of such artists as Monet, the French divisionists and other non-German, contemporary painters. Although the whole enterprise came to an end in 1904 as a result of financial difficulties, Kandinsky had both taught at the Phalanx school and served as President of the group. For the next few years he travelled; it was during this period that he visited Paris and became acquainted with the work of the Fauves. But when he returned to Munich, he became involved, in 1909, in setting up another collaborative venture – the Neue Kunstler–Vereinigung (NKV), or New Artists Association – along with Gabriele Münter, Alexei von Jawlensky (1864–1941) and others of his friends. The idea of forming the association was first mooted during the summer of 1908 when the three friends were staying in Murnau. Like Phalanx, this too was to be an association devoted to bringing its members' work before the public and, in addition, to exhibiting the work of contemporary figures from other countries.

French Influences

Like Kandinsky, Alexei von Jawlensky was a Russian. A former officer in the Imperial Guard, he had come to Munich in 1896 to study painting. It was here, when they were both art students, that the two became friends. Jawlensky too had spent time in France, and had seen the first public exhibition of

254 ALEXEI VON JAWLENSKY   Summer Evening in Murnau
1908–09.

Jawlensky painted this tiny landscape while he was staying with Kandinsky and Münter in their cottage at Murnau. It burns with dark glowering intensity for beyond the hills the dying sun has illuminated a towering, distant cloud in fiery orange, though the hills and valley are cut off from its light. The forms of field, tree and hillside are losing their definition, their edges beginning to blur, as a closer, darker cloud hovers over them – as well as over the spectator – striking out the daylight with striated, parallel strokes of dusky grey and violet. The sun-drenched Mediterranean canvases of Matisse and Derain never hinted at the ominousness of night's approach that is sensed so strongly here by Jawlensky.

Fauvism at the Salon d'Automne in 1905. In 1906 he had met the Dutch painter Jan Verkade (1868–1946), by then a monk in the Benedictine monastery at nearby Beuron, but who had spent much of the 1890s in Pont-Aven learning from Gauguin's disciples. It was from Verkade that Jawlensky learnt the simplified, painterly techniques first applied in the 1880s by Emile Bernard (1868–1941), Paul Gauguin (1848–1903) and Paul Sérusier (1864–1927) and then taken up by the Nabis in Paris.

In 1907 Jawlensky completed his education, as it were, in contemporary or recent French developments by returning to Paris to visit Matisse. The same year he also met Sérusier at Beuron. All these influences are evident in his subsequent work, particularly the landscapes he painted while staying with Kandinsky and Münter in Murnau during the summers of 1908 and 1909 (see plates 254, 264, 265 and 266). Kandinsky was later to recall with gratitude his friend's enthu-

siasm in sharing with himself and Münter all he had learnt from these contacts and travels.

If at this early point Jawlensky encouraged Kandinsky to pursue with boldness and determination the depiction of increasingly subjective and abstract responses to nature, he never crossed over himself into the realm of non-objective representation that Kandinsky would shortly enter. In fact, at the point when Kandinsky was in the process of breaching this threshold and trying to set up at the same time yet another association – this time the Blaue Reiter – Jawlensky, against all expectation, declined to follow. He never participated in the Blaue Reiter exhibitions nor contributed to the *Almanac*. After the outbreak of war, when the group's activities foundered, Jawlensky had in any case been forced to flee Germany as a former officer in the Russian army. He moved to St Prex in Switzerland, on the shores of Lake Geneva. It was here that he produced some of his most haunting landscapes, like *Night in St Prex (see plate 251)*, some of which threatened, but never managed to take the step into abstraction. Jawlensky certainly entertained the highest beliefs for his painting. At one point he said: 'Art is nostalgic for God.'[16] But unlike Kandinsky, his search for the divine expressed itself through the tangible; his was to be an indirect imaging of the absolute, one that concentrated more on the search – on longing – than on the arrival itself.

The seeds of the Blaue Reiter were sown in 1910 at the second NKV exhibition organized by Jawlensky and Kandinsky. Displaying paintings as modern as Kandinsky's *Study for Composition 2 (see plate 269)* and many of Jawlensky's most audacious Murnau landscapes, together with a pretty comprehensive list of modern French pictures, the exhibition attracted a vitriolic response from the press. One painter, however, wrote a highly sympathetic review and sent it in to the gallery; a pamphlet was quickly published in which this review was printed alongside a reprint of one of the more hysterical articles that had previously appeared in the press. Franz Marc, the author of the piece, had been bowled over by Kandinsky's *Study for Composition 2* in particular. Before long the two painters met; they became firm friends. When, in 1911, Kandinsky resigned from the NKV as a result of a disagreement about its hanging policy, it was with Marc – and old friend Münter – that he founded the Blaue Reiter in retaliation – as a more progressive competitor.

Franz Marc had initially wanted to become a priest. He had then begun studying for a degree in philosophy before finally deciding to become a painter. He had travelled to both Paris and Brittany, and had gone back to Paris once more in 1907;

255 FRANZ MARC Deer in a Monastery Garden 1912.
The presence of the moon in the top left-hand corner, and the muted tone of the colours indicate that this is a night scene. Furthermore, it is a landscape consciously hidden from the senses of man, a daylight animal, and revealed only to a solitary deer. The diagonal grid and multiple facets through which Marc has organized the scene, and which he has taken from contemporary French and Italian painting, are used here to establish a crackling, connecting web between deer, landscape and moon. It is as though all these different forms of nature begin to communicate at night in a language far beyond human comprehension.

thus he was fully aware of the advances made by the Fauves, and of other leading tendencies within the French avant garde. By the time he met Kandinsky and Jawlensky, Marc, too, was passionately interested in rediscovering a spiritual direction for contemporary painting.

Kandinsky had turned to music – in all its variations – as the closest analogy to the spiritual inner world that he wanted to penetrate and then express through his painting. Marc, meanwhile, chose to look elsewhere. To quote Robert Rosenblum again:

Marc considered the creation of art as a vehicle for the expression of ultimate truths that were quasi-religious in character. For Marc, however, the primary metaphor of these spiritual metaphors was not landscape or the human figure, as it had been for Munch, Hodler and Van Gogh, or for Friedrich, Runge, and Blake, but rather the animal, a symbol that he thought could provide another sentient creature through which man might once again recapture his lost contact with the forces of a God-given nature, almost reversing the direction of Darwin's theory of evolution.[17]

Marc himself was to write:

Is there a more mysterious idea for an artist than the conception of how nature is mirrored in the eyes of an animal? How does a horse see the world, or an eagle, or a doe, or a dog? How wretched and soulless is our convention of placing animals in a landscape which belongs to our eyes, instead of submerging ourselves in the soul of the animal in order to imagine how it sees?[18]

In *Anna Karenin* (written 1875–77), Leo Tolstoy (1828–1910) produces an extraordinary description of an early-morning duck shoot. Having described the mist hanging over the marshes, the squelch of boots in the mossy, soggy ground, and his hero Levin's anxiety that his hunt should be successful, the narrative suddenly switches for a few paragraphs to describe the pursuit purely from the point of view of his dog. Unable to see above the reeds, the dog's experience is solely dictated by its sense of smell, and (for it knows, as Levin does not, exactly where the duck is hiding) by its frustration that its master is unable to understand its frantic indications as to where the duck is lying. Tolstoy's narrative then switches back just as suddenly to Levin's human viewpoint, and the reader is left feeling slightly dizzy at this rapid and totally unexpected change of perspectives. Children's books and Walt Disney excepted, it is rare to find such a powerful instance of creative empathy with the animal kingdom either in literature or the visual arts. Marc's paintings are exceptional in this regard. Thus, in a picture like *Deer in a Monastery Garden (see plate 255)* Marc shows us the deer from behind, with the panorama of the landscape stretched out in front of it – in other words, we are encouraged to see the landscape from the animal's point of view.

The construction of the picture shows how quickly and effectively Marc was able to turn contemporary, stylistic innovations to his own account: thus, the division of the garden itself into diagonally oriented, interlocking facets, creates a maze in which to hide the deer as it turns its head to stare at the large white moon in the top left-hand corner. He had evidently studied the catalogue of the first Futurist exhibition, which had toured to Berlin earlier that year. He had also studied the work of Delaunay, who had shown two paintings at the first Blaue Reiter exhibition in 1911 and whom Marc had visited in Paris in October 1912. Marc had earlier written enthusiastically to Kandinsky about Delaunay's 'Window' pictures *(see plate 202)*: 'He is working towards truly constructive pictures, eliminating representation altogether: pure fugues of sound one might say.'[19] While both Delaunay and the Futurists had recognized the expressive potential of the Cubists' formal innovation, however, whereby all the elements of a composition were dissolved into a number of interpenetrating planes and then re-organized on a diagonal grid, Marc adapted this stylistic trait to his own symbolic programme. Animals, embedded in their surroundings and partaking of the same pictorial rhythms as nature herself, became ciphers for a state of innocence and inherent reciprocity with the natural environment which mankind – a material and industrial animal – had spurned *(see plates 256, 275, 276 and 277)*.

A Plea for Apocalypse

Delaunay's example was also to be of crucial importance for two other artists closely involved in the Blaue Reiter group: August Macke (1887–1914) and Paul Klee (1879–1940). Macke trained as an artist in Düsseldorf between 1904 and 1906. The following year he travelled to Paris to acquaint himself with all the most modern artistic tendencies. The trip was a revelation. He wrote to Bernhard Koehler, his future wife's uncle, who had provided him with the necessary funds to travel (and who was later to pay the printing costs of the

256 FRANZ MARC Vermilion Greeting 1913.
Animals even inhabit this postcard that Marc sent to Kandinsky in April 1913: 'Dear K., Hartley is coming on Monday; I have arranged to meet him at the Goltz Gallery, where he has some pictures. Why don't the two of you come along as well: maybe we can all go and eat somewhere. We are travelling back on Wednesday evening. Vermilion greetings. F. Marc.' (in Armin Zweite, with Annegret Hoberg, The Blue Rider in the Lenbachhaus, Munich, *Munich, 1989, opposite plate 13.) Neither the lunch, Hartley nor the Goltz Gallery are remembered today as significant. But what a delicious card for such a mundane message.*

Almanac) to explain: 'It means as much to me perhaps as two years' work. I see everything quite differently, everything has a kind of elevation such as I have never experienced before – no more brown sauce paintings for me.'[20] In other words, Macke had determined to abandon the dark palette encouraged by his teacher to concentrate on the bright, spectral colours favoured by the Impressionist and Post-Impressionist generations. Perhaps the enthusiasm Macke expressed in this letter to his benefactor might have been a little premature for a portrait he painted as late as 1910 still displays a traditionally academic, though nonetheless competent, technique *(see plate 258)*.

By 1911, however, everything had changed. The Galerie Tannhäuser in Munich had mounted a Matisse exhibition in 1910 and its impact on Macke's subsequent production was, if not profound, then certainly immediate *(see plate 280)*. Macke had also that year introduced himself to Marc, having visited an exhibition in Munich of the older artist's work – Marc's first one-man show, in fact. It was not until 1911 that

257 AUGUST MACKE Zoological Garden I 1912.
Macke met Franz Marc in 1911, and through him was introduced to the
work of Kandinsky, Jawlensky and others of the NKV. He was evidently
influenced by Marc's paintings, but whereas Marc's animals are only ever
seen in the wild, Macke relocates them in an urban setting. The human
figure had also been banished from Marc's work; here, on the other hand,
Macke pictures six bowler-hatted city gentlemen standing easily among the
glowing colours of parakeets, parrots, deer and pelican. Figures, animals
and setting have all been subtly organized within a delicate, Cubist
structure. Tropical paradise has thus been urbanized and domesticated.

Macke met Kandinsky and it was during that year that his
painting began to show the influence of his new friends and
colleagues (see plates 257 and 278). The somewhat bewildering
variety of stylistic influences discernible in his work of these
years can be explained by the fact that Macke was still very
much in the process of developing his own artistic personality. His brief involvement with Kandinsky and Marc, however,
was to bring him to maturity (see plate 259), although he
could not agree with their more abstract tendencies. For
Macke, like Jawlensky, was always suspicious of a purely
abstract painting. He preferred to let any spiritual content his
works might embody speak through epiphany, as he
explained in the *Blaue Reiter Almanac*: 'Unfathomable ideas
express themselves in comprehensible forms comprehensible
through our senses as stars, thunder, flowers, as form. Our
senses are the bridge between the unfathomable and the
comprehensible.'[21]

Macke's final metamorphosis came in the spring of 1914
when he travelled to Tunisia with his friend, the artist Paul
Klee (see plate 279). Swiss-born, Klee had trained as an artist
in Munich, and it was there that he befriended Macke and
through him met Kandinsky in 1911. He had not shown any
paintings at the first Blaue Reiter exhibition, being more of a
draughtsman than a painter at the time, but he did show
some of his graphic work at the second exhibition and had a
number of his drawings reproduced in the *Almanac*. It was
Klee, in fact, who was the first of the Blaue Reiter artists to
make the pilgrimage to Paris to meet Delaunay. Although this
was in 1912, the full impact of the expressive potential of
colour was not to reveal itself to him until the trip to Tunisia
in 1914. Klee's painting – as opposed to his graphic work –
had always been distinguished by the fineness of his touch
and the delicacy of his colour (see plate 281). It was in Tunisia,
however, that he first applied these qualities, in his character-

istically refined and naïve manner, to the geometrical
schemata of Delaunay's lyrically Cubist compositions (see
plates 282 and 283).

Perhaps Germany's rapid industrialization in the last quarter
of the nineteenth century was in part responsible for the determined way that the Blaue Reiter artists presented their public
– through their work – with a set of aspirations that contradicted the pervading materialist philosophy. Their paintings
did not overtly display the polemical tone that seems to have
motivated the artists of Die Brücke: Kirchner's *Five Women in
the Street* (see plate 8), for example, seems a vicious attack on
urban chic, while Macke's *Milliner's Shop* (see plate 259) offers a
more subdued image of the mesmerizing power of city fashions. Nevertheless the Blaue Reiter artists were consciously
reacting to current political and social trends. And indeed at
times it has seemed possible to see in some of their paintings
premonitions of the war that was about to engulf Europe – in
Improvisation No. 30 (Cannons), for example, painted by
Kandinsky in 1913 (see plate 271). When Arthur Jerome Eddy
of Chicago, who bought the painting, asked Kandinsky what
the cannons meant, the artist replied:

258 AUGUST MACKE Farmboy from Tegernsee 1910.
This portrait displays the sort of conservative, academic style from which
so many turn-of-the-century young artists were trying to break away. And
yet, even with its subdued colours, consistent shadows and realistic pose,
Macke's portrait would still probably not have met with the approval of the
establishment. The boy's coat has been painted with barely any modelling,
and his hands are only very schematically described. The boy himself is
unusually tense and suspicious – perhaps he was reluctant to hold a pose.
Ultimately, for all its conservatism, the relatively flat colour areas almost
begrudgingly reveal the influence of Matisse, whose paintings Macke had
studied in Paris two years earlier.

The designation Cannons, selected by me for my own use, is not to be conceived as indicating the 'contents' of the picture. These contents are indeed what the spectator lives, or feels while under the effect of the form and colour compositions of the picture . . . The presence of the cannons in the picture could probably be explained by the constant war talk that had been going on throughout the year. But I did not intend to give a representation of war; to do so would have required different pictorial means.'[22]

Marc's *The Fate of the Animals*, also painted in 1913, seems similarly prescient. For the deer, horses, foxes and swine have been transfixed in some terrible, final conflagration *(see plate 274)*. Once again the hinged, coloured facets and diagonal structures that characterized Delaunay's limpid and poetic transformation of Cubism's austere formal language have here been transformed into an image of the holocaust.

Marc subtitled the picture 'And all being is flaming suffering', which suggests that the sharp diagonal axes of red and orange were to represent some sort of heavenly fire sent to consume the earth. In fact the painting itself was to suffer fire damage in 1916, as though unable to contain the purgative heat it had generated. A large proportion of its left-hand side was restored by Klee. Nevertheless, Marc's apocalyptic image was not without hope. For the critic Frederick Spencer Levine has convincingly argued that the painting represents: 'a plea for apocalypse; the expression of a longing for the destruction of the present world of corruption, evil and degeneration, and its replacement with a world of innocence, goodness and purity'.[23]

Marc joined the German army in August 1914. It was in 1915 from the front that he wrote to Bernhard Koehler about the picture: 'It is like a premonition of this war, at once horrible and stirring. I can hardly believe that I painted it.'[24]

Macke was killed in action in France in September 1914; Marc too was to be consumed in the apocalypse he himself had invoked, for he fell at Verdun in 1916. Kandinsky and Klee, who had not been born in Germany, were forced to leave the country and only returned after Germany's defeat in 1918. The Blaue Reiter movement, however, had come to an end long before.

Universal Beauty

Almost until 1900 the atom . . . so far as science was concerned, [was] merely a hard solid unstructured sort of infinitesimal billiard-ball, or, as Lucretius had described it two thousand years earlier, *solido atque aeterno corpore*.[25]

In the last years of the nineteenth century this view of the atom, the building block of the universe, fundamentally unchanged since Roman times, was to undergo drastic revision. The discovery of the electron in 1897, and of radiation the year before in 1896, revealed that the atom was not some irreducible, elemental essence; rather, it was a complex and composite structure. The somewhat more detailed experiments conducted by Ernest Rutherford (1871–1937) in 1911 disclosed that the atom was in fact: 'A structure largely empty and consisting of a minute but massive central nucleus, with a positive electrical charge, surrounded at a distance by a peripheral shell of negatively charged electrons – a kind of solar system in miniature. Matter seemed, therefore, to be mostly empty space'.[26] Though subsequent discoveries have shown the matter actually to be even more complex than this,

at the time such ideas were disturbing enough, to say the least. One commentator noted that Rutherford's results constituted 'the greatest change in our idea of matter since the time of Democritus'.[27] Artists, of course, were not unaffected by these changes.

Kandinsky looked back in 1913 at some of the events that had proved decisive in conditioning his development as an artist, and he recalled at that stage the momentous effect that contemporary research on the composite structure of the atom had had on his sensibility:

The collapse of the atom was equated, in my soul, with the collapse of the whole world. Suddenly, the stoutest walls crumbled. Everything became uncertain, precarious and insubstantial. I would not have been surprised had a stone dissolved into thin air before my eyes and become invisible. Science seemed destroyed: its most important basis was only an illusion, an error of the learned, who were not building their divine edifice stone by stone with steady hands, by transfigured light, but were groping at random for truth in the darkness and blindly mistaking one object for another.[28]

259 AUGUST MACKE   Milliner's Shop   1913.
A lone woman in a city street, elegantly slender in her blue dress, stares into a shop window entranced by some hats. On the surface it is a prosaic scene, but Macke lends it a peculiar, emblematic force. This is not a crowded commercial street; the woman is alone. Her stare, completely uninterrupted, assumes the stillness of meditation. And the white tones just to the right of her right elbow serve to diminish the barrier of the glass, bringing her closer to her fashionable ideal. Thus, her gaze makes this a forceful generic image of aching desire. But the woman will soon walk on and the spell will be broken.

The experience was to undermine Kandinsky's faith in material reality. It would encourage him, however, as an artist, to begin to depict his conception of those essentially unstable forces that lay behind or beneath the surface of appearances. At the same time, though, miles to the north of Kandinsky's adopted Munich, Piet Mondrian (1872–1944) in Holland was working from a similar premise, striving to realize an abstract art that could speak directly of truths hidden from the eye, a conception of the world that operated beyond the realm of the senses.

For Kandinsky the intuitive gesture, expressed in colour and line, was the means chosen to function as the pictorial analogy for these unseen, explosive energies. Kandinsky's new harmony was convulsive; his vision informed by notions of upheaval and apocalypse. For Mondrian, on the other hand, painting was to be reduced to its essence. He employed the barest minimum of basic, fundamental elements –

260   PIET MONDRIAN   Windmill in Sunlight   1908.

Mondrian often chose to paint lone, isolated objects, describing them from a low viewpoint in order that they impose themselves on the spectator, suggesting that they hold a more than ordinary significance; the windmill is treated in this way, just as the chysanthemum was before it (see plate 285). Mondrian limits his palette here to the three primary colours, in a reductive intensification of divisionist practice which he had learned from Jan Toorop. The power of this angry red, as it spills out from the windmill into the field around it, however, places this canvas closer in feeling to the excesses of the French Fauves than to the calmer, more serene paintings of Toorop.

vertical and horizontal, black and white – and created contrasts by juxtaposing these non-colours with the three primary colours.

These pictorial quintessences, constantly held in a continuous and infinitely varied equilibrium, would thus speak of an unseen, imperturbable order. This was Mondrian's concept of universal beauty:

Disequilibrium means conflict, disorder. Conflict is also a part of life and of art, but it is not the whole of life or universal beauty. Real life is *the mutual interaction of two oppositions of the same value but of a different aspect and nature.* Its plastic expression is universal beauty.[29]

Only with such an exalted metaphysical notion could anyone spend almost thirty years of their life painting grids and rectangles.

Piet Mondrian (originally spelt Mondriaan) received his formal art education in Amsterdam after he had persuaded his strict Calvinist father that he wanted to become an artist. And it was here, in Amsterdam, that he settled when he had finished his training. He managed to earn his keep by teaching, supplementing his income by selling some of his paintings. At this stage his work contained no hint of what was to come. It was only after the turn of the century, when Mondrian was in his thirties, that anything like a progressive style can be discerned in his painting; for Mondrian's path to an abstract art, like Kandinsky's, was rooted in years of the careful and meticulous study of nature.

If his later abstract works seem to exude a classic calm and stability, Mondrian's earlier studies reveal more a romantic's desire to distil from nature anthropomorphic and introspective images of a decidedly morbid character (*see plates 284 and 285*). His landscapes at this time are similarly uncluttered by the bustle of life; indeed they are never populated. Spurning the city crowds, he was attracted to the flat and lonely coastal scenery of Zeeland, north of Amsterdam. Between 1908 and 1911 he spent each summer there, and he would go back briefly between 1914 and 1915. In 1908 he met the painter Jan Toorop (1858–1928) (*see chapter 1*), who introduced him to the divisionist style, and Mondrian applied himself to using the technique in his painting with characteristic intensity. Immediately his work displayed a change; divisionism's potentially dry, disciplined mannerism ceded to all the exuberance of Fauvism (*see plates 260, 286 and 287*).

Mondrian had rejected his father's rigid Calvinism by becoming an artist. His naturally philosophical, speculative temperament, however, led him to investigate alternative standpoints that lay outside the dogmatic and doctrinaire boundaries of this severe brand of Christianity. The artist was particularly attracted by the writings of Rudolf Steiner (1861–1925), whose mystical and idealist philosophy of Theosophy provided the cosmological framework within which he was to evolve his spartan, abstract formulae. Mondrian joined the Dutch Theosophical Society in 1909 and its impact is clearly evident in some rather programmatic paintings he made soon afterwards – the triptych *Evolution*, for example (*see plate 261*). However, if Theosophy was to provide Mondrian with a philosophy, it was Cubism that would help him develop a pictorial language (or, as Mondrian called it, a plastic expression) capable of translating its precepts into painterly form.

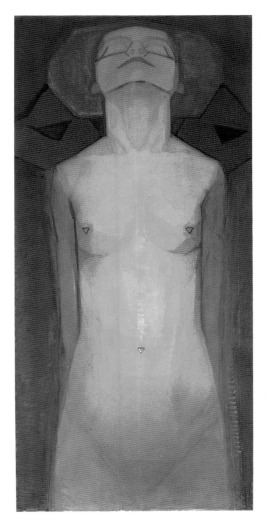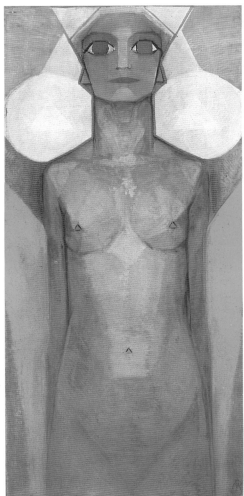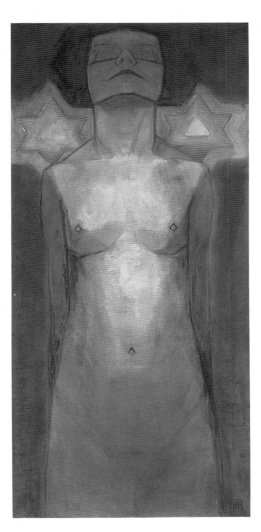

261   PIET MONDRIAN   Evolution   1910–11.

There is a clear progression from the left and right panels to the central one in this Theosophical triptych. A young female nude, with eyes closed and head raised in the two flanking sections, opens her eyes and stares straight ahead in the central panel, as though finally fully born. Moreover, the heads of the two supporting figures are enclosed in shadow while that of the central nude is fully lit. Some of the sacred, geometric figures of the Theosophists appear above her shoulder: the hexagram and the triangle enclosed within a circle – all emblematic signs of her spiritual journey.

Mondrian had exhibited his work in Amsterdam with an avant-garde association of painters known as the Moderne Kunstkring, or Circle of Modern Art. Foreign artists were also invited to participate in these group exhibitions, and it was his exposure to contemporary French painting at these shows that determined the Dutch artist to travel to Paris. He arrived there late in 1911 and stayed until 1914 when he was obliged to return to Holland to visit his sick father. The outbreak of war prevented him from going back.

For any artist anxious to acquaint himself with the most modern painterly idioms, Paris was able to offer a potentially bewildering variety of dialects at that date. The Cubist works of Georges Braque (1882–1963) and Pablo Picasso (1881–1973) were on almost permanent display at Kahnweiler's gallery; the Futurists were generating their own scandalous reputation at their infamous exhibition at Bernheim-Jeune's; and the various responses to Paul Cézanne's (1839–1906) legacy proposed by Léger and Delaunay were to be seen at the Indépendants. Mondrian methodically set about sorting out this multitude of stimuli. He settled on the Left Bank, close to Léger and Delaunay, but it was to the more austere, monochromatic Cubism of Picasso and Braque, the Lords of

Montmartre on the other side of the city, that he turned *(see plates 262 and 263)*. Everything he had done previously – and Mondrian was now forty years old – appeared now to have been a preparation. It was in Paris that Mondrian changed the spelling of his surname, dropping the second 'a', as if permanently to mark this tranformation of his artistic identity.

He returned to one of his favourite subjects – the tree – translating its rhythms into his newly adopted Cubist style, ignoring every other contingency *(see plates 290 and 291)*. In the same manner, he also reworked his Zeeland seascapes, painting them from memory in Paris in 1912.

In Shakespeare's *The Winter's Tale* (Act IV, scene iv), the shepherd Florizel says to his love, the disguised princess Perdita:

When you do dance, I wish you
A wave o' th' sea, that you might ever do
Nothing but that; move still, still so,
And own no other function.

The rhythm of the second couplet, echoing the quiet cadence of the sea's movement as the lines pivot on the repetition of the word 'still', crystallizes Florizel's love into an image of perpetual graceful movement. The rhythms of nature become the living image of a love conceived of as eternal. Something of this fascination with the sea's continual oscillation between rest and movement, its rhythm both ordered and unpredictable, asymmetric yet pregnant with suggestions of a larger, eternal symmetry that defies rational exposition, informs Mondrian's post-Cubist sea paintings. He pursued the same subject when he was forced to remain in Holland by the outbreak of war, though with a painterly vocabulary now reduced

still further to a series of marks and signs (*see plate 289*). He limited himself only to black vertical and horizontal lines; yet the mathematical code of the right angle allowed him to describe minute organic variations within a law that is always, but never mechanically obeyed.

Steiner's Theosophy had described creation itself as the result of the conflict of polar opposites – masculine and feminine, spirit and matter. Henceforth, these fundamental oppositions existed for Mondrian in dynamic equilibrium; their pulse constituted the structure of the universe. The pictorial means Mondrian chose – vertical and horizontal, black and white – could give palpable form to this music of the spheres, discernible in nature's visible manifestations. To use the words he jotted in his sketchbooks at the time, it was simply a matter of progressing from an outer to an inner image:

If one has loved the surface of things for a long time, later on one will look for something more. However, this 'something more' is on the surface. The interior of things shows through the surface: thus as we look at the surface the inner image is formed on our soul. It is this inner image that should be represented. For the natural surface of things is beautiful, but the imitation of it is without life.[30]

So far, however, Mondrian had been distilling purely organic rhythms. No matter how abstract his means, he was still painting from nature. In the movement of the sea or the structure of a tree, nature might provide symbols that could be translated into 'inner images' of universal beauty, but these images were tied to the specific. They were not yet pure painterly expressions of Steiner's dynamic equilibrium:

Looking at the sea, sky and stars, I represented them through a multiplicity of crosses. I was impressed by the greatness of nature, and I tried to express expansion, repose, unity . . . But I felt that I still worked as an Impressionist, and expressed a particular feeling, not reality as it is.[31]

This was the impulse that decided Mondrian, as a natural progression, to step into a completely abstract art that contained no references, however vestigial, to nature (*see chapter 9*). Mondrian had to serve an apprenticeship before he could earn the right to paint rectangles.

262   PIET MONDRIAN   Still-Life with Gingerpot I   1911–12.
263   PIET MONDRIAN   Still-Life with Gingerpot II   1911–12.
When, in his early works, Mondrian had chosen to describe the sea and trees, he had essentially already found the subjects that were to occupy him for the rest of his life. For he saw in them the outward manifestations of those universal rhythms or structures that lay behind or beneath the world of appearances. It was in Paris in 1911, however, that he was to take the decisive steps towards developing a painting style that was suitable for the expression of these mystical notions. Once again, it was Cézanne's painting that provided the key. Cézanne had painted numerous still-lifes with a blue-glazed gingerpot as the central motif. The gingerpot in the first of these still-lifes, together with the palette of blues and greens, and the division of objects into simplified planes of colour make this painting a deliberate act of homage. It was painted soon after Mondrian's arrival in Paris. In the second version, Mondrian distilled the Cubists' development of Cézanne's achievements. Twenty years or so of radical French painting have been appropriated by this serious Dutchman in just two canvases. It is a remarkable demonstration of self-imposed, educational concentration.

NOTES

[1] Jack D. Flam (ed.), *Matisse on Art*, London 1973, 140.

[2] Ibid, 112-13.

[3] Robert Rosenblum, *Modern Painting and the Northern Romantic Tradition*, London, 1975, 138.

[4] Barry Herbert, *German Expressionism: Die Brücke and Der Blaue Reiter*, London, 1983, 99.

[5] Kenneth C. Lindsay and Peter Vergo (eds.), *Kandinsky: Complete Writings on Art, Volume One (1901–1921)*, London, 1982, 212-13.

[6] Barry Herbert, op. cit., 153.

[7] Ibid, 115.

[8] In George Heard Hamilton, *Painting and Sculpture in Europe, 1880–1940*, The Pelican History of Art, Harmondsworth, 1981, 303.

[9] Maurice Denis, 'Définition du Néo-Traditionnisme', in *Art et Critique*, 23 August, 1890.

[10] From 'Reminiscences', 1913, in Kenneth C. Lindsay and Peter Vergo (eds.), op. cit., 370.

[11] From *Concerning the Spiritual in Art*; ibid, 154.

[12] From 'Reminiscences', 1913: ibid, 363.

[13] Ibid, 370.

[14] From *Concerning the Spiritual in Art*; ibid, 193.

[15] Ibid, 218.

[16] Peter and Linda Murray, *A Dictionary of Art and Artists*, Harmondsworth, 1959, 212.

[17] Robert Rosenblum, op. cit., 139.

[18] Franz Marc, *Briefe, Aufzeichnungen und Aphorismen*, I, Berlin, 1920, 121; ibid, 141.

[19] In Armin Zweite, with Annegret Hoberg, *The Blue Rider in the Lenbachhaus, Munich*, Munich, 1989, opposite plate 9.

[20] In Barry Herbert, op. cit., 144.

[21] In Armin Zweite, with Annegret Hoberg, op. cit., opposite plate 98.

[22] Arthur Jerome Eddy, *Cubists and Post-Impressionism*, Chicago, 1914, in George Heard Hamilton, op. cit., 209–10.

[23] Frederick Spencer Levine, *An Investigation into the Significance of the Animal as a Symbol of Regression and the Representation of the Theme of the Apocalypse in the Art of Franz Marc*, Master's Thesis, Washington University, St Louis, June 1972, 53.

[24] In Barry Herbert, op. cit., 187.

[25] David Thomson, *The New Cambridge Modern History*, Volume XII, Cambridge, 1969, 103–04.

[26] Ibid.

[27] Ibid.

[28] From 'Reminiscences', 1913, in Kenneth C. Lindsay and Peter Vergo (eds.), op. cit., 364.

[29] Piet Mondrian, 'Plastic Art and Pure Plastic Art', 1937, in Herschel B. Chipp, *Theories of Modern Art*, London and Los Angeles, 1968, 354.

[30] In Michel Seuphor, *Piet Mondrian: Life and Work*, London, 1957, 117.

[31] Piet Mondrian, 'Towards a True Vision of Reality'; ibid, 120.

264 ALEXEI VON JAWLENSKY   Girl with Peonies   1909.
*The deep red of the peonies is barely distinguishable from the colour used
for the girl's blouse, though here it has been marginally lightened by the
addition of orange. Both these reds are set alight by the green background,
though the two complementaries are kept apart by an untidy, thick black
contour. Flecks of blue on the blouse, the flowers and lace collar relieve
these vast areas of uninterrupted colour. Blue is also used to model the
yellows of face, arms and hands. Yet for all this exuberance, the girl turns
her head away from us, a little shy.*

266 ALEXEI VON JAWLENSKY   Still-Life with Fruit   1910.
*It is strange how everything here seems to lean a little to the left. Yet,
in this utterly simplified still-life, this slight diagonal tilt has an
extraordinarily enlivening effect. It creates a sense of latent energy,
contained and constrained by the four edges of the canvas. Cézanne had
used this technique before (see plate 174), and Matisse had painted still-
lifes of comparable simplicity (see plate 130) – both crucial precedents
for Jawlensky. Yet he differs from their example, both in the heaviness
of his touch and, despite the purity of his palette, in the darker tonality
of his colours.*

265 ALEXEI VON JAWLENSKY   Portrait of the Dancer Alexander
Sacharoff   1909.

*Apparently Sacharoff once turned up at Jawlensky's studio in full stage
make-up and costume – the occasion when this arresting portrait was
painted. He took the cardboard panel away with him, with the paint still
wet, afraid that Jawlensky would retouch it later. Sacharoff stares out,
provocatively androgynous, challenging us to decide upon his gender.
Jawlensky uses the same vivid red-green opposition as was employed in the
construction of Girl with Peonies. He had probably learnt this technique
during his time in Paris, as it is evident in the similarly bold portraits
painted by Matisse, The Green Line (see plate 139) in particular.*

267 WASSILY KANDINSKY Motley Life 1907.

Set against a black sky, a fortified Russian city looks down on a crowded, panoramic valley, filled with people and activity. Some kind of total, comprehensive narrative about life is intended. Old and young, woman and man, priest and layman mingle happily in the foreground. From the middle distance to the background, beneath the profile of a red squirrel sitting on a branch, fighting men on foot and horseback fill the valley, preparing for an early burial in the cemetery close by. Kandinsky has darkened the tones of his colours; they seem to be giving out a last, phosphorescent glow before finally being extinguished by the black of sky and forest.

268 WASSILY KANDINSKY Kochel: Graveyard and Rectory 1909.

Despite the season and the subject, there is nothing morbid about this small, intense oil painting: 'For the red blood reigns in the winter's pale', as Autolychus puts it in The Winter's Tale *(Act IV, scene iii). Dazzling blues, enlivened by the oranges of the houses, fall as shadows across the snow, and in the foreground, deeper blues, whites and reds describe a snow-laden bush. Bright colour is used to describe reflected light on white snow and while the bulk and weight of the snow itself is suggested by the heavy application of paint, a lively contrast is created.*

270 WASSILY KANDINSKY Composition 4 1911.
Two lances in front of a castle divide the composition in two. To the left, mounted cossacks clash on rearing horses above blue gun-batteries; to the right, two reclining figures look on. Kandinsky wrote of this work: 'The whole composition is intended to produce a very bright effect, with many sweet colors, which often run into one another (resolution), while the yellow, too, is cold. The juxtaposition of this bright-sweet-cold tone with angular movement (battle) is the principal contrast in the picture.' ('Reminiscences', 1913; in Kenneth C. Lindsay and Peter Vergo (eds.), Kandinsky: Complete Writings on Art, Volume One (1901–1921), London, 1982, 384.)

269 WASSILY KANDINSKY Study for Composition 2 1910.
Kandinsky described his 'Compositions' as highly calculated and reasoned works which in their final state reveal nothing of their lengthy gestation, despite having been matured over time in studies like this one. Thus, in Study for Composition 2 *we see Kandinsky in the process of slowly abstracting numerous recognizable forms. In fact, this study contains a panoramic narrative similar to that of some of Kandinsky's much earlier works like* Motley Life *(see plate 267). In front of the onion domes of a Russian church in the top left-hand corner, two figures look down on two horses – one white and one blue – colliding in combat in the centre. To the right, others flee from this battle beneath the drooping branches of a willow.*

271 WASSILY KANDINSKY Improvisation No. 30 (Cannons) 1913.

In a letter to the picture's owner, Arthur J. Eddy, Kandinsky recalled that he painted this work: '. . . rather subconsciously in a state of strong inner tension. So intensively did I feel the necessity of some of the forms, that I remember having given loud-voiced directions to myself, as for instance: "But the corners must be heavy!" . . . Whatever I might say about myself or my pictures can touch the pure artistic meaning only superficially. The observer must learn to look at the picture as a graphic representation of a mood and not as a representation of objects.' (In Kenneth C. Lindsay and Peter Vergo (eds.), Kandinsky: Complete Writings on Art, Volume One (1901–1921), London, 1982, 403.)

272 WASSILY KANDINSKY Autumn II 1912.
A turreted château to the left overlooks a river surrounded by trees. Their mirrored reflections in the water flatten the attenuated expression of a three-dimensional space. To the right, image and reflection join, cutting across the diagonal, separating line of the embankment, thus confusing the spectator's spatial orientations still further. It is quite easy, however, to relate the colours and shapes to the crisp, pristine freshness of a sunny autumn day. For all the deliciousness of Kandinsky's colours, this canvas has not moved much further away from nature towards abstraction than Sérusier's The Talisman of 1888 (see plate 83).

274 FRANZ MARC The Fate of the Animals 1913.
In the area damaged by fire in the bottom right-hand corner, four deer seem to escape the conflagration that consumes all the other animals. The central tree, traversing the canvas from bottom right to top left, has also been identified as a symbol of hope: '[It is! the mythical Yggdrasil, the world-ash tree from Nordic cosmology, which, with the four deer at the right, will survive and provide the hope for the resurrection of a new, cleansed race after this terrible apocalypse.' (Robert Rosenblum, Modern Painting and the Northern Romantic Tradition, *London, 1975, 145.)*

273 WASSILY KANDINSKY Composition 6 1913.
Kandinsky abandoned his remaining ties with nature most effectively when, as in this picture, he removed any suggestion of an horizon. Having been planning this work for over a year, he painted it quite quickly – finishing most of it within two or three days. Conceived as an expression of the idea of the Deluge it was always intended by Kandinsky to be an hopeful apocalypse: 'What . . . appears a mighty collapse in objective terms is, when one isolates its sound, a living paean of praise, the hymn of that new creation that follows upon the destruction of the world.' ('Reminiscences', 1913; in Kenneth C. Lindsay and Peter Vergo (eds.), Kandinsky: Complete Writings on Art, Volume One (1901–1921), *London, 1982, 388.)*

275 FRANZ MARC Red Roe Deer II 1912.

What is it that these two deer have sensed or smelled, with their noses turned upwards to the breeze that blows the fat clouds above? Whatever it is, it is not for us to know. For, as they would in all Marc's animal paintings, these beasts inhabit their surroundings totally, sharing in the rhythms of that environment in a way that is not permitted to us. Tree, hill, clouds and grass: all flow with the same curves as the gracefully intertwined bodies of the deer. They exist as an ideal of sentient, natural innocence, in a state of intuitive harmony with the landscape. We can only aspire to this perfection.

276 FRANZ MARC The Tiger 1912.

Like the deer Marc painted so often, this tiger seems to sense something outside the picture, though we will never know what it is. Unlike the deer (see plate 275), however, the tiger's body is not fragmented into Cubist shards. It is the sharp planes of the animal's tense, poised muscles that seem to determine the size of those describing the undergrowth in which it hides. In other words, the apparently aggressive nature of the tiger means that it is responsible for shaping its own environment, whereas the more passive deer becomes part of, indeed is almost shaped by its surroundings.

277 FRANZ MARC The Birds 1914.
'Very early on I saw human beings as "ugly"; animals seemed to me purer,
more beautiful, but even in them I found so much that was ugly and
contrary to feeling that, following an inner compulsion, my paintings
instinctively grew more schematic and abstract.' (Marc, in a letter to his
wife, 1915; in Armin Zweite, with Annegret Hoberg, The Blue Rider in
the Lenbachhaus, Munich, Munich, 1989, opposite plate 11.) Marc
forces three white birds into two overlapping diagonal grids, but in many
ways they seem incidental to the colouristic and linear forces of the
painting. Perhaps, though, they were meant to rise, phoenix-like, from
this explosive, Futurist scaffold.

278 AUGUST MACKE Indians on Horseback 1911.

In a passage to the left, blues from the sky slip downwards, disrupting the illusion of space by cutting off the peak of a hill from the foreground. The simplification of the forms into naïve hieroglyphs – whether trees, houses or figures – and the introduction of arbitrary shifts in colour (in the wall of the house on the left, for example) demonstrate how Macke at this stage was adopting more and more avant-garde techniques. Moreover, it is as though these stylistic shifts have been effected purely because Macke believed that his choice of an imaginary 'primitive' scene demanded a comparable style.

279 AUGUST MACKE Kairouan I 1914.
During his two-week trip to Tunisia with Klee, Macke painted thirty-seven watercolours and made over a hundred drawings. This subtle, smoky watercolour is built up of delicate greys, mauves and yellows and the scene is given some sort of structural cohesion by being overlaid with uninsistent vertical washes of colour. These and the overall transparency of the paint reveal the influence of Delaunay. In the foreground, naïvely drawn camels appear in silhouette. They almost seem like hieroglyphs; indeed, the whole image could almost be an illustration in some ancient, forgotten manuscript.

280 AUGUST MACKE Flowers in the Garden – Clivia and Geraniums 1911.
Macke's choice of flower and foliage here lends this painting a somewhat vicarious exotic flavour; but for the terracotta pots, we could be being given a glimpse of some distant, tropical undergrowth. And as if to chide this greenhoused jungle into a more abandoned life, Macke nudges the pots to one side, upsetting their civilized balance. The composition of the image is founded upon that most sensual of complementary pairings – red and green. Yet the greens are cooled, in places, with pale blues. Macke painted this work in his garden in Bonn; complete liberation would only burst forth when he left Europe to paint in Tunisia.

281   PAUL KLEE   Little Port   1914.

Subtle juxtapositions of tone and colour do all the work in this painting, for there is little or no line or shading to describe differences in space and light. Hazy purples and blues describe the far shore, distant hills and sky. Further forward, the pointed prows of the boats and the spindly timbers of a small jetty are put down in nutty reds and browns. Yellow and green foliage joins boathouse to far shore. It is all very simply done. Although it is frequently observed that there are no straight lines in nature, Klee's little scene is built up entirely out of straight-edged bands of colour. His limited means, however, are perfectly suited to expressing the finest nuance.

282   PAUL KLEE   Garden in St Germain, The European Colony in Tunisia   1914.

The sky, plant and stone form a scene that threatens to divide itself into little squares of colour. These incipient squares and overlappings were to become progressively more stylized and schematic in Klee's later work. Here, they retain a rough, patchwork-like quality as Klee followed the example of Delaunay, and ultimately of Cézanne, to translate into paint his responses to the intense African sun pouring down on this garden. Evidently by this time Klee was also beginning to enjoy the effects that could be achieved by brushing a transparent wash of slightly lighter tone over just one part of a composition – the blue, for example, to the left and right of the central roof.

283 PAUL KLEE Föhn in Marc's Garden 1915.

*Klee divided his motif into transparent, overlapping lozenges with
increasing confidence and sophistication. The wall of fellow artist Marc's
house stands along the right-hand edge; dark trees surround the red roof
of a smaller, distant building; and looming over everything is a violet
mountain. Everything in this honeycombed structure is connected,
however, both by shape and colour, whether in the foreground or further
away. Klee painted this watercolour when he was staying with Marc
at his cottage near Kochel, while his friend was on leave from the army.
The Föhn, incidentally, is a warm, dry wind that blows down from the
Bavarian alps.*

284   Piet Mondrian   The Red Cloud   1907.

A sole red cloud provides the only bright colouristic touch in this dirty,
brown and grey landscape. Mondrian positions the horizon low down in
his composition, thus creating a vast sense of scale, an infinite expanse of
sky bearing down on this desolate, flat terrain. There is little life within
this dreary land, either natural or human, and this absence lends the cloud
an even greater significance, making it a solitary signal of a more vivid
existence that floats high above the earth, distant and inaccessible.

286   Piet Mondrian   The Blue Tree   1909–10.

In some of his early works, Mondrian shows himself to be van Gogh's heir.
That other Dutchman's drawing style provides the only precedent for the
succinct, graphic intensity achieved by Mondrian here (see plate 91). Both
artists were able to draw out of a single motif an expression of those forces
felt by each to be animating the whole of nature. Mondrian's tree even
seems to retain the aura or halo of which van Gogh spoke when he
described his portraits, as the turbulent, vigorous sweeps of the branches
charge the air around them.

285 PIET MONDRIAN Dying Chrysanthemum 1908.
*Central, isolated and imposing, this flower has been described by
Mondrian as if the secrets of nature could be discovered, or symbolized, in
the study of the microcosm. Van Gogh had done much the same in his
studies of sunflowers. And the same idea can also be found in the mystical
writings of Rudolf Steiner which Mondrian is known to have read.
Mondrian's chrysanthemum leans feverishly to the left, its liquified petals
touching a funereal, black, vertical band. Further down the stem, the
leaves droop, their fibres' resilience and vigour turned to lifeless torpor.*

287 PIET MONDRIAN Sea at Sunset 1909.
Mondrian's early subjects define themselves repeatedly as images of extreme Romanticism. Here the viewer finds him- or herself standing on the very edge of land looking out to the horizon. In an abrupt change of scale Mondrian has moved away from the microcosm of an individual plant to present its opposite – an infinite expanse of sea stretching out beyond the shoreline, the horizon curving beneath a huge empty sky shot with yellow from the setting sun. Again, this bleak and enormous space is totally uninhabited: man is felt to be dwarfed and minimized by nature's vast indifference.

288 PIET MONDRIAN Dune V 1909–10.
The lone dune threatens to cover the entire surface of the canvas, reducing the sea, whose horizon we glimpse towards the left, to a thin wedge of blue. Indeed, the characteristic low viewpoint Mondrian has adopted lends this dune, despite the flat calm of the brushwork, an upward dynamic thrust; as though the land were attempting to blot out both sea and sky in some prehistoric convulsion of natural forces long before the appearance of human or even vegetable life. For not even a lone plant populates this desolate landscape; its very remoteness seems to have suggested to Mondrian faint memories or echoes of the earth's earliest history.

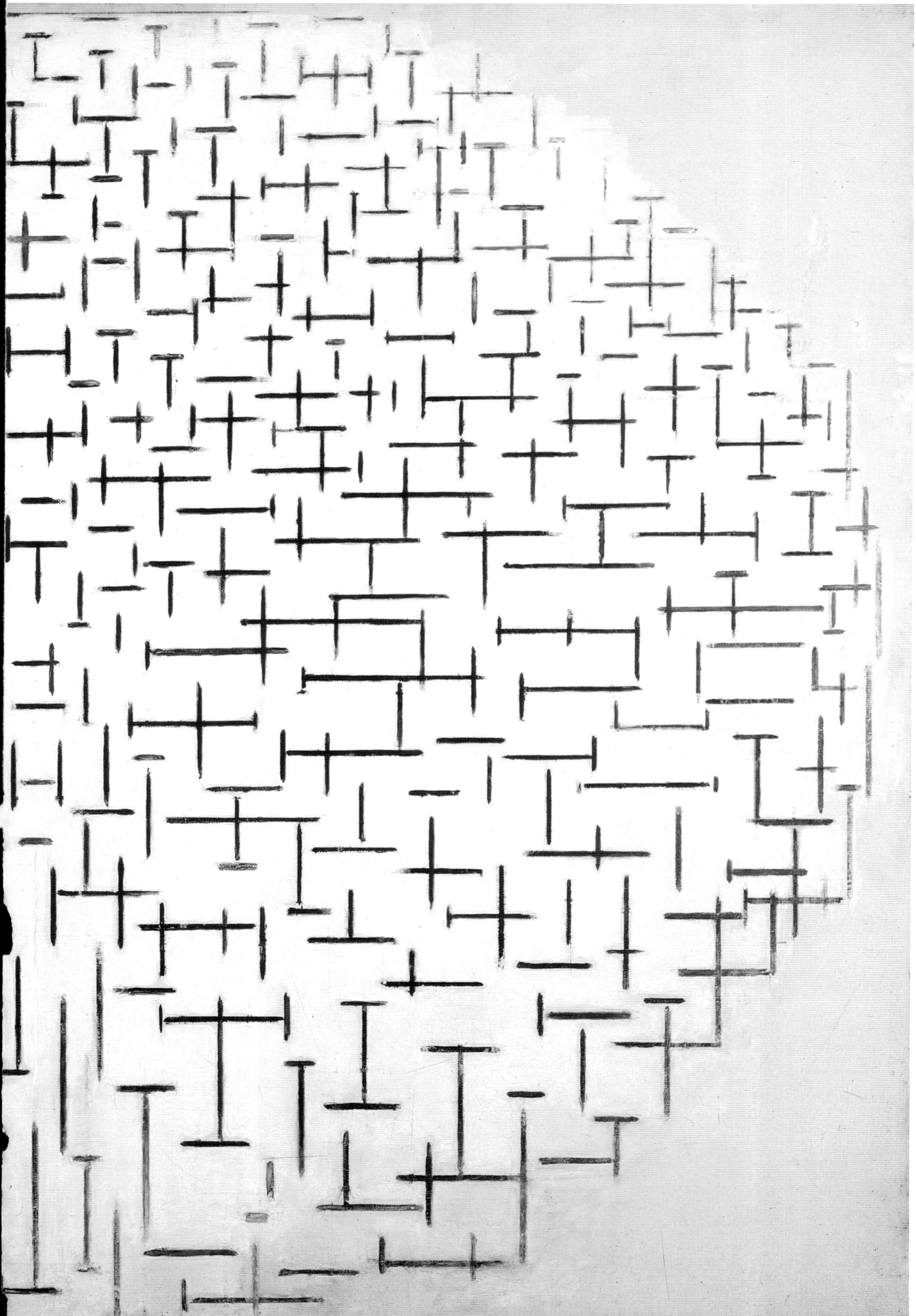

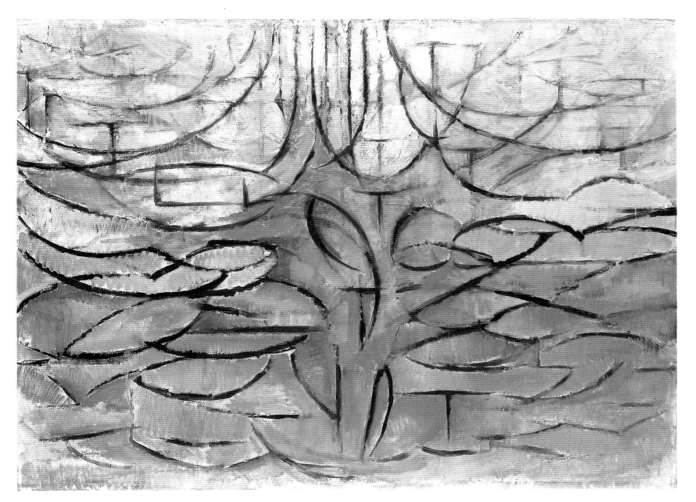

290 PIET MONDRIAN Flowering Apple Tree 1912.
Using the reductive pictorial syntax that he had learnt from Cézanne and the Cubists, Mondrian channelled all the gay exuberance of a tree blossoming in spring into a series of curved black lines laid over a grey background. Some of the spaces in between the branches he shaded with greens and ochres. With these spartan means, Mondrian expresses a lyrical excitement at nature's annual renewal; for the top edge of the canvas cannot contain the vertical rush of lines spilling out from the centre of the picture.

289 PIET MONDRIAN Composition No. 10, Pier and Ocean 1915.
As Mondrian's pictorial vocabulary becomes progressively more simplified, the spectator's viewpoint moves steadily further towards the heavens. For while in The Sea at Sunset we stand at ground level (see plate 287), looking out across the water, here we are given a bird's-eye view of the waves hitting shore and pier. Mondrian had already shown during his stay in Paris that he was capable of the utmost concentration in his distillations of Cézanne and Cubism. Here he has taken a step further to add an other-worldly detachment to his armoury. It is a detachment, a rarified and contemplative attitude, in which he now invites us to share.

291 PIET MONDRIAN Composition No. 3 1913.
The simplification of every element in a painting to a series of complex, interlocking planes, as well as the centripetal nature of the motif, means that Mondrian has had to let his composition fade somewhat towards the four corners. The Cubists had experienced the same problem (see plate 164), and both they and Mondrian were to experiment with oval formats in an attempt to rectify this situation. Here, though, this difficulty notwithstanding, Mondrian's delicately organized planes of faint blues, greys, ochres and greens, gently brushed in over the white of the canvas, convey a startlingly vivid impression of light playing over leaves, branches and twigs.

293   OSKAR KOKOSCHKA   The Bride of the Wind
(The Tempest)   1914.
Kokoschka immersed himself energetically in Berlin's fashionable social
circles and soon fell into an affair with Alma Mahler, the wife of the
composer. It was this relationship, as it reached its final stages, that he
chose to symbolize in this large, allegorical painting. While she sleeps
calmly, Kokoschka lies awake with his fingers nervously intertwined,
all around acidic flashes of white amidst the otherwise gloomy blues
and greens express his awful, neurotic premonitions.

292   OSKAR KOKOSCHKA   Portrait of Herwarth Walden   1910.
Kokoschka arrived in Berlin from his native Vienna in 1910 and soon got
to know two of the city's leading impresarios of modern painting: Paul
Cassirer and Herwarth Walden. Cassirer had formerly been director of the
National Museum but by 1910 was an influential dealer. During that
year Walden set up a publishing house and a journal, both called Der
Sturm, and in 1912 he opened an art gallery of the same name. With
these enterprises Walden was to become a major force in modern German
art. Kokoschka had seen some of van Gogh's portraits in 1906. In his
portrait of Walden he attempts to reveal the personality of his sitter using
distortions of form and colour that were reminiscent of the Dutchman's
style. But Kokoschka's means are coarser and rawer than van Gogh's:
despite the slashed, nervous lines, especially those in red, which portray
a man of intense, restless energies, Walden is presented in muddied,
dirty colours.

Chapter 7

Northern Lights

It was not revolution, as perhaps we might expect, that caused the art world in Russia to be overturned and a radically new avant-garde tradition to be born – as the result of a laborious process in which developments in the west were assimilated into a number of indigenous traditions and quite independent artistic impulses. The complex origins of this Russian modernism are rooted in the 1880s, in the period that was dominated by a group of realist painters known as the Wanderers. The artists Ilya Repin (1844–1930) and Vassily Surikov (1848–1912) were the leading lights. Taking as their inspiration the painters of the late Renaissance, Repin and Surikov produced huge set-pieces in the style of Veronese and smaller historical genre scenes reminiscent of British mid-Victorian painting. This was the style that was to dominate the decade. It was against this backdrop, therefore, that a trio of artists were thrown into profile in the mid-1880s. Mikhail Vrubel (1856–1910), Valentin Serov (1865–1911) and Konstantin Korovin (1861–1939), each the possessor of a very different talent, can together be held responsible for the birth of an artistic tradition in Russia that grew out of everything that was happening in the rest of Europe, activities that would later be described generally as Post-Impressionism.

Korovin had visited Paris in 1885 and discovered the work of the Impressionists. He quickly assimilated their technique and thereafter for the rest of his career remained an Impressionist painter. From the early Tissot-like genre scenes (James Tissot 1836–1902) that he produced in the 1880s to the later, more fluid townscapes, he was always concerned with the depiction of light. In 1901 he became a professor at the Moscow College of Painting, Architecture and Sculpture and it was as a teacher that, along with Serov, Korovin helped to shape the avant garde in Russia between 1890 and 1920. Between them they tutored virtually every single painter that emerged as a leading figure of the avant garde before the Great War.

The early life of both the future masters was focused on Abramtsevo. An artistic colony had been established here in

294 KASIMIR MALEVICH Bather 1910.
Perhaps it is his peasant origins that often makes the primitivism of Kasmir Malevich seem more authentic than that of his contemporaries Larionov and Goncharova. Like Larionov, he had abandoned a straightforward Impressionist approach in 1908. The monumentality of this bather, however, unlike the greater intimacy in the images of the other artists, seems to presage and understand the prominent position assumed by Malevich at the forefront of the Russian avant garde at the outbreak of the First World War.

the 1860s by Baron Savva Mamontov, the railway baron who owned the estate. Serov had lived here since the premature death of his composer father in 1871. Directly after his father's death Serov had been taken to Paris by his mother. It was while he was there, at the age of six, that Serov had received his first drawing lessons – from no less a master than Ilya Repin. From the age of ten, when he was back in Russia, Serov had effectively been brought up by the Mamontov family at Abramtsevo and continued to have lessons with Repin. When he was thirty-two years old Serov went to teach at the Moscow College, remaining there until 1909. His paintings, for the most part portraits of peasants and performing artists, remain very much reminiscent of the style of the French painter Jules Bastien-Lepage (1848–1884).

A more difficult figure to position neatly in a history of art is the Russian artist of Polish-Danish descent, Mikhail Vrubel. He had entered the St Petersburg Academy of Art in 1880, and became a close friend of Serov from the late 1880s onwards. When Vrubel was introduced to Mamontov in 1890 the web was made complete. Vrubel's art, which was heavily influenced by Byzantine decoration, was crucial to the creation of the impetus which fuelled the rise of a Russian avant garde. Vrubel by-passed the naturalism and Impressionism of his colleagues, instead moving directly from Repin's realism to Art Nouveau – by way of Byzantium. In 1884 he had been commissioned to help restore the Byzantine murals in the Church of St Cyril in Kiev. Although he never actually painted the walls, in the course of making an exhaustive series of preliminary working drawings, Vrubel discovered a new approach to art, rooted in a style far older than those then in vogue. Unlike Serov, Vrubel turned away from the idyllic countryside favoured by the Impressionists and the Wanderers, away from the natural colours that formed an integral part of the world they observed. Instead, between 1889 and 1902, his palette comprised the colours of a fantasy world, a world of demons and legends; the world of Russian folklore seen anew through the eyes of Symbolism. In a statement that echoes the voice of Maurice Denis (1870–1943), the Nabis painter who was to receive great acclaim in Russia in the first decade of the twentieth century, Vrubel emphasized the importance of the picture surface: 'Byzantine painting differs fundamentally from three-dimensional art. Its whole essence lies in the ornamental arrangement of form which emphasises the flatness of the wall.'[1]

Moreover, it was Vrubel who was chiefly responsible for defining in Russia the important role of colour and and its power to evoke emotions. Russian painting between 1900 and 1920 is inextricably linked with the other arts: music, drama and most importantly poetry. As the Symbolist poet Alexandr Blok (1880–1921), put it:

Russia is a young country and her culture is a synthesis . . . The writer should not forget the painter, the architect and musician . . . In Russia, painting, music, prose and poetry are inseperable from one another, and equally at one with philosophy, religion, philanthropism and even politics.[2]

Vrubel combined his love of the passionate poetry of Mikhail Yurevich Lermontov (1814–1841) with the Byzantine art he had seen in Kiev and subsequently in Venice. In particular he was inspired by Lermontov's poem 'The Demon', which he first illustrated in 1890. His subsequent pictures – demons with huge heads and staring eyes, as in his *Demon Seated* (*see plate 307*), for instance – were to an increasing extent shaped by Lermontov's words. Being himself another tortured spirit and writing frequently on the role of the artist, Vrubel provided a major source of inspiration to the Russian avant garde between 1890 and 1910. Even when he painted studies of plants as a means of relaxation, he could not help but explore their form in an almost abstract style; the fevered brushstrokes and clashes of colour seem almost to presage Cubism and Futurism. Essentially, though, Vrubel is best described as a romantic Symbolist. Blok's description of his sunsets bears witness to this: 'As though through a broken dam, the blue-lilac twilight of the world bursts in, to the lacerating accompaniment of violins and tunes reminiscent of gypsy songs.'[3]

295 ALEXANDER BENOIS Stage Design for Petrushka 1911.
The work of Alexander Benois was instrumental in transforming the formal appearance of Russian art in the 1900s. This is an example of his late work, a design for fellow Russian Igor Stravinsky's (1882–1971) ballet Petrushka. Benois and other artists of the World of Art movement developed from his stage designs a number of devices which provided an alternative to traditional means of depicting space and perspective. The side-wings, framing curtain and use of objects in the middle distance all recur in paintings by Benois and his fellow artists, pointing the way towards the two-dimensionalism that would characterize the work of later generations of Russian twentieth-century artists.

Although it is unlikely that his own philosophy was shaped by the Symbolism emerging in France during the late 1880s, it was in such ideals that his heart lay. As a personality Vrubel seems to have been one of those romantic, doomed figures that emerge time and again among the artistic community of his generation. He is one with Gauguin, Munch, van Gogh and Klimt. From 1900 to 1910 he suffered from recurrent bouts of mental illness and eventually died insane in a mental institution. As a theorist, however, like Paul Henri in America and Sickert in Britain, Vrubel provided the verbal and intellectual stimulus for the birth of modernism in Russia. One might well compare Vrubel's importance to Russian art with that of Cézanne in the West.

The World of Art and the *Golden Fleece*

The radical changes in Russian art that were occasioned by Vrubel's example can only be understood, however, when set against the backdrop of the Mir iskusstva, or World of Art movement, which was the Russian equivalent of French Art Nouveau and German Jugendstil. Largely the brainchild of the painter Alexander Benois (1870–1960), this movement was to flourish between 1897 and 1906.

Benois, a Franco-German Russian from St Petersburg, had attended the St Petersburg Academy from 1890. It was here that he met fellow artist Lev Rosenburg, better known under his assumed name of Leon Bakst (1866–1924). The two men came to dominate a literary and artistic society known as the Nevsky Pickwickians from this date. Comprised of young men, the society was concerned with 'self-education', independent of the art academies. During the winter of 1890 they were joined by a disaffected young legal student called Sergei Diaghilev (1872–1929), who was taking music lessons from Rimsky-Korsakov (1844–1908) at the time. In 1891 Benois travelled to Munich to learn about contemporary art and Diaghilev went to Paris where he was attracted not to the work of the Impressionists but rather to that of Puvis de Chavannes (1824–1898) and the Symbolists. When these two returned to St Petersburg the group reformed and was joined by both Serov, who had known Bakst since they had studied together in St Petersburg, and by his fellow painter Korovin, from the Mamontov circle. Serov now began to paint in a more decorative manner. By 1900 he was producing portraits in which the sitter is shown in silhouette and, with a vibrancy which rivals the northern radicalism epitomized by Munch; his portrait of M. N. Ermolova (*see plate 318*) is typical of this period. By 1901, with the arrival of the art student Nicholas Roerich (1874–1947), the group was complete. The group also became friendly, during that year, with a French diplomat called Charles Birle. He showed them the work of some of the early French rebels, notably Georges Seurat (1859–1891), Vincent van Gogh (1853–1890) and Paul Gauguin (1848–1903). From this time onwards European painting was to play an increasingly important role in their art.

In 1895 Diaghilev travelled abroad again. He bought paintings as he went, and, on his return, began to give serious thought to becoming an art administrator. It was with this in mind that he put together two exhibitions in 1897: one comprised English and German watercolours, the other was dedicated to Scandinavian painting. Benois had returned to Russia from Paris in 1896; he had been studying art there for two years. Under the leadership of Diaghilev the re-formed group re-named itself Mir iskusstva, meaning World of Art. They launched a magazine of the same name, financed in part by Mamontov and partly by the famous arts patron Princess Tenisheva, and the first edition appeared in October 1898. Benois wrote a critique of the Impressionists. Diaghilev wrote an informal declaration of the group's aims in which he said that beauty was the only possible justification for art. The logo of the group – a mountaintop – was designed by Bakst and it was chosen to reflect the group's high spiritual intentions. A romantic nostalgia pervaded the whole publication, tempered by various Symbolist views; indeed, the work of the French Symbolist poets Charles Baudelaire (1821–1867) and Paul Verlaine (1844–1896) was printed alongside that of similarly minded Russian poets. Illustrations were mainly Art Nouveau in style, but also included work by Claude Monet (1840–1926), Edgar Degas (1834–1917) and Puvis de Chavannes. The emphasis, however, tended to be rather more German than French, for the artistic influence of France only began to dominate Russian art after 1904. Meanwhile, the group continued its activities. In 1898 Diaghilev masterminded another exhibition, this time of Russian and Finnish painting; among the Russian artists whose work was exhibited were Korovin, Serov and Vrubel. The following year the exhibition was repeated, but the boundaries had been expanded by this stage to incorporate French artists too – including Puvis de Chavannes, Monet and Degas, and by this stage the American expatriot James McNeill Whistler (1834–1903). The work of Germans Arnold Böcklin (1827–1901) and Adolf Menzel (1815–1905) was also exhibited.

Perhaps a more important direct influence on Russian painting was that which resulted from the involvement of the World of Art artists in the Russian theatre. In 1899 Benois and Bakst were commissioned to design together the set and costumes for two productions at the Hermitage Theatre. It was the start of a close working relationship both between the artists themselves and between them and the stage. Over the next fifteen years this creative forum was to produce a style of set design that would have a major impact on painting. Their main achievement was to be able to render depth and space without the use of perspective. To achieve this on stage Benois used in his set designs such devices as side wings and unusual viewpoints, reflected images and silhouettes (see plate 295). His shapes became purely decorative. As such artists as Benois grew more and more involved in theatre design, so these tricks of the stage quickly made their way into the painters' vocabulary. Foreground foliage would be used to frame the picture and viewpoints would be chosen that were similar to those used in the theatre, viewpoints which also echoed those favoured by some of the Impressionists, Degas and Gustave Caillebotte (1848–1894) in particular. At the same time as this new influence emphasized the Byzantine flatness taught by Vrubel, and other painters, including Korovin, were drawn into work for ballet productions. Nevertheless, despite its background importance in opening up contacts with the West and in suggesting such technical innovations as these, the World of Art movement should not be seen as a coherent whole, striving against the Academy in the name of Symbolism. For this it never was. It was left to others to achieve this and one among these individuals in

296   VICTOR BORISOV-MUSATOV   Two Seated Women 1899.

Following the death of his teacher Gustav Moreau in 1898, Victor Borisov-Musatov returned from Paris to Moscow. He was fortunate enough to be invited to paint on the estate of a local landowner at his home town of Saratov. This was the perfect location for the artist as he explored the new painting styles that he had discovered in France. The estate formed a focal point for artists and community alike. Here we see Borisov-Musatov experimenting with his technique, as he tackles his favourite subject matter: women. His customary tight handling of the paint is looser here, and broad brushstrokes combine with subtle colour to describe the atmosphere of quiet contemplation.

particular – the artist whom we might be tempted to describe as the first Russian painter really to compare with his European avant-garde contemporaries.

Victor Borisov-Musatov (1870–1905) had studied both at the Moscow College and at the St Petersburg Academy, before starting work in Moscow in 1892. Thus he can be said to have assimilated the teachings of both schools. Between 1895 and 1899 he studied at the atelier of Gustave Moreau in Paris, alongside Henri Matisse (1869–1954), Albert Marquet (1875–1947) and Henri Manguin (1874–1949) – the future Fauves. There were some fifty students in the class; working within Moreau's tenet that each artist should be allowed to discover himself; they ranged from the chic to the anarchic. It seems, however, that rather than befriending the Fauves, Borisov-Musatov began to read the poetry of Verlaine, and was taken with the work of Bastien-Lepage and Puvis de Chavannes. When Borisov-Musatov returned to Russia after Moreau's death in 1898 he produced a series of strange, contemplative works in the grounds of a local landed estate, dominated by a derelict Neo-classical mansion at the top of a tree-lined hill. Puvis de Chavannes's preoccupation with historical costume has been replaced by ruined, aged architecture. In these ghostly evocations of a past age, painted in a soft, mood-evoking palette of blue and grey tones, Borisov-Musatov's crinolined ladies, apparently weighed down with

297   Photograph of Shchukin's house in Moscow   1912.
The Moscow industrialists Serge Shchukin and Ivan Morozov provided the Russian avant-garde artists of the early twentieth century with an unique opportunity to discover the exciting developments taking place in French art during the period. Shchukin in particular displayed a discerning taste in his astonishing collection, which included works by Picasso, Matisse, Monet, Renoir and Cézanne. We can see here just a few of his treasures, including several works by Gauguin. The view is dominated, however, by three Matisse paintings – Conversation in the centre and Nasturtiums and 'The Dance' to the left. Matisse himself travelled to Moscow to instal his Music and Dance (see plate 161) in this house.

care, wander through the otherwise empty parklands in images which are at once both decorative and symbolist. Borisov-Musatov's women never talk, those in *The Reservoir* (*see plate 319*) for instance, but in a quasi-sacred inaction maintain their forlorn existence. His works were a success abroad and in 1904 he had a one-man show in Germany. The following year he was among the exhibitors at the Salon de la Société des Artistes Français in Paris.

It was during this year – 1905 – that Russia experienced a ghastly foretaste of what was to come some twelve years later. There was an abortive revolution. Nevertheless this unsuccessful social revolution heralded a decade of revolutions within the Russian art world. And art movements from the rest of Europe succeeded each other as the dominant influence in Russian art with bewildering rapidity.

World of Art had opened up the frontier with Europe, and in the wake of the turmoil of 1905 a new generation of collectors began to buy European work. Prominent amongst them was Sergei Shchukin, who had bought a Monet from Paul Durand-Ruel (1831–1922) in 1897 and had gone on to purchase works by Edouard Manet (1832–1883), Camille Pissarro (1830–1903), Alfred Sisley (1839–1899), Degas and Henri Fantin-Latour (1836–1904) from him. He had bought his first Cézanne in 1904. Other paintings followed by Gauguin, van Gogh, the Nabis, André Derain (1880–1954) and Matisse. Shchukin met Matisse, who was later to paint his portrait through Derain. In 1908 Matisse in turn introduced him to Pablo Picasso (1881–1973). Along with Shchukin the other great collector of the period was Ivan Morozov. Generally more cautious than his compatriot, he collected vast amounts of work. He also met Matisse, through Shchukin, in Paris in

1908. By this date the houses of these two collectors were filled with the best of French contemporary art, although Morozov eschewed that of Picasso, preferring to limit himself to Gauguin, Cézanne, Denis, Pierre Bonnard (1867–1947) and Edouard Vuillard (1868–1940). He commissioned the last three to paint huge panels specifically for his house.

The two collectors did not keep their treasure houses to themselves, but invited the public inside, allowing artists and students to experience first hand this new artistic French revolution. Shchukin's house (*see plate 297*) was open to all-comers on Saturday afternoons and the works it contained caused a stir from the first day it opened its doors. It is impossible to over-estimate the contribution made by the critical faculties of these two outstanding collectors to the development of Russian modernist art during the period. Even at the time the impact of this fantastic array was obvious: Serov, the frustrated teacher of the next generation of the avant garde described his students' reaction to Shchukin's collection:

After such spice the diet of the school was insipid. There was no alternative but to give up the course, because they [the young painters] did not want to hear any more, each of them stewed in his own way and refused to learn.[4]

There was one particularly exciting aspect to these great collections. For as fast as the public came to recognize the work of these previously unknown painters, so Shchukin acquired more paintings. These included Matisse's *Harmony in Blue* (which was actually altered to red simply on order to match the collector's dining room!), his *Nymph and Satyr* and *Music and Dance*. The artist himself installed this last in Shchukin's house in 1911, travelling to Moscow specifically for the purpose. This artist's paramount importance to the Russian avant garde can possibly in part be explained by the fact that Shchukin's interest in both him and his work was unending.

It was not by such philanthropic means alone that Russian artists came to know of European developments. From 1881 onwards other smaller exhibitions of French and German art were frequently held in Moscow and St Petersburg. Wassily Kandinsky (1866–1944) had seen one of Monet's grainstacks paintings at a small trade fair in Russia in 1891. Sadly a lack of documentary evidence makes it hard to gauge the importance of such relatively small exhibitions. Undoubtedly they were influential, however, particularly when regarded in conjunction both with the private collections, the fact that artists had the scope to travel extensively and the growing interest in art magazines.

World of Art published its last edition in 1904, filling it with the work of the Impressionists; its contributors had gone their separate ways. To some extent, its place was taken by a new magazine called *Zolotoe Runo*, or *Golden Fleece*, which lasted from 1906 to 1909. It is significant that the magazine's sixth edition in 1909 was devoted in its entirety to Matisse, including a translation of his 'Notes d'un Peintre', originally published in 1908. For the moment, however, Russian artists looked closer to home for inspiration.

In 1906 Diaghilev organized a show in Moscow of the work of Borisov-Musatov, who had died two years before. Uniquely, the exhibition contained not only the work of Borisov-Musatov himself, but also that of his followers. For the most part these were ex-students of Serov and Korovin

298   MARTIROS SARYAN   Self-Portrait   1907.
The many sides of Martiros Saryan are apparent in this intense self-portrait, painted several years after his return from Paris in 1900. At this stage Saryan is still working with the palette he had seen in France in the work of Gauguin. But to this he brings something of his own – the bold primitivism of Eastern art and particularly that of Persia. It might be said that Saryan was establishing his own form of Fauvism in Russia, paralleling that developing in France. This Eastern strain was one that he would continue to develop for the rest of the decade with further visits to Egypt and Turkey.

from the Moscow College; having assumed the title of Alaya roza, meaning Scarlet Rose, at their previous exhibition in 1904, they now changed their name to Golubaya roza, meaning Blue Rose. As such a colour change in the title might suggest, the show was overwhelmingly Symbolist in feeling. It included works by Pavlov Kuznetsov (1878–1968), Natalia Goncharova (1881–1962), Mikhail Larionov (1881–1964) and Martiros Saryan (1880–1972).

A year later Kuznetzov would host an exhibition in his own house devoted exclusively to the work of the group. Yet it is not only for this reason that Pavel Kuznetsov deserves greater attention as an individual artist. Having studied under Serov and Korovin in Moscow he later took private lessons in Paris. In 1904 he exhibited at the Salon d'Automne in Paris. But by 1905 he had moved away from an Impressionist style towards a more abstract expression of his feelings in paint. Where Kuznetsov's works are weird, disturbing allegorical treatises on birth and death, filled with intertwined forms and staring faces, unborn children and demonic figures, they combine the decorative tonalities of Borisov-Musatov with the moody introspection of Vrubel.

All the members of the Blue Rose group were subject to this combination of influences. In an article published in *Golden Fleece No. 1* in 1908, one of them, Nikolai Milioti

(1874–1962) attempted to define their objective; it was, he proposed: 'To bring clarity into the chaotic state of affairs'.[5] Meanwhile, the editor of the magazine *Apollon*, meaning Art, described the group as: 'Heralds of the new primitivism to which our modern painting has come'.[6]

Despite the unearthly look that is common to all their paintings, the philosophy of the Blue Rose was essentially optimistic about the nature of mankind. The stillness of their paintings is not the silence of death but that of the mystery of being – the mystery of the Symbolists.

The Russian Symbolism of painters like Kuznetsov was to last but a few years. Other, more basic forces were at work. Of the other Blue Rose artists, the most important to the development of an avant-garde tradition in Russia were Saryan, Larionov and Goncharova.

The paintings of Saryan, an Armenian ex-student of the Moscow College, are close in composition to the work of Derain; they also have something in common with the work of the Blaue Reiter artist Franz Marc (1880–1916) and the German Expressionist Erich Heckel (1883–1970) although they pre-date both. Saryan, whose self-seeking nature is well conveyed in his *Self-Portrait* of 1907 (*see plate 298*), had begun his career as a realist before adopting an Impressionist style in the early 1900s. He had, in all probability, seen the works of Matisse in Shchukin's house, and these may be seen as playing a powerful role in the shaping of his art, qualifying and supporting the urge towards primitivism that was rising throughout Europe – both East and West – at this time.

In 1906 Diaghilev had the idea of organizing an exhibition of contemporary Russian painting in Paris. He wrote to Benois, then resident in Paris, on 20 April 1906: 'Can you not test the lie of the land? The French will be really foolish if they refuse. I take it upon myself to show them the real Russia.'[7] The French were not foolish and during the autumn of that year, in twelve of the rooms of the Grand Palais, specially decorated for the occasion by Bakst, 750 works by some 53 Russian artists were displayed. Vrubel had a room to himself. Larionov helped Diaghilev to set up the show and it succeeded not only in attracting the French public, but also in bringing other Russian artists to Paris: Kandinsky, Alexei von Jawlensky (1864–1941), Kuzma Petrov-Vodkin (1878–1939) and Kuznetsov among them.

The publication of *Golden Fleece* that autumn further emphasized this growing sense of internationalism. From the outset this journal had been published in both French and Russian; in 1908 this link was reinforced even more strongly when *Golden Fleece* organized the first of three important exhibitions in Moscow. The paintings of the French Impressionists were accompanied by those of Henri de Toulouse-Lautrec (1864–1901), Cézanne, Matisse, Georges Braque (1882–1963), Henri Rouault (1871–1958) and the Nabis. And alongside this group of French painters stood a selection of Russian painters. Among the French works exhibited were many of those that had made such an impact at the Fauve Salon d'Automne in 1905, including Matisse's *View of Collioure* (*see plate 140*) and his initial sketch for *Le Bonheur de Vivre* (*see plate 134*). Derain showed four London scenes. And there were also paintings by Kees van Dongen (1877–1968) and Marquet. In the Russian section there were works by Kuznetsov, Saryan, Goncharova and, most dominantly, Larionov, who showed some twenty canvases. All the Russian works were characterized by the same general trend: away from the realism inspired by Borisov-Musatov and towards the primitive. While some artists, like Kuznetsov chose to look to Gauguin, Saryan, whilst admitting some sort of debt to Matisse, was clearly looking to the East and his Armenian origins. His travels to Persia and Egypt served to emphasize both how close his taste was to that of the Frenchman and yet that there was an independent spirit at work in his art.

That Saryan and others adopted new and bold colours at this time clearly indicates that there was certainly something of the Fauves' influence apparent in their art. This sense of international cross-fertilization was taken a stage further in 1909 when an exhibition was mounted in which the Russian artists were not segregated as before, but shown among the French. The crowd-puller this time was Braque's *Nu Debout*. It was during this year that the famous edition of *Golden Fleece* containing important extracts from Matisse's 'Notes d'un Peintre' was published.

It would be short-sighted, however, despite their obvious importance, to place undue emphasis on the influence of the French at this time. There was another energetic force at work. An indigenous tradition of Russian folk art, that of the icon and the ancient religious fresco, now began to appeal to such artists as Petrov-Vodkin and Kuznetsov.

Petrov-Vodkin had been a student of Serov in Moscow. Significantly he had also worked in Munich. In 1905 he travelled to Africa and while he was there he was exposed to primitive art for the first time. He was deeply impressed. On his return to Russia, Vodkin had become associated with the Blue Rose group, although he refused to exhibit with them. His *Red Horse Swimming* (*see plate 310*) exhibits all the influences upon his art: Byzantine painting, primitive sculpture and the work of Matisse. In both the composition and the tension created between the figures the picture bears a strong resemblance to the French artist's *Dance* (*see plate 161*), which Vodkin would undoubtedly have known from its prominent place in Shchukin's house. Vodkin's work is somehow flatter than that of Matisse, however, and his figures seem to hark back to an older tradition of Western painting.

It is in the work of the artist Natalia Goncharova that this new enthusiasm for an indigenous primitivism is most apparent. It was her work, together with that of Larionov, which dominated the third *Golden Fleece* exhibition of 1909–10. Here, in a backlash against excessive French influence, only works by Russians were displayed. Despite their common roots in Serov and Borisov-Musatov, the work of these two artists differed significantly from that of their contemporaries. Once again, in the space of only a few years, the Russian avant garde had swiftly abandoned one style of painting in favour of another.

Primitives and the Donkey's Tail

Primitivism emerged as a force in Russian art in 1910, when the group known as the Knave of Diamonds held their first exhibition. The core of the group included Pyotr Konchalovsky (1876–1956), Ilya Mashkov (1881–1944), Aristarkh Lentulov (1882–1943), Robert Falk (1886–1958), Larionov and Goncharova. The ideas which bound them together were essentially negative. For not only were they

299   PYOTR KONCHALOVSKY   Portrait of Georgy Yakulov   1910.
The unadulterated primitivism which was to reach its Russian apogee in the work of Goncharova is also evident in this extraordinary portrait of the artist Yakulov. Konchalovsky shows us his friend as a fashionably dressed young aesthete, seated on a velvet cushion, in front of a wall hung with oriental swords and pistols. The sitter did indeed have a large and renowned collection of such weaponry. Although the primitive, almost demonic appearance of his sitter seems essentially Russian, the artist's muted palette appears to nod an acknowledgement to France, but definitely towards Cézanne rather than Matisse.

against the constraints of the Academies, but also against the Symbolists, and what they saw as the excesses of Art Nouveau contained in the World of Art movement. Their protest took the form of a reversion to a crudely primitive style of painting that had its foundation in Russian folk art. They found inspiration in religious wall paintings, shop signs, toys and the popular Lubki prints, as well as in religious and political tracts and song sheets. They also looked beyond Russia to the primitive elements of Die Brücke in Germany and to Gauguin's work in France. Foreign work for the show was chosen by the French critic Alexandre Mercereau and among those he invited to participate were Derain, van Dongen, Braque, Fernand Léger (1881–1955), Kandinsky, Jawlensky, Marc and Ernst Ludwig Kirchner (1880–1938).

Konchalovsky, one of the Russian exhibitors, who was Surikov's son-in-law, had studied at St Petersburg Academy and then in France where he had been impressed by the work of Matisse and Cézanne. The primitivist style of his *Georgy Yakulov* (*see plate 299*) was typical of his work of the next few years; after that he began to move towards a form of Cubism similar to the painted collages produced by Picasso.

Mashkov specialized in still-life and portraiture, his particularity angular style and monumental figures well-suited to the primitivist ethic. He had studied under Serov in Moscow, where apparently he had angered his master by painting his nude studies with green armpits. But Mashkov's major source of inspiration was in sign painting. Thus, in his still-life *Fruit on a Dish* of 1910 (*see plate 312*) he uses the same bright colours and bold, dark outlines as would have been found on traditional Russian shop signs. Lentulov had studied in Kiev and St Petersburg and by 1910 had already shown alongside Goncharova and Larionov at smaller exhibitions, notably at The Wreath show at St Petersburg in 1908. In 1911 he travelled to France and Italy; he was influenced by Albert Gleizes (1881–1953) and Henri le Fauconnier (1881–1946), and indeed in 1912 developed in his painting a form of Cubism. Falk, from Moscow, had received private tuition from Mashkov as well as studying at the Moscow College under Korovin and Serov. Having started to paint in the distinctive Moscow Impressionist manner he too moved steadily towards a rhythmic, lyrical Cubism, though one that was directly inspired by Cézanne.

Among the other artists to show at the first Knave of Diamonds exhibition were the Burliuk brothers, David (1882–1967) and Vladimir (1886–1916). These two artists from Kharkov had studied in Odessa, Munich and Paris. In 1907 they met Goncharova and Larionov for the first time and with them arranged the exhibition The Wreath, which included the work of the two future primitives and that of the Blue Rose painters. The brothers were formidable, flamboyant characters, embodying all the youthful excitement that pervaded Russian art throughout this period. At this stage the public were as much drawn to the antics of the young avant-garde artists walking along the street with their faces painted, wearing spoons as buttonholes, making outrageous declarations, being expelled from art schools – as to their art. Vladimir Burliuk took this flamboyant behaviour to an extreme, and being a professional wrestler, carried a pair of dumbells with him wherever he went.

In 1908 the Burliuk brothers moved to St Petersburg. They began to gather around them the core of a coherent Russian avant garde, and later that year organized another exhibition. Entitled 'The Link', this show again brought together the work of Goncharova and Larionov, with paintings by Lentulov and themselves. Both brothers were also poets, serving to underline once more the strong links at this time between Russian art and literature; the work of Russian futurist poet Vladimir Mayakovsky (1894–1930), for instance, who self-consciously attacked with his fellow poets what he saw as the artificial sophistication propounded by the World of Art movement. It was from this core of artists that the Knave of Diamonds movement emerged in 1910.

Two members of the group stand out as being of greater importance than the others to the development of the Russian avant garde: indeed, Mikhail Larionov and Natalia Goncharova can be seen as the true founders of neo-primitivism in Russia. It was they, more than any of the other artists, who looked to an indigenous tradition, adapting these Russian art forms according to the theories and teachings then current in contemporary Russian and German painting.

Although a movement towards simplicity had been evident at the shows organized by the *Golden Fleece* since April 1908, it had only come to the fore in 1909 at the group's third exhibition, one that provided the necessary backdrop for the debut of this new style of painting. Larionov and Goncharova

were, of course, well respected there. Larionov, the son of an army doctor, had studied at the Moscow College, where he had painted in the then-favoured Impressionist style; however, he was expelled for non-attendance. His first neo-primitive works are landscapes and views of his own home town, descriptions of events in its everyday life, although many of his pictures also portray life in the army, reflecting his own national service. In paintings such as his *Soldier in a Wood* (*see plate 308*) the figures are stiff and wooden, no more than childrens' toys, yet at the same time they possess an earthy sense of reality. Natalia Goncharova was Larionov's wife and companion. The poet Pushkin's great grand-daughter, she had studied science in Moscow before moving to the College in 1898 to study art under the World of Art sculptor Pavel Trubetskoi (1866–1938). It was here that she met Larionov and from that time onwards the two were inseparable, travelling extensively together to England, Spain and Italy between 1900 and 1904. During the early years of the century Goncharova painted in a Nabis-influenced style, but she soon turned to producing primitivist paintings of peasants, workers and country life (*see plate 309*). As early as 1905 Goncharova's very simplistic style also bears traces of Byzantine icons; the religious sentiments evident in her work thus also creates a link with the contemporary work of Die Brücke in Germany. If her paintings are even more severe in appearance than those of her husband, they are still more

300   MIKHAIL LARIONOV   Relaxing Soldier   1911.
By the time he painted this picture, Larionov had made considerable progress. Gone now are the fevered brushstrokes evident in his earlier attempts at neo-primitivism. They have been replaced by a new lyricism and a bold move towards two-dimensionality. Larionov's early subjects were often taken from army life. The son of an army doctor, he had himself had first-hand military experience during his own national service. The soldiers he paints are a curious combination: the children's toy mixed with the raw earthiness of the Russian peasantry; and then harks back to the popular Lubki books, which played such an important part in inspiring the primitive style in Russian art.

The new group's first exhibition was held in Moscow in March 1912. Goncharova and Larionov were joined by other artists, including the expatriot Marc Chagall (1887–1985) and the two painters who would force Russia to adopt and accept a modernist tradition: Kasimir Malevich (1878–1935) and Vladimir Tatlin (1885–1953).

'The True Freeing of Art'

Malevich came from a peasant family. He trained in Kiev until 1900, arrived in Moscow in 1905 and studied there in the atelier of the artist Roerburg until 1910. Malevich came into contact with Larionov in 1908; before that he had painted in an Impressionist style tinged with a few stylistic details drawn from the Nabis. From 1908, however, he painted images of the peasantry in the manner of Larionov and Goncharova, and with the sparsest use of line in works like his *Bather* (see plate 294) created monumental figures which also owe something to Cézanne. By 1911 Malevich had refined these images still further. Using a smoother technique in which his paint resembled polished metal, he produced figures that looked like simple, rounded blocks of matter. The *Knife Grinder* (see plate 322) illustrates the inevitable conclusion of this continual refinement: figure and background become one, realism is sacrificed utterly to rhythm and form. Although this and others of Malevich's paintings resemble Leger's work of the same date, they are definitely the product of Malevich's own individual development rather than a borrowing from the Frenchman's visual vocabulary.

Vladimir Tatlin, the other leading artist of the Donkey's Tail, had run away to sea at the age of eighteen before going to Moscow to paint in 1910. He showed thirty-four theatrical costume designs at the exhibition but it was in the following year that Tatlin began to make his mark – with primitivist paintings in the style of his *Fishmonger* (see plate 320). He was invited to show his work at the resurrected World of Art exhibitions, and his paintings of that year show both a refinement of form similar to that seen in Malevich's work of this period and a similar reverence for Cézanne. Tatlin also visited Berlin and Paris in 1913, and while in the French capital he was inspired by Picasso to produce the first of his 'painted reliefs'. In these he attempted to translate Cubism into sculpture; they presage his revolutionary constructions of the 1920s.

Larionov had been working during the previous year on some extraordinary new works, in which actual figurative form was completely subordinated to rhythm and line (see plate 321). Almost abstract compositions, these most closely resemble the work of the Futurists in Italy. At the opening of the exhibition, called 'The Target', in 1913, Larionov publicly announced the birth of another new art movement: Rayonism. He boldly declared:

The style of Rayonnist painting promoted by us, is concerned with spatial forms which are obtained through the crossing of reflected rays from various objects, and forms which are singled out by the artist . . . The ray is conventionally represented on the surface by a line of colour . . . From here begins the creation of new forms, whose meaning and expression depend entirely on the degree of saturation of a colour-tone and the position in which it is placed in relation to other tones . . . from here begins the true freeing of art.[9]

301   NATALIA GONCHAROVA   The Weaver   1913.
The subordination of the individual to the machine, which is the subject of this comparatively mature work by Goncharova, heralds a new age in Russian painting. Here the artist goes even further than Malevich in her fragmentation of the image, giving us just a glimpse of the operative of the complex machine that fills the picture plane; there is a sharp silhouette at the centre of the canvas. Whilst obviously looking back to Picasso's Cubism, Goncharova seems to prepare the way for the new, non-figurative imagery test-run by Malevich later that year.

decorative. The couple visited Paris in 1906 and in the years before 1910 they gradually managed to combine a whole gamut of styles: Borisov-Musatov and Vrubel were combined not only with Cézanne, van Gogh and the Fauves but also with Byzantine and Russian folk art.

The involvement of Goncharova and Larionov in the Knave of Diamonds was short-lived; they maintained a belief that the rest of the group had taken too much from the French, and disengaged themselves in 1911. They vehemently declared that the cradle of all art lay in the East and soon afterwards refined their own art more pointedly towards primitivism. Unlike Gauguin, Matisse, Cézanne and the Germans, however, the Russians did not look to such exotic examples as Tahiti, Africa and India; instead they turned to their own native culture. The break was made official at a discussion on contemporary art organized by David Burliuk in Moscow in February 1912. Larionov stood up and attacked Burliuk as a 'decadent follower of Munich'.[8] Goncharova and Larionov self-consciously moved away from the group, naming their own rebel faction the Donkey's Tail.

302   RICHARD BERGH   The Dying Day   1895.
*The work of Richard Bergh, so well summed-up in this picture of 1895,
was important in keeping alive the Nordic tradition of spirituality in
painting. His theme is death and suffering, seen against the backdrop of
the setting sun of the Norwegian summer. The death of the season is
married to the death of the body in a work whose figures are depicted
with a similar monumentality to the landscape in which they are placed.
Formally, while the figures owe much to the High Renaissance painting
and sculpture which Bergh so much admired, they also seem to have
something in common with the peasants in early works by van Gogh,
and even if Bergh is not looking directly at the tormented Dutch master,
he most certainly displays a knowledge of van Gogh's own mentors
of the Hague School of painters.*

Goncharova had also been experimenting herself, and
between 1911 and 1914 when she departed with her husband for Paris, she produced a number of striking paintings
including *The Weaver* (*see plate 301*), which use Cubist form
and dynamic line to suggest movement, in a similar way to
the Futurists and in line with Larionov's Rayonist theories.

If all this was not radical enough, 1913 was also marked by
a rather more far-reaching development in Russian art.
Malevich had moved on from his *Knife Grinder* (*see plate 322*)
which he labelled 'Cubo-Futurist'. And whilst producing
painted collages that emulated those by Picasso in 1912 (*see
plate 323*), he had simultaneously been developing his own
new theory of painting. The figures in his work had become
less important than form, while the painted planes themselves
had grown to hold the utmost interest for him. Malevich
reached his conclusion in what he called Suprematism. Here,
the natural progressive analysis of form into geometrical shape
became purely emblematic. He explained it:

*The Suprematists have deliberately given up the objective representation of
their surroundings in order to reach the summit of the true 'unmasked' art
and from this point to view life through the prism of pure artistic feeling.*[10]

In these new Suprematist works Malevich used only the
square, the rectangle, the circle, the triangle and the cross,
the purest of these being the square. Although the first of his
works to be produced along these radically new lines was

only exhibted in 1915, it seems likely that it was actually
painted, as he claimed, in 1913. *Black Square* may have
emanated from the minimal backdrop of a bisected black
square that Malevich had been contemplating for a production of the modernist opera *Victory over the Sun*, produced in
St Petersburg in December 1913. Whatever its roots it represents the most significant single breakthrough in Russian
avant-garde art. Once Malevich had painted *Black Square* and
the *Black Square and Red Square* (*see plate 324*), there could be
no turning back from pure abstraction. The face of art had
changed forever.

A Golden Age

If in Russia the birth of a truly modernist idiom in art did not
occur until the early 1900s, in Scandinavia its emergence was
slower still. It is not until after 1910 that we are able to talk
about any Scandinavian country possessing a school that
reflected the developments displayed at either of Roger Fry's
notorious exhibitions. There had been exceptions among the
Scandinavian naturalists of the 1890s, influenced as they
were by Bastien-Lepage. Most notable was the Swedish artist
Richard Bergh (1858–1919), who produced spare, contemplative, almost Symbolist images; the figures in his *Dying Day*
(*see plate 302*), for instance, have the sculptural intensity of
Michelangelo and embody the Nordic spirit which characterizes all Scandinavian art. In a similar vein to Bergh's work is
that of the Danish artist Vilhelm Hammershoi (1864–1916),
who from the late 1880s was painting tonal, intimist interiors,
in which the quiet, sepulchral figures of silent women owe
something to Vermeer as well as to the native Nordic tradition
(*see plate 326*). In his landscapes, however, Hammershoi
shows us quite another dimension, imbuing simple views of
his homeland with a deep spirituality which cannot altogether
be defined as Symbolism (*see plate 327*). A similar feeling is
discernible, though in a rather different context, in the work
of another free spirit in Scandinavian art at this time. Eugene
Jansson (1862–1915) abandoned popular, pretty, rustic
visions to embrace in his work a visionary social truthfulness;
his paintings of tenement blocks and industrial suburbs (*see

303   EDVARD MUNCH   The Sick Child   1885–86.
This early work by Munch marks the emergence of what can be regarded as his quintessential style. Here he abandons his early realism to embrace the two-dimensionality that would become typical of his later work. Munch has clearly been thinking along similar lines to Gauguin and the Nabis; he uses flat planes of colour, simple forms and a simplified palette of pale greens, browns and oranges, enhanced with just a dash of red. His purpose, however, is not simply formal, but spiritual. Fuelled by the memory of his sister's childhood illness and death, he paints an image of intense power which points the way to his later achievements.

plate 325) are described in a simple style similar to that of the Nabis. Jansson was joined in his choice of subject matter by the playwright August Strindberg (1849–1912), who late in life produced a number of urban landscapes in dark tones (*see plate 329*) together with several curious anthropomorphic works that seem possessed of all the Angst and emotion present in his plays (*see plate 328*). In their use of non-figural imagery, both men present us with a variation of the classic Nordic art form called the Stamning, meaning – roughly translated – an evocation of nature whose mood and atmosphere has some deeply personal significance for the creator. In Stamning a house is not simply a building but a symbol of death, a tree a sign of life. It is part of the great Northern Romantic tradition of spiritual introspection seen earlier in the work of Caspar David Friedrich and later taken up by the German Expressionists. This deeply personal form of art found its apotheosis in late nineteenth-century Scandinavia in the work of the Norwegian Edvard Munch (1863–1944).

A detailed examination of Munch's life is not within the scope of the present work. However, he is of paramount importance in any examination of early twentieth-century painting in Scandinavia and such was his influence on the next generation of Scandinavian artists that his work should be given its proper place. From his teens Munch had painted in a style alternately similar to early van Gogh and to that

prevalent among the fashionable *plein-air* painters. In 1881 he began to study art in Oslo and by 1885 something quite new had emerged in his work; the intense, thoughtful melancholy mood of his *The Sick Child* (see plate 303), foreshadows the mood of much of Munch's painting in the 1890s. For it is in the work that he produced after 1892 that Munch developed the style that would influence so many of his fellow Scandinavian artists.

In 1889, on his first visit to Paris, his first reaction had been to paint several canvases in the style of Monet. It was at the end of this year that Munch took his most momentous step, abandoning the Impressionists and finding in the work of Gauguin the natural way to express the thoughts that had preoccupied him for some years. These were thoughts that were paralleled in the work of Søren Kierkegaard (1813–1855), Franz Kafka (1883–1924) and Sigmund Freud (1856–1939), and shaped by the illness which had plagued Munch's childhood. Together with the memories of the death of his sister, they were to haunt him throughout his life. *Melancholy* (see plate 330), which dates from the end of 1891, is one of the first of these canvases; it is painted with the same large forms and blocks of colour that were favoured by Gauguin and Bernard.

304   EDVARD MUNCH   The Scream   1893.
The influence of the Japanese print on Munch's painting is once more obvious in this, probably his most famous image. The figure walking across a bridge that recedes sharply into the picture plane was a subject that had been painted many times by such Impressionist artists as Monet and Sisley. Munch brings to the motif his unique approach. The head of the central figure, no more than a ghastly death's head, is emphatically brought to our attention by the formal pointers of both bridge and river. The blue swirl of the river snakes through a background where perspective has been sacrificed to the abstract qualities of the red sky and green ground. The whole picture seems to throb with all Munch's own mental agony; perhaps he had at last found the means to express himself fully.

In 1892 Munch travelled to Berlin to exhibit fifty of his pictures. The show closed after a week, being described by the critics as: 'An insult to art'.[11] Munch found the artistic atmosphere of the city more conducive to his art, however, than that of either Oslo or Paris. He stayed for three years. During his stay Munch met Strindberg and through him became involved in a love affair with Dagny Juell, the lover of the Polish author Stanislaw Przybyszewski (1868–1927). This terrible triangle of love and jealousy was to form the foundation of many of his most intense paintings, not least *The Scream* (*see plate 304*). It also explains in part the pervading hopelessness of his *Dance of Life* (*see plate 332*), which makes a good contrast to Matisse's exuberant, southern treatment of the subject in 1909–10 and Derain's of 1906 (*see plates 161 and 147*). Munch threw himself into the artistic life of Berlin in the 1890s. He frequented the Black Piglet beer hall, and after an evening here, he would work late into the night in his small studio room by the candlelight which permeates his canvases of this time with its eerie yellow-green glow.

Returned to Norway in 1908, Munch succeeded in freeing Scandinavian painting from the prison of realism. *The Sun* (*see plate 331*), well illustrates how he adopted and adapted the techniques of Gauguin and van Gogh to convey basic emotions: jealousy, hate, despair, sexuality, bitterness, love and ultimately the madness which plagued him throughout his tortured life. Some of the clearest evidence of Munch's legacy is seen in the work of Robert Storm Petersen (1882–1949) who, in his variously witty and pathetic images of prostitutes, married the bold palette of Munch, the line of Rouault and the low-life subject matter favoured by Lautrec.

Another artist to abandon naturalism was Ivar Arosenius (1878–1909). He had studied at the Konstakademia in Stockholm from 1898, before leaving to join the radical Artist's Association school under Richard Bergh. By 1901 he was finding his inspiration in Swedish folk art. Between 1904 and 1905 Arosenius was in Paris, where he saw the work of the Fauves; he immediately absorbed their bright palette into his work and thus his *Noah's Ark* (now in the Nationalmuseum, Stockholm), although still painted in a style reminiscent of Denis, in its orgiastic idyll bears comparison with Matisse's *Bonheur de Vivre* (*see plate 134*) of two years earlier. Along with Munch, the Fauves, and in particular Matisse, now became the most profoundly important force in the creation of an avant-garde art in Scandinavia. The essential difference between the Fauves and their Scandinavian compatriots lay in their divergent views on the role of colour. While Derain and Matisse chose to celebrate colour for itself, the Nordic artists turned to the Northern Romantic tradition and to the expressive use of colour, articulated as theory by Kandinsky, and best exemplified in the work of the German Expressionists. Before the Scandinavian painters were able to create such works, however, they had to possess the necessary artistic vocabulary. For this they looked to Paris.

Although Norway had been looking to France for inspiration since the 1880s, it was the Swedes who took the first actual steps towards Paris. The Swedish artist Carl Palme (1879–1960) had studied under Kandinsky at the Phalanx school in Munich between 1901 and 1904 and, having travelled to Italy, ended up in Paris. He began to mix with the international art set there, including the American painters Patrick Henry Bruce (1880–1937) and Max Weber (1881–1961), and

305 ARVID FOUGSTEDT Matisse teaching Scandinavian artists in his studio 1910.

It was above all to Henri Matisse that the young artists of the Scandinavian avant garde looked in the early years of the century, and few images demonstrate the god-like status they bestowed on him better than this drawing of the master teaching in his studio. From left to right we see Carl Palme, Rudolf Levey (the school's 'massier'), Matisse himself, the woman artist Sigrid Hjerten, Isaac Grünewald (palette in hand), Per Krohg (in profile) and the tall bearded figure of Birger Simonsson. Interestingly, the master is instructing his pupils in life drawing. And it is not surprising that his preoccupation with this subject also features frequently in that of the Scandinavian modernists of this period.

the collector Gertrude Stein, through whom he also met Matisse and Picasso. In 1907 Palme encouraged Matisse in a plan to teach him and other foreign students then resident in Paris, and in January 1908 Matisse opened his school in the rue de Sèvres with Palme as his first pupil (*see plate 305*). By the autumn the Scandinavians had arrived in force, and by the following year Matisse was teaching some twenty Swedes and Norwegians – about half of the class. Among his pupils were the Swedes Isaac Grünewald (1889–1946), Nils von Dardel (1888–1943) and Birger Simonsson (1883–1938), and the Norwegian Per Krohg (1889–1965).

In 1909 the young artists, led by Simonsson, formed themselves into an association called De Unga, meaning The Young Ones. Two years later this group was superseded by De Atta, meaning The Eight. Calling themselves the 'Swedish Expressionists', these artists – among them Grünewald, Dardel and Grünewald's wife Sigrid Hjerten – formed the Swedish avant garde in the years immediately preceding the First World War. Grünewald perhaps most clearly reflects the group's inspiration in his borrowings from Cézanne, Matisse and Munch (*see plate 317*) and it is of some significance that he showed at the Sonderbund exhibition of Expressionism in Cologne in 1912. It was not until 1913 that Dardel began to explore Cubism, and the achievements of Braque and Picasso did not really affect Swedish art until after that date.

The Danes, on the whole, did not choose to study in Paris, and Danish art retained its traditional bias until the first years of the First World War. Harald Giersing (1881–1927) was experimenting with Post-Impressionist ideas in 1906 and had seen the work of Die Brücke artists in Germany in 1909, his *Judgement of Paris* (*see plate 333*) bearing a strong resemblance to the early work of Kirchner. Sigurd Swane (1879–1973)

306 NILS VON DARDEL   Rue Ville de Paris, Senlis   1912.
Although Nils von Dardel had studied under Matisse, his style in this
painting seems to be closer in feeling to the pale tonality and light touch of
Cézanne. With its simplified palette, heightened only by the blue and red
of the tricolour and soldier's uniform, this townscape takes on an abstract
quality curiously close to the painted collages produced by Picasso during
his synthetic Cubist period of the same year. Von Dardel's masterly
evocation of the winding town street, however, is almost Braque-like in
its studied repetition of rooftops and chimneys.

fell under the spell of the Fauves after he had met Giersing
in Paris in 1907; he combined their style with that of
Munch in such powerful images as his *Jacob's Dream* (*see plate*
334). Other young artists from Denmark who made contact
with the European avant garde included Karl Isakson
(1878–1922), Olaf Rude (1886–1957) and William Scharff
(1886–1959), who were all in Paris in 1911 and although
they had met Picasso, were more influenced by Cézanne. The
Futurist exhibition held in Copenhagen in 1912 also seems to
have had little direct effect on Danish art.

Similarly, among Finnish artists the move towards modernism
did not really happen until 1912 when Tyko Sallinen
(1879–1955) exhibited a number of his paintings in a new
style which combined the influence of Munch seen in his work
of the previous year with that of Cézanne. Like the Danes, no
Finnish artists studied under Matisse, and it was also their misfortune to be on the verge of discovering Cubism when the First
World War curtailed artistic movement throughout Europe.

Of all the Scandinavian countries, however, it is in Norway
that the trend towards modernism can be considered
strongest before the First World War. The Norwegians had
long looked to France and by 1910 a Parisian art education
was a pre-requisite for any aspiring Norwegian artist.
Furthermore, partly as a result of the country's comparatively

recent (1905) separation from Swedish rule, there was no
established academic tradition in Norway; the radical stance
of the younger artists thus seemed to be a logical progression
rather than a rebellion.

As early as 1903 Norwegian artists such as Henrik Rom
(1887–1919) were painting in a style somewhere between that
of Lautrec and Cézanne that also owed something to the individualism of Munch. It is important to recognize that while in
other countries his art was still seen as unpalatable and modern, when Munch returned to Norway in 1908, he was
received as a proven master. Jean Heiberg (1884–1976),
another Norwegian artist, also returned to his native country in
1908. He had been studying at the Académie Colarossi in Paris
and latterly under Matisse, to whose studio he now advised his
contemporaries to hurry. One of these was Per Krohg, who had
lived in Paris since 1897, attending the Académie Colarossi
where his father Christian was on the teaching staff. Krohg now
began to paint in a decidedly colourist style, although this was
quickly superseded in 1911 by the earthier palette and slight
Cubist influence of his *Night* (*see plate 314*). On the whole,
however, it was Matisse who now became the dominant influence in Norwegian art as he had in Sweden. Yet this was not a
case of simple borrowing. For, apparently, Matisse's role in all
Scandinavian painting had not been forged by the Fauves. In
his essay 'Matissismen' in the journal *Dagens Nyt* in October
1909, Christian Krohg made the Scandinavian position clear:
'Matisse . . . resembles Edvard Munch, but lacks his greatness
. . . Munch is the father of Matissism.'[12]

This belief in the pre-eminence of home-grown genius
peaked in 1914 with the birth of The Fourteen. This group,
which included Sorensen, Heiberg, Axel Revold (1887–1962)
and Rudolph Thygesen (1880–1953) (*see plate 316*), seemed
to herald a great future for Norwegian art. As the Swedish art
historian David Moselius confidently declared: 'Nowhere
North of France is there such good art as the Norwegian.'[13]
Moreover, in his review of the group's 1914 exhibition, his
Norwegian counterpart Einar Lexow predicted: 'A coming
golden age for Norwegian painting'.[14]

NOTES

[1] Mikhail Vrubel in a letter to his sister, 24 May 1890, in S. Yaremich,
Vrubel, Moscow, 1911.

[2] *Sobraniye sochinenii v8-mi tomakh*, Vol. 6, Moscow, 1962, 175-6.

[3] M. Gorlin, 'The Interrelation of Painting and Literature', in *Russia-Slavonic
and Eastern European Review*, London, 1946, 146-7.

[4] Valentin Serov, in conversation with Chtcherbatov, in Chtcherbatov, *Art
in Russia*, New York, 1955.

[5] N. Milioti, *O Soyuse-Zolotoe Runo No. 1*, Moscow, 1908.

[6] Sergei Makovsky, *Golubaya Rosa, Zolotoe Runo, No. 5*, Moscow, 1907.

[7] Sergei Diaghilev in a letter to Alexander Benois, 20 April 1906.

[8] Mikhail Larionov, text of speech at Contemporary Art Discussion,
Moscow, February 1912, quoted in Camilla Gray, *The Russian Experiment in
Art*, London, 1962, 132.

[9] *Oslinni Khvost i Mishen*, Moscow, 1913.

[10] G. Habasque, 'Les Documents inédits sur les débuts de suprematisme',
in *Aujourd'hui: art et architecture*, No. 4, Paris, 1955.

[11] Josef Paul Hodin, *Edvard Munch*, London, 1972, 61.

[12] C. Krohg, *Matissismen*, Dagens Nyt, Kristiania, 14 October 1909, in M.
Werenskiold, *De Forste heroiske ar 1910–1920*, exhibition catalogue, Oslo,
1986.

[13] C.D. Moselius, in M. Werenskiold, op. cit.

[14] E. Lexow, *De 14, Kunst og Kultur*, Kristiania, 1914, 51-61.

307 MIKHAIL VRUBEL   Demon Seated   1890.

Mikhail Vrubel was to Russian painting of the 1890s what van Gogh was to that of France and Munch to that of Norway. His tortured genius, which played such an important role in shaping the development of an avant-garde tradition in Russia, is embodied in the central figure of this painting. Vrubel was obsessed with the poetry of the Russian romantic master Mikhail Lermontov and in particular by his poem 'The Demon'. The huge demons which fill his canvases from 1890 until his death in 1910 seem to reflect all the mental torment of Vrubel himself, who ended his days in a lunatic asylum.

308 MIKHAIL LARIONOV Soldier in a Wood 1908.
*Mikhail Larionov and his wife Natalia Goncharova are two of the
most important figures in the development of twentieth-century Russian
painting. Here, in an early example of his primitive period, we can see the
giant steps he had taken away from the light, Impressionist style which
he had favoured in the earlier years of the century. The overall feeling is
overwhelmingly decorative, although, because Larionov had not yet
entirely cast off the heavily worked Impressionist technique of his
early work, the entire picture surface is covered with brushstrokes
that suggest foliage.*

309 NATALIA GONCHAROVA Peasants 1911.

Perhaps the greatest exponent of neo-primitivism in Russia in the 1900s was Natalia Goncharova, who in 1915 married Larionov with whom she had studied at the Moscow College. This painting is a perfect example of the rhythmic, planar style which she made her own before 1912, based on the indigenous peasant art of her homeland. Here we see figures and forms lifted from religious icon and lubki alike as the two bearded peasants wearing traditional dress, cross the surface of a work which also possesses similarities to those of Matisse in composition, simplicity of form and dramatic juxtaposition of colour.

310 KUZMA PETROV-VODKIN Red Horse Swimming 1912.

While a knowledge of Matisse's work of 1910 appears to be evident in the colour and simplicity of form present in this painting by the erstwhile pupil of Serov, other influences are also in play. The artist had been in Africa six years previously and had been much taken with the primitive art which he had seen there. The attenuated form of the boy in the foreground, and the unreality of his impossible mount support this new primitive impulse and point also to the two-dimensional qualities of Serov's later works garnered from the Russian Byzantine tradition. In its sheer boldness the picture seems to indicate Petrov-Vodkin's later role as the teacher of the next generation of Russian modernists.

311 MIKHAIL LARIONOV   Evening after the Rain   1908.
That the influence of the French had a long-lasting hold on the Russian
avant garde is shown in this work by Larionov, which dates – surprisingly
– from the same year as his excursion into primitivism. Despite the
naïve simplicity of the figures, which show the artist's attempt to break
free from these constraints, his formal debt is still to Cézanne, while in
colour Larionov is clearly looking to the Fauves, and in particular to
Derain's images of the Seine painted in 1905.

312 ILYA MASHKOV Fruit on a Dish 1910.
Still-life was a favourite subject for Mashkov, another of Serov's pupils, and between 1903 and 1920 he painted numerous images of fruit in similar settings to this. Here we see him at his most French. The apples, oranges and peaches are painted with little attempt to depict a third dimension, suggesting the work of painters like Bernard. The painting also bears comparison with Konchalovsky's work of the same period; indeed the two artists were working together in a close professional relationship.

313 HENRIK SORENSEN Variety Artist 1910.
*In this painting we can see just how Henrik Sorensen provided such
a strong link between Matisse and the young generation of Scandinavian
artists. At the time it was painted Sorensen was still a pupil at Matisse's
school. In pose, subject matter and above all in colour, it is close to the
work of his tutor. Along with others by Sorensen, this painting was
exhibited in Stockholm in 1911, and while it caused a storm among the
critics, it was a succès d'estime among the more progressive artists.
In 1914 Sorensen became a member of The Fourteen. His advice to many
young artists – to travel to Paris and study Matisse – was instrumental
in shaping the character of an avant-garde 'modernist' art in Norway.*

314 PER KROHG Night 1911.
*Per Krohg was the son of the famous Swedish painter Christian Krohg,
who taught at the Académie Colarossi. From the age of eight he grew up
in Montparnasse and thus was no stranger to the French art world. This
head start stood him in good stead during the second decade of the century
when the artistic climate was unsettled and unsettling. His work of the
period displays a greater sophistication and surety of handling than many
of his countrymen. Between 1910 and 1911 he evolved quickly from
essentially a colourist's style to a manner closely related to the Cubists'.
This moody study, in which the folds of the model's gown take on an
almost landscape-like angularity, bears witness to this.*

312

315 AXEL REVOLD Italian Woman 1913.
*Revold was one of the Norwegian artists advised by Henrik Sorensen
to study under Matisse in Paris. He did so between 1908 and 1910. This
painting illustrates the transition his work went through when Revold
abandoned the Fauve-influenced style that had pervaded his work, in
favour of the Cubist manner which he embraced after 1913. A certain
looseness of handling and the green face of Matisse's early Fauve works is
still present here, although we can detect a tentative experimentation with
early Cubist ideas in the blocked-out shadows of the arm and dress.*

316 JEAN HEIBERG Portrait of Rudolph Thygesen 1913.
Heiberg was the first Norwegian artist to study with Matisse. The effect of
the Frenchman's teaching can still be seen in this portrait of the painter
Thygesen, despite the fact that it was painted some three years after
Heiberg left Paris. The essentially decorative quality of the work owes
much to Matisse, as do the two-dimensional quality of the simply coloured
background and the pose of the sitter. Thygesen was not, like Heiberg, one
of Matisse's pupils; he studied instead at the Académie Colarossi under
Christian Krohg. However, he was a member of The Fourteen and at the
time this portrait was painted in 1913, he had visited Italy and Germany,
where he had been much impressed by the work of the self-confessed
Expressionists.

317 ISAAC GRÜNEWALD Iván by the Armchair 1915.
This painting demonstrates Grünewald's strong allegiance to the work
of Matisse, with whom he had studied in Paris from 1909 to 1911. The
sharply angled planes of the interior, its incised and simply painted
decorations, and the sinuous pose of the sitter are all common
characteristics of his teacher's work. The palette, too, is strikingly close
to such works as Matisse's La Desserte, Harmonie Rouge, painted in
1909. The face in particular is described in such a way as to echo the
simplicity of line and expression favoured by Matisse and seen
throughout his work.

318 VALENTIN SEROV Portrait of M. N. Ermolova 1905.
By 1905, when he painted this portrait of the great Russian tragédienne, Valentin Serov had abandoned the Impressionist style of his earlier work in favour of a new and bold manner through which he imbues the sitter with a sense of dignity and real presence. Rather than concentrate on the play of light upon form, Serov depicts Ermolova in silhouette, the great black mass of her body sharply contrasted against the flat plane of the pale wall. A cleverly positioned mirror that reflects the opposite corner of the room forms his only concession to volume and space.

319 VICTOR BORISOV-MUSATOV The Reservoir 1902.
A painting that dates from late in Borisov-Musatov's career, The Reservoir displays the mood of melancholy that pervades his entire output. Two female figures stand on the banks of the reservoir; they do not speak, but gaze dreamily into space. Typically they are dressed in period costume – that of the 1830s, the era for which he longed. The composition is purely two-dimensional and decorative, the canvas being given its shape by the lyrical double arc of the pool. Thus this work places the artist as a bridge between the World of Art painters and their decorative work inspired by theatrical design and the spirituality of the Blue Rose group.

321 MIKHAIL LARIONOV Glass 1912.
As Malevich was beginning to fragment his figures into formalist constructions, Larionov was moving away from neo-primitivism towards an entirely new art form. He called this concept Rayonism. It is seen in its early exuberance in this canvas, where the artist takes the conventional theme of a still-life and attempts to depict the rays of light which fall on the objects within the picture in a way that the Impressionists would never have dreamed of. It also hints at the purely abstract art which was soon to emerge in the north of Europe.

320 VLADIMIR TATLIN Fishmonger 1911.
Vladimir Tatlin's brand of primitivism is quite different from that of Goncharova and her fellow members in the Donkey's Tail movement. Here, although he gives his fishmonger the simple facial construction that his contemporaries would employ in their pictures, Tatlin is much more concerned with the formal construction of the image as a whole. The fishmonger himself is only one component in a spiral composition which leads our eye from top left, through the two bending figures, up through the man's body and down through the fish's tail, to the blunt conclusion of its decapitated torso.

322 KASIMIR MALEVICH Knife Grinder 1912.
During 1911 Malevich refined his monumental primitivist figures (see
plate 294) into forms made up of a series of geometric solids. Bodies
became cylindrical, women's skirts rhomboid, a sheaf of corn a golden
segment. The Knife Grinder, produced the following year, demonstrates
the inevitable conclusion of this impetus. Malevich fragments each of the
solids into a number of sections which, playing with each other with an
extraordinary, almost Futurist dynamism, blur the distinction between
background and figure.

323 KASIMIR MALEVICH An Englishman in Moscow 1914.
Although this painting dates from the year after Malevich's radically
abstract minimalist works of 1913, it should be seen rather as an
intermediate step in his art, for it developed alongside, rather than after,
his non-figurative paintings. Using an artistic language derived from
Picasso's Cubist works of the same period, with which he was familiar,
Malevich conveys to us, in an almost surreal image, the sensations
experienced by his top-hatted Englishman in the Russian capital. Thus,
here, we see variously, a fish, a Russian church, a sabre, a saw, a candle,
a mandolin and numerous disjointed letters and words, including the
slogan 'Riding School', over his shoulder.

324 KASIMIR MALEVICH Black Square and Red Square 1915.
It is now more or less regarded as fact that Malevich's celebrated Black
Square *of 1913 and the other subsequent geometric Suprematist pictures*
which followed in its wake came about as the result of his designs for
Kruchenin's Futurist opera Victory over the Sun, *which opened at the*
Luna Park Theatre in St Petersburg in December 1913. While the opera
is now lost in obscurity, Malevich's design for the backcloth – a simple
black square bisected by a diagonal – is one of the most famous images
in art history, having provided the spark for his move to abstraction,
the step which was to have such importance for the development of
the modernist movement throughout the world.

325   EUGÈNE JANSSON   Riddarfjärden in Stockholm   1898.
This painting, from Jansson's late, blue period of the turn of the century,
represents the culmination of his art. Here we see the inevitable conclusion
of the increasing simplicity of Jansson's work discernible from the 1890s.
Having concentrated upon stark, suburban subject matter, Jansson
gradually moved on to depict the imagined world of his own dreamscapes.
In such paintings as this, while his apparent subject is his native
Stockholm, he in fact shows us the timeless landscape of his own
imagination, in which air and water meet, often with the prospect
of an unattainable 'Nirvana' at their point of meeting.

326 VILHELM HAMMERSHOI The Baker's Shop 1888.
An unmistakable subject of nineteenth-century Scandinavian painting and indeed of all northern painting of that time, is the quiet interior with a figure, usually seen from behind. It is found in the paintings of Caspar David Friedrich in the 1820s, Moritz von Schwind in the 1850s and here in Hammershoi. While, formally, the pose and theme have their roots in the work of such Dutch seventeenth-century painters as Vermeer and de Hooch, Hammershoi brings to his subject the ethereal appearance lacking in earlier renderings and emphasizes the essentially contemplative nature of this intimate scene.

327 VILHELM HAMMERSHOI Landscape from Lejre 1905.
The intense solitude seen in Hammershoi's interiors is also carried over into his landscapes. In all of these works, executed with an even, light technique, a mysterious peace is the central theme. Whether he is depicting the human figure or the landscape, Hammershoi is the master of mystery in painting, continually asking us to enquire further about the content of his work. Here, in this depiction of his homeland of Zetland, Hammershoi imbues the three clumps of trees with an almost human dimension, suggesting in their partly hidden masses, in conjunction with the clouds which grow larger as they near us, the possibility of movement and change.

328 AUGUST STRINDBERG Lonely Poisonous Mushroom
1893.

*Strindberg's obsession with the position of man in the universe is evident
in this extraordinary painting: the focal point of what in formal terms we
must call a landscape becomes no more than a tiny mushroom. With no
attempt at realism the artist covers his canvas with the same complete
abandon that had characterized his earliest landscapes, but now he does
not feel the need to give the spectator even the merest hint of where his
vision actually started. Instead we are presented with an almost abstract
work in which the only real object becomes the mushroom itself; it acts as
the medium for Strindberg's own emotional isolation in a way similar
to that later embraced by Abstract Expressionism.*

329 AUGUST STRINDBERG The City 1900.

*It is perhaps not generally known that the great Swedish playwright
August Strindberg was also an accomplished painter, although it was in
this artistic milieu that he preferred to be known. Like Jansson, Strindberg
initially confined himself to the landscape, taking as his subject matter the
industrialized towns and cities. His technique, however, is far removed
from that of his contemporaries, displaying a bold use of paint, which he
applies straight from the tube in huge swathes of impasto. Strindberg uses
the palette knife to achieve an effect which conveys a similar emotion
to that portrayed in his writings. Here, for example, a tortured, stormy
sky rages above an equally agitated foreground, or is it the sea, while the
city itself, the apparent subject of the painting, is seen in the far distance,
given its true position in the natural order.*

330 EDVARD MUNCH Melancholy 1891.
The effect of Munch's visits to Paris between 1889 and 1891 is apparent in this painting. Tendencies he first expressed in The Sick Child (see plate 303) are here brought to maturity. Munch had been looking at the work of Gauguin, Bernard and other Nabis painters and also at the work of Japanese printmakers who had been such a strong influence on the Impressionists. The viewpoint and composition of this painting, in which the figure in the foreground is represented only by a head, and the angle of the beach is used to suggest depth and recession, are common features of many Japanese prints. The use of simplified form and outline suggests Gauguin, however, and the restrained palette echoes the muted colours of the Nabis.

331 EDVARD MUNCH The Sun 1909–11.
In his mature work, Munch began increasingly to move towards an abstract preoccupation with the power of nature. In this painting, one of a series of monumental murals that he executed for Oslo University between 1908 and 1909, Munch looks directly into the sun, the source of light, the painter's life-blood. It shines on the horizon of a landscape painted in the style of Gauguin, casting its rays with a jewel-like intensity. Once again he depicts the sun's reflection in the water as a simplified cruciform shape. In its power to evoke the natural spirituality to be found in nature, it is the most obvious assertion of Munch's declared intention to make his spectators 'take off their hats as though they were in church'.

332 EDVARD MUNCH Dance of Life 1899.
While he was in Berlin for the exhibition of his work in 1892, Munch had met and fallen in love with Dagny Juell, the wife of Polish writer Stanislaw Przybyszewski. The terrible love triangle that evolved over the next few years was to feature throughout his future work. Here he pictures an archetypally happy couple waltzing through life, while two observers stand at the side. One in white is happy, the other sad, in black; they represent the two sides of Munch's own polarized emotions. It might be said that in Jungian terms, all these emotions are being kept in check by the couple. In the background, against the sea, we see the reflected setting sun, an emblematic crucifix clearly indicative of Munch's theosophical frame of mind.

333   HARALD GIERSING   Judgement of Paris   1908–09.
This is one of Giersing's most important early works; he alludes here to the
work of his contemporaries and forebears both in France and in Germany.
Giersing was in Paris in 1906 and 1907, where he saw the work of
Gauguin; his use of outlines in this painting demonstrates the influence
of the would-be savage. In addition he had been exposed to the work of
the artists of Die Brücke in Germany, and something of their early
looseness of handling might also be present here. Significantly, the artist
has relocated the mythological subject of the title into a present-day
environment, and the decadence and bohemian attitude of the figures –
both nude models and the single, seated, clothed man – also suggest
a German model.

334 Sigurd Swane   Jacob's Dream   1911–12.
The Danish painter Sigurd Swane was one of the most Expressionist of
this generation of Scandinavian artists. He had met Giersing at the
Danish Royal Academy of Fine Arts, where he studied from 1899 to 1903;
it is interesting to note that both artists shared an attraction for the work
of their German contemporaries. Here, in one of numerous versions,
Swane takes a subject favoured by the Old Masters and reinterprets it in
a loose style and in vivid colour. The liberating influence of Munch is also
evident, together with a Fauve-inspired colour theory, based in
strong contrasts.

Chapter 8

The English-Speaking World

Although it was in Britain in 1910 that Roger Fry's (1866–1934) 'Post-Impressionist' exhibition gathered and displayed the most modern tendencies emerging in the European art world, this was an extraordinary event; for even at that date, generally speaking, the British art world – and certainly the public – knew little of the influential changes that had been taking place on the Continent since the 1870s. Nevertheless, the new, disquieting developments that emerged in British art in the wake of Roger Fry's two Post-Impressionist exhibitions of 1910 and 1912 were not as limited as Fry and his exhibition co-organizer Clive Bell (1881–1964) suggested by their selection for the English group represented at the second exhibition; the work of Duncan Grant (1885–1975), Vanessa Bell (1879–1961) and Percy Wyndham Lewis (1882–1957) made up the major part of this section.

These modernist developments were brought about by the actions of several very different and distinct groups, together with a number of isolated, though important individual artists. Like all revolutionaries, those who spearheaded the artistic revolution that occurred in Britain between 1910 and 1914 and which dragged British art kicking and mewling into the modern world, were in fact united only by their opposition to the old order.

As the British art world entered the twentieth century, it basically resembled that of the eighteenth century. History painting and portraiture were still regarded by the establishment as the highest forms of painting. All other subject matter – landscape, genre and still-life – were subordinated to these two, just as they had been in the days of Sir Joshua Reynolds (1723–1792).

Edwardian painting was severely restrained in terms of colour, and thus James McNeill Whistler (1834–1903) represented to his peers the pinnacle of possible artistic achievement. For in Whistler's teaching it was tone, rather than

335 DUNCAN GRANT The Tub 1912–13.

Grant's own favourite, this picture marks the zenith of the artist's move towards a Byzantine two-dimensionality. It relates closely to his Adam and Eve *of 1913 (now lost), sharing with that image a figural monumentality and simply decorated background. The hatched detail and the boldly outlined breasts and ribs also suggest that Grant had been looking further than Italy and the Middle East for inspiration – to Africa perhaps. Yet even in this work we find the abiding appeal of the Fauves; the figure resembles those of Derain's* Three Bathers *of 1908 (see plate 149).*

colour that mattered, and the technique behind his once scandalous aestheticism was rooted in the painterliness of the seventeenth-century old masters Diego Velásquez (1599–1660) and Sir Anthony van Dyck (1599–1641). The brilliant primaries so beloved of the Impressionists were anathema to his disciples, who went so far as to devise a complex numbering system for the gradations of tonality in their paintings. Tonality was everything to the Edwardians. What relief there was in this accomplished though arid atmosphere was provided from the 1880s by Sir George Clausen (1852–1944) and other emulators of the work of the French painter Jules Bastien-Lepage (1848–1884). So popular were his softly painted rural idylls with the art-buying public that, in 1883, one critic had noted: 'Everyone today paints so much like M. Bastien-Lepage that M. Bastien-Lepage seems to paint just like everyone else.'[1] It was these artists who served to 'civilize', and to a great extent to anaesthetize the *plein-air* techniques of the Impressionists, providing a more accessible version for a British public who were still buying Jean-Baptiste Camille Corot (1796–1875) and Jean-François Millet (1814–1875).

During the late 1880s the only rivalry that existed within what might loosely have been described as an artistic avant garde in Britain was entirely unconnected with the momentous developments taking place across the English Channel. The Bastien-Lepage and Clausen naturalist camp was challenged by a nascent British Impressionism embodied in the work of the *bête noire* of Edwardian art Walter Richard Sickert (1860–1942), together with his few followers, most notably Philip Wilson Steer (1860–1942). Having seen the paintings of Edgar Degas (1834–1917) in Paris in 1885, Sickert promoted the artist's work in Britain, praising in particular his use of unexpected, informal viewpoints and exhibiting his paintings at the New English Art Club from the late 1880s to the mid-1890s; his own paintings of music halls in the 1890s bear witness to his debt to the Frenchman. However, this short flirtation with modern Continental trends on British Impressionism's part lasted only some five years. By 1895 those artists who had championed the Impressionists were back among the shadows, fearful lest they might lose what remained of their artistic credibility at home. Sickert alone refused to compromise; embittered, he retired to France.

In the clutches of reactionaries once more, British art bowed again to the Old Masters. Pre-eminent in the realm of portraiture were William Nicholson (1872–1949) and John Singer Sargent (1856–1925). At the Slade School – established in 1871, but by the turn of the century considered the most important art college in London – young artists fell under the spell of arch snob Henry Tonks (1862–1937), learning from him the draughtsmanship of Jean Antoine Watteau (1684–1721), and the colour values of Velásquez, Francisco Goya (1746–1828) and van Dyck. It was a repressive regime and, as with all dictatorships, while outwardly all seemed orderly, underneath the surface a force of counter-revolution was gathering strength.

During 1905 Paul Durand-Ruel (1831–1922) held a major exhibition of French Impressionist work at London's Grafton Gallery. By this date even such artists as Sargent, safe in their painterly tradition, were championing the Impressionists. Alongside the paintings by Alfred Sisley (1839–1899), Claude Monet (1840–1926), Edouard Manet (1832–1883), Camille Pissarro (1830–1903) and Pierre Auguste Renoir (1841–1919), however, there were several disturbing works on the walls of the Grafton Gallery by the hitherto unknown artist Paul Cézanne (1839–1906). The critic Frank Rutter (1876–1937) thought he remembered having seen some of Cézanne's works at the Salon d'Automne the year before, but confessed to having been unimpressed. Later in his memoirs, he described the general reaction to the 'colourless daubs' displayed at the Grafton:

336 WALTER RICHARD SICKERT The Gallery of the Old Bedford c. 1895.

When Sickert painted this picture, he was still under the influence of the French Impressionists; Degas's penchant for the unusual viewpoint and the world of the theatre can both be detected here. Using just two or three colours, all based upon a single brown tone, Sickert successfully recreates the smoky, crowded atmosphere of the music hall which made it such an attractive place for him. Sickert had only entered the Slade School of Art at the age of twenty-one, after starting his professional life as an actor; the smell of greasepaint was to draw him back to his first love again and again throughout his career.

Hullo! What's this? What are these funny brown-and-olive landscapes doing in an impressionist exhibition? . . Who are they by? Oh, *Cézanne* . . . He's not very strong on drawing, is he? . . . I don't like his colour. Let's go back and look at the Monets.[2]

Meanwhile, the critic of the *Daily Mail* called Cézanne an amateur. The artist did not stand a chance with the English public: it was too soon. Rutter himself admitted that in 1905: 'We were far too busily occupied trying to persuade the pundits of modern art to accept Manet, Monet, Degas and Renoir.'[3] What really mattered, however, was that Cézanne's work had been made available, offering tempting suggestions to a few admirers of what was happening on the Continent.

Significantly, it was also in 1905 that Sickert returned to England. The artist was encouraged to make the move by the young artist Spencer Frederick Gore (1878–1914) when he visited Sickert in his lodgings in Dieppe. Gore, an ex-Slade pupil, had fired Sickert's imagination with news of a new generation of British painters who, although they felt that something must change, clearly required a figurehead. Sickert rose to the challenge and took rooms in Camden Town – a particularly seedy area of London at that date – in order to fulfil his new role. Here he continued to paint in the style he had developed on the Continent, taking as his subject matter the low life of his surroundings – local prostitutes, for instance, and music-hall interiors (*see plate 336*).

The group that gathered round Sickert over the next two years contained some of the most influential figures in early twentieth-century British painting. His closest disciple was Gore, who now turned to focus on similar themes, but other painters rallied to him, amongst them Harold Gilman (1876–1919). By 1907 the small group of friends had become a society; they called themselves the Fitzroy Street Group after the address of their leader's studio. Over the next three years the group expanded to include painters from a wider circle, among them such diverse talents as Augustus John (1878–1961) and Robert Bevan (1865–1925). In 1910 the extended group renamed themselves the Camden Town Group. In the same year Sickert declared his purpose and that of the group as a whole in a statement that castigated all the conservatism that had characterized English art during the 1880s and 1890s:

The more art is serious, the more it will tend to avoid the drawing room. The plastic arts are gross arts, dealing joyously with gross material facts . . . and while they flourish in the scullery or on the dunghill, they fade at a breath from the drawing room.[4]

A Matter of Emotion

Perhaps the most significant of Sickert's disciples in the context of European avant-garde painting was Robert Bevan. Born in 1865, Bevan was one of the small but influential and today neglected group of British artists who benefited from direct experience of the most advanced art in France before its discovery by their peers in England in 1910. He had studied at Westminster before going to the Académie Julian in Paris. From 1893 to 1894 Bevan lived in Brittany, and here, at Pont-Aven, he was deeply impressed by the work of Paul Gauguin (1848–1903) who returned briefly to France from Tahiti in

August 1893 due to lack of funds. It has been suggested that the two artists might well have met and become friends in February 1894. Whether or not Bevan actually knew Gauguin, the effect of the would-be primitive on the younger artist's work was of lasting importance.

In 1897 Bevan married the Polish artist Stanislawa de Karlowska (1876–1952), and the two set up home in London. His response to his exposure to contemporary French painting, however, is clearly evident in his painting *The Courtyard* (*see plate 350*), which he executed while staying with his wife's family in Poland between 1903 and 1904. In the work of few British artists of this period do we find such brightness and fearless use of primary colour. Sadly, Bevan must have realized that in painting this picture, he had gone too far for the British public and ran the risk of alienating himself. Several years ahead of its time, the work was savagely attacked when it was hung in Bevan's one-man show at the Baillie Gallery in London in 1905, and he subsequently retreated into the more familiar Sickertian palette of early Camden Town. Flirtations with divisionist techniques notwithstanding, it is not until Bevan's series of paintings of Cumberland Market painted in 1915 (*see plate 352*), that we again see such boldness in his work.

Among the few other artists who had been exposed to the modernist tendencies in French painting before Fry's 'discovery' of Post-Impressionism in 1910, four in particular stand out as being of lasting importance: one Englishman, one Irishman and two Scots.

John Duncan Fergusson (1874–1961) had been in Paris in 1895 at the Académie Colarossi but at this stage, like so many of his contemporaries, he was caught in the spell of Velásquez and Whistler. However, he mixed with café society in Montparnasse and even after he returned to his native Edinburgh, he would still spend every summer in France. Indeed, the call of the boulevards was such that in 1907 Fergusson was to settle permanently in Paris.

In 1904 Fergusson persuaded his fellow Scot S. J. Peploe (1871–1935) to join him in Brittany. Peploe, like Bevan, had studied at the influential Académie Julien in Paris from 1894. Like Fergusson, he had at first been influenced by Manet and the Old Masters. On his return to the British Isles, however, Peploe began to produce – along with Fergusson – some extraordinary paintings entirely unrelated to the cloistered tonalities of the British mainstream. Fergusson's works were shown in 1905 at the Baillie Gallery in London where, interestingly, Bevan's Gauguinesque *Courtyard* (*see plate 350*) had been savaged the previous year. In his introduction to the catalogue Fergusson wrote:

The painter, having found the beauty of nature, ceases to be interested in the traditional beauty, the beauty of art . . . Art being purely a matter of emotion, sincerity in art consists of being faithful to one's emotions.[5]

Interestingly, this idea of abandoning traditional beauty pre-dates Clive Bell's thesis on the subject in his influential book entitled *Art* (1914), by some nine years, and Fergusson's concept of the artist-philosopher must be seen as the direct result of the artist's contact with French artists in Paris. When, in 1908, he had a joint exhibition with Peploe at the Baillie Gallery, the full extent of this contact became apparent. It is highly likely that both artists had visited the Salon d'Automne

337 JOHN DUNCAN FERGUSSON At My Studio Window 1910. *By 1910 Fergusson's work had developed considerably. While the influence of Matisse is still apparent, Fergusson has moved on, as we might expect, from the French master's early portrait style to develop a more mature understanding of form. This painting resembles work produced by Matisse after 1907, or even that of André Derain. Fergusson places his model against a backdrop; the view of the trees in the street is framed by the window frame on one side and on the other by the curtains. Using a limited palette Fergusson manages to create an harmonious whole; the simplified tubular and cylindrical forms of the model's body are echoed in the pattern of the curtain and in the organic forms which he abstracts from the foliage.*

of the Fauves of 1905, for after this date their palettes took on a Fauve character. Henri Matisse (1869–1954) was a particular influence on Fergusson; the significance of his shocking *Woman in a Hat* of 1905 (*see plate 126*) in the Scotsman's *Closerie des Lilas* and *At My Studio Window* (*see plate 353 and 337*) is obvious. Peploe, on the other hand, while his *Landscape at Cassis* of 1913 (*see plate 354*) still has strong echoes of André Derain (1880–1954), seems to have turned to Georges Braque (1882–1963) for inspiration in his 1910 painting of the *Harbour at Royan*. His *Still-Life* of the same year (*see plate 355*), inspired once again by Cubism, seems to go a stage further.

Matthew Smith (1879–1959) was another British artist – though an Englishman this time – who benefited from direct exposure to France and its art world. An older-than-average student at the Slade in 1905, Smith was humiliated by Tonks for his poor draughtsmanship. In 1908, aged thirty, he fled to live in Gauguin's shadow at Pont-Aven. The Tahitian exile's influence once again proved pervasive and by 1912 Smith was producing paintings almost wholly inspired by his mentor, as is evident in his *Lilies* (*see plate 357*). Although Smith's technique only became as bold as many of his fellow British painters during the 1920s, his Post-Impressionist inclinations seem to have emerged earlier than most – both in the period immediately before the First World War, and indeed during the years of hostilities, in works such as his Fitzroy Street nudes of 1916.

Perhaps the most remarkable of all the British artists to fall under the spell of France at an early stage in his career was the Irishman Roderic O'Conor (1860–1940). O'Conor had left Ireland in 1889; he lived first at Grez, where he painted in a naturalist style similar to the early work of John Lavery (1856–1941), and later at Pont-Aven. He painted a series of small panels here in 1892 (*see plate 356*), in which his bold palette rivalled that of the Fauves some thirteen years before they were to be unleashed upon the French public. While in technique O'Conor's brushstrokes resemble those of Monet, it is undoubtedly the influence of Vincent van Gogh (1853–1890) which dictates his use of such extremes of colour. Nevertheless, there is something more here than mere imitation; there is something that is purely O'Conor's, which gives these paintings an importance they are often denied. Following Gauguin's return from Tahiti in 1894, he and O'Conor became close friends, although the artist–savage failed to persuade his young friend to return with him to the South Seas. Whether O'Conor knew Bevan, who was also living in Pont-Aven at this time, is not recorded, but such a relationship seems more than likely.

O'Conor lived the rest of his life in Paris and his visibility and influence in Britain was limited to exhibitions at the Allied Artists' Association, founded in 1908 by Frank Rutter on the pattern of the French Salon des Indépendants. However, in 1913 he did visit Cassis, the haunt of Derain, and so may well have met Peploe and Fergusson, who were working there at the time. Certainly, by the 1920s O'Conor knew many of the Bloomsbury painters and entertained Matthew Smith and others on their frequent trips across the Channel.

While these few artists had individually been making strides in their respective experiments with contemporary techniques, they remained unable to influence the mainstream, for they lacked the necessary support of critics and dealers. It was the critics who heralded the birth of a British avant garde. Roger Fry had first been alerted to the worth of the new art being produced in France not by his discovery of any one particular painter but by the review in the *Burlington Magazine* of a little-seen show of Impressionist pictures at the International Society in January 1908. Fry responded to the criticism levelled in the revue against what it described as: 'The extreme old age of Impressionism . . . the stage of positive disintegration . . . In [the picture] of M. Matisse the movement reaches its second childhood.'[6]

The author of this review likened the 'neo-Impressionists' to the later artists of the Renaissance. Fry, drawing on his knowledge of Renaissance art history, was angered by this analogy and suggested that the change more closely resembled the move away from the naturalism of Roman art to the more spiritual qualities of the art of Byzantium. Fry called Gauguin and Cézanne proto-Byzantines. It was welcome support, but where had Fry been for the previous six years? Had he not seen Cézanne's paintings at the Grafton Gallery in 1905, nor the work of Bevan, Fergusson and Peploe at the Baillie Gallery? Matisse's work had been prominently shown at various fashionable dealers' galleries in Paris since 1905, and a few months after Fry's letter thirty pictures exhibited by

338   STANLEY SPENCER   The Apple Gatherers   1912.
This work, shown at the Contemporary Art Society in 1913, was painted during the Christmas holidays of 1911–12 at Spencer's home village of Cookham. He started to paint it in his parent's house in the main street, but when this began to fill up with relations, he moved his easel to an abandoned cottage which had been the Old Ship Inn. In the picture a couple 'discover' each other whilst gathering apples at the edge of the village. When the painting was exhibited it was greeted with praise. The painter Henry Lamb (1883–1960) wrote to Spencer, congratulating him on his achievement, and eventually bought the painting for £30. Indeed, the same monumental treatment of figures can be found in much of Lamb's own work of this period.

Matisse at the Salon d'Automne were favourably reviewed by no less a paper than *The Times*. Three works by Gauguin and two by Matisse had also been included in a small exhibition in Brighton only a few months before Fry organized his own 1910 show in London.

Fry most certainly knew of Cézanne. He had in fact proclaimed in 1906 that Cézanne 'touches nothing of the finer issues of imaginative life'.[7] It was only in the course of the next two years that Fry's attitude was to change completely.

Nonsense Pictures

The cynic might say that Fry only took up the cause of the avant garde when he realized that it was safe to do so, although his 1910 show was certainly still a shock for the art world and public alike. Certainly it provoked a number of British artists to experiment, but it thus becomes evident that in 1910 many of the artists today commonly regarded as the key British Post-Impressionists, and at the time accorded much publicity by Fry – notably Bell, Grant and Lewis – were relatively unaware of the avant-garde tendencies developing in France before Fry's show. Indeed, while several of her compatriots had actually been working on the Continent at the nerve centre of modernist painting activity, Vanessa Bell's retrospective reflections on the events of 1910 are most revealing: 'How can one possibly describe the effect of that first Post-Impressionist exhibition on English painters at that time? . . . London knew little of Paris.'[8]

Several books were published in the wake of the show, of which the most influential was that by Frank Rutter, entitled *Revolution in Modern Art*.

It was not until Fry's next show, however, the celebrated second Post-Impressionist exhibition of 1912, that the full extent of British reaction to this new artistic phenomenon became evident. Vanessa Bell's husband Clive, who jointly organized the exhibition with Fry, wrote in his introduction to the catalogue:

Mr Fry and Mr Grant are true, plastic artists . . . Theirs is an art that stands on its own feet instead of leaning upon life and herein it differs from traditional English art, which, robbed of historical and literary intent, would cease to exist. It is just because these Englishmen have expelled or reduced to servitude those romantic and irrelevant qualities that for two centuries have made our art the laughing stock of Europe, that they deserve as much respect and almost as much attention as superior French artists who have had no such traditional difficulties to surmount.[9]

Meanwhile, the reviewer in *The Times* wrote:

On the whole the English pictures are inferior to the French, just where we should expect them to be, in the rendering of mass and form . . . If Post Impressionism becomes popular in England we shall have hundreds of nonsense pictures.[10]

Chief among the works he classed as 'nonsense pictures' were those by Fry, Grant, Bell and Wyndham Lewis. Fry, Grant and Bell had been exhibiting together since 1905 when Vanessa Bell founded the Friday Club. The club continued to be one of the few unifying elements in avant-garde British art of the period, linking these so-called Bloomsbury artists with the other diverse strands which made up the complex web of the British avant garde. A more important link was the Allied Artists' Association, founded by Frank Rutter – the English Indépendants – which had shown the work of Wassily Kandinsky (1866–1944) in England as early as 1909.

The Camden Town artists maintained a more consolidated and official conservative stance, and by and large the separate groups kept their distance. Such meetings, therefore, were few, and the British painters who exhibited at the second exhibition were only loosely associated. Nevertheless Spencer Gore, whom the organizers clearly considered sufficiently radical, was asked to exhibit. Both in his mural for the celebrated Bohemian café The Cave of the Golden Calf, which he executed in the same year, and his *Gauguins and Connoisseurs* (*see plate 361*), Gore revealed an audacity unusual among the more restrained tendencies of his Camden Town colleagues. Another curious and puzzling inclusion was that of Stanley Spencer (1891–1959), whose monumental *Apple Gatherers* (*see plate 338*) and *John Donne Arriving in Heaven* received a mixed reception.

Despite knowing of the existence of the two Scots painters in Paris, Fry had omitted the work of Fergusson and Peploe. His neglect was noted by the critic P. G. Konody:

It is difficult to understand why no place has been found in Grafton Street for the very interesting work of Messrs Peploe and Fergusson . . . they at least have made up their minds to work in two dimensions, whereas the Grafton Street Post Impressionists still frequently waver between the two and three dimensional.[11]

A closer look at the works shown by Grant and Bell reveals the different ways in which the two artists had been affected by Fry's first exhibition.

Although he had been in Paris in 1906 and 1907 Duncan Grant had not visited either the Gauguin or the Cézanne exhibitions, and was apparently unaware of the activities of the Fauves. Evidently, however, he met Pablo Picasso (1881–1973) and Matisse in 1909 and in the space of two years, he moved away from the Edwardian tonalities of his early portraits and flirtations with Camden Town to adopt a divisionist technique; moreover, the Byzantine composition of his *Queen of Sheba* (*see plate 359*) echoes Roger Fry's 1908 verdict on Matisse. Equally Byzantine in composition, Grant's *Footballers* of 1911 (*see plate 360*) was also exhibited in the 1912 show. It has been suggested that Grant painted both of these canvases in response to a trip to Rome and Istanbul in April 1911, during which he studied both the Sistine Chapel and Byzantine mosaics. There is, however, a certain affinity between the *Footballers* and the monumentality of Derain's paintings of dancers and bathers (*see plates 147 and 149*) and, in the *Queen of Sheba*, a similar closeness in both technique and feeling to Matisse's *Luxe, calme et volupté* and Derain's *L'Age d'Or* of 1904 and 1905 (*see plates 68 and 69*).

Nevertheless, the most exciting aspect of the work of Grant and Bell was their search for original inspiration. Grant's *The Tub* (*see plate 335*), albeit possibly inspired by Picasso's example, has obvious origins in African sculpture. Grant and Bell

339 VANESSA BELL Bathers Screen 1913.
The abstraction of the coastline visible in Bell's Studland Beach (*see plate 358*) *is given greater emphasis in this screen, created for the Omega Workshops in 1913. Here, in a way suggestive of Cézanne at his most refined, the hills, fields and valleys are given shape by the simplest of lines. Planes overlap and colours jar to suggest recession, while in the foreground four figures disport themselves in a manner reminiscent of Kirchner's* Figures Walking into the Sea *of the previous year (see plate 236). Here, however, all of the figures are female. The work harks back to innumerable Old Master paintings of the idyllic fantasy world of classical mythology, although the actual form of the figures shows the influence of African sculpture as well as of Picasso's* Les Demoiselles d'Avignon *of 1907 (see plate 194), of which Bell was undoubtedly aware.*

340 AUGUSTUS JOHN Llyn Treweryn 1911–12.
It is pointless, even supposing it was possible, to attempt to place Augustus
John within the confines of any single artistic group; and this situation is
very much the result of John's deliberate isolationism. He had been
entertained briefly by Fitzroy Street, but in 1912 he both refused to show
at the second Post-Impressionist exhibition and resigned from the Camden
Town Group, finally making a conscious break from the English avant
garde. Instead, John decided to remain a member of the New English Art
Club – in the Impressionist and realist mainstream. Although he had
assimilated something of the naïve formalism of Gauguin, this painting
illustrates that his style was much better suited to the older tradition.
Indeed, his involvement with the new modernist tradition was ever fated
to be a mere flirtation.

began to look to such primitive and archaic examples partly
as a result of the relative caution of the Camden Town
painters when compared with the extravagances of the
Fauves. The particular artistic coterie they figureheaded – the
Bloomsbury Group – was one of the most influential products of the impact of Post-Impressionism on Britain.

Vanessa Bell came to Post-Impressionism a little later than
Grant, first using a primary palette in 1910. By 1912, in
Studland Beach (see plate 358), her figures have become simple
forms and blocks of colour, and her screen entitled *Bathers in
a Landscape* (see plate 339) shows this abstraction of the
human figure carried a stage further. Here she parallels African
sculpture in forms reminiscent of Picasso's *Les Demoiselles
d'Avignon* and Matisse's dancers (see plates 161 and 194).

This screen was just one of many decorative pieces produced by the Omega Workshops, set up in July 1913 by
Roger Fry as a centre for fine craftsmanship. He intended to
revive the ideals of William Morris's (1834–1896) Arts and
Crafts Movement, whilst creating products characterized by
the new simplicity of the modernists. The Bloomsbury artists,
including Grant, Bell, Fry, Lewis, and on occasion Gore, decorated and designed a variety of household objects in a distinctive, primitive style. And indeed, Omega enjoyed a limited
success and even received commissions from a number of
leading society figures of the day to decorate entire rooms.
However, lack of technical skills eventually outweighed artistic
bravura and the workshops were forced to close after only six
years. Moreover it was after an acrimonious argument in
October 1913 over a decorative commission that Percy
Wyndham Lewis, Frederick Etchells (1886–1973) and

Edward Wadsworth (1889–1949) left Omega and split from
the Bloomsbury Group, forming the Rebel Art Centre in the
spring of 1914.

This new partnership established by the Omega secession-
ists signals the final and most extreme phase of British avant-
garde painting before the First World War. But before
examining this we should place it in the context of the artistic
developments which had taken place within the Camden
Town Group since 1910.

From Camden Town to Vorticism

Although they might seem tame when compared with the
striking and savage primitivism of Grant's *The Tub*, the works
produced by the Camden Town Group between 1910 and
1914 should not be underestimated. These painters' reputations have suffered because of their association with Sickert,
scoffed at by Bell for his dark palette and domestic subject
matter. But there is much more to them than that. The group
was anything but conservative; it had itself come about as a
reaction to the New English Art Club's disapproval of Fry's
first Post-Impressionist show. Despite its apparent coherence
the group – like Bloomsbury – was never really a movement,
but rather a statement of protest. Thus, while on the one

341 MALCOLM DRUMMOND In the Cinema 1912–13.
Having studied at the Slade School and later, from 1908, under Sickert
at Westminster, Malcolm Drummond – a little-known Camden Town
painter – initially worked in an Impressionist style close to that of Sickert.
From 1910, however, he moved away from such looseness, concentrating
instead on a simplification of form, although at first he continued to paint
in the same dark tones as his master. By the time Drummond painted
this picture, in a style even simpler than previously seen in his work, he
had left the gloom behind and taken up a brighter palette. Here the darker
tones are specifically employed to convey atmosphere as the eerie glow of
the cinema screen is reflected in the faces of the audience.

hand Wyndham Lewis could be said to have belonged to the Omega Workshops, he was also briefly a member of the Camden Town Group, as was Augustus John.

John himself is a curious figure in his connections with Post-Impressionism. Despite his obvious assimilation of the teachings of Gauguin, evident in his relatively early portrait of Liyn Treweryn (*see plate 340*), he is best seen outside the context of any movement, making his way quite independently, like Spencer, through twentieth-century British art. There are, however, artists whose work can most definitely be said to embody a certain style which is Camden Town.

One such artist is Malcolm Drummond (1880–1945), an original founder member of the Camden Town Group. In works such as *In the Cinema* (*see plate 341*), he demonstrates a confidence in the handling of light coupled with a purely modernist emphasis on planes of colour. Compare this with Sickert's works of 1909 (*see plate 349*) and the difference is immediately apparent. A basic split can be seen within the group between those artists who remained closest in style to the Impressionists and those who displayed a clear attraction to more experimental Continental trends. Standing beside Sickert in the first category were, among others, Lucien Pissarro (1863–1944), Walter Wesley Russell and – before 1911 – Spencer Gore. The core of the latter group comprised Bevan, Lewis and Karlowska; they were joined by Gore in 1911 when he became bolder, and he was followed a year later by Charles Ginner (1878–1952), and in 1913 by Harold Gilman. The general impetus in the latter group was towards a simplification of colour and composition. Robert Bevan's *Cab Yard at Night* of 1910 (*see plate 351*), is a good early example: the artist is here at the end of a divisionist phase and is already moving towards the style which was to make his later work so distinctive.

The Camden Town Group held its first exhibition at the Carfax Gallery in June 1911 and at this stage the division between the two camps within the group was not yet defined. It was not until their second exhibition six months later that the split became evident. Unsurprisingly, perhaps, the use of bright contrasts of colour was here most clearly pronounced in the work of Spencer Gore. His *Balcony at the Alhambra* (*see plate 342*) juxtaposes deep blues and azures against a strident ribbon of crimson to powerful effect, breaking away abruptly from the subdued tones that still characterized Sickert's work of the period. Here is evidence instead of Gore's revitalized interest in his erstwhile mentor Gauguin. These ideas, tentatively explored in 1911, were consolidated by Gore and his colleagues during 1912. Gilman travelled to Sweden where he began to use a bright primary palette dominated by mauve, yellow and blue applied in wide areas of colour. During his stay in Sweden he lent his house at Letchworth to Gore who, during the summer, painted several canvases in which his use of colour planes verges almost on abstraction (*see plate 363*). These views of the station and the cinder path were the most radical yet painted by any Camden Town artist; they anticipate not only the work of the Vorticists but also that of many artists of the following decade.

By 1913 the members of the Camden Town Group had begun to pursue more individual paths, and the group became less coherent. Gilman returned from Sweden using a more vivid palette (*see plate 362*). He and Gore held a joint show. Ginner, now more than ever painting in the tradition of

342 SPENCER GORE The Balcony at the Alhambra
c. 1911–12.
Gore had been instrumental in persuading Sickert to return to England, and in the years immediately following 1908 he adopted the master's dark palette and subject matter. By 1911, however, whilst still choosing to describe a music hall interior – a typical subject much favoured by Sickert – Gore had abandoned the dark tones of his erstwhile mentor in favour of what might be called truly modernist colour. This was largely the consequence of the artist having seen pictures by Gauguin and Matisse at the first Post-Impressionist exhibition at the Grafton Gallery in 1910. The influence of Gauguin is particularly evident both in the bright crimson swathe which cuts through the picture from top to bottom and in the viewpoint, which is placed above the spectator's head.

van Gogh (*see plate 343*), went abroad to paint with Gore and Bevan in Dieppe. Sickert, meanwhile, in an effort to keep the group together, amalgamated the Camden Town and Fitzroy Street groups to form the London Group in 1913–14, with Gilman and Bevan on the committee. Before the first exhibition of 1914, however, both Sickert and Pissarro had resigned. Nevertheless, the disintegration of the Camden Town Group by no means implied a set-back for British modernism. On the contrary, its members were free now to indulge in greater artistic freedoms, and as one movement died in 1913, another emerged.

Wyndham Lewis's quarrel with Fry was not only about money; the two men were becoming increasingly polarized in matters of taste. The Fauves were no longer the only avant-garde French painters to influence the English art world. Cubism had taken hold and in March 1912 Frank Rutter had mounted an exhibition of Italian Futurist art at the Sackville Gallery. The public, by now inured to such events, were not quite as shocked as they had been by Fry's Gauguins two years earlier, although one critic described it as 'Nightmare art'.[12] Fry himself was unimpressed:

What the Futurists have yet to learn . . . is that great design depends upon emotion . . . As yet the positive elements in their creed, their love of speed and of mechanism, have failed to produce that lyrical intensity of mood which alone might enable the spectator to share their feelings.[13]

Wyndham Lewis did not agree. And his opinion was shared by other artists including Wadsworth and Etchells, and Christopher Nevinson (1889–1946) who, in Paris, had studied under Matisse and met Picasso. When Lewis broke with the Omega Workshops in October 1913, he and his supporters founded the Rebel Art Centre in Great Ormond Street and began to articulate their own version of Futurism: Vorticism.

In December 1913 an exhibition was held of English Post-Impressionists, Cubists and others in Brighton Art Gallery. It sought to span all the various styles then prevalent. The Camden Town section included works by Sickert, Bevan, Gore, Ginner, Gilman, Pissarro and others, while the Cubist room included Wadsworth, Etchells, David Bomberg (1890–1957), Nevinson, Lewis and the sculptor Jacob Epstein (1880–1959). In his introduction to the exhibition catalogue Lewis wrote:

All revolutionary painting today has in common the rigid reflection of steel and stone in the spirit of the artist . . . People are invited, in short, to change entirely their idea of the painter's mission, and penetrate, deferentially, with him into a transposed universe as abstract as, though not different from, the musician's.[14]

During the following three years Lewis wrote extensively, defining the principles of the Vorticist movement and launching vitriolic attacks on all those who ridiculed it. In June 1914 he published the first edition of *Blast*, a periodical aimed at the the new art public; the Vorticist manifesto was outlined in detail in this first issue. *Blast* was not the first magazine to be produced by the artistic avant garde in Britain during this period of renewal; in the summer of 1911 the writers and collectors John Middleton Murry (1889–1957) and Michael Sadler (1888–1957) had founded *Rhythm*, a quarterly magazine on art, literature and music, edited by J. D. Fergusson. In its Bergsonian stance, which emphasized the power of human intuition, however, *Rhythm* was entirely different to Lewis's machine-age *Blast*, and that contrast serves to underline the division between the Fauves and the Cubists within British modernist art circles.

Lewis soon found other artists rallying to his call, notably the painter William Roberts (1895–1980) and the sculptor Henri Gaudier-Brzeska (1891–1915). Moreover, the scope of the movement widened when the imagist poets Ezra Pound (1885–1972) and Thomas Ernest (T.E.) Hulme (1883–1917) also declared themselves to be Vorticists. Vorticism represents the most extreme tendency of British modernist activity during the pre-war period. Bomberg's great geometric essay *In the Hold* and Lewis's *The Crowd (Revolution)* (see plates 364 and 366) both go far beyond even the abstract canvases produced in the same year by Bell and Grant (see plates 344 and 335).

The presence in the Vorticist ranks of two sculptors added a powerful dimension to the movement. Jacob Epstein, a founder of the London Group, had long been influenced by primitive models; the pieces he produced for the British

Medical Association in 1907–08 and his dynamic winged figure for the tomb of Oscar Wilde (1854–1900) in Paris in 1912 still proved controversial. Born in France, Gaudier-Brzeska added a certain cosmopolitanism to the group. His sculpture, founded upon a system of geometric shapes, was characterized by a strong sense of movement; his *Red Stone Dancer* of 1913 is a good example. Epstein produced his grotesque but unforgettable *Rock Drill* (see plate 345) in the same year. This is a steely-faced monster that seems to ride in emphatic sexual violence upon the earth, threatening destruction and death to all who stand in its way – a visual metaphor almost for the great holocaust that was to engulf the world only two months after Lewis published his manifesto. On 10 August 1914 Austria declared war on Serbia and within a year Lewis's worship of the glory of the machine age – and by implication all that Vorticism stood for – had been discredited in the mud of the battlefields of Flanders.

The New World

During the four years between the first Post-Impressionist exhibition and the outbreak of the First World War, an artistic revolution similar to that which had turned the British art world on its head was taking place across the Atlantic. The

343 CHARLES GINNER The Circus 1913.
If his contemporaries amongst the Camden Town Group looked to Gauguin and the Nabis, Charles Ginner's attention was focused on the work of van Gogh. In The Circus, which was exhibited at the Allied Artists' Association in 1913, the artist's technique is tighter than it had been in any of his pre-1910 work, and yet Ginner still retains the painterliness and heaviness of application that mark him out as disciple of van Gogh. Ginner began to be more conscious of the effect of light and to experiment with the sharp contrasts in tone evident here only after his trip to Paris with Gilman and Frank Rutter in 1911.

344 VANESSA BELL Abstract Painting 1914.
Despite Wyndham Lewis's rift with the Omega artists in 1913, this did not preclude Vanessa Bell and Duncan Grant from the abstract impetus which emerged in British art during that year. Bell uses a breathtakingly simple two-dimensional composition reminiscent of Malevich, in which any form and recession is left to be suggested by the power of colour alone. In many ways more radical even than those of Lewis, this canvas is just one of a number of experimental works produced by both Bloomsbury artists at this time. The essential difference between Bell's abstraction and that of Lewis lies in the difference in emotional structure. While Lewis emphasizes the violence of his forms, Bell's oeuvre is peaceful and contemplative; suffusing her work is a lyrical harmony that anticipates the School of Paris and the Abstract Expressionists of the 1950s.

birth of modernism in America, however, was an even more laboured and gradual affair than it had been in Britain.

The expatriate American James McNeill Whistler made an important contribution to the changing face of art in the 1870s and 1880s (*see plate 367*), and yet it was some ten years after the the Impressionist dealer Durand-Ruel had been forced by the Franco-Prussian War to establish an English base in London that America mounted its first exhibition of Impressionist painting. Slow to start, the artistic avant garde in America continued to develop, but constantly at a stage several years behind that of its transatlantic cousins. While a few isolated Americans who made Paris their home between 1904 and 1910 did espouse aspects of the avant-garde painting being developed there, in New York – the focus of artistic activity in America – the forces of reaction managed to maintain control until the Armory Show in 1913. Even then abstract art did not really emerge in America until well after the war, although – obviously – there were a few exceptions. Despite their eventual ascendancy, the Americans cannot be said to have played a key role in the creation or development of the modern movement.

Nevertheless, important seeds were sown in America during the early years of the twentieth century – the fruit once again of Impressionism – most notably in the work of the

American Impressionists and realists, and specifically by a small group of artists who called themselves the Ash-can School – a declaration of their commitment to the depiction of the dirtiest, most unpleasant aspects of everyday life. Inspired by the Impressionist painter turned realist Robert Henri (1865–1929), and bound together by their commitment to modern urban subject matter, the Ash-can School was still only a loose association of painters. Amongst their number, however, was the group known as The Eight. As the name suggests, the group which gathered around Henri in his studio at 806 Walnut Street, Philadelphia, comprised eight artists, including John Sloan (1871–1951) and Everett Shinn (1876–1953). Their enemy was academicism. When their work was rejected by the National Academy in 1907 they followed the example of their European forebears and staged an independent exhibition. This show, held at the Macbeth Gallery in New York in February 1908, set the pace for the future. The American art establishment was put into a state of consternation and The Eight were attacked in the art press as 'The apostles of ugliness'.[15] More hysterically they were described as 'Henri's revolutionary black gang'.[16] In 1909

345 JACOB EPSTEIN Rock Drill 1913–14.
By the time he carved this memorable monument to modernism in 1912, Epstein was already a figure of some controversy; he had rocked the art world in 1908 with his work for the façade of the headquarters of the British Medical Association in the Strand and again in 1912 – this time in Paris – with his monument to Oscar Wilde. In this work Epstein takes his customary angularity to a new extreme. The violence and energy of Wyndham Lewis's beloved machine age is embodied in the well-muscled trunk and hideous face – half-robot, half-African primitive mask – of this figure. Rather than a celebration of the new age, however, the sculptor saw this as a plea for sanity; indeed he later described it in his autobiography as 'the terrible Frankenstein's monster we have made ourselves into'.
(Percy Wyndham Lewis, Rude Assignments, London, 1950, 148.)

346 JOHN SLOAN   Sunday, Women Drying their Hair   1912.
The first steps towards the development of an artistic avant garde in America, as in many other countries, were actually taken by painters of a realist school. John Sloan was pre-eminent amongst the American realist painters; he was one of the Ash-can artists, disciples of the Impressionist Robert Henri. Ostensibly a crusader in the name of Socialism, Sloan's images of working-class life in urban America were, in fact, somewhat patronizing; here he shows us a trio of young girls on the roof-tops of New York. While Sloan's style seems closest to that of the Nabis, it is not as a formalist that he is at his best, but rather as a chronicler of the life in the city's own Bohemian quarter around Sixth Avenue.

Henri established his own school on Broadway and this became the cradle for an American avant garde. Henri's words were often more radical than his painting and indeed it is as a teacher rather than as an artist that he is vitally important in the development of American modernism. His bold advice encouraged a spirit of adventure:

Do not be afraid of new prophets or prophets that may be false . . . Go in and find out. The future is in your hands . . . Be willing to paint a picture that does not look like a picture.[17]

Henri's philosophy was based on the idea that man was innately good and developed only through his own experience. Life was for living, for finding out: 'All art that is worthwhile is a record of intense life.'[18] The works of Henri and his disciples amongst the Ash-can School reflect this belief; they represent, influenced by Degas and Henri de Toulouse-Lautrec (1864–1901) and displaying something of a kindred spirit with the Camden Town painters, the everyday life of the urban poor. Here again we see the music halls and the women washing portrayed by Sickert and Gilman. However, the New Yorkers' style is not as disparate as that articulated by the Camden Town set, and it lacks the Gauguinesque colour of Bevan and Gore. And yet this vision of the urban poor, produced between 1905 and 1914, is essentially a hopeful one.

The Ash-can artist who most clearly took up Henri's advice was John Sloan. A liberal social crusader, he nevertheless always stood well back from active political involvement, and

such works as his *Sunday, Women Drying their Hair* (*see plate 346*) are imbued with a detached and at times patronizing sympathy for the downtrodden. Although he never left America, his works betray the influence of Honoré Daumier (1810–1879) and Lautrec, and his later paintings have something in common with Edouard Vuillard (1868–1940) and the Nabis. Everett Shinn is perhaps closest to Sickert in his preoccupation with the music hall, particularly in his *London Hippodrome* (*see plate 368*). Of the others only the working-class Eugene Higgins (1874–1958), who had been in Paris in 1904, can be said to have produced anything remarkable in his grim paintings of the urban poor; in their pale tone and sculptural quality they recall the blue period of Picasso.

George Bellows (1882–1925) took Shinn's realism a step further. He succeeded, in his *The Big Dory* (*see plate 369*), for instance, in reconciling his own tendency towards the radical in art with a form of social realism that gained widespread acceptance in American artistic circles and paved the way for the arrival of more extreme art forms. And one other artist amongst this second generation of realists is of interest: Rockwell Kent (1882–1971). The paintings he produced, which portray both the vastness of the countryside (*see plate 370*), and the bustle of urban life, display a style which bears comparison with the early work of Munch and which may owe something to the Nabis.

The battle in 1907 between The Eight and the Academy, which provoked their subsequent exhibition, also marks the start of a conflict that eventually resulted in the Armory Show of 1913. The split with the Academy having been established, a new tradition of anti-Academic painting grew up and was served by a series of exhibitions: at the Macdowell Club in 1909 and 1910, and the Independent Artists' Exhibition in April 1910, a show that was held in a loft at 29 West 35th Street, New York City.

Art for Art's Sake

While The Eight were declaring their independence, theorists were at the same time compounding the ideas that would provide the justification for future American modernism. Moreover, just as Roger Fry was galvanizing artists in England, so in America the photographer and art dealer Alfred Stieglitz (1864–1946) was doing the same. In 1905 he had opened his 291 Gallery, at 291 Fifth Avenue, New York City, in order to promote new photography. Gradually, however, he took up the wider cause of the avant garde. In 1908 he displayed drawings by Auguste Rodin (1840–1917) and Matisse – the first time they had been brought to America. The former were received with caution but the latter, predictably, provoked critical abuse. Stieglitz rose to the challenge and began to show works by other European modernists, although it is interesting to note that he had laughed at the Cézannes shown at the Bernheim-Jeune Gallery – just as Fry had done. Now he took up the banner of 'art for art's sake' with vigour and, along with the Europeans, began to show the work of a number of American artists recently returned from Europe.

Max Weber (1881–1961) was one such newcomer to Stieglitz's fold. A Russian emigré who had settled in New York in 1891, Weber had gone to Paris in 1905 to study at the Académie Julian. He had visited the Salon d'Automne of

1906 and had been struck by the work of Cézanne. He had also met Picasso, whose experiments with primitive inspiration Weber had wholeheartedly embraced in his own work. Moreover, he had become friendly with Robert Delaunay (1885–1941) and had studied under Matisse from 1907 to 1908, learning from him the brilliant colours of Eastern art. It was Weber who introduced the New York painters to the work of the Fauves. He also broadened Stieglitz's mind to the possibilities of European art experiments, although his own style between 1908 and 1911 (see plate 372) is similar to that of Picasso's Les Demoiselles d'Avignon (see plate 194), and after that developed into a sort of analytical Cubism.

Soon after his return to New York, Weber held a small exhibition in the basement of the Haas Gallery. This show was largely ignored and it was only when he exhibited with Stieglitz in 1910 at the 291 Gallery that Weber was brought into the public eye. Even then his work was attacked by the critics. In the New York Tribune Royal Cortissoz wrote that his paintings were:

Untrue to nature, ugly and quite uninteresting . . . Post-Impressionism in the light of this exhibition need cause no alarm; it is only a bore.[19]

Among Weber's co-exhibitors with Stieglitz in 1910 were four other painters who were to exert a profound influence on American avant-garde painting: Alfred Maurer (1868–1932), John Marin (1870–1953), Marsden Hartley (1877–1943) and Arthur G. Dove (1880–1946).

Alfred Maurer had also studied at the Académie Julian. He had been to Paris as early as 1897 (shortly after Bevan and Peploe) and later lived there intermittently until the outbreak of war in 1914. A regular visitor to the Stein household, he had met the Fauves there in about 1907, and the meeting had provoked a profound change in his work. Hitherto Maurer's style had been heavily influenced by Whistler; now it became markedly Fauvist. It was this latter style that characterized the paintings (see plate 373) shown by Stieglitz at the 291 Gallery from 1909. And yet, once again, Maurer's new style provoked derision. One critic wrote:

Frankly, of all the forms of imbecility that have overtaken youth time out of mind, these are the limit . . . to take this seriously is to write oneself down an ass. There is no health, sanity, intelligence, beauty or harmony in the performances.[20]

A new artistic tradition had arrived in America. And as their French forebears had met in Parisian cafés, so now its champions – Stieglitz, Marin, Maurer, Weber, the proto-Cubist Dove and the critics Charles Caffin and Marius de Zayas – met at the Holland House restaurant in the Prince George hotel. Yet it was not from within this circle but from outside that the impetus that would bring this avant-garde art to the notice of the American public came.

On 17 February 1913 an exhibition opened at the Armory of the 69th regiment on Twenty-fifth street and Lexington Avenue in New York City. It was known simply as the Armory Show. Although the brainchild of three realist painters – Jerome Myers (1867–1940), Walt Kuhn (1877–1949) and Elmer MacRae (1875–1955) – it was largely the achievement of one man: the artist Arthur Bowen (B.) Davies (1862–1928). Inspired by the controversial Independent

Artists' Exhibition of 1910, Myers, Kuhn and MacRae had conceived the idea of holding a large exhibition of American art during a joint show at the Madison Gallery in 1911. As a means to this end they formed a group of twenty-five artists: the Association of American Painters and Sculptors. All that was lacking was a figurehead and thus Davies was asked to accept the presidency.

Davies had all the necessary attributes. He was a liberal thinker. He had a broad knowledge of the art of the past as well as of contemporary painting. He was himself experimenting at the time with Cubist techniques – in such paintings as Dream (see plate 347) and Dancers (see plate 371). Most importantly, however, with his influential connections, he could raise the necessary money.

It was Davies who decided to widen the scope of the show, making it an overview not only of American art but also of the art of Europe. In 1912 he sent Kuhn to the exhibition of the Cologne Sonderbund, a show that contained a wide spectrum of contemporary European art. Kuhn was able to earmark certain exhibits for the American show there, before going on to Paris where, with Davies and Maurer, he met Marcel Duchamp (1887–1968) and his brother Jacques Villon (1975–1963), and the dealer Ambroise Vollard (1868–1939).

The stage was set and the show which opened at the Armory in February of the following year was a blockbuster (see plate 348). Its 1,600 exhibits were organized by nation. The American section contained not only the work of the realists but also that of younger avant-garde artists from the Stieglitz circle who had helped to organize the exhibition. There were the Fauve-inspired works by Marin and other even more extreme practitioners. Maurer's work hung with that of Marsden Hartley who had progressed, after an early preoccupation with divisionism, to exhibit with the Blaue Reiter in Berlin in 1913 before returning to America for the Armory

347 ARTHUR BOWEN DAVIES Dream 1908.
One of the most interesting American painters of the pre-war generation, Arthur Davies was born in New York in 1862. His importance is threefold: as a Symbolist painter, as a radical modernist and as the man largely responsible for masterminding the Armory Show of 1913. This painting illustrates his early style, reminiscent of the Symbolism of Puvis de Chavannes. Davies's major interest was in line and form used in conjunction with soft tones. But, importantly, he also looked to earlier traditions, echoing the art of the Early Renaissance in the chilly formality of his attempts to achieve the perfect composition.

348 Photograph of the Armory Show 1913.
The Armory Show of February 1913 was of seminal importance to the development of modern art in America. Here, for the first time under one roof, the American public – and in particular American artists – were exposed to the full spectrum of nineteenth-century French art from Ingres to Cézanne. It was a shock. The eclectic mixture of works in so many diverse styles drove the critics into a furore. They called it variously 'derivative', 'depraved', 'gauche' and 'monstrous'. However, the show's impact both on the artists, and on the more open-minded members of the public was enormous. If any single event changed the course of the history of art in America, then it was the Armory Show.

Show. (Returning to Germany after the show Hartley developed a decorative abstract technique with Expressionist undercurrents [*see plate 374*].) There was the Synchronism of Stanton Macdonald Wright (1890–1973) (*see plate 375*), which paralleled the Orphism of Frenchman Delaunay whom they claimed to have anticipated. Macdonald Wright had studied colour theory at the Académie Julian and had first showed the results of his theorizing in Munich and at the Bernheim-Jeune Gallery in Paris in 1913.

The European section was heavily biased in favour of France, tracing the development of French art from Jean Auguste Dominique Ingres (1780–1867) and Eugène Delacroix (1798–1863) through Daumier and Corot to Manet, and thence to the Impressionists, divisionists and Symbolists. Twentieth-century representatives of French painting included the Dutchman van Gogh (18 works), Cézanne (13) and Gauguin (12). Significantly, there were also forty Fauve paintings exhibited – with a strong emphasis on Matisse. And most vitally, perhaps, the Cubists were here, represented by Picasso, Braque and Fernand Léger (1881–1955). And Delaunay was also exhibited. From Germany came the Expressionists, primarily Ernst Ludwig Kirchner (1880–1938), while Edvard Munch (1863–1944) represented Norway and Kandinsky Russia.

Notable by their absence were the Futurists, Die Brücke and the Blaue Reiter. On the whole, however, the exhibition was an outstanding achievement and it represented a good cross-section. Surprisingly, perhaps, it was only after the show had been open three weeks that the critical fury which the organizers had expected began to surface, the victim of the most violent attacks being a work by the French future Dadaist Marcel Duchamp, *Nude Descending a Staircase* (*see plate 392*). The piece seemed incomprehensible; *Art News* even offered a prize for the best explanation of it. Like Fry's second Post-Impressionist show in London the previous year, this exhibition was seen by some critics as a manifestation of anarchy. Edward Dangerfield wrote:

That which is good in art is that which is obedient. That which is beautiful is that which is reverent – obedience to law, order, principle – reverence toward that which is behind, above and transcends law – God!.[21]

The academician William Merrit Chase (1849–1916) railed at Matisse, calling him the 'charlatan and faker'.[22] And typical of the reactionary feeling which swept the conservative press was Royal Cortissoz's comment: 'Post Impressionist, Cubist, or Futurist, however they may be designated, their cue is to turn the world upside down.'[23]

The original organizers were terrified by the outcome. Myers was bewildered: 'Davies had unlocked the door to foreign art and thrown the key away.'[24]

When it closed in New York, the Armory Show went on tour, its reputation preceding it. In Chicago students burned effigies of a Matisse painting; in Boston the show lost money. Nevertheless, the impact of the Armory Show on American art cannot be overstated. Some 300,000 people had visited the exhibition and in its wake more and more galleries began to hang the work of both American and European modernists. In the space of one month America had made up for ten years of isolation. Things would never be the same again.

NOTES
[1] Lucien Pissarro, 1883, in *Burlington Magazine*, London, 1949.

[2] Frank Rutter, *Art in My Time*, London, 1933, 111.

[3] Ibid, 114.

[4] W. R. Sickert, *A Free House*, London, 1947.

[5] J. D. Fergusson, introduction to catalogue for exhibition at the Baillie Gallery, London, 1905.

[6] Review in *Burlington Magazine*, London, February 1908, 272-3.

[7] Roger Fry, in *The Athenaeum*, London, 13 January 1906.

[8] Vanessa Bell, Memoir VI, ms collated by Angelica Garnett; quoted in F. Spalding, *Vanessa Bell*, Macmillan, London, 1983, 92.

[9] Clive Bell, introduction to catalogue for the 'Second Post-Impressionist Exhibition', London, 1912, 9-12.

[10] Unsigned review in *The Times*, London, 4 October 1912.

[11] P. G. Konody, in the *Observer*, London, 27 October 1912.

[12] P. G. Konody, in the *Pall Mall Gazette*, London, 1 March 1912.

[13] Roger Fry, in *The Nation*, London, 9 March 1912.

[14] Percy Wyndham Lewis, in the *Egoist*, London, 1 January 1914.

[15] Quoted in Milton W. Brown, *American Painting*, Princeton, New Jersey, 1955, 12.

[16] Ibid.

[17] Robert Henri, in *The Art Spirit*, New York, n.d.

[18] Ibid.

[19] Royal Cortissoz, in the *New York Tribune*, in M.W. Brown, op. cit.

[20] Milton W. Brown, op. cit., 43.

[21] Edward Daingerfield, in the *American Magazine of Art*, New York, June 1917.

[22] Royal Cortissoz, in *Century*, New York, April 1913.

[23] F. J. Mather, in *The Nation*, New York, 6 March 1913.

[24] Jerome Myers, *Artist in Manhattan*, New York, 1940.

349   WALTER RICHARD SICKERT   Dawn, Camden Town
1909.

Sickert painted this moving work just four years after his return from
France in 1905. It is one of a series of paintings he produced at this time
that was inspired by the infamous 'Camden Town Murder' of September
1907; Emily Dimmock, a woman of dubious reputation, was murdered
in the vicinity of his studio. The pictures all share a common theme: a
couple are depicted in a cramped bedroom, in melancholy attitude.
Generally, the female is nude, as she is here, and the male clothed. The
Observer described the scene: 'a British navvy, fully dressed, and a dirty
complexioned woman with nothing to cover her at all sitting back to back
upon a small bed in an East London attic'. (Quoted in Wendy Barron,
Christies catalogue, 1988, 84.) Apart from the location the author of the
piece was quite right. But that was what Camden Town was all about.
Whatever the truth of the situation, the picture generated critical outcry.

350 ROBERT BEVAN   The Courtyard   1903–04.

*This early work by Robert Bevan is remarkable for its bold use of colour
clearly derived from the work of Gauguin. Although painted in Poland at
Szeliwy, on the estate of Bevan's wife Stanislawa de Karlowska, it might
almost be a farm at Pont-Aven. Bevan had in fact been to the artistic
colony in Brittany between 1893 and 1894 and had fallen under the spell
not only of Gauguin himself, who returned briefly from Tahiti in 1894, but
also of the French painters still working there. Sadly, the picture was not
well received when it was exhibited in London in 1905 and Bevan
retreated into a more sedate, Impressionist-influenced style which was
to characterize most of his work for the next ten years.*

352 ROBERT BEVAN   Showing the Paces, Aldridges
c. 1913–14.

*Between 1911 and 1914 Bevan often took horses as his theme, in this case
the horse sales at Tattersall's rooms in Knightsbridge. These animals
were not, of course, racehorses, but the beasts essential to everyday life in
the Edwardian city, just as the motor car is to our own age. Here the artist
is beginning to re-emerge from his more restrained style. He displays once
again an unabashed use of planes of colour, and now takes this a stage
further; clearly influenced by developments in France, he introduces an
angularity into his work that was to become his distinctive trademark.*

351 ROBERT BEVAN Cab Yard at Night 1910.
Between his early phase of conservative Impressionism and his later bright, planar paintings, Bevan worked for a period with a divisionist style. Such a technique is particularly effective here as the artist tries to create the atmosphere of a smoggy evening in one of Edwardian London's many cab yards. The deep purple of the shadow, into which Bevan mixes strokes of green, is illuminated by the light from a cab lamp, which converts it to a sickly yellow. Bevan used this yard – Ormonde Place, St John's Wood – as the setting for at least two other paintings; with a somewhat Impressionist concern, he attempted to capture the varying effects of light at different times of day.

353 JOHN DUNCAN FERGUSSON   Closerie des Lilas   1907.
*Omitted from Roger Fry's second Post-Impressionist show of 1912, John
Duncan Fergusson is undoubtedly one of the most underrated British
artists active during the first decade of the twentieth century. Only recently
has he begun to recover from this lack of early public exposure. Fergusson
had been aware of French avant-garde painting since his student days in
Paris in 1895, but it was only after 1904, when he returned to visit the
city, that his style began to change significantly. In this work, set outside
the celebrated Parisian restaurant of the title, Fergusson presents the
spectator with his Scotsman's interpretation of Matisse's famous green-
faced portraits of his wife – produced two years before. This is in fact
a portrait of the American artist Anne Estelle Rice, whom Fergusson
had met in Paris earlier in 1907.*

354 S. J. PEPLOE Landscape at Cassis 1913.
*In 1913 Fergusson left Paris and went to the south of France, for he
believed his art might benefit from a change of light. Another Scottish
painter S. J. Peploe, who had studied at the Académie Julian before joining
his fellow Scot in Brittany in 1904, and working with him intermittently
in Paris after 1907, accompanied him. In Cassis Peploe experimented
further with the style he had begun to use in Brittany two years earlier.
This landscape, in its simplified trees and buildings made up of sharply
opposed planes, shows the influence of Cézanne. The colours too are
somewhat Cézannesque, although there is still something here of the
Fauves.*

355 S. J. PEPLOE Still-Life 1913.
*Although painted in the same year as his Cassis landscape (see plate
354), this remarkable still-life demonstrates a further development in
Peploe's work. Despite both its immediate impression and the fact that
a contemporary critic chose to describe it as 'cubistic' when it was first
exhibited, this is not – strictly speaking – a Cubist painting. It is still to
Cézanne that Peploe turns, in his formal organization of the canvas and
the cool tonality of his palette. Using the canvas simply as a two-
dimensional plane, Peploe creates a suggestion of spatial depth purely
in the arrangement of the colours themselves.*

356 RODERIC O'CONOR   Field of Corn at Pont-Aven   1892.
In 1892 the Irish painter Roderic O'Conor produced a number of small landscapes at Pont-Aven in Brittany. Executed in wild, pure colour, these pictures are unique in British art, pre-dating even Bevan's Gauguinesque Courtyard of 1905 (see plate 350) in their outspoken boldness. O'Conor was a cosmopolitan figure; having been educated in England, he had studied under Charles Carolus-Duran (1837–1917) in Paris from 1889. Here, using the painterly technique of van Gogh coupled with Gauguin's palette, O'Conor anticipates the early colour experiments made by Matisse some six years later and ultimately developed in the work of the Fauves after 1900.

357 MATTHEW SMITH   Lilies   1913.
Having entered the Slade School of Art at the comparatively late age of twenty-six, Matthew Smith was severely ridiculed by Henry Tonks for his poor draughtsmanship. Disillusioned but not discouraged, he decided to go to Paris. It was here, at the school run by Matisse, that Smith discovered the art that was to shape his own work. Although he did not truly mature as an artist until the 1920s, in this early still-life Smith seems already to have begun to assimilate a French sense of colour. There is also a hint of that vibrancy which was to make his later works so distinctive.

358 VANESSA BELL Studland Beach 1912.
Although Vanessa Bell had been painting in a style loosely influenced by
that of Gauguin since late in 1910, this painting is the boldest statement
to date to reflect such an interest. To a greater extent than in her Bathers
of the previous year, she uses here large areas of paint and bold outlines,
giving the painting a feeling of abstraction. This is qualified by the
curiously mystical character of the sculptural figure standing at the
bathing tent. In a manner she was to develop both in her work for the
Omega Workshops and in her later painting, Bell suggests the presence
of actual people simply by describing a hat on top of the mass of a dress.

359　Duncan Grant　The Queen of Sheba　1912.

Grant was experimenting with various different techniques throughout 1912. Having executed a number of works in the style of Gauguin and Cézanne, he turns his attention in this painting to a divisionist technique, albeit taking as his theme a subject favoured by the Old Masters. In a manner reminiscent of Derain's L'Age d'Or of 1905 (see plate 69), he uses large dots and dashes to provide the decorative background for his two figures, who are described with closer brushstrokes. The formal composition and two-dimensional quality of the work may suggest the legacy of Grant's visit to Rome and Istanbul in April of the previous year.

360　Duncan Grant　Footballers　1911.

Further evidence of the importance of Grant's trip to Turkey and Italy is found in this work of 1911. It was originally painted as a commission, together with a companion piece entitled Bathing, for the walls of the students' dining room at London's Borough Polytechnic. The generic title of the two pieces was London at Play, a theme also described by other artists at this date. The boys here, however, do not resemble Londoners, but rather the heavily muscled youths of Michelangelo's Rome. Moreover there is also something Fauve about the style of the work; in particular Derain's sinuous bacchic dancers of 1906 (see plate 147) spring to mind.

361 SPENCER GORE Gauguins and Connoisseurs at the Stafford Gallery 1911–12.

In this picture Gore describes the exhibition of works by Gauguin and Cézanne held at the Stafford Gallery in Duke Street in November 1911, organized at the suggestion of the collector Sir Michael Sadler. Gore provides us with portraits of Augustus John (head and shoulders, foreground) and Philip Wilson Steer (centre, with stick), while on the far wall are three paintings by Gauguin: (left to right) Manao tupapau, Agony in the Garden and Jacob and the Angel (see plates 22 and 21). By this time the British public was immune to the relative restraint of Gauguin and Cézanne and the most important effect of the show was to turn the two painters into 'Old Masters'. Indeed the Observer described the exhibition as 'in no way bewildering'. (P.G. Konody, 'Cézanne and Gauguin' in the Observer, 3 Dec 1911; quoted in Bullen, 248.)

362 HAROLD GILMAN Tea in a Bed-Sitter 1913–14.

Gilman's approach – like Gore's during the same period – altered dramatically while he was in Sweden in 1912. In this painting, set in his rooms at 47 Maple Street, Gilman portrays two women taking tea. The empty chair and the contemplative pose of the two figures suggest that he had been looking at current developments in Scandinavian art; the all-pervading inspiration of Munch, then at its height throughout Scandinavia, and in particular in Norway, which Gilman visited in 1913, may well have been influential. He has abandoned here the rich colours of his earlier paintings in favour of an overall tonality, in particular a jarring combination of blues and mauves.

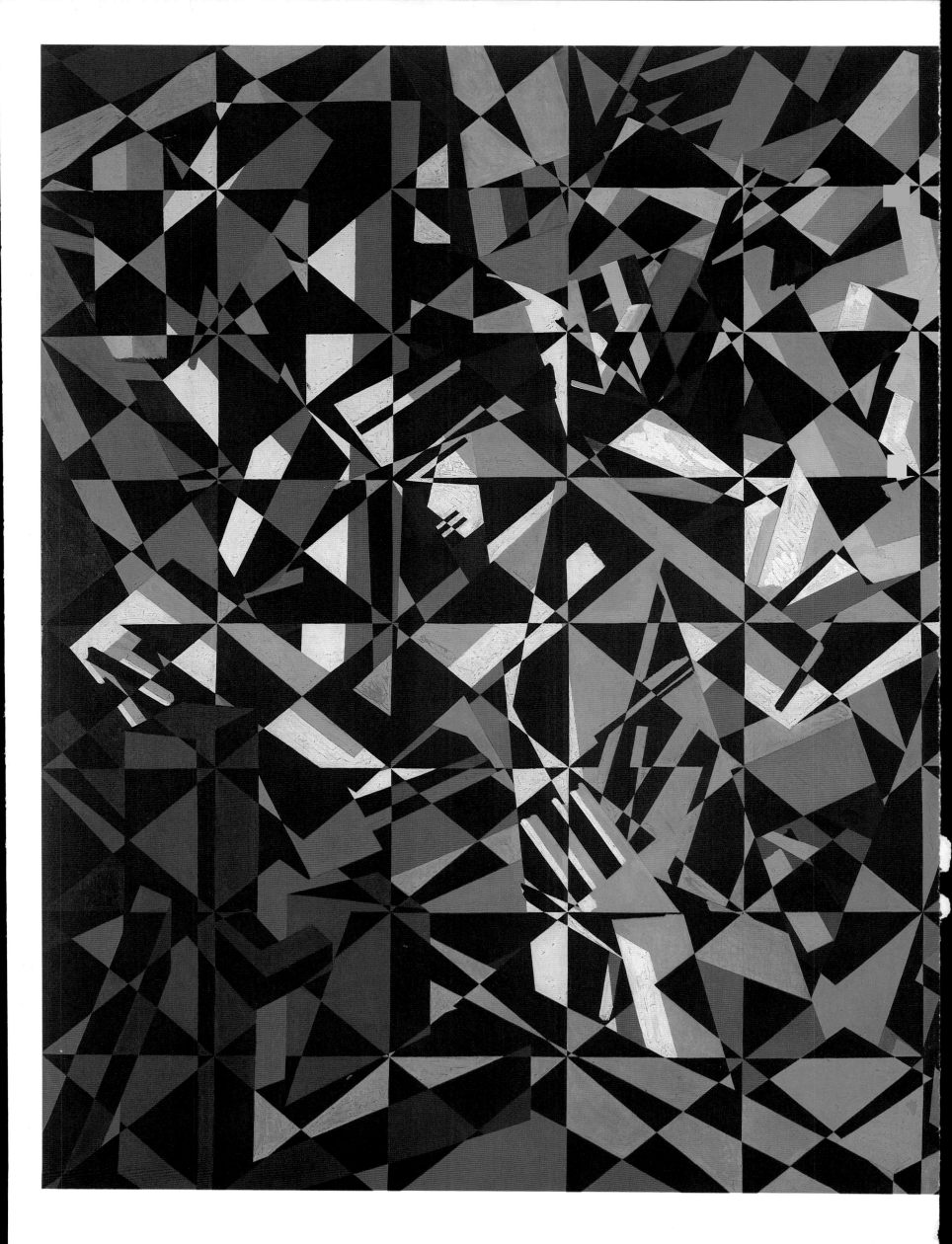

363 SPENCER GORE Letchworth Station 1912.
When Harold Gilman made a trip to Sweden in 1912, he lent his recently built house in Letchworth to Gore. It was here, at 100 Wilbury Road, that Gore's painting style underwent a great change. He started by painting a picture of Gilman's house, and then went on to paint various scenes around the town; the bright red roofs and white walls of the new garden-city made a profound contrast with the green fields around. Two paintings amongst the series are the most celebrated: that of The Cinder Path *and this image of the spick-and-span, newly finished railway station. Using an almost Cubist technique, Gore represents fields and houses in a series of flat planes, setting them off against one another in a riot of colour – brighter than he had ever used before.*

364　David Bomberg　In the Hold　1913–14.

This shocking image was abstracted by Bomberg from a series of studies for the subject that he executed in 1913. In the earlier works the formal basis for the construction is still apparent. The central motif is of two men: one to the left of the foreground, discernible in blue in the finished work, wearing a hat and looking to the left, his arms spanning the canvas in an almost cruciform shape, and the other on the right, his left leg described here in a diagonal of red and yellow to the bottom right. They are moving cargo at the mouth of a ship's hold, while beneath them the sharp parallel lines of the fingers of two hands reach up to help. Bomberg has cleverly adapted the age-old device of squaring up a study before transferring it onto canvas, using it as scaffolding to create an entirely new way of looking.

365 PERCY WYNDHAM LEWIS Composition 1913.
*In this archetypically Vorticist watercolour, Lewis takes the architecture of
the modern city and turns it on its head. Lewis, unlike Bomberg in his* In
the Hold *(see plate 364), no longer feels the need here to refer directly to
his figurative inspiration. Essentially, it is an image of violence: a series of
interrelated planes, taken in conjunction with their colour – or lack of it –
suggest depth and rhythm, within an explosion of modernism and
machine-age metal that runs from the bottom left-hand corner to the top
right. The only possibly identifiable figurative reference is the slightly
façade-like motif in the centre at the bottom of the painting.*

366 PERCY WYNDHAM LEWIS The Crowd (Revolution)
1915.
*In this oil painting Lewis tempers the pure abstraction of his earlier work
(see plate 365) by including several figures in the bottom left-hand
corner. They appear like robots, close to the form of Epstein's* Rock Drill
*(see plate 345). And yet the one really discernible visage is locked in a
ghastly scream. Above him flies a tricolour, suggesting that if this semi-
abstract landscape is meant to be somewhere specific, then that place is
France. In the 'background' it is also possible to make out the first few
disjointed letters of a word – ENCU. What is this word if it is not
'enculer', French slang for 'bugger'? In every way this is a violent
painting; it is filled with the implied invective of the title and hints of
falling masonry could even suggest the toppling of the establishment.*

368 EVERETT SHINN The London Hippodrome 1902.
Everett Shinn must surely have been to Edwardian America what Sickert was to England. Another Ash-can artist, Shinn concentrated on street subjects and – as here – on the interior of the music hall in particular, echoing Sickert's interest in the work of Degas. Unlike the Englishman, however, Shinn became increasingly caught up in the world of the theatre; sadly, in later years, he tended to specialize in decorative commissions. It is in his early work that we see him at his strongest, using a loose style and displaying a confident understanding of lighting effects; the height of the balcony and the trapeze artist suspended in mid-air are both described more than competently. Moreover, Shinn creates here a sense of the exciting yet dingy atmosphere of the music hall.

367 JAMES MCNEILL WHISTLER Falling Rocket 1874.
Although he lived for most of his life in Britain and his work most closely approached French painting in feeling, Whistler was an American. Laying claim to the leadership of the American avant garde, he was openly embracing the aesthetic realist tradition exemplified by his style. If anyone can be said to have been responsible for laying the foundations for the rise of modernism in America then it must ultimately be Whistler, with his insistence on the importance of tone, despite the fact that the first generation of these American painters still had to experience for themselves the light, Impressionist style to which Whistler was essentially opposed. In this early work, which is so close to future abstract experiments, it is possible to see the skeleton of the new way of looking, even if he did create it, as Ruskin accused him, by having 'flung a pot of paint in the face of the public'.

369 GEORGE BELLOWS The Big Dory 1913.
The critics, and subsequently the conservative public of middle-class America, may have dismissed the artists of the Ash-can School as 'apostles of ugliness', (in Milton W. Brown, American Painting, Princeton, 1955.) but George Wesley Bellows managed to bridge the gap between the new art and a reluctant public. It became Bellows's responsibility to introduce realism to the Academy and, thus, he can be seen as having subverted American taste from within the cultural machine itself. While others of the group seemed Bohemian and disreputable, Bellows was an all-American family man; it was on account of his spotless character rather than his art that he was deemed acceptable. And as soon as he was accepted, scenes like this were seen not as subversive glorifications of the working class, but as charming and typical illustrations of 'the American way'.

370 ROCKWELL KENT   The Road Roller   1909.

Although Rockwell Kent began his painting career in a similar way to Bellows, he was even further removed from the self-righteous approach of Sloan and others of the Ash-can School. While Bellows chose to elevate the urban in the realm of art, it was the vastness of America's great open country that most strongly inspired Kent's greatest work. This painting is a typical example. The sheer weight of the great road roller, which will create the new transport arteries for the progress of modern civilization, is conveyed by the straining of the team of horses as they haul it across the great plains.

371 ARTHUR BOWEN DAVIES Dancers c. 1910.
Quite another side of Davies's complex character is apparent in this
work, which was painted only two years after his Dream (see plate 347).
Davies was a well-travelled intellectual and knew the work of his
contemporaries amongst the European avant garde. Here he is
experimenting with a style far removed from his earlier Symbolism: the
rhythm of Matisse meets the angularity of Cézanne and the Cubists. He
never quite allowed himself, however, totally to abandon the realism which
lay at the root of his art and, thus, although he was vitally important in
the introduction of European avant-garde painting into America (through
the Armory Show), it may be said that Davies's earlier painting style was
the more successful.

372 MAX WEBER Figure Study 1911.
*Like many Americans, Max Weber was an immigrant – from Russia, in
his case – and thus his art has a certain cosmopolitanism about it that
is lacking in the work of many of his new compatriots. Whilst studying at
the Académie Julian in Paris in 1905, Weber had been taken by the work
of Cézanne, which he had seen at the Salon d'Automme of that year.
This, combined with both what he learned subsequently during his time at
Matisse's school and a knowledge of the work of Picasso, produced some
of the most radical paintings of early American modernism. This painting
is a good example; here the planes of Cézanne meet Picasso's demoiselles
from Avignon and the primitivism common to European avant-garde
painting of the period.*

373 ALFRED MAURER Fauve Landscape with Tree 1930.
*While Weber shows the American reaction to Cézanne and the Cubist
impulse (see plate 174), Alfred Maurer's work demonstrates the
influence of the Fauves. Maurer had also attended the Académie Julian
and had come across the Fauves and their work through his friendship
with Gertrude Stein in 1907; although this picture dates from two decades
later, the style still bears witness to this earlier influence. In its use of spare
but spontaneous brushstrokes and unbridled colour, it suggests both the
work of Vlaminck between 1905 and 1906 and that of Matisse from 1904
and 1905.*

375 STANTON MACDONALD WRIGHT Oriental. Synchromy in Blue Green 1918.

One of the most radical forms of avant-garde painting in America is seen in the work of Stanton MacDonald Wright. Between 1913 and 1915, along with his fellow artist Morgan Russell, Wright developed a form of pure abstraction, in which the formal technique of Cézanne was rationalized into a system of chromatics. The two artists combined recent theories on colour with their study of the purity of Oriental art to create a style that they christened Synchromism. First shown by Russell in Paris in 1913, this style parallels the results of similar experiments being undertaken at this time by the French Orphist artist Robert Delaunay.

374 MARSDEN HARTLEY Painting No. 5 1914–15.

Marsden Hartley encountered modernism relatively late; under the tutelage of William Merritt Chase in New York. Having digested his master's particular brand of Impressionism, Hartley adopted a similar style himself between 1907 and 1908. Then, in 1909, he moved on to a form of romantic Symbolism and exhibited at the 291 Gallery. In 1912 he travelled to Paris. When he returned to America he met Stieglitz; he exhibited at the dealer's gallery along with Weber and Maurer. It was in Germany, however, that Hartley found his true artistic direction. He first visited the country in 1914 and, impressed by the Munich Expressionism of Kandinsky, he began to develop an abstract style that was, however, only to last a few heady years. The formalist abstraction of this painting can be seen as an early manifestation of this style.

Chapter 9

Civilized Carnage

The First World War and the Bolshevik Revolution brought the Post-Impressionist age to a close. These two climactic events, which so drastically conditioned the course of the new century, have irrevocably cut us off from the particular world in which these works were produced. Twenty million casualties in Europe alone, twenty-eight million in Russia – in retrospect, the appalling figures lend a certain innocence to even the most extreme avant-garde painting prior to 1914.

Retrospectively too, however, it has been possible to see in certain of the works examined in this volume prophecies of that war's terrible destruction. It is tempting to view Cubism's fragmentation of the world of appearances, for example, as somehow prophetic of the disintegration – political, geographical and moral – that the war wreaked on the European status quo:

Things fall apart; the centre cannot hold;
Mere anarchy is loosed upon the world,
The blood-dimmed tide is loosed, and everywhere
The ceremony of innocence is drowned . . . .[1]

The first of these lines from William B. Yeats's (1865–1939) poem 'The Second Coming' may be seen as an interesting poetic parallel to the Cubists' shattering of the object. Nevertheless, Cubism did not discard the shattered shards of the bottle or the newspaper of the café still-life, but rather reorganized them on a geometric grid, offering not mere, bloody anarchy but a new and complex order. Yeats's poem goes on to speak, however, with a doomed voice that is utterly alien to Cubism's intellectually playful, witty and experimental nature. Pablo Picasso (1881–1973) and Georges Braque (1882–1963) developed their Cubist style between 1909 and 1914; 'The Second Coming' was first published in 1928.

Wassily Kandinsky (1866–1944) and Franz Marc (1880–1916) quite consciously presented more deliberately

376 KURT SCHWITTERS Spring Picture 1920.
In the interlocking, diagonal grid-like structure with which he has organized his materials in this collage – scraps of newspaper, bus and tram tickets, corrugated cardboard and other bits of useless waste – Schwitters was obviously influenced by the Cubists. Just to the left of the centre, he includes a somewhat cryptic reference to the season of the title: '1 MAR' suggests the spring. Above this he has also pasted in a half-hidden signature. Yet, over all these papers he has put down roughly painted patches of blue and greens – a suggestion, perhaps, that this rubbish can yet provide a fertile soil for natural growth.

apocalyptic images of final cataclysm and conflagration (*see plates 273 and 274*). These, though, were more symbols expressing a hope in spiritual regeneration than hellish forecasts of the muddy slaughter on the Eastern and Western Fronts. The Futurists positively glorified war in their manifesto of 1909.

It is important to remember, however, that before 1914 no one – except Lord Kitchener (1850–1916) – envisaged a major European war as being anything other than glorious, decisive and, above all, quick. All these pleas for apocalypse and all the theatrical celebrations of the machine's military potential were made before it had become apparent just what terrible destruction and what seemingly endless, futile loss of human life would be involved (*see plate 386*). When all the horrific implications of war did emerge it was inevitable that an entirely different kind of artistic response would be felt to be necessary.

Before concluding, however, with a brief look at some of the pre-war avant garde's more radical reactions to the war, and at their development in its wake, it would seem appropriate to spend a little time considering exactly what Post-Impressionism was.

Collective Individualism

'Post-Impressionism' was a term born out of exasperation. It was chosen, or rather invented by Roger Fry (1866–1934) in 1910 as the title of an exhibition of recent, avant-garde French painting held at the Grafton Gallery in London. Two years later he used the neologism again, this time for an exhibition which included work by artists from all over Europe. Fry was confronted by a problem; he needed to find a term under which a cluster of varied artists' endeavours might meaningfully be grouped. Although he originally preferred 'Expressionism', Fry was eventually coerced into choosing a strictly temporal, historical term. Desmond MacCarthy (1878–1952), who was secretary to the exhibition committee, records how, with an exhibition to promote, a deadline to meet, and an unhelpful journalist to placate, Fry finally, after some fruitless discussion, lost patience: ' "Oh, let's just call them post-impressionists: at any rate, they come after the impressionists." '[2] The term passed quickly into the English language and established firm roots; despite the complaints of some scholars as to its non-exact and all-embracing character, it has remained there ever since.

377 LUDWIG MEIDNER Apocalyptic City 1913.
'The earth quakes and folds, the city is shaken to its foundations . . .
Houses collapse, great ravines appear in the streets, a fiery storm blows
up. Minute human figures flee in panic, not knowing where to escape . . .
This tremendous quaking . . . seems to break forth from the earth . . . and
at the same time to plunge down on it from the menacing cloud
formations.' (Wieland Schmied, in German Art in the 20th Century,
London, 1985, 26.) Meidner painted a series of these apocalyptic
cityscapes in 1912 and 1913. They have since become eerie, and
disturbingly specific, premonitions of the war's destruction.

Thus, Post-Impressionism, like 'Fauvism' and 'Cubism', was a title chosen not by the artists concerned but rather by a literary figure seeking to classify in words what he felt to be significant and new. Christenings of this kind have tended to distort our retrospective view of events as they actually unfolded; it is easy to suggest that several individuals shared collective aspirations when in fact no such aims existed. 'Post-Impressionism' is actually a little more complicated even than this. For while the critic who coined the terms 'Fauvism' and 'Cubism' came from the same country, and even the same city, as the artists he was seeking to classify, Fry was English and the work he was christening was initially all French, and then latterly European. Furthermore, whereas the labels 'Fauvism' and 'Cubism' were later adopted by the artists themselves, the same could not be said of 'Post-Impressionism'.[3] Indeed, of the artists whose works were shown at either or both of the two Grafton exhibitions, many had already been dead for several years.

Here, an important characteristic of Post-Impressionism becomes apparent. For, unlike Fauvism or Cubism, the term did not describe one consistent style of painting practised by a coherent, nor even an incoherent group of artists. The label,

as its prefix clearly states, is merely a chronological one; it describes those artists who came after the Impressionists. Perhaps this should not be a cause for alarm. But in recent years a number of writers have worried that it has established a rather false historical distinction between the Impressionists and their immediate followers in the European avant garde.

Fry asserted that there was a reaction amongst the avant garde against the Impressionists' obsessive interest in optical reality; he was not wrong in this assertion, but perhaps a little simplistic. The edges were more blurred than he implied. Paul Cézanne (1839–1906), Paul Gauguin (1848–1903) and Georges Seurat (1859–1891), for example, had all shown their paintings at one or other of the Impressionist exhibitions. Furthermore, by the 1880s and 1890s many of the Impressionists themselves were beginning to modify their *plein-air* painting practices of the 1870s (*see chapter 1*). And as late as March 1912, a French critic called Jacques Rivières, who was a friend of many of the Parisian avant-garde artists, could still write:

In spite of appearances, painting has not yet emerged from impressionism. All art is impressionist that aims at representing, instead of the things themselves, the sensation we have of them; instead of reality, the image by which we become aware of it; instead of the object, the intermediary that brings us into relation with it.[4]

Clearly the issue is a little more complicated than too ready an acceptance of Fry's term and its implications might suggest.

The propriety of the term 'Post-Impressionism' thus qualified, it is still possible to make a number of general points about avant-garde European painting between the 1880s and the outbreak of the First World War.

The first, most impressive characteristic that can be noted is the increasingly subjective position adopted by these artists in their choice of themes and subjects. Painters had always, in the past, maintained close contact with society's political structures, and thus either the Church or the State – at the top of this pyramid – had also determined the kinds of subjects that artists would depict; in history or narrative painting, therefore, which was considered the most exalted genre of painting, subjects would be taken principally from the Bible or from classical mythology. But through their antagonism to the Academy, the avant garde severed all the painter's connections with the traditional patron; and in so doing it found itself with no single, defined ideology to promote or express. The materialism of their new bourgeois patrons certainly could not provide them with one. Isolation thus forced the avant-garde painter to turn inwards, to look to his own private, personal feelings, thoughts and responses as the only proper basis for a painting.

A very brief glance at artists' production during an earlier period will underline this new phenomenon. For instance, it is clear that throughout the sixteenth and seventeenth centuries, the crisis brought on by the Reformation and the Council of Trent determined the nature of much of the subject matter of the greatest, contemporary European painting. Michelangelo Buonarroti (1475–1564) and Jacopo Tintoretto (1518–1594) in the sixteenth century, as well as El Greco (1541–1614), Bartolomé Murillo (1617–1682) and Peter Paul Rubens (1577–1640) in the seventeenth were all essentially conditioned by these debates. No such precise, established theological or philosophical thread unifies the choice of subjects of the many different artists considered in this book. Rather the opposite, in fact, for the period is characterized by the multiplicity of subjects that inspired them. The artists of Die Brücke looked to Friedrich Nietzsche (1844–1900), Piet Mondrian (1872–1944) to Rudolf Steiner (1861–1925); Marc turned to animals. Henri Matisse (1869–1954) depicted an exotic, decorative paradise. Vincent van Gogh (1853–1890) formulated his own faith in a natural divinity, while Emil Nolde (1867–1956) found inspiration in a highly personalized Christianity. Gauguin attempted to become an Oceanic savage, while Edvard Munch's (1863–1944) paintings were fuelled by his own neuroses. Most revealing of all, perhaps, was Cubism. For what Picasso and Braque did was none other than to pursue an intensely introspective examination into the nature of art itself. Cubism remains the purest example of the Post-Impressionist artist's obligation to turn inwards for inspiration. For rather than explore or even indulge in their own subjective responses to the world around them, Picasso and Braque conducted a rigorous enquiry into the nature of their chosen vocation.

If, on the one hand, there is an emphatic individualism about these artists' works, it is equally noticeable that they also tended to operate in groups. This is not as paradoxical as it seems. Given their isolation from the establishment, avant-garde artists were obliged to come together in order to survive. In the face of widespread neglect and indifference, collective action was crucial. Hence, in every country examined in this book, there appeared purpose-built exhibition fora in which the avant garde were able to bring their work before the public. France led the way with the Salon des Indépendants and the Salon d'Automne. Everyone else followed: Les Vingt in Belgium, Die Brücke and the Blaue Reiter in Germany, the Secession exhibitions in Germany and Austria, the Donkey's Tail and Golden Fleece in Russia, and the New English Art Club in Britain. The avant garde's ability to create its own independent, collective institutions manifested itself in other ways too (see Introduction), through the rising importance, for instance, of the critic, the dealer and the art press.

One other example of this avant-garde collectivism, one that prevailed despite all the thematic divergences between the different groups involved, also deserves to be mentioned. This was the tendency for particular styles evolved by individual artists rapidly to assume the nature of a common currency amongst the avant-garde community. Thus Seurat's divisionism influenced scores of artists across Europe throughout the 1880s, 1890s and even in the first years of the new century. He bitterly resented the development for it threatened to undermine the unique value of his discoveries: 'The more numerous we are, the less originality we shall have, and the day when everybody uses this technique, it will no longer have any value and one will look for something else.'5 Despite Seurat's misgivings, however, divisionism took root in Belgium, Germany, Holland and Italy.

Other French artists suffered the same fate. Indeed, a brief glance at the chronology which follows this chapter will indicate the importance of Paris throughout this period as an artistic centre, as painters continued to be attracted to the city from all over Europe and America. From the middle of the first decade of the twentieth century to the outbreak of war, Cézanne's painting influenced countless artists from London to Moscow. It became, more than any other single artist's work, the inspiration for numerous subsequent innovations and developments across the breadth of Europe. Collectively, both the Fauves – Matisse in particular – and the Cubists proved nearly as influential as Cézanne had individually in their impact on the growth of avant-garde painting outside France. Germany and Russia were conspicuously receptive to these works in particular.

It is particularly interesting at this point to note the stylistic internationalism of the European avant garde and its total disregard for nationalist politics. While Germany and France were rapidly heading towards war on the political stage, for example, the canvases of Cézanne and Matisse were exerting a profound influence on the artists of Die Brücke and the Blaue Reiter. The free exchange of stylistic ideas seems to have been more or less totally unaffected by the worsening political situation. In 1912 Germany clashed with France over their respective colonial interests in Morocco. During the same year Matisse sold three pictures he had painted on a trip to Morocco to a Russian merchant called Ivan Morosov (see plate 163). As Russia was France's ally in the complex system of treaties and alliances then dividing and unifying the major European powers, Matisse's choice of a Russian rather than a German patron is hardly surprising. Yet the German artist August Macke (1887–1914) was completing his artistic apprenticeship at exactly this time and his work bears witness to the powerful influence both of Matisse (see plate 280) and of another French painter, Robert Delaunay (1885–1941) (see plate 257). Moreover, Macke was certainly not the only German artist to turn to the French in this way (see chapters 5 and 6).

378　FERNAND LÉGER　L'Avion Brisé　1916.
Léger fought as a sapper at Verdun in 1916 and then on the Aisne front, where this drawing was made. He was gassed the following year and invalided out of the army. With green fields above, the orange wing of the crushed aeroplane dominates this strangely depopulated scene, while a tangled wheel is half-covered by the wreckage. Léger's emotional attitude to his subject seems neutral. In others of his war paintings, Léger depicted soldiers playing cards in the trenches. He never, however, focused his efforts on the actual suffering. Such detachment reveals the rigid and exalted nature of his own artistic vocation.

This kind of internationalism amongst the avant garde is evident in other areas too: the widespread interest in 'primitive' art provides another example. Artists from nearly all the countries dealt with in this book explored the art of ancient and/or other cultures in their efforts to develop a language particularly suited to their expressive requirements. Gauguin, Matisse, André Derain (1880–1954), Braque and Picasso in France; Ernst Ludwig Kirchner (1880–1938) and the artists of Die Brücke in Dresden and Berlin; Kandinsky and the Blaue Reiter in Munich; Natalia Goncharova (1881–1962) and Mikhail Larionov (1881–1964) in Russia: all these artists were profoundly influenced by art that lay resolutely outside mainstream European traditions. Such an imaginative, cultural emigration was a pan-European phenomenon.

These three characteristics of the European avant garde – subjectivity, group action and a stylistic internationalism irrespective of nationalistic politics – can all be accounted for by the avant-garde artist's isolation from the rest of society. Having spurned the questionable benefits afforded by the Academy, avant-garde painters were obliged to fend for themselves as a community, to create anew all the traditional structures and securities they had lost.

For all the self-imposed isolation of the avant garde, however, it would yet be a mistake to suppose that these artists remained cocooned from life outside their various studios. Though the style of their work might suggest a certain insulation from the worsening political situation in Europe, they were, in fact, affected as much as anyone else. Nationalistic feelings did not entirely pass them by. In 1908, for example, the director of the Nationalgalerie in Berlin was dismissed for

his policy of buying pictures by modern French artists; Kirchner wanted to revive a specifically German art; and Nolde was partly influenced by anti-Semitic sentiments. And as early as 1908, Guillaume Apollinaire (1880–1918) found himself obliged to defend French avant-garde painting in overtly nationalistic terms:

Foreign countries possess portrait painters and landscapists etc., but at the moment France alone is producing examples of that honest, healthy and splendid art which stuns the world as it unfolds and which will be to the lasting honour of the twentieth century.[6]

Moreover, in both 1910 and 1912, it became something of a commonplace in the Parisian press to attack Matisse for being 'un-French'. Critics noted with relief that it was mainly Russians, Americans and Scandinavians who studied at his school and that his influence was more strongly felt in Berlin than in Paris.[7] Here, within the rivalries and coteries of the avant garde, the seeds of war had also taken root.

'May it Burn in their Lousy Souls'

On 28 July 1914 Austria declared war on Serbia. By 31 July Austria, Germany and Russia had fully mobilized their respective armies. On 1 August Germany declared war on Russia. Her declaration of war against France followed two days later and the German armies marched into Belgium. On 4 August Great Britain, bound by treaty to defend Belgian neutrality, declared war on Germany.

On the Eastern Front the Russian army, after some early success was rebuffed by Austria and Prussia. To the west, meanwhile, after the German army had failed to outflank the French and British, a network of trenches stretching northwards from Switzerland to the sea drew up the two armies in opposing lines. By the end of August the stalemate was clear and the four-year-long war of attrition commenced.

By the end of the war the scale of the destruction all this had wrought had reached virtually incomprehensible proportions. In December 1918, one month after the Armistice had been signed, the American Red Cross compiled a report on the devastation of the various *départements* of north and eastern France, where the bulk of the war on the Western Front had been waged. They made the following calculation:

The total building done throughout France before the war in any one year was less than 7 per cent of the building that would have to be done to replace what has been destroyed in the invaded departments. Therefore if no building were to be done elsewhere in France after the war, and reckoning that 500,000 of the building tradesmen would be available to work in the devastated regions, it would take over twenty years to rebuild.[8]

The full economic and industrial might of the civilized world had been brought to bear in this war. A variety of novel and efficient applications of new technology had been introduced into play: torpedoes, mines, the machine-gun, heavy artillery, barbed wire, gas, the aeroplane (*see plate 378*) and the tank. Their effects had never been seen before. Although there are many statistics that could be cited to indicate the scale of the cost in human lives, one may suffice: on the first day of the Battle of the Somme (1 July 1916), the British suffered

379 OSKAR KOKOSCHKA The Knight Errant 1915.
Kokoschka volunteered for the Dragoons in 1914 when he broke up with his lover Alma Mahler. Two years later – a year after this picture was painted – he was severely wounded on the Eastern Front. There was something hopelessly romantic about his decision to join the cavalry. And, similarly, as the title suggests, Kokoschka seems to be casting an ironic glance back at Romantic traditions in this painting. For this particular knight errant, alone, wounded and without a horse, lies in a devastated landscape. This symbolic self-portrait was to prove horribly prophetic of future, more physical injuries.

380 HENRI MATISSE Open Window, Collioure 1914.
Matisse painted this stark work soon after the outbreak of war. Faint lines on the blue indicate the window's slats; a diminutive diagonal to the right suggests a sense of space; beneath the expanse of black towards the lower edge of the canvas, the railings of a balcony are just visible. Matisse had already painted many views from his window and was to paint many more. It was a subject that gave him the opportunity to depict a landscape from the quiet and calm of the studio, to study nature with detachment and equanimity. Here, however, the view has been painted over in black and is lost to us.

60,000 casualties, and by the end of this particular five-month battle the French, British and German armies had together lost over a million men.

Many of the men mentioned in this book saw active service during the war. Apollinaire, Umberto Boccioni (1882–1916), Henri Gaudier-Brzeska (1891–1915), Marc and Macke lost their lives. Oskar Kokoschka (1886–1940), Braque and Fernand Léger (1881–1955) were seriously wounded. Others either volunteered or were called up: Kirchner and Max Beckmann (1884–1950) who were both discharged following nervous breakdowns, Eric Heckel (1883–1970) who was a volunteer medical orderly, Otto Mueller (1874–1930), Karl Schmidt-Rottluff (1884–1976), Paul Klee (1879–1940), Ludwig Meidner (1884–1966), Maurice de Vlaminck (1876–1958), Othon Friesz (1879–1949) who worked in camouflage, Raoul Dufy (1877–1953) who drove a military postal van, Derain who was a driver in the artillery, Charles Camoin (1879–1965), Jean Metzinger (1883–1956), Marc Chagall (1887–1985), Giorgio de Chirico (1888–1978), Filippo Marinetti (1876–1944), Luigi Russolo (1855–1947), Max Ernst (1881–1976), Kurt Schwitters (1887–1948), Paul Nash (1889–1946), David Bomberg (1890–1957), Christopher Nevinson (1889–1946), Mark Gertler (1892–1939) and Percy Wyndham Lewis (1884–1957).

Not all of these artists drew specific inspiration from their war experiences. Indeed, one of the most poignant and terrifying

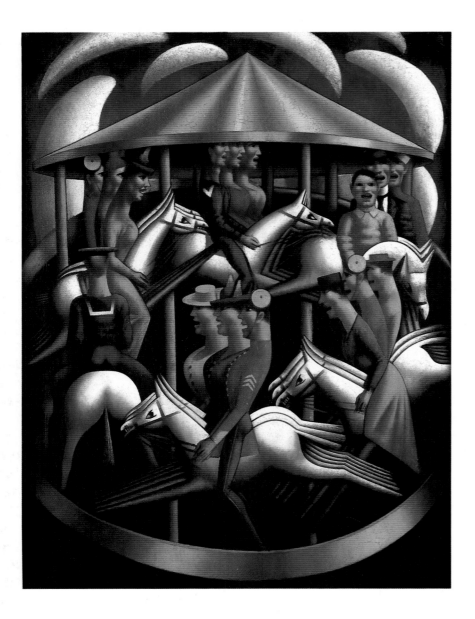

381 MARK GERTLER The Merry-Go-Round 1916.
D. H. Lawrence saw a photograph of this picture soon after it was finished. He wrote to Gertler: 'Your terrible and beautiful picture has just come. This is the finest picture you have ever painted; it is the best modern picture I have seen: I think it is great and true, but it is horrible and frightening. I'm not sure I wouldn't be too frightened to come and look at the original.' (In John Ferguson, The Arts in Britain in World War One, London, 1980, 73.) The fairground setting painfully satirizes the inane jollity with which so many people went to war. Those same people are now trapped, puppet-like, in the war's endless, mechanical revolutions.

images was produced by an artist who was not exposed to the slaughter at the front (*see plate 379*). The experiences of the trenches were, however, directly reflected in the work of Kokoschka, Léger, and Nash (*see plates 379, 378 and 386*), while others depicted it in a more symbolic manner (*see plates 387, 381 and 401*).

Paul Nash decided to become an artist only after a series of professional disasters. He failed to gain entry to the Royal Navy, then thought briefly about a career first in architecture and then in banking, before eventually becoming an art student in London. In 1914 he joined the Artists' Rifles. He spent the first three years of the war in Britain but in 1917 he was sent to Ypres, where he later became an official war artist. In November that year he wrote to his wife:

We all have a vague notion of the terrors of a battle, and can conjure up with the aid of some of the more inspired war correspondents and the pic-

tures in the *Daily Mirror* some vision of a battlefield; but no pen or drawing can convey this country – the normal setting of the battles taking place day and night, month after month. Evil and the incarnate fiend alone can be master of this war, and no glimmer of God's hand is seen anywhere. Sunrise and sunset are blasphemous, they are mockeries to man, only the black rain out of the bruised and swollen clouds all through the bitter black of night is fit atmosphere in such a land. The rain drives on, the stinking mud becomes more evilly yellow, the shell holes fill up with green-white water, the roads and tracks are covered in inches of slime, the black dying trees ooze and sweat, and the shells never cease. They alone plunge overhead, tearing away the rotting tree stumps, breaking the plank roads, striking down horses and mules, annihilating, maiming, maddening, they plunge into the grave which is this land; one huge grave, and cast upon it the poor dead. I am no longer an artist interested and curious, I am a messenger who will bring back word from the men who are fighting to those who want the war to go on for ever. Feeble, inarticulate, will be my message, but it will have a bitter truth, and may it burn in their lousy souls.[9]

Nash's description of the wastes of the Ypres front is pierced with a sense of violent disgust at the desecration of the landscape. Indeed, as a landscape painter first and foremost, his war paintings concentrate more on the war's ravages of nature than on the men who had to fight in these surroundings. Yet an angry barb with a slightly more political flavour flashes forth at the end of the passage quoted above. And a similar sense of anger seems to have inspired the war paintings of Mark Gertler and Max Beckmann. All these artists, however, made their protests in the artist's traditional medium of oil and canvas. There was at the same time a loosely knit group of artists working in different cities in Europe and America who were to push their peculiarly violent protests much, much further. Their diverse actions, exhibitions, artistic and literary stunts were to become known as Dada.

The Rotten Pie of Human Flesh

Dada was born in neutral Switzerland early in 1916. In February a German poet and philosopher called Hugo Ball (1886–1927) opened the Cabaret Voltaire in Zürich. Following a precedent set by the Futurists, the cabaret operated as a cross between a night-club and an arts society, a place where writers and artists were invited to read their work, hang their pictures, and play their music. Ball was soon joined by some other notable figures, amongst them Tristan Tzara (1886–1963), Jean (Hans) Arp (1887–1966) and Richard Huelsenbeck (1892–1966). The Cabaret Voltaire was an immediate success.

When the Socialist International split in 1915 – some believed that the Socialists should make a collective stand against hostilities, while the majority followed their respective governments into war – it was in Switzerland that those opposed to the fighting established the Socialist International Commission. Moreover, numerous painters, poets and musicians disaffected by the war had also gathered in Zürich. The Cabaret Voltaire thus provided a focal point for all the anger and disgust felt by these artists as they saw the war completely betraying all civilized values. And indeed it was precisely these feelings of protest that inspired the outrageousness of the Cabaret Voltaire evenings. As the poet and painter Jean Arp later recalled:

In Zürich in 1915, losing interest in the slaughterhouse of the world war, we turned to the Fine Arts. While the thunder of the batteries rumbled in the distance, we pasted, we recited. we versified, we sang with all our soul. We searched for an elementary art that would, we thought, save mankind from the madness of these times.[10]

This 'elementary' art was christened Dada; the name was used as the title for a journal, and later for an art gallery, the Galerie Dada in Zürich. Apparently, the name was found by accident as Ball and Huelsenbeck were leafing through the pages of a German–French dictionary. In characteristic Dada fashion, however, Arp provided an alternative account of how the name was chosen:

I hereby declare that Tristan Tzara found the word on February 6, 1916, at six o'clock in the afternoon; I was present with my twelve children when Tzara for the first time uttered this word which filled us with justified enthusiasm. This occurred at the Café de la Terrasse in Zürich, and I was wearing a brioche in my left nostril.[11]

Whatever its origin (the word is the French for hobbyhorse, the Rumanian for yes, or apparently, in colloquial French, a child's first utterance), the naïve sound of the word seemed perfectly suited to the subversive, nonsensical nature of these artists' various activities.

Ball, for example, recited one of his phonetic poems at the Galerie Dada early in 1917. Dressed in a massive costume of shiny cardboard, so large that he was unable to move and had to be carried on to the stage, Ball began to intone: 'gadji beri bimba glandridi laula lonni cadori . . . .'[12] On another occasion, Tzara, Huelsenbeck and Marcel Janco (b.1895) recited three different poems simultaneously in German, French and English – at the tops of their voices. Arp exhibited collages that he had made by tearing up pieces of coloured paper, dropping them onto a larger piece of paper, and sticking them where they had fallen (see plate 403).

Similarly pointless and subversive acts took place in other cities, especially after the war, as the original group living in Zürich began to disperse. Huelsenbeck moved back to Berlin where he started a review entitled Der Dada, published a manifesto and gave numerous public lectures. Tzara moved to Paris in 1918 where he also published a Dada manifesto. At one of the first Dada evenings in Paris, drawings made by the painter Francis Picabia (1879–1953) on a blackboard were brought on to the stage, only to be rubbed out by the poet André Breton (1896–1966) (see plate 391). In Hanover Kurt Schwitters started making collages out of rubbish that he picked up off the city's streets (see plate 376). In 1920 the painter Max Ernst held a Dada exhibition in his native Cologne. The entrance to the show was through a gentleman's lavatory, and on the opening night guests were then met by a young girl, dressed in a white communion dress spattered with blood, reciting erotic poetry. Ernst had also attached an axe to one of his sculptures by a piece of rope, along with a label inviting spectators to smash it.

Two important points should be noted about these endeavours. Firstly, they illustrate the Dadaists' belief that the artist was free to create his poetry, sculpture or painting out of anything at all. Secondly – and perhaps more crucially – these activities were intended as attacks, with art as the target, on the whole bourgeois society that had made the war possible.

Poetry that was noisy and meaningless; an exhibition that the spectators would themselves destroy; pictures made according to the laws of chance or out of the detritus of the modern city: all these activities undermined traditional notions of what art was, how it should function, and how valuable it should be considered (see plate 400). By attacking such established and cherished ideas, the Dada artists could signal their rejection of the society that had produced both them and the war. For, when seen in this context, even the most outrageous and obscene of Dada's stunts became polite and tame:

People act as if nothing had happened. The slaughter increases, and they try to cling to the prestige of European glory. They are trying to make the impossible possible and to pass off the betrayal of man, the exploitation of the body and soul of the people, and all this civilised carnage as a triumph of European intelligence . . . They cannot persuade us to enjoy eating the rotten pie of human flesh that they present to us . . . They cannot expect us to confuse the increasingly disastrous apathy and cold-heartedness with heroism. One day they will have to admit that we reacted very politely, even movingly. The most strident pamphlets did not manage to pour enough contempt and scorn on the universally prevalent hypocrisy.[13]

382 FRANCIS PICABIA Portrait of Cézanne 1920.
Cézanne was, without question, the most influential painter of his generation in Europe. In 1919, a year before Picabia made this portrait, Wyndham Lewis wrote in a review: 'Ungrateful as it seems, one must say that it is a misfortune that all the diversity of art and human talent of a generation should have depended on this one old man . . . Is there any lack of apples on tables? Do jugs abound? Yes, they are everywhere in this exhibition, as in every other modern exhibition of the last eight years.' (Wyndham Lewis, The Caliph's Design, London, 1919, 8, 52.) Picabia has portrayed the master as an ape, nature's most talented mimic.

383 MARCEL DUCHAMP   In Advance of a Broken Arm   (1915)
1945.

The snow shovel and its title interact with each other here to create an ominous sense of latent, but ill-defined violence. Who will wield its cutting edge? Will it be the spectator himself or will another's aggression make the spectator a victim? The question remains unanswered, as does that surrounding this object's precise status. Sitting in a New York hardware shop before Duchamp bought it, it was just a snow shovel. By buying it and bringing it into a museum, Duchamp forced it into the world of fine art. Here it remains, not because of any intrinsic artistic value it might have, but simply because the artist Duchamp chose to go through this particular set of processes with this particular object.

The Dada artists were not the only ones to feel the enormous, catastrophic weight of the war. The novelist Henry James (1843–1916) wrote at the same time: 'To have to take it all now for what the treacherous years were all the while really making for and *meaning* is too tragic for words.'[14] In other words, was all the experimentation and innovation of the European avant garde in the years before 1914 really only leading to the unprecedented destruction of this war? If so, then it was certainly nothing less than a bad joke, deserving only of contempt and ridicule.

Some of Dada's most memorable images were made by two exiled Frenchmen, Marcel Duchamp (1887–1968) and Francis Picabia, when they were living in America. Duchamp began his career as an artist in a conventionally avant-garde manner, his work bearing the influence of Cézanne (*see plate 390*). He then developed a style that fused something of both

Cubism and Futurism, and he showed his work along with the other Cubists at the Section d'Or exhibition in Paris in 1912 (*see plate 399*). During the following year Duchamp took a job as a librarian in the Bibliothèque Sainte-Geneviève in Paris; as an artist, meanwhile, he almost completely gave up all conventional forms of painting and drawing. Instead he began a long series of studies that was eventually to lead to his most highly regarded and influential construction: *The Bride Stripped Bare by her Bachelors, Even* (*see plate 28*). It was also in 1913 that he mounted a bicycle wheel on a stool in his studio (*see plate 385*). At the time it was simply an unimportant, private joke; indeed, Duchamp was later to say: 'It was just a distraction. I didn't have any special reason to do it, or any intention of showing it, or describing anything.'[15] This absurd object was later, however, to inspire some of Dada's most disconcerting accomplishments.

At the outbreak of war, Duchamp was found unfit for military service. In 1915 he travelled to New York where, following the success of *Nude Descending a Staircase* (*see plate 392*) at the Armory Show of 1913, he was hailed as a master of the European avant garde. It was here that the disturbing artistic potential of the bicycle wheel was first realized: Duchamp simply bought and then exhibited a series of ordinary, commercially manufactured objects which he named 'Readymades'. Thus, in 1915 Duchamp purchased a snow shovel from a New York hardware store, entitled it *In Advance of the Broken Arm*, signed and exhibited it (*see plate 383*). Other 'Readymades' followed: a bottle rack and, perhaps most famously, a porcelain urinal entitled *Fountain*, signed and exhibited in 1917 under the pseudonym 'R. Mutt'. In an article published following the furore caused by this last, one of Duchamp's friends defended his actions:

Whether Mr. Mutt with his own hands made the fountain or not has no importance. He CHOSE it. He took an ordinary article of life, placed it so that its useful significance disappeared under a new title and point of view – created a new thought for that object.[16]

Duchamp's 'Readymades' constitute the single most radical and subversive artistic act dealt with in this book. On the one hand, being mass-produced and machine-made, they challenged every accepted notion of the value of artistic skill, the artist's display of manual dexterity and craftsmanship which for centuries had given the art-object a value which separated it from and raised it above the everyday. It was in their shameless subversion of all those special qualities with which tradition had imbued sculpture, drawing and painting, that these 'Readymades' became so important to the Dada movement.

Duchamp also described his 'Readymades' as 'brain-facts'. In so doing, he was demonstrating his belief that the work of art is – or should be – primarily the result of an act of mental, not manual, creativity; indeed, what makes the 'Readymades' important is nothing more than the fact that Duchamp chose them. In the creation of any work of art, he maintained, the mind should take precedence over manual skill. In this way, Duchamp's 'Readymades' hovered with disturbing ambiguity somewhere between life and art. Moreover, over the years, they have continued to shock, puzzle and tease. In the 1930s, years after it was first exhibited, Duchamp's snow shovel was included in a retrospective exhibition of his work at a museum in Philadelphia. When the exhibition was being dismantled, in order to facilitate its move to its next destination, the shovel was found to have disappeared. It was discovered later in the hands of a workman; he had found it propped up against a wall, and had taken it outside to clear some snow from a path. The shovel had to be sent to the conservation department because the signature was found to have been nearly worn away. After this brief foray into the real world, the piece was safely restored to the world of art.

In 1919 Duchamp returned briefly to Paris where he became involved with André Breton and the short-lived Parisian Dada movement. It was here at this time that he made one of his most deliberately iconoclastic Readymades: a reproduction of Leonardo da Vinci's (1452–1519) *Mona Lisa* with a moustache and goatee beard drawn on it, and the letters 'L.H.O.O.Q.' inscribed across the bottom (*see plate 384*).

In 1912 André Salmon (1881–1969) had defended the Cubists' innovative distortions of traditional concepts of beauty and pictorial propriety: 'Deprived of the Smile, we could only recognise the Grimace. For too long, perhaps, the smile of the Gioconda was the Sun of Art.'[17] In other words, Salmon was pointing out that the Cubists were reforming and revising those beliefs and values which had made Leonardo's *Gioconda* (or *Mona Lisa* as it is called in English) for so many years the epitome of art, the highest example of the painter's craft. Duchamp went one stage further by completely rejecting all such beliefs or values. He implied that the famous smile that brushes over the *Mona Lisa*'s lips was nothing more than the flush of excitement at the prospect of imminent sexual fulfilment. For the letters 'L.H.O.O.Q.', when recited quickly in French, translate into an obscene pun: 'Elle a chaud au cul.'

Dada's stance was very much anti-art (*see plate 382*). Pieces such as Duchamp's *L.H.O.O.Q.* or Ernst's sculpture with the attached axe were made as provocative gestures rather than as finished works of art. In fact, Ernst himself was later to say:

A Dada exhibition. Another one! What's the matter with everyone, wanting to make a musuem piece out of Dada? Dada was a bomb . . . can you imagine anyone, around half a century after a bomb explodes, wanting to collect the pieces, sticking it together and displaying it?[18]

Despite Ernst's dismay, the mechanisms of the art world, its institutions and its literature, have all proved hungry enough to absorb and preserve at least some of Dada's angry, ephemeral gestures. They have also proved able to confer upon them, though not without occasional confusion (in the case of Duchamp's shovel), the status of an art object.

Dada's irony and invective, then, was dependent for its effect on the bourgeois society it was ridiculing. Duchamp's *L.H.O.O.Q.*, for example, relied on the esteem in which society held a painting by da Vinci. If it brilliantly attacked the society that had made such reverence possible, it yet remained unable to provide any alternative system of beliefs or values. Dada's energies were purely self-destructive. For as one commentator of the movement has written, emphasizing the full tautological cycle that Dada's nihilism put into play: 'The true Dadaists were against Dada.'[19] The movement was thus never destined to last very long, and its various manifestations in Zürich, Paris, New York, Berlin, Cologne and Hanover died out by about 1922.

Nevertheless, many of the Dadaists' disruptive artistic

384 MARCEL DUCHAMP L.H.O.O.Q. 1919.
Duchamp described this work as 'a combination Readymade and iconoclastic Dadaism'. (Marcel Duchamp in Anne d'Harnoncourt and Kynaston McShine (eds.), Marcel Duchamp, exhibition catalogue, New York, 1973, 243.) It is indeed iconoclastic in a number of ways. It attacks accepted notions of artistic craftsmanship – the reproduction of a work of art has become the work itself. It also transforms the most famous woman of Western painting into a transvestite, and suggests that her well-known enigmatic smile is merely the outward sign of inner lasciviousness.

activities were to inspire their successors, the Surrealists. Arp's use of the laws of chance in his collages was a device subsequently taken up by many Surrealists, both writers and painters (*see plate 388*). And Duchamp's illogical fusion of objects taken from the real world – in his bicycle wheel, for instance – was another influential predecessor of many Surrealist collages and constructions (*see plate 389*).

Surrealism differed from Dada, however; for in place of nihilism it offered a system. André Breton, who founded the movement in Paris in 1924, defined this system in his *Surrealist Manifesto*, published in the same year:

Pure psychic automatism, by which one intends to express verbally, in writing or by any other method, the real functioning of the mind. Dictation by thought, in the absence of any control exercised by reason, and beyond any aesthetic or moral preoccupation . . . Surrealism is based on the belief in the superior reality of certain forms of association heretofore neglected, in the omnipotence of dreams, in the undirected play of thought.[20]

The Surrealists thus committed themselves to the artistic revelation of the irrational workings of both the unconscious and subconscious strata of the human mind. As Surrealism continued as a major force in European literature and the visual arts well into the 1930s, any detailed treatment of the movement lies beyond the scope of this book. However, the peculiar style of later Surrealist painters such as Salvador Dali (1904–1989) and Réné Magritte (1898–1967) did depend enormously on the work of an Italian artist named Giorgio de Chirico, whose early paintings were shown at the first Dada exhibition in Paris in 1921 (*see plates 393, 394 and 395*). Later described by Breton as 'the supreme Surrealist painter',[21] de Chirico was actually only associated with the movement for a short while. Between 1911 and 1919, when he was painting his highly disturbing, eerie and dream-like visions, de Chirico's work seemed to have few, if any precedents; it was only after the Surrealists established their position that his painting found a wide, appreciative audience.

Plato and Madame Cézanne

The revolutionary stance assumed by the Dadaists was maintained by the Surrealists – not least in their brief association with Communism, though in the event this did not last very long. Yet despite the apparently unavoidable confrontational politicization of art wrought first by the Dadaists and then carried on by the Surrealists, four of the most famous figures who came to maturity before World War I continued to develop their painting after the war according to principles they had established for themselves pre-1914.

Kandinsky and Mondrian, for example, continued to paint in an abstract style which they hoped might provide a new spiritual direction for humanity. Indeed their idealism only seems to have been deepened by the war's atrocities. Having previously been working in Paris, Mondrian was forced by the outbreak of war to remain in his native Holland. During the war years, however, he and two friends – the painter Theo van Doesburg (1883–1944) and the architect Jacobus Johannes Oud (1890–1963) – formed a group called De Stijl, meaning The Style.

De Stijl was committed to the belief that the artist, and architect, could help bring about new and ideal social conditions through creating a new visual environment. Mondrian's pre-1917 paintings already contain glimpses of this environment – based on the purity of forms employed by the artist. After that date, however, Mondrian reduced his vocabulary still further; he limited himself to white, black and the three primary colours, placing coloured squares or rectangles – encased within a black grid of horizontal and vertical lines – on a white ground. It was with these spartan painterly means that Mondrian painted his most characteristic works: geometric maps of an unseen, pure and ordered universe whose minimal forms could suggest, but never fully define this infinitely expansive and yet mathematically perfect conception (*see plates 396 and 397*).

The formal austerity that characterized the work of De Stijl was undoubtedly influenced in part by the group's Dutch Calvinist background. The source of such ideas can, however, be traced even further back. In his ideal republic, Plato (*c.* 427–348 BC) had maintained that he would banish the artist

385 MARCEL DUCHAMP Bicycle Wheel (1913) 1951.
A wheel that revolves but remains static and a stool you cannot sit on: there is something deliciously absurd, and not a little humorous about the joining of these two objects. Duchamp left the original version in Paris when he sailed for New York in 1915. He made a replica for his New York studio in 1916, but this was also lost. Nevertheless, there are now eleven different replicas in existence around the world of this forerunner of the 'Readymades', Dada's essential anti-art gesture. Many are in national museums. Most of these were made by the artist during the 1960s when his work attracted much attention from the first generation of Pop artists.

and forbid the artistic representation of anything other than the most basic, and hence the most perfect, geometric forms. Something of this neo-Platonic strain of thought was also to affect Kandinsky's post-war production.

Kandinsky had left Germany to return to Russia in 1914. In 1921 he moved back to Germany and the following year he took up a teaching post at Walter Gropius's (1883–1969) highly influential Bauhaus School of Architecture and Design, where he remained until it was closed by the Nazis in 1933. The Bauhaus had been established in 1919, and initially its teaching had been based on passionately Expressionist principles. In 1922, however, it came under the influence of the ideas of De Stijl; Theo van Doesburg, the Dutch group's leading theorist, lectured there during that year to great and lasting effect. Moreover the school's commitment to the geometrically stark and austere was reinforced when a newcomer to its fold, the Russian Constructivist El Lissitzky (1890–1941) began to contribute to the debate. This new stylistic and ideological impetus affected Kandinsky's paintings of the 1920s; he left behind the sweeping, organic fury of his pre-war abstractions and began to produce works that, though they lost little of their predecessors' élan, were yet more mathematically precise in their composition (see plates 398 and 399).

If the concentration of activity that emerged with the Bauhaus reinforced Germany's major importance to the European avant garde, Paris still remained its central and most important focus. Picasso had remained in the French capital throughout the war and afterwards he initially appeared to temper the ferocity, both stylistic and thematic, of much of his pre-war production, turning instead to a gentle, yet monumental, classicism (see plate 402). Yet his genius had always seemed too mercurial to remain for very long pointed in any one direction. And indeed, it was not long before he painted some of his most violently distorted images; his Large Nude in a Red Armchair (see plate 405), displays a figure spread in obscene agony over the armchair of the title. One arm hangs over the arm-rest, the other is twisted around her screaming head in a pose traditionally expressive of pain. The shrill, bright colours of this otherwise quite luxurious interior finally only seem to act as a chorus to her suffering.

Like Picasso, but without his forays into the violent, Matisse also spent much of the 1920s tempering the restless experimentation that had characterized his pre-war work; the pictures he produced during this period exude an opulence and luxury that bears easy comparison with much eighteenth-century French painting (see plate 404). Indeed the female nude, with one arm raised above her head, and seated in an ornate interior, became one of Matisse's favourite themes during the years following the war.

Picasso's Large Nude in a Red Armchair seems to take on an added significance at this point. For in this picture, Picasso has attacked Matisse on his home territory – taking one of his colleague's favoured subjects and destroying its haughty luxury in order to create instead a potent image of agonized suffering.[22] As early as 1908 Matisse had defined his aims, saying that he wanted to produce a consoling, decorative art that avoided troubling or disturbing subject matter. This, whatever Matisse's greatness – and Picasso was the first to admit that – is a limited view, and one shared by all idealist art. Perhaps, though, it may be a little inaccurate to call Picasso's work an attack; rather it is a demonstration of the artist's ability to use the same subject in such a way as to proclaim an utterly different conception both of art's function and potential, and even of man's inner state. It is also, therefore, in its own way, a mark of Picasso's respect for Matisse that he should so criticize him – as though Picasso understood Matisse's intention and felt that it needed refuting, that debate was necessary, that it was too important simply to leave untouched.

For the rivalry between these two painters mellowed somewhat over the years into a profound but still slightly suspicious respect. Apparently Matisse used to send little gifts of oranges to some of his friends. Picasso, who was one of the recipients, understood why. For of all the different fruit that Matisse might have chosen, the orange, with its fiery skin and succulent flesh, provided the most concise symbol of that ideal world of sunny and colourful luxury that Matisse wanted to portray. Picasso used to keep these oranges in the reception room of his Paris apartment; but when anyone tried to take one of them, he would explain that they were not for eating. They were Matisse's oranges.

One further point remains to be made. Picasso, as we have seen, had already implicitly criticized Matisse's understanding of Cézanne as far back as 1907; for as Matisse developed his decorative idylls from his Cézannesque Blue Nude (see plate 150), Picasso moved swiftly from Les Demoiselles d'Avignon (see plate 194), which also had its roots in Cézanne, into the rigours of Cubism. In 1929, when the Large Nude in a Red Armchair was painted, Picasso seems to have decided to re-address this contentious issue. Whilst obviously drawing on Matisse's nude, Picasso also seems to be looking to another source – to Cézanne. More specifically he seems to be turning to one of the portraits Cézanne made of his wife: Madame Cézanne in a Red Armchair (see plate 13). Although Cézanne's portrait now hangs in Boston, Massachusetts, both Picasso and Matisse could have seen it in Paris when it was exhibited there in 1907. Three years later it was shown at Roger Fry's first Post-Impressionist exhibition, where it unintentionally became part of another, altogether different artistic debate.

NOTES

1 In John Hayward (ed.), The Penguin Book of English Verse, London, 1956.

2 Desmond MacCarthy, 'The Art-Quake of 1910', The Listener, 1 February, 1945.

3 J. B. Bullen (ed.), Post-Impressionists in England, London and New York, 1988, Introduction.

4 Jacques Rivière, 'Sur les tendances actuelles de la peinture', Revue d'Europe et d'Amérique, (1 March 1912), in Ellen C. Oppler, Fauvism Re-examined, doctoral dissertation, Columbia University, 1969, 79.

5 In John Rewald, Post-Impressionism: from Van Gogh to Gauguin, London, 1978, 104.

6 Guillaume Apollinaire, in L. C. Breunig (ed.), Chroniques d'Art 1902–1918, Paris, 1960, 51.

7 See, for example, André Salmon, La Jeune peinture française, Paris, 1912, 20.

8 In Shepard B. Clough, Thomas and Carol Moodie (eds.), The Economic History of Europe: Twentieth Century, London and Melbourne, 1969, 61.

9 In John Ferguson, The Arts in Britain in World War One, London, 1980, 105.

10 Hans Arp, 'Dadaland', On My Way, New York, 1948, 39.

11 In George Heard Hamilton, Painting and Sculpture in Europe, 1880–1940, Harmondsworth, 1981, 366.

12 In Dawn Ades, 'Dada and Surrealism', in N. Stangos (ed.), Concepts of Modern Art, London, 1985, 116.

13 Hugo Ball, diary entry, 1916, in Dawn Ades, Dada and Surrealism Reviewed, An Outline by Dawn Ades, Arts Council of Great Britain, London, 1978.

14 In George Heard Hamilton, op. cit., 365.

15 In Anne d'Harnoncourt and Kynaston McShine (eds.), Marcel Duchamp, exhibition catalogue, New York, 1973, 270.

16 Beatrice Wood, The Blind Man, 2 (May 1917), in Calvin Tomkins, The World of Marcel Duchamp, New York, 1939.

17 In Edward F. Fry, Cubism, 1966, 84.

18 In Dawn Ades, Dada and Surrealism Reviewed, op. cit.

19 Alan Young, Dada and After: Extremist Modernism and English Literature, Manchester, 1981.

20 In Dawn Ades, 'Dada and Surrealism', op. cit., 124.

21 In Hugh Honour and John Fleming, A World History of Art, London, 1982, 591.

22 See Kenneth Clark, The Nude: A Study of Ideal Art, London, 1956, 351.

386 PAUL NASH We are Making a New World 1918.
The trees remain unidentifiable stumps within this churned and pitted country, the shell craters ridged like waves. In this stark, symmetrical and emblematic landscape, broad, flat rays of light break over the earth from a centrally positioned sun. Although this picture was painted in the last year of the war, it would seem too glib to imagine that the sunrise was intended to indicate the beginning of a new, more hopeful era. For we are just as free to see the desolate landscape itself as the new world referred to by Nash in the title.

387 PAUL KLEE Sad Flowers 1917.
Furled curtains in the top two corners reveal a fantastic theatrical performance. Stylized, nervously drawn flowers descend gently upon a mountain landscape. In the bottom left-hand corner a tear drops from a dislocated eye, while below that a heart is about to be pierced by an arrow. The drooping flowers of the title, moreover, have been subtly anthropomorphized: male to the left and female to the right. 'The whole range of creation is addressed in this combination of the human and the vegetable; and, in the final analysis, it is creation that is mourning its own destruction.' (Ernst-Gerhard Guse (ed.), Paul Klee: Dialogue with Nature, Munich, 1991, 62.)

2 enfants sont menacés par un rossignol /M. ernst

388 ANDRÉ MASSON Fish Drawn in the Sand 1927.
*In 1926 Masson began to adapt Arp's chance techniques, or 'automatism'
as André Breton dubbed it, to his own more violently expressive needs.
Thus, in a work such as this, he would begin by pouring glue in random
patterns over a canvas. He would then scatter sand, sometimes of different
colours, over the glue and then, with a few painted brushstrokes, use the
forms and shapes suggested by this procedure to complete the image. He
would add a title right at the end. Remarkably vivid textures would result
from these processes. More than that, though, the combination of using
chance and by-passing the artist's rational control of his means was
intended to release a more intuitive understanding of the subject.*

389 MAX ERNST Two Children are Threatened by a Nightingale
1924.
*Ernst took the title of this work from the beginning of a prose poem he had
recently written. As in de Chirico's paintings, the causal relationships
between the figures and the setting remain unexplained. Any spectator's
perception of the image would be drastically affected, however, if the title
were learned only after an initial reaction had been established. Now, once
again, the spectator seems coerced into imagining some awful, violent
conclusion that is all the more frightful for being unseen. The unusual
blend of 'real' and painted elements is equally disconcerting. One girl runs
after the innocuous-looking nightingale with a large knife in her hand,
while another lies unconscious, and a faceless man abducts a child over
the roof. Ernst's work contains all the unexplained ambiguities of a
nursery rhyme.*

390 MARCEL DUCHAMP Portrait of the Artist's Father 1910.
'1909 and 1910 were the years of my discovery of Cézanne, who was then acclaimed only by a minority. This portrait of my father was done in 1910 and is a typical illustration of my cult for Cézanne mixed up with filial love. Thanks to . . . constant financial help from my father, I was able to concentrate freely on this influence of Cézanne which lasted about two years and opened new vistas for my general development.'(Marcel Duchamp in Anne d'Harnoncourt and Kynaston McShine (eds.), Marcel Duchamp, exhibition catalogue, New York, 1973, 243.)

391 FRANCIS PICABIA I See Again in Memory My Dear Udnie 1914.
Picabia did not confine his artistic activity to the ephemeral gestures of the Dada evenings; he also worked in more traditional media. The title of this painting suggests that the artist is recalling, with some regret, an idealized past lover. If this is so, he has created a peculiarly disturbing, fluid mechanism to stand as an image of her in his memory. In a subversive reduction of the artist's romantic lyricism, hoses, springs and spark plugs stand in for the lover's more usual attributes. Like the Futurists, the Dadaists gave machine imagery a central role in their work. Unlike them, however, they used it to create an especially caustic irony.

392 MARCEL DUCHAMP Nude Descending a Staircase 1912.
'Nude Descending a Staircase . . . was the convergence in my mind of various interests among which the cinema, still in its infancy, and the separation of static positions in the photochromographs of Marey in France and Muybridge in America. Painted, as it is, in severe wood colors, the anatomical nude does not exist, or at least cannot be seen, since I discarded completely the naturalistic appearance of a nude, keeping only the abstract lines of some twenty different static positions in the successive action of descending.' (Marcel Duchamp in Anne d'Harnoncourt and Kynaston McShine (eds.), Marcel Duchamp, exhibition catalogue, New York, 1973, 256.)

393 GIORGIO DE CHIRICO   Portrait of Apollinaire   1914.
Born in Greece of Italian parents, Giorgio de Chirico arrived in Paris in
1911, having studied and travelled in Greece, Italy and Germany. It was
there that his strangely silent and illogically mysterious paintings attracted
the attention of the critic Guillaume Apollinaire, who bought a number of
them in 1913. During the following year de Chirico painted Apollinaire's
portrait. It was later to be celebrated as a strange prophecy, for the white
target painted over the temple of the black silhouette pinpointed the spot
where Apollinaire was to be wounded by a piece of shrapnel in the trenches
– the wound from which he was to die in 1918.

394   GIORGIO DE CHIRICO   The Uncertainty of the Poet   1913.

395   GIROGIO DE CHIRICO   The Song of Love   1914.
De Chirico's memories of his travels in Italy clearly proved a fundamental inspiration for the deserted piazzas, classical architecture and statuary that populate his work. He brought these elements together in blatantly impossible groupings: a torso and a bunch of bananas, a classical head and a rubber glove. Yet these juxtapositions prompt multiple interpretations, often sexual in nature, where human relations are represented by the inanimate and reduced to the absurd. For, indeed, a human presence will only rarely disturb these quiet scenes. At the same time, however, the threat of latent violence seems to reside in the dark shadows of a portico; the dream always seems to be on the verge of turning into a nightmare. Somehow, even the thinness of the pigment, which betrays no discernible relish in the medium on the part of the artist, contributes to the evocation in these paintings of a disquieting serenity, or sometimes, perhaps, of infinite ominousness.

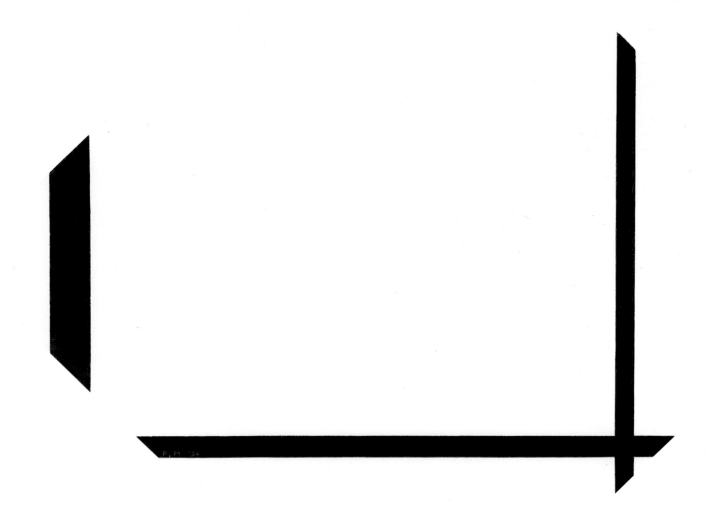

396   PIET MONDRIAN   Composition in a Frame   1929.

397   PIET MONDRIAN   Fox-Trot A   1930.

Mondrian never renounced the European artist's traditional materials of oil and canvas. This may seem a little strange, given the purity of his formal means and the uncompromising nature of his modern, Utopian ideals. Nevertheless, using this medium allowed him to create effects whose subtlety and variety is belied by the minimalism of his adopted vocabulary. His whites are not always pure. His lines are not always completely straight, nor are they of uniform thickness. In some of the earlier paintings they do not quite reach the edge of the canvas. When they do, as they do here, it seems as though the grids continue, unseen, past the edges of the canvas. What the spectator sees, therefore, is but a glimpse of a larger, ordered, geometric but unpredictable and infinite whole. Mondrian had proscribed himself the use of the diagonal, but by tilting his canvas at an angle of 45 degrees he could avail himself of its dynamic properties. Thus, in Fox-Trot A, using only three lines and a white ground, he is able to create a sense of extraordinary dynamism because we can see the corner of another right angle just below the lower left-hand edge.

398 WASSILY KANDINSKY Variegated Circle 1921.

399 WASSILY KANDINSKY Three Sounds 1926.
When Kandinsky returned to Germany from Russia in 1922, he brought
Variegated Circle *back with him. The restless energies, sweeping*
diagonals and flaming colour of his pre-war work still survive at this date
– in a painting like Composition 6, *for example (see plate 273). The*
title of Three Sounds *makes explicit, too, Kandinsky's predeliction for*
comparing similarities between his abstract paintings and music.
However, the way in which he has organized these elements on the canvas
has changed. As early as 1911 he had written about basing an abstract or
non-objective painting on the basic geometrical shapes – square, triangle
and circle – but these only made their appearance in his work nearly ten
years later, in Variegated Circle. *And as he introduces them, the last*
vestiges of faintly recognizable, natural forms disappear. While,
theoretically at least, this brings his painting closer to that of Mondrian
or the Russian Constructivists, fundamental differences still remain.
Kandinsky's new geometries appear loud, brash and explosive when
compared with their paintings of the same period.

391

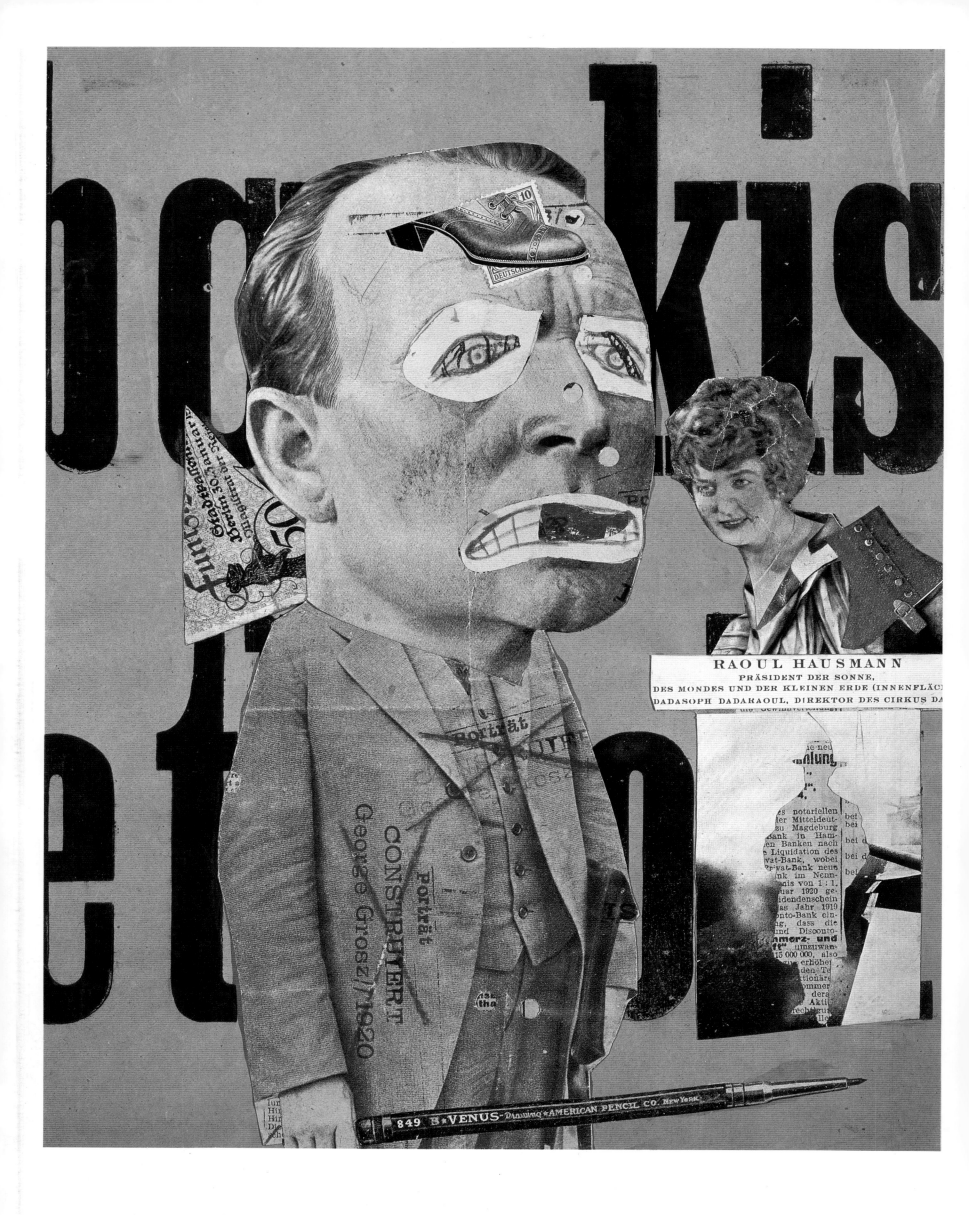

400 RAOUL HAUSMANN The Art Critic 1919–20.

The critic was bound to find himself the target of Dada's attacks. For as his importance as mediator between artist and public grew, he was also becoming increasingly powerful. It was ultimately the critic, after all, who conferred value on art in a number of different ways: aesthetic, historical, moral, and financial. Hausmann's ferocious, self-important critic has a fragment of a 50 mark note sticking out of his neck. Warrior-like he brandishes his pencil like a spear. However, the word 'Venus' is clearly discernible on the body of the pencil. That, and the part of his anatomy which it is mimicking, betray the hidden nature of his vocation.

401 MAX BECKMANN The Night 1918–19.

The grotesqueness of the protaganists of this drama, and the extreme violence of the action seem inexplicable. On the far left a shadowy, half-obscured figure hoists the noose that is strangling the last gasps of breath from the man lying on the table. Another figure, bandaged and clenching a pipe between his teeth, is in the act of breaking this same man's wrist, while to his right, a half-naked prostitute sinks slowly to the floor with her arms raised and legs splayed to echo her neighbour's. Yet the scene is presented as a modern crucifixion with the prostitute as the Magdalen, and the strangled man as the thief. There is no Christ.

402 PABLO PICASSO   Mother and Child   1921.
In 1918 Picasso married Olga Koklova, a dancer from Diaghilev's Ballet Russe company. In February 1921 – the year this massive picture was painted – their son Paolo was born. Safely enfolded in his mother's enormous legs, the child leans back to look into her noble, calm face; he reaches back towards her with one small, yet Herculean arm. With the other hand gripping his foot, he unconsciously mimics the position of his mother's right arm. This tender moment, probably inspired by Picasso's new role as a father, is given monumental and tranquil expression. Picasso translates his own experience into timeless, classic form.

403 JEAN (HANS) ARP   Collage Arranged According to the Laws of Chance   1916–17.
Ultimately, the exploitation of the laws of chance in the creation of a work of art was not, for Arp, merely an iconoclastic snipe at traditional notions of artistic craftsmanship. Chance, he said, 'embraces all laws and is unfathomable like the first cause from which all life arises [and] can only be experienced through complete devotion to the unconscious'. (Hans Arp, On My Way, New York, 1948, 77.) The accidental ways in which torn pieces of paper fell to the ground would sometimes only act as initial suggestions. He would then manipulate and exploit these random variations in the elaboration of the finished work, as he has here.

404　Henri Matisse　Nude Seated on a Sofa　1923.
This large, modestly posed nude sits in slightly incongruous, bourgeois
surroundings. Venus has arrived in the suburbs. She has arranged herself
on a red sofa, while the patterned hanging on the wall behind subtly
suggests that her original environment may have been more exotic and
colourful. Yet these are dim reminders of a distant mythological land that
Matisse no longer chooses to portray. This modern Venus is also simply a
model posed in a domestic interior.

405　Pablo Picasso　Large Nude in a Red Armchair　1929.
The red armchair, the yellow star-shaped pattern on the green wall and
the empty frame or mirror in the top left-hand corner suggest that Picasso
had Cézanne's Portrait of Madame Cézanne in a Red Armchair (see
plate 13) in mind when he painted this ferocious nude. The subject itself,
however, together with the partial view on to the balcony to the right,
indicate that he was actually addressing himself more to Matisse. Matisse,
a more decorous artist altogether, however, never painted orifices, which
probably explains why Picasso gave them such a central emphasis here.

Chronology

WALTER SICKERT sees paintings by EDGAR
    DEGAS in Paris
VLADIMIR TATLIN born (d. 1953)
VAN GOGH paints *The Potato Eaters*

1886
Eighth and last Impressionist exhibition in
    Paris
Second Salon des Indépendants, Paris
    (hereafter held annally)
First exhibition of French Impressionist
    artists' work in America
FREDERICK ETCHELLS born (d. 1973)
GAUGUIN visits Brittany for first time
OSKAR KOKOSCHKA born (d. 1980)
AXEL REVOLD born (d. 1962)
OLAF RUDE born (d. 1957)
SIGNAC meets van Gogh
VAN GOGH arrives in Paris

1887
MARCEL DUCHAMP born (d. 1968)
GAUGUIN travels to Martinique
JUAN GRIS born (d. 1927)
AUGUST MACKE born (d. 1914)
CLAUDE MONET visits London
SEURAT's *La Grande Jatte* shown in Brussels

1888
GIORGIO DE CHIRICO born (d. 1978)
GAUGUIN in Pont-Aven, Brittany, where he
    paints *Vision after the Sermon: Jacob and the
    Angel*. He is visited by EMILE BERNARD
PAUL SÉRUSIER also visits Gauguin; he
    paints *The Talisman*
VAN GOGH leaves Paris for Arles. He is
    visited by GAUGUIN, who leaves after an
    argument. VAN GOGH's first attack of
    madness
NILS VON DARDEL born (d. 1943)

1889
Exposition universelle in Paris; MAX
    LIEBERMANN exhibits and founds Berlin
    Secession
GAUGUIN organizes an exhibition of his and
    other artists' works at Café Volpini, Paris
ISAAC GRÜNEWALD born (d. 1946)
PER KROHG born (d. 1965)
HENRI MATISSE decides to become a painter
OTTO MODERSOHN settles in Worpswede
    and establishes artists' colony with
    MACKENSEN and H. AM ENDE
MUNCH's first visit to Paris coincides with his
    first one-man show in Oslo
RODERIC O'CONOR leaves Ireland for Grez,
    Brittany
SÉRUSIER, MAURICE DENIS and PIERRE
    BONNARD form the Nabis, later joined by
    EDOUARD VUILLARD and XAVIER
    ROUSSEL
VAN GOGH enters an asylum in St Rémy
EDWARD WADSWORTH born (d. 1949)

EMILE ZOLA – *Germinal*

1886
FÉLIX FÉNÉON defends SEURAT in *La Vogue*
JEAN MORÉAS publishes *Symbolist Manifesto*
    in *Le Figaro*
FRIEDRICH NIETZSCHE – *Beyond Good and
    Evil*
EMILE ZOLA – *L'Oeuvre*

1887
JULES LAFORGUE dies (b. 1860)
STÉPHANE MALLARMÉ – *Poésies*
RICHARD WAGNER – *Lohengrin* – first Paris
    performance

1888
T.S. ELIOT born (d. 1965)

1889
LUDWIG WITTGENSTEIN born (d. 1951)

cylinder motorcar engine

1886
Statue of Liberty unveiled in USA
GLADSTONE introduces Irish Home Rule bill
First Indian National Congress meets
Fluorine discovered

1887
Work begins on Eiffel Tower, Paris
QUEEN VICTORIA's Golden Jubilee
GENERAL BOULANGER's coup fails in Paris

1888
WILLIAM II becomes Emperor of Germany
BENJAMIN HARRISON (1833–1901) elected
    US President
Kodak box camera launched
Jack the Ripper murders six women in
    London

1889
Exposition universelle in Paris
ADOLF HITLER born (d. 1945)
May Day becomes annual holiday in France
Moulin Rouge opens in Paris
Invention of cordite
Archduke RUDOLF, CROWN PRINCE OF
    AUSTRIA. commits suicide

1890

ALEXANDRE BENOIS enters St Petersburg
    Academy
DAVID BOMBERG born (d. 1957)
SERGEI DIAGHILEV joins World of Art,
    St Petersburg
STANTON MACDONALD-WRIGHT born
    (d. 1973)
SEURAT's *Le Chahut* shown at the Salon des
    Indépendants
VAN GOGH moves to Auvers, close to Dr
    Gachet. Commits suicide – 29 July
VRUBEL meets MIKHAIL LERMONTOV and
    paints first picture – of *The Demon*

1891

BENOIS visits Munich
DIAGHILEV visits Paris
HENRI GAUDIER-BRZESKA born (d. 1915)
GAUGUIN leaves for Tahiti
WASSILY KANDINSKY fails to recognize the
    subject of a MONET at a show in Moscow
MONET exhibits grainstack series at PAUL
    DURAND-RUEL's gallery,
SEURAT organizes memorial exhibition of
    VAN GOGH's work at Salon des
    Indépendants, Paris
STANLEY SPENCER born (d. 1959)
WEBER settles in New York

1892

Foundation of Munich Secession
VICTOR BORISOV-MUSATOV working in
    Moscow
MATISSE enrols as a student at the Ecole des
    Beaux-Arts under Gustave Moreau
MONET begins Rouen Cathedral series
MUNCH exhibits in Berlin, stays until 1898
EMIL NOLDE teaching at St Gallen
O'CONOR working in Pont-Aven
RENOIR exhibition at PAUL DURAND-
    RUEL's gallery, Paris
SIGNAC moves to St Tropez

1893

Foundation of Dresden Secession
ROBERT BEVAN in Pont-Aven until 1894
GAUGUIN arrives back in France; Tahitian
    paintings met with ridicule in the press
PÈRE TANGUY dies (b. 1894)
AMBROISE VOLLARD opens a gallery in the
    rue Laffitte, Paris

1894

Foundation of an artists' colony in Dachau
FERDINAND HODLER exhibits at Munich
    Secession
MODERSOHN and PAULA BECKER exhibit at
    Berlin Kunsthalle
OTTO MUELLER enters Dresden Academy
O'CONOR meets GAUGUIN
S.J. PEPLOE studying at Académie Julian

1890

Mercure de France founded by VALLETTE
Théâtre d'Art founded by Fort
MAURICE DENIS publishes 'Définition du
    néo-traditionnisme' in *Art et Critique*

1891

Revue Blanche founded by Natanson brothers
THOMAS HARDY – *Tess of the d'Urbervilles*
A.-J. HUYSMANS – *Là-Bas*
ARTHUR RIMBAUD dies (b. 1854)

1892

WALT WHITMAN dies (b. 1819)

1893

The last of EMILE ZOLA's *Le Rougon-
    Macquart* series of novels is published
STÉPHANE MALLARMÉ – *Vers et Prose*
GUY DE MAUPASSANT dies (b. 1850)
HIPPOLYTE TAINE dies (b. 1828)
PYOTR TCHAIKOVSKY dies (b. 1840)

1894

CLAUDE DEBUSSY – *L'Après-midi d'un faun*
RUDYARD KIPLING – *The Jungle Book*

1890

WILLHELM II dismisses Bismarck
Worldwide flu epidemic
First steel-framed building erected in Chicago
Idaho and Wyoming become US states

1891

Triple Alliance of Austria, Germany and Italy
    renewed for twelve years
Treaty signed between France and Russia
GENERAL BOULANGER commits suicide
Famine in Russia

1892

Viscose discovered
RUDOLF DIESEL (1858–1913) patents internal
    combustion engine
GLADSTONE elected Prime Minister of Britain

1893

HENRY FORD (1863-1947) and BENZ construct
    four-wheeled cars
World Exhibition in Chicago
CLEVELAND elected US President for second time
Independent Labour Party formed, Bradford,
    England
Panama Canal corruption trial, Paris

1894

President CARNOT of France assassinated by
    Italian anarchist
ALFRED DREYFUS (1859-1935) arrested on
    charge of treason and imprisoned on Devil's
    Island
TSAR NICOLAS II ascends throne in Russia
LUMIERE brothers – AUGUSTE (1862–1954) and
    LOUIS (1864–1948) – invent cinematograph

1895

BORISOV-MUSATOV working with Moreau in
  Paris
J.D. FERGUSSON studying at Académie
  Colarossi, Paris
GAUGUIN returns to the South Seas
MODERSOHN and BECKER exhibit at Munich
  Glasspalast
WILLIAM ROBERTS born (d. 1980)
SIGNAC shows *Au Temps d'Harmonie* at Salon
  des Indépendants
VOLLARD's first Cézanne exhibition

1896

ANDRÉ BRETON born (d. 1966)
KANDINSKY and ALEXEI VON JAWLENSKY
  arrive in Munich from Russia

1897

Foundation of Vienna Secession
BEVAN marries Stanislawa de Karlowska
DIAGHILEV mounts exhibitions of English and
  German watercolours and of Scandanavian
  paintings
PER KROHG settles with his family in Paris
MAURER studying at Académie Julian, Paris,
  living in Paris on and off until 1914
VALENTIN SEROV teaching at Moscow College
SERGEI SHCHUKIN buys his first MONET from
  PAUL DURAND-RUEL

1898

Foundation of Berlin Secession
IVAR AROSENIUS studying in Stockholm
BECKER moves to Worpswede
BORISOV-MUSATOV returns to Russia
DIAGHILEV mounts an exhibition of Russian
  and Finnish paintings
GAUGUIN completes *Where Do We Come From?*
  What Are We? Where Are We Going?
RENÉ MAGRITTE born (d. 1967)
GUSTAVE MOREAU dies (b. 1826)
MUNCH travelling in Europe until 1908
NOLDE working with ADOLF HÖLZEL, Munich
PIERRE PUVIS DE CHAVANNES dies (b. 1824)

1899

BENOIS and LÉON BAKST commissioned to
  design set for Hermitage Theatre
DERAIN meets MATISSE at Académie Carrière
NOLDE in Paris
ALFRED SISLEY dies (b. 1839)

1900

Exhibition of work of HENRI DE TOULOUSE-
  LAUTREC in Dresden
BECKER visits Paris
DERAIN meets MAURICE DE VLAMINCK
PECHSTEIN enters art school, Dresden
PICASSO first visits Paris
VRUBEL has mental breakdown

1895

Trial of OSCAR WILDE
Venice Biennale founded
Promenade concerts founded in London by
  SIR HENRY WOOD
THOMAS HARDY – *Jude the Obscure*

1896

First performance of ALFRED JARRY's *Ubu roi*
  in Paris
EDMOND DE GONCOURT dies (b. 1822)
GIACOMO PUCCINI – *La Bohème*

1897

GAUGUIN's 'Noa Noa' published in *Revue
  Blanche*

1898

Launch of *World of Art* magazine
THOMAS HARDY – *Wessex Poems* – his first
  collection of verse to be published
STÉPHANE MALLARMÉ dies (b. 1842)
H.G. WELLS – *The War of the Worlds*
EMILE ZOLA – 'J'accuse'

1899

SIGNAC's *D'Eugène Delacroix au néo-
  impressionnisme* published in book form

1900

JOSEPH CONRAD – *Lord Jim*
SIGMUND FREUD – *The Interpretation of
  Dreams*
FRIEDRICH NIETZSCHE dies (b. 1844)
OSCAR WILDE dies (b. 1854)

1895

End of Sino-Japanese war
X-rays discovered
Cuban war of independence vs. Spain
GUGLIELMO MARCONI (1874-1937) invents
  radio telegraphy

1896

First modern Olympic Games held in Athens
ANTOINE HENRI BECQUEREL (1852–1908)
  discovers radioactivity
Klondike gold rush, Canada
Treaty signed between Russia and China

1897

J.J. THOMSON (1856–1940) discovers the
  electron
Exposition universelle in Brussels
QUEEN VICTORIA's Diamond Jubilee
Graeco-Turkish war

1898

Opening of Paris Metro network
PIERRE (1859-1906) and MARIE CURIE
  (1867-1934) discover radium
FERDINAND VON ZEPPELIN (1838–1917)
  builds first airship
Spanish-American war

1899

Orange Free State and Transvaal declare war
  on Britain to start second Boer War
Second Hague Peace Conference
WILLHELM II visits England
DREYFUS pardoned

1900

Boxer Rebellion (unsuccessful) in China
Relief of Mafeking besieged by the Boers for
  217 days
Exposition universelle in Paris
UMBERTO I of Italy murdered by anarchist
VLADIMIR ILYICH LENIN (1870–1924) flees
  Russia

1901

BECKER marries OTTO MODERSOHN
DENIS shows his *Hommage à Cézanne* at
    Salon des Indépendants
HECKEL meets SCHMIDT-ROTTLUFF in
    Chemnitz
KANDINSKY founds Phalanx group in Munich
KOROVIN elected professor Moscow College
CARL PALME studying under KANDINSKY in
    Munich until 1904
PICASSO settles in Montmartre, Paris
TOULOUSE-LAUTREC dies (b. 1864)

1902

PECHSTEIN enters Dresden Academy

1903

First Salon d'Automne, Paris (hereafter held
    annually)
Munich Secession exhibition in Dresden
BEVAN in Poland
GAUGUIN dies (b. 1848)
KIRCHNER studying in Munich
MODERSOHN-BECKER in Paris
PISSARRO dies (b. 1831), MATISSE attends
    funeral
TATLIN runs away to sea

1904

Scarlet Rose exhibition in Moscow
AROSENIUS living in Paris until 1905
BORISOV-MUSATOV exhibits in Germany
CÉZANNE retrospective at Salon d'Automne
SALVADOR DALI born (d. 1989)
FERGUSSON and PEPLOE painting in Brittany
SPENCER GORE visits SICKERT in Dieppe
HECKEL enters Dresden School of Architecture
EUGENE HIGGINS in Paris
PAVLOV KUZNETSOV exhibits at Salon
    d'Automne
SHCHUKIN buys his first Cézanne

1905

Foundation of Die Brücke in Dresden
VANESSA BELL founds Friday Club
BEVAN and FERGUSSON exhibit in London
BORISOV-MUSATOV exhibits in Paris
DERAIN, MATISSE and KANDINSKY exhibit
    at Salon d'Automne
DURAND-RUEL shows Impressionist
    paintings at Grafton Gallery, London
FERGUSSON and PEPLOE probably visit Salon
    d'Automne
HECKEL begins work as an architect
VON JAWLENSKY visits Salon d'Automne, Paris
KASIMIR MALEVICH studying under
    Roerburg in Moscow
MODERSOHN-BECKER in Paris
SICKERT returns to England
LEO and GERTRUDE STEIN buy MATISSE's

1901

THOMAS MANN – *Buddenbrooks*

1902

JOSEPH CONRAD – *Heart of Darkness*
ANTON CHEKHOV – *Three Sisters*
EMILE ZOLA dies (b. 1840)

1903

GEORGE ORWELL born (d. 1950)

1904

Last edition of *World of Art* magazine
ANTON CHEKHOV – *The Cherry Orchard*
JOSEPH CONRAD – *Nostromo*

1905

JEAN-PAUL SARTRE born (d.1980)
LOUIS VAUXCELLES christens MATISSE,
    DERAIN et al the 'Fauves' in an article in
    Gil Blas

1901

Death of QUEEN VICTORIA, succeeded by
    EDWARD VII
Motor-bicycle launched
Social Revolutionary party founded in Russia

1902

Treaty between Britain and Japan
LEON TROTSKY (1879–1940) escapes from
    Siberia and flees to London
Portugal declares itself bankrupt
End of Boer War

1903

Entente Cordiale between Britain and France
    settling outstanding colonial disputes
ALEXANDER I of Serbia assassinated
First flight made by WRIGHT brothers –
    WILBUR (1867–1912) and ORVILLE
    (1871–1948)
First motor taxis in London

1904

Russo-Japanese war breaks out
THEODORE ROOSEVELT (1858–1919)
    elected US President
Exposition universelle in St Louis

1905

ALBERT EINSTEIN (1879–1955) formulates
    theory of relativity
First European cinema opens, in London
End of Russo-Japanese war

Woman in a Hat
ALFRED STIEGLITZ opens 291 Gallery,
    New York
MATTHEW SMITH enters Slade School of Art
VAN GOGH exhibition in Dresden
WEBER studying at Académie Julian, Paris

1906
CÉZANNE dies (b. 1839)
DERAIN visits London, probably for the
    second time, at Vollard's bidding
DIAGHILEV mounts exhibition BORISOV-
    MUSATOV and the Blue Rose in Moscow
    and Russian painting in Paris
GONCHAROVA and LARIONOV visit Paris
DUNCAN GRANT in Paris until 1907
KIRCHNER issues *Die Brücke Manifesto*
MATISSE's *Bonheur de Vivre* hung at Salon des
    Indépendants
MATISSE visits Algeria
MATISSE meets PICASSO at Steins' flat in Paris
MODERSOHN-BECKER in Paris
MUNCH and French Post-Impressionist
    exhibitions in Dresden
NOLDE and PECHSTEIN join Die Brücke
PICASSO paints *Portrait of Gertrude Stein*
WEBER sees CÉZANNE's paintings at Salon
    d'Automne

1907
Vienna Secession exhibition in Dresden
Foundation of Fitzroy Street Group
Foundation of The Eight
DAVID and VLADIMIR BURLIUK meet
    GONCHAROVA and LARIONOV
CÉZANNE watercolour exhibition at
    Bernheim-Jeune Gallery, Paris
CÉZANNE retrospective at Salon d'Automne
FERGUSSON settles in Paris
VON JAWLENSKY meets MATISSE in Paris
KANDINSKY, MACKE and MARC visit Paris
KUZNETSOV exhibits at the Blue Rose, Moscow
MATISSE exhibits *Blue Nude* at Salon des
    Indépendants
ALFRED MAURER meets Fauve painters
    through GERTRUDE STEIN
PALME instrumental in persuading MATISSE
    to start teaching
PECHSTEIN visits Italy and France
PICASSO sees African sculpture at Trocadéro
    museum and repaints parts of *Les
    Demoiselles d'Avignon*
SIGURD SWANE meets GIERSING in Paris
WEBER meets DELAUNAY and studies under
    MATISSE in Paris until 1908

1908
First Golden Fleece exhibition
The Wreath exhibition, St Petersburg
'The Link' exhibition, St Petersburg
THE BURLIUKS move to St Petersburg
Show of Impressionist art at International
    Society Exhibition in London
The Eight exhibit at the Macbeth Gallery,
    New York

1906
First edition of *Golden Fleece*; includes Blue
    Rose article
ROGER FRY criticizes PAUL CÉZANNE in
    The Nation

1907
HENRI BERGSON – *L'Evolution Créatrice*
JOSEPH CONRAD – *The Secret Agent*

1908
BRAQUE's L'Estaque landscapes earn the
    analogy with 'cubes' in the Parisian press
E.M. FORSTER – *A Room with A View*
ROGER FRY defends CÉZANNE and MATISSE
    in the *Burlington Magazine*
HENRI MATISSE publishes his 'Notes d'un
    peintre' in *La Grande Revue*

1906
First dreadnought launched
First motor-racing Grand Prix held in France
Earthquake in San Francisco
Reform laws in Russia

1907
Hague Peace Conference
First comic strip launched in *San Francisco
    Chronicle* (Mr Mutt)
GRIGORI RASPUTIN (?1871–1916) gains
    influence at the Russian court

1908
Boy Scout movement founded by LORD
    BADEN POWELL (1857–1941)
Model T Ford produced
Olympic Games in London
Bulgaria proclaims independence

Exhibition of RODIN drawings at 291 Gallery, New York
BRAQUE paints in L'Estaque and exhibits at DANIEL-HENRI KAHNWEILER's gallery
FERGUSSON and PEPLOE exhibit in London
HEIBERG returns to Norway from Paris
KANDINSKY and GABRIELE MÜNTER buy cottage in Murnau
MALEVICH meets LARIONOV
PIET MONDRIAN meets JAN TOOROP
IVAN MOROSOV meets MATISSE
MUNCH returns to Norway
NOLDE leaves Die Brücke
PICASSO paints *Three Women*
PICASSO and his friends hold banquet in honour of HENRI ROUSSEAU
MATISSE opens art school in Paris
SHCHUKIN meets Picasso
MATTHEW SMITH visits Pont-Aven, Brittany
VAN GOGH and Fauve exhibitions in Dresden

1909

Exhibition of Matisse drawings at 291 Gallery, New York
BRAQUE and PICASSO start working together
HECKEL visits Italy
KANDINSKY shows at Allied Artists', London
KANDINSKY founds Neue Kunstler-Vereinigung (NKV) with GABRIELE MUNTER and VON JAWLENSKY
MONDRIAN joins Dutch Theosophical Society
SHCHUKIN commissions MATISSE's *La Danse*

1909

Futurist Manifesto appears on front page of *Le Figaro*
DIAGHILEV launches Ballet Russe in Paris
C. KROHG publishes 'Matissismen' in *Dagens Nyt*
HENRI MATISSE's 'Notes of a Painter' appear in the last edition of the *Golden Fleece*. It is also published in Germany

1909

LOUIS BLÉRIOT (1872–1936) flies across the English Channel
Selfridge's store opens in London
WILLIAM HOWARD TAFT (1857–1930) becomes US President
Cure discovered for syphilis
Bakelite invented, named after Belgian-born US inventor

1910

Foundation of the Camden Town Group
First Independent Artists Exhibition, New York
Die Brücke moves to Berlin
Second NKV exhibition
Berlin Secession rejects Die Brücke, foundation of Neue Secession
ROGER FRY and CLIVE BELL meet on train
FRY's 'Manet and the Post-Impressionists' opens in London
KIRCHNER, HECKEL and PECHSTEIN paint together in Moritzburg
LÉGER meets PICASSO
MACKE introduces himself to MARC
MATISSE exhibition in Berlin
MUELLER joins Die Brücke
PECHSTEIN sees GAUGUIN paintings in Dresden
TATLIN moves to Moscow to paint
HERWARTH WALDEN founds journal – *Der Sturm* – in Berlin
WEBER exhibits at 291 Gallery, New York

1910

Futurist Manifesto appears in Italian press
E.M. FORSTER – Howard's End
LEO TOLSTOY dies (b. 1828)
E.M. WORRINGER – *Form Problems of the Gothic*

1910

Suffragettes march on Westminster
EDWARD VII dies, succeeded by GEORGE V
DR HAWLEY HARVEY CRIPPEN (b. 1862) executed – first criminal to be apprehended by radiotelegraphy
Revolution in Portugal
Tango gains in popularity in USA and Europe

1911

Cubism emerges as a movement at Salon des Indépendants and Salon d'Automne
First Blaue Reiter exhibition Munich
First and second Camden Town Group exhibitions, London
The Eight formed in Paris
DUNCAN GRANT travels in Italy and Turkey

1911

WASSILY KANDINSKY – *Concerning the Spiritual in Art*
First edition of J.D. FERGUSSON's *Rhythm*

1911

ERNEST RUTHERFORD (1871–1937) formulates atomic theory
Revolution in central China under CHIANG KAI-SHEK
ROALD AMUNDSEN (1872–1928) from Norway is first man to reach South Pole
Italo-Turkish war

MACKE and PAUL KLEE meet KANDINSKY
FILIPPO MARINETTI, UMBERTO BOCCIONI,
 LUIGI RUSSOLO and CARLO CARRÀ join
 GINO SEVERINI in Paris
MATISSE visits Moscow
MONDRIAN arrives in Paris
EMIL NOLDE visits JAMES ENSOR in Ostend
PECHSTEIN leaves Die Brücke

1912

Futurist exhibition at Bernheim-Jeune Gallery,
 Paris, which then travels Europe
Cubists, but without BRAQUE or PICASSO,
 show at Section d'Or exhibition, Paris
Second Blaue Reiter exhibition in Munich
Die Brücke leave Neue Secession
Die Brücke exhibition in Cologne
Sonderbund exhibition of Expressionist art in
 Cologne
FRY's second Post-Impressionist exhibition in
 London
HAROLD GILMAN visits Sweden and Norway
SPENCER GORE staying in Letchworth in
 Gilman's house
KLEE, MACKE and MARC meet DELAUNAY in
 Paris
WALT KUHN visits Europe with ARTHUR
 DAVIES and MAURER; they meet DUCHAMP
 and VOLLARD
LARIONOV forms Donkey's Tail which holds its
 first exhibition in December
MALEVICH and TATLIN exhibit at the Donkey's
 Tail show
NOLDE completes his *Crucifixion*
FRANK RUTTER exhibits the Futurists in
 London
EGON SCHIELE arrested on pornography charge

1912

KANDINSKY and MARC (eds.) – *Der Blaue Reiter
 Almanac*
EMIL NOLDE begins book on primitive art

1912

War in the Balkans
ROBERT FALCON SCOTT (1868–1912) 'of
 the Antartic' reaches South Pole
Titanic hits an iceberg off Newfoundland on
 her maiden voyage and sinks with loss of
 1,513 lives
Royal Flying Corps founded

1913

Die Brücke comes to a formal close
Opening of Omega Workshops; FRY's argument
 with PERCY WYNDHAM LEWIS
Exhibition in Brighton of English Post-
 Impressionists, Cubists and others
Armory Show opens in New York and travels to
 other American cities
LARIONOV announces birth of Rayonism
MACDONALD-WRIGHT exhibits in Munich and
 Paris
MALEVICH paints *Black Square*
MATISSE visits Morocco
MATISSE's *Blue Nude* burnt in effigy in Chicago
MAURER exhibits with Blaue Reiter in Berlin
NOLDE visits New Guinea
O'CONOR, FERGUSSON and PEPLOE painting
 in Cassis
TATLIN visits Paris and Berlin

1913

Modernist opera entitled *Victory over the Sun*
 staged in St Petersburg with backdrop
 designed by KASIMIR MALEVICH
D.H. LAWRENCE – *Sons and Lovers*
THOMAS MANN – *Death in Venice*
MARCEL PROUST – *A la Recherche du temps perdu*

1913

Mohandas Karamchand 'MAHATMA'
 GANDHI (1869–1948) arrested
Jet propulsion discovered
Zip fastening becomes popular
Foxtrot becomes fashionable on the dance
 floor

1914

Foundation of The Fourteen
KLEE and MACKE visit Tunisia
LARIONOV and GONCHAROVA visit Paris
LEWIS founds Rebel Art Centre
MARC and KIRCHNER conscripted into the
 German army

1914

First edition of *Blast* – Vorticist manifesto
GUILLAUME APOLLINAIRE describes
 CÉZANNE's watercolours as the most potent
 influence on contemporary painting
CLIVE BELL – *Art*
JAMES JOYCE – *The Dubliners*

1914

World War I breaks out
Germany occupies Brussels and Lille
Russians defeated at Tannenberg
Battle of the Marne and first Battle of Ypres

Bibliography

EXHIBITION CATALOGUES
(listed chronologically)

Rubin, William, *Dada, Surrealism and their Heritage*, New York: Museum of Modern Art, 1968, rpt 1977.

Gordon, Irene (ed.), *Four Americans in Paris: The Collections of Gertrude Stein and Her Family*, New York: Museum of Modern Art, 1970.

Schneider, Pierre (ed.), *Henri Matisse, Exposition du centenaire*, Paris: Grand Palais, April–September 1970, Réunion des musées nationaux, Paris, 1970.

Seckel, Helene (ed.), *Paris – New York*, Paris: Centre Georges Pompidou, Paris, June–September 1971, Editions des musées nationaux, Paris, 1971.

d'Harnoncourt, A., and McShine, K. (eds.), *Marcel Duchamp*, New York: Museum of Modern Art, 1974.

Elderfield, John, *The 'Wild Beasts', Fauvism and Its Affinities*, New York: Museum of Modern Art, 1976.

Rubin, William (ed.), *Cézanne: The Late Work*, New York: Museum of Modern Art, 1977.

Hulten, Karl, and Gunnar, Pontus, *Paris – Moscow*, Paris: Centre Georges Pompidou, 1979.

House, John, and Stevens, MaryAnne (eds.), *Post-Impressionism: Cross Currents in European Art*, London: Royal Academy,1979–80.

Peter Vergo et al, *Abstraction: Towards a New Art, Painting 1910–1920*, London: Tate Gallery, 1980.

Barron, Stephanie, and Tuchman, Maurice, *The Avant Garde in Russia*, Los Angeles: County Museum of Art, 1980.

Joachimedes, C., Rosenthal, W., and Schmied, W., *German Art in the Twentieth Century*, London: Royal Academy, 1985.

Moffet, Charles, et al, *The New Painting, Impressionism 1874–1886*, Fine Arts Museum of San Francisco, 1986.

Gaber-Abrahamsen, Martha, Plesner, Marriamet and Hort, Patrick, *Dreams of a Summer Night*, London: Hayward Gallery, Nordic Council of Ministers, 1986.

Baron, Wendy (ed.), *The Camden Town Exhibition at Christie's*, London, 1988.

The Art of Paul Gauguin, Washington DC: National Gallery of Art, 1988.

Nordic Council of Ministers, *The Scandinavian Modernism Exhibition*, Goteborgs, Kunstmuseum, Gothenburg, Rizzoli, New York, 1989.

Cowling, Elizabeth, and Mundy, Jennifer, *On Classic Ground, Picasso, Léger, de Chirico and the New Classicism, 1910–1930*, London: Tate Gallery, Tate Gallery Pulbications, 1990.

Krumrine, Mary Louise, with Boehm, Gottfried, and Geelhaar, Christian, *Paul Cézanne: The Bathers*, trans. John Mitchell and Dorothy Kosinski, with Meret Meyer and Isabel Feder (eds.), Basel: Museum of Fine Arts, 1989, Thames and Hudson, London, in association with the Kunstmuseum Basel/Eidolon, 1990.

Bomford, D., Kirby, J., Leighton, J., and Ashok, R., *Art in the Making: Impressionism*, Yale University Press, 1991.

Freeman, Judi, *The Fauve Landscape*, London: Royal Academy, 1991.

BOOKS AND ARTICLES
(listed alphabetically by author)

Appollinaire, Guillaume, *Chroniques d'art 1902–1918*, L.C.Breunig (ed.), Gallimard, Paris, 1960.
———————— *Les Soirees de Paris*, 2 vols., Slatkine Reprints, Geneva, 1971.

Baigell, M., *A History of Amercian Painting*, Thames and Hudson, London, 1971.

Baron, Wendy, *The Camden Town Group*, Scholar, London, 1979.

Barr, Alfred H. Jr., *Matisse: His Art and His Public*, Museum of Modern Art, New York, 1951, rpt. [Arno Press, New York] 1966.
———————— *Picasso: Fifty Years of His Art*, Museum of Modern Art, New York, 1946, rpt 1980.

Bell, Clive, *Art*, Chatto and Windus, London, 1914.

Benjamin, Roger, *Matisse's 'Notes of a Painter': Criticism, Theory and Context, 1891–1908*, Studies in the Fine Arts: Criticism, no.21, UMI Reserve Press, Ann Arbor, 1986.

Benois, Alexandre, *The Russian School of Painting*, Laurie, London, 1919.

Billcliffe, Roger, *The Scotish Colourists*, John Murray, London, 1989.

Bird, Alan, *Russian Painting*, Phaidon, Oxford, 1987.

Bowlt, John E., *Russian Art of the Avant-Garde*, Thames and Hudson, London, 1988.

Brown, Milton W., *American Painting*, Princeton, New Jersey, 1955.

Buchheim, Lothar Gunter, *Die KG Brücke*, Feldafing, Munich, 1956.

Bullen, J.B. (ed.), *Post-Impressionists in England*, Routledge and Kegan Paul, London and New York, 1988.

Burgess, Gelett, 'The Wild Men of Paris' in *The Architectural Record*, XXVII, no. 5, (May 1910), 401–14.

Cézanne, Paul, *Paul Cézanne, Correspondance*, John Rewald (ed.), Grasset, Paris, 1978.
———————— *Paul Cézanne: Letters*, John Rewald (ed.), trans. Seymour Hacker, Hacker Art Books, New York, 1984.

Chamot, Mary, *Russian Painting and Sculpture*, Pergamon Press, Oxford, 1969.

Chassé, Charles, *The Nabis and their Period*, trans. Michael Bullock, Lund Humphries, London, 1969 [La Bibliothèque des arts, Paris, 1960].

Clark, Kenneth, *The Nude, A Study of Ideal Art*, John Murray, London, 1956, rpt. [Book Club Associates, London] 1973 .

Clough, Shepard B., Moodie T., and Moodie C. (eds.), *Economic History of Europe: Twentieth Century*, Macmillan, London and Melbourne, 1969.

Cobban, Alfred, *A History of Modern France, Volume 3: 1871–1962*, Harmondsworth: Penguin, 1965.

Cork, Richard, *Vorticism, Vol. 1*, Fraser, London, 1976.

Daix, P., and Rosselet, J., *Picasso: The Cubist Years, 1907–1916, a catalogue raisonné*, Thames and Hudson, London, 1979.

Denis, Maurice, *Theories 1890–1910. Du symbolisme et de Gauguin vers un nouvel ordre classique*, Rouart et Watelin, Paris, 1912, rpt. [revised edition Olivier D'Allones (ed.), Hermann, Paris] 1964.
———————— *Nouvelles théories, sur l'art moderne, sur l'art sacre, 1914–1921*, Rouart et Watelin, Paris, 1922.

Derain, André, *Lettres à Vlaminck*, Flammarion, Paris, 1955.

Doran, P.M. (ed.), *Conversations avec Cézanne*, Macula, Paris, 1978.

Dostoevsky, Fyodor, *The Idiot*, trans., Penguin, London, 1955.

Dube, Wolf-Dieter, *The Expressionists*, Thames and Hudson, London, 1972.

Elderfield, John, *Matisse in the Collection of the Museum of Modern Art, New York*, Museum of Modern Art, 1978.

Escholier, Raymond, *Henri Matisse*, Librairie Floury, Paris, 1937.

Farr, Dennis, *English Art 1870–1940*, Oxford University Press, Oxford, 1984.

Fawcett, Trevor, and Phillpot, Clive (eds.), *The Art Press*, The Art Book Company, London, 1976.

Fénéon, Félix, *Au-delà de l'impressionnisme*, F. Cachin (ed.), Hermann, Paris, 1966.
———————— *Félix Fénéon, Oeuvres plus que complètes*, 2 vols., Joan U. Halperin (ed.), Librairie Droz, Geneva, 1970.

Ferguson, John, *The Arts in Britain in World War I*, Camelot Press, Southampton, 1981.

Finke, Ulrich, *German Painting*, Manchester University Press, 1974.

Flam, Jack D. (ed.), *Matisse on Art*, Phaidon, London and New York, 1973.
———————— *Matisse, The Man and His Art, 1869–1918*, Thames and Hudson, London, 1986.

Fourcade, Dominique, *Henri Matisse, Ecrits et propos sur l'art*, Hermann, Paris, 1972, rpt. [with revisions and corrections] 1989.
———————— 'Autres Propos de Matisse' in *Macula*, no. 1, (1976), 92–115.

Fry, Roger, *Vision and Design*, Chatto and Windus, London, 1920.
———————— *The Letters of Roger Fry*, 2 vols., Denys Sutton (ed.), Chatto and Windus, London, 1972.

Gauguin, Paul, *The Writings of a Savage*, New York, 1974.
———————— *The Intimate Journals of Paul Gauguin*, London, 1985.

George, Waldemar, *Larionov*, Editions art moderne, Paris, 1966.

Giry, Marcel, *Le Fauvisme: ses origines, son évolution*, Ides et Calendes, Neuchatel, 1981.

Gise, Ernst-Gerhard (ed.), *Paul Klee: Dialogue with Nature*, Prestel, Munich, 1991.

Golding, John, *Cubism: A History and an Analysis, 1907–1914*, Faber and Faber, London, 1959, rpt. [2nd edn.] 1967.
———————— 'Fauvism and the School of Chatou: Post-Impressionism in Crisis' in

Proceedings of the British Academy, LXVI, (1980), 85–102.

Goldwater, Robert, *Symbolism*, New York, 1979.
———————— *Paul Gauguin*, New York, 1957.

Gordon, Donald E., *Kirchner*, Harvard University Press, Cambridge, Mass., 1968.
———————— *Modern Art Exhibitions, 1900–1916*, Selected Catalogue Documentation, 2 vols., Prestel, Munich, 1974.
———————— *Expressionism*, Yale University Press, New Haven, 1987.

Gray, Camilla, *The Russian Experiment in Art*, Thames and Hudson, London, 1968.

Green, Christopher, *Léger and the Avant-Garde*, Yale University Press, New Haven and London, 1976.

Grohmann, Wilhelm, *Kirchner*, Thames and Hudson, London, 1961.

Haftmann, Werner, *Painting in the Twentieth Century*, 2 vols., Prestel-Verlag, Munich, 1965, rpt. [trans. Janet Seligman, Lund Humphries, London] 1980.
———————— *Emil Nolde*, Faber and Faber, London, 1959.

Hamilton, George Heard, *Painting and Sculpture in Europe, 1860–1940*, The Pelican History of Art, Harmondsworth: Penguin, 1967, rpt. [3rd edn.] 1981.

Hauser, Arnold, *The Social History of Art: Volume 4 – Naturalism, Impressionism, The Film Age*, trans. Stanley Godman, Routledge and Kegan Paul, London, 1989.

Heller, Reinhold, *Munch: His Life and Work*, John Murray, London, 1984.

Herbert, Barry, *German Expressionism: Die Brücke and Der Blaue Reiter*, Jupiter Books, London, 1983.

Hobhouse, Janet, *Everybody Who Was Anybody: A Biography of Gertrude Stein*, Weidenfield and Nicolson, London, 1975.

Hodin, Josef Paul, *Edvard Munch*, trans., Thames and Hudson, London, 1972.

House, John, *Monet, Nature into Art*, Yale University Press, New Haven and London, 1986.

Hunkin, Harry, *The Group of Seven*, Edinburgh, 1979.

Jaffe, Hans, *Piet Mondrian*, Thames and Hudson, London, 1970.

Jähner, H., *Kunstgruppe Brücke*, Kohlhammer, 1984.

Kaplanova, Sofya, *Vrubel*, Aurora, St Petersburg, 1975.

Kandinsky, Wassily, *Complete Writings on Art, Volume One (1901–1921)*, Kenneth C. Lindsay and Peter Vergo (eds.), Faber and Faber, London, 1982.

Kent, Niel, *The Triumph of Light and Nature*, Thames and Hudson, London, 1987.

Lethève, Jacques, *Impressionistes et symbolistes devant la presse*, Armand Colin, Paris, 1959.

Liberman, Alexander, *The Artist in His Studio*, The Viking Press, New York, 1960, rpt. 1974.

Loevgren, Sven, *The Genesis of Modernism, Seurat, Gauguin, Van Gogh and French Symbolism in the 1880s*, Hacker Art Books, New York, 1959, rpt. [with revisions] 1983.

Mauclair, Camille, *Trois crises de l'art actuel*, Bibliothèque-Charpentier, Paris, 1906.
———————— *Les Etats de la peinture française de 1850–1920*, Payot et Cie., Paris, 1921.

McConkey, Kenneth, *Irish Art 1860–1960*, Phaidon, London, 1990.

Myers, Bernard Samuel, *Expressionism*, Thames and Hudson, London, 1957.

Naylor, Gillian, *Bloomsbury*, Octopus, London, 1990.

Neff, John, *Matisse and Decoration, 1906–1914: Studies of the Ceramics and the Commissions for Paintings and Stained Glass*, unpublished doctoral thesis, Harvard University, Cambridge, Mass., June 1974.

Nicholson, Benedict, 'Post-Impressionism and Roger Fry' in *Burlington Magazine*, XCIII (January 1951), 11–15.

Nietzsche, Friedrich, *Thus Spoke Zarathustra*, trans., Penguin, London, 1961.

Olivier, Fernande, *Picasso et ses amis*, Librairie Stock, Paris, 1933.

Oppler, Ellen C., *Fauvism Re-examined*, unpublished doctoral thesis, Columbia University, 1969.

Perry, Gillian, *Paula Modersohn-Becker*, Women's Press, London, 1979.

Pople, Kenneth, *Stanley Spencer*, Collins, London, 1991.

Raymond, Marcel, *From Baudelaire to Surrealism*, Methuen, London, 1973 [Editions A.A. Correa, Paris, 1933].

Read, Herbert, *Art Now*, Faber, London, 1933.

Reff, Theodore, 'Cézanne and Poussin' in

Journal of the Warburg and Courtauld Institutes, XXIII, (January 1960), 150–74.
————— 'Cézanne's Constructive Stroke' in *Art Quarterly*, XXV, (1962), 214–27.
————— 'Cézanne et Poussin' in *Art de France*, III, (1963), 302–310.
————— 'Matisse: Meditations on a Statuette and Goldfish' in *Arts Magazine*, no. 51, (November 1976), 109–15.

Rewald, John (ed.), *Paul Cézanne*, trans. Margaret H. Liebman, Spring Books, London [n.d.].
————— *Paul Cézanne, Correspondance*, Grasset, Paris, 1978.
————— *Cézanne, The Watercolours, a catalogue raisonné*, Thames and Hudson, London and New York, 1983.
————— *A History of Impressionism*, 4th rev. edn., Secker and Warburg, London, 1973.
————— *Studies in Impressionism*, Irene Gordon and Frances Weitzenhofer (eds.), Thames and Hudson, London, 1985.
————— *Studies in Post-Impressionism*, Irene Gordon and Frances Weitzenhofer (eds.), Thames and Hudson, London, 1986.
————— *Cézanne and America: Dealers, Collectors, Artists and Critics, 1891–1921*, Thames and Hudson, London and New York, 1989.

Rilke, Rainer Maria, *Rainer Maria Rilke: Letters on Cézanne*, trans. Joel Agee, Fromm International Publishing Corporation, New York, 1985, rpt. [Jonathan Cape, London] 1988.
————— *Worpeswede Monographie*, Insel Verlag, Leipzig, 1903.

Rivière, Jacques, *Etudes, nouvelle revue française*, Marcel Rivière et Cie, Paris, 1911.

Roethl, Hans K, *Kandinsky*, Phaidon, Oxford, 1979.

Rosenblum, Robert, *Modern Painting and the Northern Romantic Tradition*, Thames and Hudson, London, 1983.

Rubin, William, 'Pablo and Georges and Leo and Bill' in *Art in America*, 67 (March–April 1979), 128–147.

Sarabianov, Dmitri V., *Russian Art*, Thames and Hudson, London, 1990.

Salmon, André, *La Jeune peinture française, Société des rentes*, Albert Messein, Paris, 1919.
————— *Propos d'Atelier*, Cres et Cie., Paris, 1922.

Schapiro, Meyer, *Modern Art, Nineteenth and Twentieth Centuries*, Chatto and Windus, London, 1978.

Schneider, Pierre, *Matisse*, trans. Michael Taylor and Bridget Strevens Romer, Rizzoli International Publications Inc., New York, 1984.

Sérusier, Paul, *ABC de la Peinture*, Librairie Floury, Paris, 1921, rpt. [with revisions] 1950.

Selz, Peter, *German Expressionist Painting*, University of California Press, Berkeley, 1968.

Shattuck, Roger, *The Banquet Years: the origin of the avant-garde in France, 1885 to World War I*, Harcourt Brace, New York, 1955, rpt. [Faber and Faber, London] 1959.

Shiff, Richard, *Cézanne and the End of Impressionism*, University of Chicago Press, Chicago and London, 1984.

Shilks, Ralph E., and Harper, Paula, *Pissarro: His Life and Work*, London, New York and Melbourne, 1980.

Sickert, Walter Richard, *A Free House*, Macmillan, London, 1947.

Signac, Paul, (D'Eugène Delacroix au néo-impressionnisme) in *La Revue Blanche*, Paris, 1899, rpt. [with introduction and notes by Françoise Cachin, Hermann, Paris] 1964.

Som, Richard D., *Anarchism and Cultural Politics in Fin-de-Siecle France*, University of Nebraska Press, Lincoln and London, 1989.

Spalding, Frances, *Roger Fry – Art and Life*, Granada, London, Toronto, Sydney and New York, 1980.
————— *Vanessa Bell*, Macmillan, London, 1983.
————— *British Art since 1900*, Thames and Hudson, London, 1986.

Stangos, N. (ed.), *Concepts of Modern Art*, Thames and Hudson, London, 1981.

Stein, Gertrude, 'Henri Matisse-Pablo Picasso' in *Camera Work*, (August 1912), rpt. in *Four Americans in Paris: The Collections of Gertrude Stein and Her Family*, Irene Gordon (ed.), Museum of Modern Art, New York, 1970, 99–102.
————— *Autobiography of Alice B. Toklas*, Harcourt Brace, New York; John Lane, The Bodley Head, London, 1933.
————— *Matisse, Picasso and Gertrude Stein, with Two Shorter Stories*, Plain Edition, Paris, 1933.

Stein, Leo, *Appreciation: Painting, Poetry and Prose*, Crown Publishers, New York, 1947.
————— *Journey into the Self: Being the Letters, Papers and Journals of Leo Stein*, E. Fuller (ed.), Crown Publishers, New York, 1950.

Steinberg, Leo, 'Resisting Cézanne: Picasso's "Three Women"' in *Art in America*, 66, (November–December 1978), 114–33.
————— 'The Polemical Part' in *Art in America*, 67, (March–April 1979), 114–27.

Talbot-Rice, Tamara, *A Concise History of American Painting*, Thames and Hudson, London, 1963.

Thomson, Belinda, 'Camille Pissarro and Symbolism' in *Burlington Magazine*, CXXIV, no. 946 (January 1982), 16–24.

Thomson, David (ed.), *The Era of Violence 1989–1945*, The New Cambridge Modern History, volume XII, Cambridge University Press, 1960.

Tisdall, C., and Bozzolla, A., *Futurism*, Thames and Hudson, London, 1977.

Tuchman, Barbara, *August 1914, The First Month of the First World War*, Macmillan, London, 1982 [Constable and Co., London, 1962].

Varnedoe, Kirk, *Northern Lights*, Brooklyn Museum, New York, 1982.

Venturi, Lionello, *Cézanne: son art – son oeuvre*, 2 vols, Paul Rosenberg, Paris, 1936.

Watney, Simon, *The Art of Duncan Grant*, John Murray, London, 1990.

Werenskiold, Marit, *The Concept of Expressionism*, trans. Ronald Walford, Universitetsforlaget, 1984.

Whitman, Walt, *Leaves of Grass*, trans., Penguin, London, 1959.

Willett, John, *Expressionism*, Weidenfeld and Nicholson, London, 1970.

Wilmerding, J., *American Art*, Penguin, London, 1976.

Zhadova, Larissa, *Malevich*, Thames and Hudson, London, 1982.

Zweite, Armin, with Hoberg, Annegret, *The Blue Rider in the Lenbachhaus, Munich*, Prestel, Munich, 1989.

List of Illustrations

The works of Jean Arp, Max Beckmann, Alexandre Benois, Emile Bernard, Carlo Carrà, Maurice Denis, Raoul Dufy, Giorgio de Chirico, Raoul Hausmann, Eric Heckel, Alexei von Jawlensky, Paul Klee, Oskar Kokoschka, Fernand Léger, Maximilien Luce, André Masson, Otto Modersohn, Otto Mueller, Piet Mondrian, Max Pechstein, Pablo Picasso, Karl Schmidt-Rottluff, Kurt Schwitters, Paul Sérusier, Paul Signac, Max Slevogt, Stanley Spencer, Edouard Vuillard are © DACS 1992.

The works of Pierre Bonnard and Francis Picabia are © ADAGP/SPADEM, Paris and DACS, London, 1992.

The works of Georges Braque, Charles Camoin, Robert Delaunay, André Derain, Marcel Duchamp, James Ensor, Jean-Abel Faivre, Othon Friesz, Albert Gleizes, Wassily Kandinsky, Per Krohg, Mikhail Larionov, Marie Laurencin, Albert Marquet, Gino Severini, Kees van Dongen, Maurice de Vlaminck are © ADAGP Paris and DACS London 1992.

The work of Max Ernst is © SPADEM/ADAGP, Paris and DACS, London, 1992.

The works of Percy Wyndham Lewis are reproduced by permission of the Estate of Mrs G.A. Wyndham Lewis.

The works of Henri Matisse are © Succession Henri Matisse/DACS 1992.

The works of Emil Nolde are reproduced by permission and are © Nolde-Stiftung Seebüll.

All pictures are referred to by plate numbers and not by page numbers.

413

379   The Knight Errant   1915.
Oil on canvas, 89.5 x 180.1 cm.
Solomon R. Guggenheim Museum, New York.

KONCHALOVSKY, PYOTR   1876–1956
299   Portrait of Georgy Yakulov   1910.
Oil on canvas, 176 x 143 cm.
State Tretyakov Gallery, Moscow.

KROHG, PER   1889–1965
314   Night   1911.
Oil on canvas, 88.5 x 115.5 cm.
J.F. Willumsens Museum, Frederikssund, Denmark.

LARIONOV, MIKHAIL   1881–1964
300   Relaxing Soldier   1911.
Oil on canvas, 119 x 122 cm.
State Tretyakov Gallery, Moscow.

308   Soldier in a Wood (The Smoker)   1908.
Oil on canvas, 84.5 x 91.4 cm.
Scottish National Gallery of Modern Art, Edinburgh.

311   Evening After the Rain   1908.
Oil on canvas, 68 x 85 cm.
State Tretyakov Gallery, Moscow.

321   Glass   1912.
Oil on canvas, 104.1 x 97.1 cm.
Solomon R. Guggenheim Museum, New York.

LAURENCIN, MARIE   1885–1956
167   Group of Artists   1908.
Oil on canvas, 64.8 x 81 cm.
Baltimore Museum of Art. Cone Collection, formed by Dr
Claribel Cone and Miss Etta Cone of Baltimore, Maryland.

LÉGER, FERNAND   1881–1955
7   The Mechanic   1911–19.
Oil on canvas, 46 x 61 cm.
Munson-Williams-Proctor Institute, Utica, New York.

177   La Noce   1911–12.
Oil on canvas, 406.3 x 327 cm.
Musée national d'art moderne. Centre Georges Pompidou,
Paris.

199   Nus dans un Paysage   1909–11.
Oil on canvas, 116.8 x 172.8 cm.
Rijksmuseum Kröller-Müller, Otterlo, Netherlands.

201   Le Réveil Matin   1914.
Oil on canvas, 100 x 81 cm.
Musée national d'art moderne. Centre Georges Pompidou,
Paris.

378   L'Avion Brisé   1916.
Wash and gouache on paper, 24.5 x 30.5 cm.
Musée National Fernand Léger, Biot.

LEWIS, PERCY WYNDHAM   1882–1957
365   Composition   1913.
Watercolour drawing on paper, 34.3 x 26.7 cm.
Tate Gallery, London.

366   The Crowd (Revolution)   c. 1915.
Oil, drawing, on canvas, 200.7 x 153.7 cm.
Tate Gallery, London.

LIEBERMANN, MAX   1847–1935
212   The Parrot Walk   1902.
Oil on canvas, 88 x 72.5 cm.
Kunsthalle, Bremen.

LUCE, MAXIMILIEN   1858–1941
20   The Iron Foundry   1899.
Oil on canvas, 113 x 161 cm.
Rijksmuseum Kröller-Müller, Otterlo, Netherlands.

MACDONALD-WRIGHT, STANTON
1890–1973
375   'Oriental'. Synchromy in Blue-Green   1918.
Oil on canvas, 91.4 x 127 cm.
Whitney Museum of American Art, New York.

MACKE, AUGUST   1887–1914
25   Large, Well-Lit Shop Window   1912.
Oil on canvas, 106.8 x 82.8 cm.
Sprengel Museum, Hanover.

257   Zoological Garden I   1912.
Oil on canvas, 58.5 x 98 cm.
Städtische Galerie im Lenbachhaus, Munich.

258   Farmboy from Tegernsee   1910.
Oil on canvas, 88 x 66.5 cm.
Städtische Galerie im Lenbachhaus, Munich.

259   Milliner's Shop   1913.
Oil on canvas, 54.5 x 44 cm.
Städtische Galerie im Lenbachhaus, Munich.

278   Indians on Horseback   1911.
Oil on wood, 44 x 60 cm.
Städtische Galerie im Lenbachhaus, Munich.

279   Kairouan I   1914.
Watercolour, 21.4 x 27 cm.
Staatsgalerie Moderner Kunst, Munich. Bayerische
Staatsgemäldesammlungen.

280   Flowers in the Garden – Clivia and Geraniums
1911.
Oil on canvas, 90 x 71.5 cm.
Städtische Galerie im Lenbachhaus, Munich.

MALEVICH, KASIMIR   1878–1935
294   Bather   1910.
Gouache on paper, 105 x 69 cm.
Stedelijk Museum, Amsterdam.

322   Knife Grinder   1912.
Oil on canvas, 79.7 x 79.7 cm.
Yale University Art Gallery, Newhaven, Connecticut.

323   An Englishman in Moscow   1914.
Oil on canvas, 88 x 57 cm.
Stedelijk Museum, Amsterdam.

324   Black Square and Red Square   1915.
Oil on canvas, 71.1 x 44.5 cm.
Museum of Modern Art, New York.

MARC, FRANZ   1880–1916
255   Deer in a Monastery Garden   1912.
Oil on canvas, 75.7 x 101 cm.
Städtische Galerie im Lenbachhaus, Munich.

256   Vermilion Greeting   1913.
Tempera on paper, 14 x 9 cm.
Städtische Galerie im Lenbachhaus, Munich.

274   The Fate of the Animals   1913.
Oil on canvas, 196 x 266 cm.
Öffentliche Kunstsammlung, Kunstmuseum, Basel.

275   Red Roe Deer II   1912.
Oil on canvas, 70 x 100 cm.
Franz-Marc-Museum, Kochel. Bayerische
Staatsgemäldesammlungen.

276   The Tiger   1912.
Oil on canvas, 110 x 101.5 cm.
Städtische Galerie im Lenbachhaus, Munich.

277   The Birds   1914.
Oil on canvas, 109 x 100 cm.
Städtische Galerie im Lenbachhaus, Munich.

MARQUET, ALBERT   1875–1947
146   Le 14 Juillet au Havre   1906.
Oil on canvas, 81 x 65 cm.
Musée de Bagnols-sur-Cèze, Gard, France.

MASHKOV, ILYA   1881–1944
312   Fruit on a Dish   1910.
Oil on canvas, 80.7 x 116.2 cm.
State Tretyakov Gallery, Moscow.

MASSON, ANDRÉ   1896–1987
388   Fish Drawn in the Sand   1927.
Oil on canvas, 100 x 73 cm.
Kunstmuseum, Bern. Hermann und Margrit Rupf-
Stiftung.

MATISSE, HENRI   1869–1954
4   Le Luxe II   1907.
Casein on canvas, 209.5 x 139 cm.
Statens Museum for Kunst, Sølvgade, Copenhagen.
J. Rump Collection.

14   Girl with Green Eyes   1908.
Oil on canvas, 66 x 50.8 cm.
San Francisco Museum of Modern Art. Bequest of Harriet
Lane Levy.

68   Luxe, calme et volupté   1904–05.
Oil on canvas, 86 x 116 cm.
Musée national d'art moderne. Centre Georges Pompidou,
Paris.

126   Woman in a Hat   1905.
Oil on canvas, 80.6 x 59.7 cm.
San Francisco Museum of Modern Art. Elise Stern Haas
Collection: Bequest of Elise Stern Haas.

128   Portrait of André Derain   1905.
Oil on canvas, 46 x 34.9 cm.
Tate Gallery, London.

130   Pink Onions   1906.
Oil on canvas, 46 x 55 cm.
Statens Museum for Kunst, Sølvgade, Copenhagen.
J. Rump Collection.

135   Le Bonheur de Vivre   1906.
Oil on canvas, 174 x 238 cm.
Barnes Foundation Merion, Pennsylvania.

138   Bathers with a Turtle   1908.
Oil on canvas, 179.1 x 220.3 cm.
St Louis Art Museum. Gift of Mr and Mrs Joseph Pulitzer Jr.

139   The Green Line   1905.
Oil on canvas, 40.5 x 32.5 cm.
Statens Museum for Kunst, Sølvgade, Copenhagen.

140   View of Collioure   1905.
Oil on canvas, 59.5 x 73 cm.
Hermitage Museum, St Petersburg.

150   Blue Nude (Souvenir de Biskra)   1907.
Oil on canvas, 92.1 x 140.1 cm.
Baltimore Museum of Art. Cone Collection, formed by Dr
Claribel Cone and Miss Etta Cone of Baltimore, Maryland.

151   Arab Café   1913.
Distemper on canvas, 176 x 210 cm.
Hermitage Museum, St Petersburg.

152   Interior with Aubergines   1911.
Distemper on canvas, 212 x 246 cm.
Musée de Peinture et de Sculpture, Grenoble.

161   La Danse I   1909–10.
Oil on canvas, 260 x 391 cm.
Hermitage Museum, St Petersburg.

163   Zorah on the Terrace   1912.
Oil on canvas, 116 x 100 cm.
Pushkin Museum of Fine Arts, Moscow.

380   Open Window, Collioure   1914.
Oil on canvas, 116.5 x 88 cm.
Musée national d'art moderne. Centre Georges Pompidou,
Paris.

404   Nude Seated on a Sofa   1923.
Oil on canvas, 58 x 61 cm.
Norton Simon Foundation, Pasadena.

Index